# THE INTERNATIONAL MARITIME ORGANIZATION
## Volume 1: International Shipping Rules

# The International Maritime Organization

## VOLUME I:

## International Shipping Rules

SAMIR MANKABADY

CROOM HELM
London • Sydney • Wolfeboro, New Hampshire

Croom Helm Ltd, Provident House, Burrell Row,
Beckenham, Kent, BR3 1AT

Croom Helm Australia Pty Ltd, Suite 4, 6th Floor,
64-76 Kippax Street, Surry Hills, NSW 2010, Australia

British Library Cataloguing in Publication Data

Mankabady, Samir
The international maritime organization.
Vol. 1: International shipping rules
1. Maritime law 2. International law
I. Title
341.7'566 JX4411

ISBN 0-7099-3591-9

Croom Helm, 27 South Main Street,
Wolfeboro, New Hampshire 03894-2069, USA

**Library of Congress Cataloging-in-Publication Data**

The International Maritime Organization.

Rev. ed. of: The International Maritime Organisation.
c1984.
Includes index.
Contents: v. 1. International shipping rules.
1. International Maritime Organization — History.
I. Mankabady, Samir.
VK1.I583I583 1986 341.7'566 86-16809
ISBN 0-7099-3591-9

Printed and bound in Great Britain
by Billing & Sons Limited, Worcester.

CONTENTS

## FOREWORD to the First Edition

Some time ago, Professor Samir Mankabady mentioned to me that he was editing a book on the work of the International Maritime Organization and he asked me to write a foreword. I welcomed the idea because it was my view that while the International Maritime Organization has developed a well co-ordinated regime of international maritime technical standards for enhancing maritime safety and for protecting the marine environment from pollution by shipping, this work has so far received the attention only of those persons who are directly engaged in international shipping. It seems to me to be extremely important that the extensive work of the IMO in the maritime technical and legal fields is brought to the attention of a much wider audience including teachers and students in institutions of maritime education, shipowners, seafarers, marine insurers, leading figures in public life who help in the formulation of maritime policies, and others.

The IMO's work is at present contained in conventions, protocols, codes of practice, recommendations and resolutions. Naturally, the contents of these documents are written in technical and specialized language. For the general reader, however, it is necessary to provide editorial comments and explanatory notes so that the endeavours of the Organization to provide a well co-ordinated maritime regime may be well understood and appreciated.

In bringing together a vast amount of original work of the IMO and in providing editorial comments and explanations, Professor Mankabady and his associates have undoubtedly rendered a unique service to the world maritime community. I must, of course, say that the editorial comments and explanatory notes represent the views and perceptions of the authors themselves. These comments and views are not and must not be taken to be the views of the International Maritime Organization or of myself personally. Possibly the views of the authors may well initiate not only interest in the IMO's work but also an interesting debate. That is an appropriate role for those who are engaged in academic work.

From my point of view, what is important is that in this volume Professor Mankabady and his associates have now presented a total picture of the work of the Organization which, I have no doubt, will be of interest to many people in different walks of life who may have an interest in maritime activity. Since the conventions and other instruments of the IMO have been quoted *in extenso*, this volume is bound to become an important reference book.

In conclusion, I wish to congratulate Professor Mankabady, a legal luminary of great distinction, and all his associates, who are renowned specialists in their respective fields, for the initiative they have taken in publishing this volume on the work of the International Maritime Organization.

C.P. SRIVASTAVA
Secretary-General
International Maritime Organization

## ABBREVIATIONS

| | | |
|---|---|---|
| ADP | - | Automatic Data Processing |
| AMVER | - | Automated Mutual-Assistance Vessel Rescue |
| ARPA | - | Automatic Radar Plotting Aids |
| BCH | - | Sub-Committee on Bulk Chemicals |
| BIMCO | - | Baltic and International Maritime Conference |
| CBT | - | Clean Ballast Tanks |
| CDG | - | Sub-Committee on the Carriage of Dangerous Goods |
| CES | - | Coast-earth station |
| CIM | - | Convention on Carriage of Goods by Rail |
| CLC | - | Civil Liability Convention for Oil Pollution Damage, 1969 |
| CMI | - | Comité Maritime International |
| CMR | - | Convention on Carriage of Goods by Road |
| COLREG | - | Convention on the International Regulations for Preventing Collisions at Sea, 1972 |
| COM | - | Sub-Committee on Radio Communications |
| COMECON | - | Council for Mutual Economic Assistance |
| COW | - | Crude Oil Washing |
| CRISTAL | - | Contract regarding an Interim Supplement to Tanker Liability for Oil Pollution Damage |
| CSC | - | International Convention for Safe Containers, 1972 |
| CSI | - | Convention Relating to Intervention on the High Seas in Cases of Oil Pollution Casualties, 1969 |
| CTBT | - | Comprehensive Test Ban Treaty |
| DE | - | Sub-Committee on Ship Design and Equipment |
| DG | - | Dangerous goods |
| DGN | - | Dangerous goods note |
| DSC | - | Digital Selective Calling |
| EEZ | - | Exclusive Economic Zone |
| EPIRB | - | Emergency position indicating radio beacons |
| FAL | - | Convention on Facilitation of Liability of International Maritime Traffic, 1965 |
| FGMDSS | - | Future Global Maritime Distress and Safety System |
| FP | - | Fire Protection |

| | | |
|---|---|---|
| GESAMP | - | Group of Experts on Scientific Aspects of Marine Pollution |
| | | |
| HF | - | High frequency |
| HNS | - | Hazardous and Noxious Substances |
| | | |
| IAEA | - | International Atomic Energy Agency |
| IAIN | - | International Association of Institutes of Navigation |
| IALA | - | International Association of Lighthouse Authorities |
| ICAO | - | International Civil Aviation Organization |
| ICC | - | International Chamber of Commerce |
| ICS | - | International Chamber of Shipping |
| IEC | - | International Electrotechnical Commission |
| IFC | - | Convention on the Establishment of an International Fund for Compensation for Oil Pollution Damage, 1971 |
| IGS | - | Inert Gas System |
| IHO | - | International Hydrographic Organization |
| ILO | - | International Labour Organization |
| IMF | - | International Monetary Fund |
| IMOSAR | - | IMO Search and Rescue Manual |
| INMARSAT | - | Convention on the International Maritime Satellite Organization, 1976 |
| INTELSAT | - | International Telecommunications Satellite |
| INTERTANKO | - | International Association of Independent Tanker Owners |
| IOPC | - | International Oil Pollution Fund |
| IOPP | - | International Oil Pollution Certificate |
| ISO | - | International Standards Organization |
| ITCOMIA | - | International Council of Marine Industry Association |
| ITU | - | International Telecommunication Union |
| IUMI | - | International Union of Marine Insurance |
| | | |
| KAP | - | Kuwait Action Plan |
| | | |
| LDC | - | London Dumping Convention |
| LL | - | Load Lines Convention, 1966 |
| LLMC | - | Limitation of Liability for Maritime Claims Convention, 1976 |
| LNG | - | Liquefied Natural Gas |
| LOT | - | Load on Top |
| LPG | - | Liquefied Petroleum Gas |
| LSA | - | Life-Saving Appliances |

| | | |
|---|---|---|
| MARPOL | - | Convention for the Prevention of Pollution from Ships 73/78 |
| MEMAC | - | Marine Emergency Mutual Aid Centre |
| MEPC | - | Marine Environment Protection Committee |
| MERSAR | - | Merchant Ship Search and Rescue Manual |
| MF | - | Medium frequency |
| MFAG | - | Medical First Aid Guide |
| MSC | - | Maritime Safety Committee |
| NAV | - | Sub-Committee on Safety of Navigation |
| NBDP | - | Narrow Band Direct Printing |
| NGO | - | Non-governmental Organizations |
| NLS | - | Noxious Liquid Substance |
| NOS | - | Not Otherwise Specified |
| NPT | - | Non-Proliferation Treaty, 1968 |
| NSPC | - | North Sea Pilotage Commission |
| OAS | - | Organization of American States |
| OCIMF | - | Oil Companies International Marine Forum |
| ODAS | - | Ocean Data Acquisition Systems |
| OECD | - | Organization for Economic Co-operation and Development |
| PAL | - | Convention Relating to the Carriage of Passengers and their Luggage by Sea, 1974 |
| PL | - | Protective Location |
| RCC | - | Rescue Co-ordination Centre |
| ROPME | - | Regional Organization for the Protection of the Marine Environment |
| RSC | - | Rescue Sub-Centre |
| SAR | - | Convention on Maritime Search and Rescue, 1979 |
| SDR | - | Special Drawing Rights |
| SFV | - | Convention for the Safety of Fishing Vessels, 1977 |
| SITPRO | - | Simplification of International Trade Procedures Board |
| SLF | - | Sub-Committee on Stability and Load Lines and Fishing Vessels Safety |
| SMB | - | Single Mooring Buoy |
| SOLAS | - | Safety of Life at Sea Convention 74/78 |
| STCW | - | Convention on Standards of Training, Certification and Watchkeeping for Seafarers, 1978 |
| STP | - | Special Trading Passenger Ships Agreement, 1971 |
| STW | - | Sub-Committee on Standards of Training and Watchkeeping |

| | | |
|---|---|---|
| TCC | - | Technical Co-operation Committee |
| TESC | - | Totally enclosed survival craft |
| TM | - | Tonnage Measurement of Ships Convention, 1969 |
| TOVALOP | - | Tanker Owners' Voluntary Agreement Concerning Liability for Oil Pollution |
| UKAEA | - | United Kingdom Atomic Energy Authority |
| UNCITRAL | - | United Nations Commission on International Trade Law |
| UNCLOS | - | United Nations Conference on the Law of the Sea |
| UNCTAD | - | United Nations Conference on Trade and Development |
| UNDP | - | United Nations Development Programme |
| UNEP | - | United Nations Environment Programme |
| UNID | - | United Nations Development Organisation |
| UTC | - | Universal Time |
| VTS | - | Vessel Traffic Services |
| WHO | - | World Health Organization |
| WMU | - | World Maritime Organization |
| WPCA | - | Water Pollution Control Act |
| WQIA | - | Water Quality Improvement Act |

# TABLE OF CASES

*Accinanto Ltd. and Others* v. *A/S J. Ludwig Mowinckels and Another* (1953) 1 Lloyd's Rep. 38.
*Aga, The* (1968) 1 Lloyd's Rep. 431.
*Anthony II, The* (1966) 2 Lloyd's Rep. 437.
*Askew* v. *American Waterways Operations*, 411 U.S.325 (1973).

*Banfield* v. *Goole and Sheffield Transport Co. Ltd.* (1910) 2 K.B. 94.
*Biche, The* (1984) 1 Lloyd's Rep. 26.
*Boucher* v. *Lawson*, Cas. Temp. Hard. 85.
*Brass* v. *Maitland* (1865) 6 E & B 470.
*Burgers* v. *M/V Tamano*, 370 F. Supp. (D.Me. 1973).

*Canadian Transport Co. Ltd.* v. *Court Line Ltd.* (1940) 2 All E.R. 112.
*Chevron USA* v. *Hammond* (1984) AMC,1028.
*Cockerton* v. *Naviera Aznar SA* (1960) 2 Lloyd's Rep. 451.
*Commonwealth of Puerto Rico et al* v. *S.S. Zoe Colocotroni* (1980) 628 Fed.
*Compania Maritima San Basilio* v. *Oceanus* (1976) 2 Lloyd's Rep. 161.
*Complaint of Tug Ocean Price Inc.* (1978) AMC,1786.
*Complaint of Harbor Towing Corp.* (1972) AMC, 597.

*Eagle, The* (1977) 2 Lloyd's Rep. 70.

*Farrandoc, The* (1967) 2 Lloyd's Rep. 276.
*Federal Steam Navigation Co. Ltd.* v. *Department of Trade and Industry (The "Huntingdon")* (1974) 1 Lloyd's Rep. 520.
*Frazer* v. *Furman* (1967) 2 Lloyd's Rep. 1.

*Garden City, The* (1982) 2 Lloyd's Rep. 382.
*Great Northern Railway Company* v. *L.E.P. Transport and Depository Ltd.* (1922) 2 K.B. 472.

*Lady Gwendolen, The* (1965) P. 294.
*Lord* v. *Goodall S.S. Co.*, 15 Fed. Cas. 884.
*Ludditt* v. *Ginger Coote Airways* (1947) A.C.233, P.C.

*Makedonia, The* (1962) 1 Lloyd's Rep. 316.
*Marion, The* (1984) 2 Lloyd's Rep. 1.
*Maritime Services Board of N.S.W.* v. *Posiden Navigation (The World Encouragement and Stolt Sheaf)* Sup.Ct. of N.S.W., Australia, LMLN, July 22, 1982.
*Maryland Casualty Co.* v. *Cushing* 347 U.S.409 (1954).

*Norman, The* (1960) 1 Lloyd's Rep. 1.

*Ocean Eagle* (1974) A.C. 1629.

*Paterson Steamship* v. *Robin Hood Mills* (1937) 59 Ll.L.R. 33.

*Portland Pipe Line Corp.* v. *Environmental Improvement Commission* (1973) AMC, 341.

*Rankin* v. *De Coster* (1975) 2 Lloyd's Rep. 84.

*Readhead* v. *Midland Railway Company* (1869) L R 4 Q.B. 379.

*Reed* v. *London and Rochester Trading Co.* (1954) 2 Lloyd's Rep. 463.

*Rose* v. *Plenty* (1976) 1 W.L.R. 141.

*Rylands* v. *Fletcher* (1868) L R 3, HL 330.

*St.John Shipping Corporation* v. *Joseph Rank Ltd.* (1957) 1 Q.B. 267.

*Truculent, The* (1952) P.1.

*Union Oil Co.* v. *Oppen* (1975) AMC, 416.

*U.S.* v. *Beatty Inc.*, 401 F. Supp. 1040 (W.D. 1975).

# INTRODUCTION

The first edition of this volume appeared in 1984. This second edition has been completely rewritten in order to provide the Reader with a reliable guide to the International Shipping Rules.

Since its establishment, the IMO has adopted hundreds of resolutions, a number of conventions and codes. These various instruments cover almost every aspect of safety at sea and the protection of the marine environment. The impact of these instruments is difficult to assess and in some cases it will be only felt after a number of years after their entry into force.

Like other international institutions, the IMO has had its disappointments. But it has certainly served as a universal forum for discussion and negotiation of many complex shipping problems. The debates and deliberations within the Organization have inspired and encouraged actions taken elsewhere.

This volume provides detailed coverage of hundreds of resolutions, the IMO Conventions, Codes and Statutory Instruments with the latest amendments. Thus, the Reader can be sure of having all the source material at the heart of Shipping law in an immediately accessible form. It is hoped that what is offered will prove to be of value to those who read these pages.

S.M.

Liverpool, 1986.

# CHAPTER I

# THE IMO: A LAW-MAKING ORGANIZATION

During the second half of the nineteenth century, several international conventions on shipping were adopted. These conventions were formulated either by intergovernmental or private bodies. Over the years, the number of organizations engaged in the preparation of rules on shipping increased substantially. Hence, it became apparent that there was a need for a body which would be able to co-ordinate and promote further measures on a permanent basis.

To meet such a need, the United Nations Maritime Conference in Geneva adopted on 6 March, 1948, the Convention which established the Inter-Governmental Maritime Consultative Organization (IMCO) as a body devoted exclusively to shipping matters. The Convention required for its entry into force the acceptance of twenty-one States, including seven with at least one million gross tons of shipping each. This requirement was fulfilled in 1958[(1)] and the lapse of ten years was due to differences of opinion as to the role of the Organization. Some States took the view that it should be limited to technical matters while others believed that the Organization should extend its activities to embrace economic matters.

IMCO is a specialised agency of the United Nations. Its members[(2)] include not only the traditional maritime countries but also those which rely largely on the shipping services of other countries. From May 22, 1982, the word "Consultative" was removed from its name and it became the International Maritime Organization (IMO)[(3)].

## (i) OBJECTIVES, FUNCTIONS AND STRUCTURE

The main objectives are:

(a) (i)"to provide machinery for co-operation among Governments in the field of governmental regulations and practices relating to the

---

(1) The First Assembly met in London in January, 1959.

(2) By April,1985, the IMO had 127 Members and One Associate Member. See the list of Member States and the date of receipt of the instrument of acceptance, Appendix I.

(3) The name of the Organization should not be pronounced as one word but as a three-letter abbreviation.

technical matters of all kinds affecting shipping engaged in international trade, to encourage the general adoption of the highest practicable standards in matters concerning maritime safety, efficiency of navigation and prevention and control of marine pollution from ships; and to deal with legal matters related to the purposes" of the Organization;

(ii) to provide for the consideration by the Organization of any matters concerning shipping and the effect of shipping on the marine environment that may be referred to it by any organ or specialised agency of the United Nations; and

(iii) to provide for the exchange of information among Governments on matters under consideration by the Organization.

Further, the Convention states among its objectives the following:

"(b) To encourage the removal of discriminatory action and unnecessary restrictions by Governments affecting shipping engaged in international trade so as to promote the availability of shipping services to the commerce of the world without discrimination; assistance and encouragement given by a Government for the development of its national shipping and for purposes of security does not in itself constitute discrimination, provided that such assistance and encouragement is not based on measures designed to restrict the freedom of shipping of all flags to take part in international trade;

(c) To provide for the consideration by the Organization of matters concerning unfair restrictive practices by shipping concerns in accordance with Part II."(1).

---

(1) When ratifying the Convention, many countries made reservations to the objectives stated in (b) and (c). The Scandinavian countries and others felt strongly against any involvement of the Organization in the economic field. They maintained that any intervention would run against their interest and be harmful to international trade.
As the shipping scene has changed since these

In order to achieve the above objectives, the Organization:

(a) considers and makes recommendations upon matters within its competence that may be remitted to it by Members, the United Nations or any specialised agency of the United Nations or by any other appropriate inter-governmental organization;

(b) provides for the drafting of conventions, agreements or other suitable instruments by convening such conferences as may be necessary and recommends the resulting instruments to Governments and to inter-governmental organizations for acceptance, implementation or enforcement as may be appropriate;

(c) performs functions assigned to it or under international instruments relating to maritime matters and the effect of shipping on the marine environment;

(d) promotes measures for the effective implementation and enforcement of international standards and regulations adopted by the Organization or contained in international instruments; and

(e) facilitates, as necessary, technical co-operation within the scope of the Organization, including the provision of services and other appropriate assistance to Governments, particularly those of developing countries.

In pursuing these objectives, the IMO has succeeded in generating a comprehensive body of rules(1)

---

reservations were made, the IMO moved into some of the commercial areas of shipping, especially those which are related to technical matters.

(1) A proposal was made by the Soviet Union for a universal international technical convention. Such a convention shall consist of a single set of articles concerning privileges and obligations of contracting parties; harmonized survey and certification provisions and technical annexes incorporating harmonized definitions and phrases.
At its 50th session, the Maritime Safety Committee (MSC) agreed that theoretically such an instru-

on safety at sea[1] and the protection of the marine environment. A second phase was essential to consolidate the work that has been done. Therefore, the Assembly adopted in November,1981, Resolution

---

ment would be very useful. Some delegations, however, felt that it would take many years to draft such a convention and then secure its entry into force. The majority view was that it would be realistic to deal with the matter in stages. See MSC 51/21, June 7, 1985. It may be preferable to have two main instruments, SOLAS and MARPOL, and under each one, secondary conventions.

(1) The MSC considered the feasibility of establishing a system of assigning an IMO identification number to each ship. It noted the following views:
   (a) Lloyd's Register six-digit number and an additional check digit could be used as an IMO identification number;
   (b) the identification number assigned to a ship should be permanently marked on the stern of the ship following the name and the port of registry of the ship;
   (c) an Assembly resolution would be an appropriate mechanism for implementation of the scheme;
   (d) there would be no significant financial implications of the proposed scheme if the Lloyd's Register number was adopted; and
   (e) Lloyd's Register of Shipping would claim indemnity against any legal liability which may be caused by any errors of the identification number.

Several delegations were of the opinion that numbers and procedures adopted by a private organization should not be used in an IMO system. Other delegations considered that the Lloyd's Register number should be used as an IMO identification number.
Some delegations proposed that the introduction of an IMO ship identification scheme should be restricted to the prevention of maritime fraud. Other delegations were of the view that the application of ship identification numbers should be extended to include matters related to safety of ships and pollution prevention. No decision was taken by the MSC on this issue. *Ibid*, pp. 41-43.

A.500 (XII) entitled "Objectives of the Organization in the 1980s", in which it called for slowing down in the development of new Conventions and the amendment of existing ones, until the maritime administrations and the shipping industries have caught up with the approved rules. The IMO would entertain proposals for new conventions or amendments to existing ones only when compelling needs exist(1).

Structure

Since there is a written text, the analysis will naturally be focused on it. Article 12 of the Convention states that: "The Organization shall consist of an Assembly, a Council, a Maritime Safety Committee, and such subsidiary organs as the Organization may at any time consider necessary, and a Secretariat."

The IMO has six main organs: the Assembly; the Council; the Maritime Safety Committee (MSC); the Marine Environment Protection Committee (MEPC); the Legal Committee and the Technical Co-operation Committee.

The Assembly: The Assembly consists of representatives from all Member States; it meets once every two years, decides upon the work programme, approves all recommendations, votes the budget to which all Member States contribute on an agreed scale of assessments, approves financial regulations, elects the Members of the Council and approves the appointment of the Secretary-General. In brief, the

(1) There have been a number of criticisms of the IMO, in particular its frequent amendments to conventions and the introduction of improved equipment. At the general meeting of the Baltic and International Maritime Conference (BIMCO), held in Madrid in May, 1983, Stanley Symor said: "time and effort are spent on the IMO committees and conferences with results of only limited effectiveness and in some cases counter-productive to original purposes." He described the work of the organization as "a patchwork of international regulations that are too often a response to incidents." He added that despite a proliferation of conventions, the world fleet safety record shows no sign of overall improvement. Mr. Symor suggested that the IMO should work more closely with the shipping industry. See Lloyd's List, May 11, 1983.

# TRUCTURE OF IMO BODIES

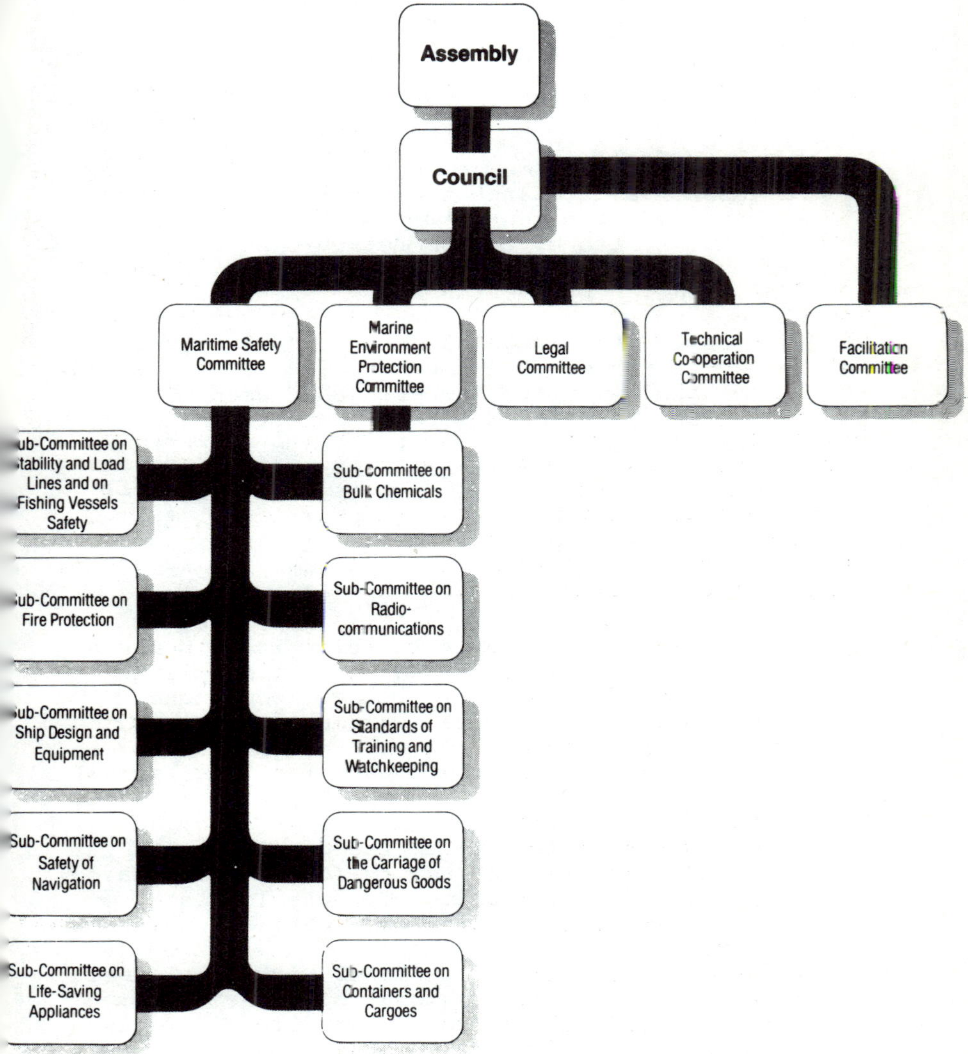

Assembly is the main legislative[1] organ. It adopts resolutions which will be recommended to Member States for action and takes decisions in regard to convening any international conferences.

<u>The Council</u>: The Council, which is the governing body of the Organization, consists of thirty-two Members[2] elected by the Assembly[3]. It meets twice a year. Between Assembly sessions, it

---

(1) In 1975, the Assembly adopted Resolution A.450 (XI) to amend the procedures of the Organization in view of the increase in its membership, the important tasks undertaken by it and the method necessary to discharge them. It states: "Texts of proposed amendments to the Convention shall be communicated by the Secretary-General to Members at least six months in advance of their consideration by the Assembly. Amendments shall be adopted by a two-thirds majority vote of the Assembly. Twelve months after its acceptance by two-thirds of the Members of the Organization, other than Associate Members, each amendment shall come into force for all Members. If within the first 60 days of this period of twelve months a Member gives notification of withdrawal from the Organization on account of an amendment, the withdrawal shall, notwithstanding the provisions of Article 58 of the Convention, take effect on the date on which such amendment comes into force."

(2) The status of the IMO was in danger of being eroded by a process of politicization. Members of the IMO used to assemble in *ad hoc* political groups in order to maximise their power and influence. However, the changes in the structure in 1982 and the enlargement of membership of the Council from twenty-four to thirty-two ensure that Member States will act in concert.

(3) In electing the Members of the Council, the Assembly shall observe the following criteria:
   (a) Eight shall be States with the largest interest in providing international shipping services;
   (b) Eight shall be other States with the largest interest in international seaborne trade;
   (c) Sixteen shall be States not elected under (a) or (b) above which have special interests in maritime transport or navigation,

exercises all the functions[1] of the Assembly in running the work of the Organization, except that of recommending to Member States regulations and guidelines for maritime safety and the control of pollution[2].

The Committees: The work of the IMO is done through the following Committees: the Maritime Safety Committee (MSC); The Marine Environment Protection

---

and whose election to the Council will ensure the representation of all major geographic areas of the world.

Furthermore, the Resolution states that:

(a) The Council shall elect its Chairman and adopt its own Rules of Procedure except as otherwise provided in the Convention;
(b) Twenty-one Members of the Council shall constitute a quorum;
(c) The Council shall meet upon one month's notice as often as may be necessary for the efficient discharge of its duties upon the summons of its Chairman or upon request by not less than four of its Members. It shall meet at such places as may be convenient.

(1) By Resolution A.500 (XII) the Assembly made directions and recommendations to the Council, in relation to the work of the Committees. The Resolution runs as follows: "Recommends that the Committees carry out their functions on the basis of the principle that provisions of new conventions or of amendments to existing conventions relating to the structure of ships should apply only to ships built after the entry into force of the instrument or instruments in question and that other provisions should not apply to ships built before the entry into force of the instrument or instruments in question unless there is compelling need and the costs and benefits of the measures have been fully considered..."

(2) See the Rules of Procedure of the Council C52/4, 20 March,1984. Under the Council's Rules of Procedure (Rule 4), the Chairman may invite non-members of the Council to attend the session as observers. As from January,1984, six official (Arabic, Chinese, English, French, Russian and Spanish) and three working (English, French and Spanish) languages are used in the IMO.

Committee (MEPC); The Legal Committee; The Technical Co-operation Committee (TCC); and the Facilitation Committee. Usually they meet twice a year for a week each time, to consider the work and the reports submitted to them by their sub-committees. They, in turn, report their findings to the Assembly through the Council.

The Maritime Safety Committee (MSC) carries a heavy load of the work of the Organization as it is responsible for the administration of ten of the IMO Conventions(1). Following Resolution A.500 (XII), the MSC reviewed its policy of work so that the emphasis is placed on the implementation of the existing rules rather than the formulation of new rules.

The Marine Environment Protection Committee (MEPC) is responsible for all matters relating to the prevention and control of marine pollution. Thus MARPOL 73/78 is one of its main occupations. Through its Sub-Committee on Bulk Chemicals, it has adopted manuals and guidelines to assist governments, the oil and chemical industries to take measures against marine pollution(2). The MEPC is active in the field of technical co-operation including the development of regional arrangements to combat pollution in cases of emergency(3). To this end, it organized seminars, workshops and training courses in this field.

---

(1) The MSC has the following ten sub-committees: (1) Sub-Committee on Safety of Navigation (NAV); (2) Sub-Committee on Radiocommunications (COM); (3) Sub-Committee on Life-Saving Appliances (LSA); (4) Sub-Committee on Standards of Training and Watchkeeping (STW); (5) Sub-Committee on the Carriage of Dangerous Goods (CDG); (6) Sub-Committee on Containers and Cargoes (BC); (7) Sub-Committee on Fire Protection (FP); (8) Sub-Committee on Ship Design and Equipment (DE); (9) Sub-Committee on Bulk Chemicals (BCH) (subsidiary of MSC and MEPC); and (10) Sub-Committee on Stability and Load Lines and Fishing Vessels Safety (SLF).

(2) See Chapter VII.

(3) It also performs such functions as are, or may be, conferred on the Organization under international conventions concerning marine pollution.

The Legal Committee is responsible for consideration of any legal matters. It prepared several conventions(1) and Protocols(2) for the Organization.

The Technical Co-operation Committee (TCC) supervises the technical assistance work; it meets once a year.

The Facilitation Committee supervises work connected with the 1965 Convention on the Facilitation of International Maritime Traffic; it meets occasionally as required.

The Secretariat: The Secretariat, which is located at the headquarters in London(3), consists of a number of officials(4) recruited on a wide geographic basis(5). They work under the leadership of the Secretary-General(6) who plays an important role in the making of a dynamic organization.

---

(1) The Legal Committee has prepared the following Conventions: the International Convention relating to Intervention on the High Seas in Cases of Oil Pollution Casualties, 1969; the International Convention on Civil Liability for Oil Pollution Damage, 1969; the International Convention on the Establishment of an International Fund for Compensation for Oil Pollution Damage, 1971; the International Convention on Civil Liability in the field of Maritime Carriage of Nuclear Material, 1971; the Athens Convention relating to the Carriage of Passengers and their Luggage by Sea, 1974; and the International Convention on Limitation of Liability for Maritime Claims, 1976.

(2) See the Protocol which substitutes the gold franc for a unit of account based on the Special Drawing Rights (SDR) of the International Monetary Fund.

(3) The building of the IMO is a Crown property leased to the Organization, with 80% of the rent met by the British Government. This is the usual arrangement for United Nations headquarters. The address of the IMO is: 4 Albert Embankment, London SE1 7SR.

(4) The Secretariat has a staff of about 270.

(5) Fifty-seven officials out of sixty professional and high posts belong to thirty-one nationalities. See JIU/REP/84/4, pp. 21,22.

(6) The Secretary-General reports to the United Nations General Assembly and to the Economic and

The duties of the Secretariat are numerous(1). It serves the Assembly, the Council, the Committees, *ad hoc* bodies, and any conference convened by the Assembly. Among its other important duties is keeping close contact with Members of the Organization for the ratification and the implementation of the IMO rules.

## The IMO Instruments

The IMO has adopted the following conventions:

- The International Convention on Load Lines (LL), 1966
- The Special Trade Passenger Ships Agreement (STP), 1971
- The International Convention for Safe Containers (CSC), 1972
- The Convention on the International Regulations for Preventing Collisions at Sea (COLREG), 1972
- The Convention on the International Maritime Satellite Organization (INMARSAT), 1976
- The International Convention for the Safety of Fishing Vessels (SFV), 1977

---

Social Council on major developments in the IMO and informs the Assembly and the Council of the discussions and decisions taken by the UN bodies which are relevant to their work.

(1) Contracts concluded by the Organization are of an infinite variety ranging from contracts for purchase, charter-parties, insurance, etc. In principle, the parties to the contract may express the law to govern it. Contracts of employment are usually made subject to the administrative law set up by the Organization. Agreements between the IMO and a State or another international organization may well be regarded as a treaty. An agreement with a private corporation may not be considered as a treaty. The parties, however, may accept to internationalize the agreement, making it subject to the general principles of law or the national law of a certain State.
The Secretariat has administrative functions such as the collection and evaluation of casualty reports. It is also the depository of numerous conventions.

- The International Convention on Standards of Training, Certification and Watchkeeping for Seafarers (STCW), 1978
- The International Convention on Maritime Search and Rescue (SAR), 1979
- The International Convention Relating to Intervention on the High Seas in Cases of Oil Pollution Casualties (CSI), 1969
- The Convention on the Prevention of Marine Pollution by Dumping of Wastes and Other Matter (LDC), 1972
- The International Convention for the Prevention of Pollution from Ships (MARPOL), 1973
- The International Convention on Civil Liability for Oil Pollution Damage (CLC), 1969
- The Convention Relating to Civil Liability in the Field of Maritime Carriage of Nuclear Material (LNM), 1971
- The International Convention on the Establishment of an International Fund for Compensation for Oil Pollution Damage (IFC), 1971
- The Athens Convention Relating to the Carriage of Passengers and Their Luggage by Sea (PAL), 1974
- The Convention on Limitation of Liability for Maritime Claims (LLMC), 1976
- The Convention on Facilitation of International Maritime Traffic (FAL), 1965
- The International Convention on Tonnage Measurement of Ships (TM), 1969

Some of these Conventions were modified by subsequent protocols or amendments.

Apart from the Conventions, the IMO formulated a number of Codes[1] and adopted over five hundred resolutions. Thus, the IMO is primarily a legislative body and a forum where Member States can express their views reflecting state or international shipping practice. It uses three different instru-

---

(1) See Appendix III.

ments: conventions[1], resolutions[2] and codes. It is commonly believed that measures contained in conventions, when ratified, are binding, while those appearing in resolutions are only recommended to Member States. Codes stand between these two instruments. In practice, this distinction is not fundamental. Resolutions may carry more weight than certain conventions, and some of the codes are incorporated into national law.

Once the convention is ratified, its provisions become mandatory on Member States. Recommendations adopted by the IMO Assembly are not, in principle, binding on governments. However, in practice, their contents may prove to be important with the result that they will be incorporated in national law. Thus generally speaking, conventions are binding when ratified, resolutions have merely an advising character, and the codes stand between the two. Some of the codes have become indispensable tools for the conduct of maritime shipping.

The issue of the preparation of the convention needs further consideration.

Preparation of the conventions: Adoption. Usually the first step is a proposal made in one of the Committees. When agreement is reached on it, the proposal is submitted to the Council which may refer it to the Assembly to have its approval to proceed with it. Once approval is given, the Committee concerned considers the matter in detail in order to

---

(1) Conventions are designed as an obligation-creating instrument when ratified. A question may arise as to what is the value of the convention in relation to a member for which it is not in force. It may be argued that the convention is not binding or perhaps it is considered as a recommendation.

(2) Resolutions lay down standards of policy. They are not binding and have not the same measure of authority; they are essentially more experimental in character. They supplement in many respects the provisions of the conventions. Recommendations are not designed for the creation of legal obligations but are exclusively standard defining instruments. They are to be communicated to all Members for consideration with a view to effect being given to them in the appropriate way by Member States. They may be considered as guides for national action.

prepare a draft instrument. It may refer the matter to one of its sub-committees for a detailed study[(1)].

The draft, when completed, is reported to the Council and Assembly with a recommendation to convene a conference to consider its formal adoption. All Member States of the IMO and also all States which are members of the United Nations or any of its specialized agencies, are invited to attend. Organizations with consultative status in the IMO are invited to send observers. The draft convention together with any comments on it by governments or interested organizations is then considered by the Conference which may approve, amend or refuse its adoption. Once it is adopted, it is deposited with the Secretary-General who sends copies to governments. The Convention is opened for signature by States, usually for a period of 12 months. Signatories may ratify or accept the Convention while non-signatories may accede to it.

Ratification: The adoption of a convention marks the first step. Before a convention comes into force and is binding, it has to be ratified by individual governments. By ratifying a convention, the government is committed to it and undertakes to give it the force of law.

Each convention stipulates the conditions which have to be made before it enters into force. The IMO conventions take a long time (sometimes five years) before coming into force. Such delay causes much concern to the Organization and some of its Members. Governments never give the reasons for not ratifying a convention. Besides, before ratifying a convention, changes in the national law may be needed or, in some cases, special facilities may have to be constructed such as the reception

---

(1) During consideration of the draft in the Committee or Sub-Committee, organizations with consultative States would bring the benefits of their practical experience to the debate and assist in the formulation of the draft. Sometimes, the whole draft is prepared by another organization. For instance, the Comité Maritime International (CMI) prepared a draft convention on Salvage to replace the 1910 Brussels Convention and submitted it to the IMO. See the text in J. of Mar. Law & Comm. Vol.12, No.4, July, 1981, pp. 550-565.

facilities outlined in the 1973 International Convention for the Prevention of Pollution From Ships.

The crucial issue is the number of ratifications stipulated by the convention(1). If a small number is required, the convention will come into force in a short time. On the other hand, it is necessary that the convention is accepted and applied by a large section of the shipping community. Otherwise it would tend to confuse rather than clarify the shipping practice since its provisions would not apply to a significant proportion of the ships it was intended to deal with.

When the conditions have been fulfilled, the convention enters into force for the States which have accepted it after a usual period of grace intended to enable all States to take the necessary measures for implementation. A government's acceptance of a convention places on it the obligation to take the measures required by it. Often national law has to be enacted or changed to enforce the provisions of the convention.

Enforcement: The enforcement of the conventions depends upon how far Member States are prepared to maintain the legal order and the IMO has no powers in this respect.

Usually when enforcing the IMO rules, the State has to adopt or incorporate them into its national legal system and to prescribe penalties for any breach.

Certain IMO conventions stipulate that a

---

(1) Although the ratification is a prerogative of individual States, and the IMO has no authority in this respect, the following measures have been taken to promote or to assist in the implementation of the conventions:
- (a) definition of "new ships" on the basis of calendar dates rather than the date of entry into force;
- (b) setting up a target date for entry into force;
- (c) providing technical assistance to developing countries;
- (d) organising seminars to explain the conventions and their impact; and
- (e) establishing machinery in the Secretariat to be in charge of the implementation of the conventions.

See IMO News, No.1, 1979, p.15.

certificate showing that the requirements are met should be kept on board the ship. The certificate could not be regarded as conclusive evidence of the adherence to the provisions of the relevant convention. It must be supplemented by port control to ensure its validity. Thus, the enforcement of the IMO conventions depends on: (a) the willingness of Member States to make sure that the IMO rules are applied in their letter and spirit; and (b) the acceptance of inspection and control of their ships in foreign ports[1].

Amendments: With the constant changes in technology, shipping conventions need to be reviewed from time to time. In early conventions, amendments came into force after a percentage of contracting states, usually two-thirds, had accepted them. The result was that more acceptances were required to amend a convention than were originally required to bring the convention into force, especially where the number of States which are parties to the convention is very large.

This percentage requirement has in practice led to long delays in bringing amendments into force. In order to remedy the situation, a new amendment procedure was devised by IMO. It is called the

---

(1) The IMO failed to take an action on port control while the EEC countries reached an agreement. On January 26, 1982, fourteen European countries signed the Memorandum of Understanding on Port State Control: Belgium, Denmark, Finland, France, West Germany, Greece, Ireland, Italy, the Netherlands, Norway, Portugal, Spain, Sweden and the United Kingdom. They have agreed to enforce in a co-ordinated manner the following instruments: the 1966 Load Line Convention, the SOLAS 1974/78 Convention, MARPOL 73/78, the 1978 Training Convention, the 1972 Collision Regulations and the ILO Convention No.147 on minimum standards for merchant vessels.
The philosophy of the EEC Agreement is to establish an effective system of enforcing safety and anti-pollution standards by means of a European port control system that would get rid of substandard ships from European ports.
The Agreement would seriously weaken the standing of the IMO although the EEC countries believe that mandatory enforcement within the community would not affect the IMO.

"tacit acceptance" procedure by which amendments enter into force at a particular time unless, before that time, objections to the amendments are received from a specified number of Parties.

The process of "tacit acceptance" is a fascinating phenomenon in its own right. It is an innovation to avoid delay in bringing the amendments to the convention into effect. In legal terms, it may be explained by saying that acceptance of the amendments occurs by mere silence. Alternatively, one can say that the State by ratifying a convention which provides for this type of procedure, waives its right to communicate its acceptance for future amendments. Against this view, it could be argued that where ratification is required for both the convention and the amendments, a State may be left in doubt and face constitutional difficulties. Again, with the "tacit acceptance" procedure, one would imagine that a convention will continue for a long period since it could be amended all the time.

Assessment of Members' contributions: The contribution of each Member State(1) used to consist of two parts: (a) basic assessment, which was fixed at a sum of US $2,000, $4,000 or $10,000 depending on that Member's percentage assessment for the United Nations budget; and (b) additional assessment, determined by dividing the rest of the budget (i.e. the budget after deducting the basic assessment of all Members and miscellaneous income) according to the proportion which that Member's merchant fleet bore to the total of world tonnage.

Several criticisms were directed to this system in particular to the fixed sum which fell far beyond an adequate contribution. Accordingly, a working group prepared in 1982 new proposals which were adopted by the Assembly.

Under the new rules, each Member's basic assessment is worked out by a rather complicated system, but it is still based on United Nations assessments. This will place a Member in one of eight categories, rather than one of three, for the calculation of the 10 per cent of the budget to be

---

(1) The Secretary-General reported to the Council (in May, 1984) that 78 States had not yet made any payment in respect of their contributions for 1984. He added that every effort is made to encourage Members to pay their contributions on time. See C52/SR.2 Nov.8, 1984, p.12.

covered by the basic assessments. Additional assessment is calculated on a tonnage basis. In order to help Member States who are beginning to build up their fleet, each Member's fleet is notionally reduced by 50,000 tons before the ratio between its fleet and the total of world tonnage is calculated.

Privileges and Immunities: Representatives of Member States: Representatives to the IMO are not accredited to the host State but to the Organization. Consequently the remedy of declaring a representative *persona non grata* is not applicable[1]. Another consequence of non-accreditation to the host State is that representatives may be received from governments not recognised by the host State.

Officials of the Organization: The immunities, privileges and facilities enjoyed by officials of the IMO are stipulated in the General Convention on the Privileges and Immunities of Specialized Agencies approved by the General Assembly of the United Nations on 21 November, 1947[2] and the Headquarters Agreement of 28 November, 1968. Section 19(a) of the General Convention provides that officials "shall be immune from legal process in respect of words spoken or written and all acts performed by them in their official capacity"[3].

A supplementary agreement was attached to the Headquarters Agreement to define the legal status of the Organization[4] and to spell out in detail "the content of certain privileges, concessions and courtesies as well as the measures for their implementation". For the purposes of privileges and

---

(1) The USSR, probably as a result of the restrictions imposed by the British Government on the number of staff accredited to its embassy in London, proposed that delegations to the IMO should be treated as an additional diplomatic mission in the same way as other bodies of the United Nations, NATO and the EEC.

(2) 33 U.N.T.S. 261-302. The Convention is a model agreement subject to variations for each specialized agency.

(3) See IMO Resolution A.10 (A) as modified by Annex XII.

(4) The inviolability of premises and archives is stated in the Agreement.

immunities, the Headquarters Agreement divides officials of the IMO in the following categories: (a) officials; (b) senior officials; and (c) the officials specifically referred to in the revised text of Annex XII to the General Convention. Thus, senior officials enjoy only "functional immunity" as opposed to a full "jurisdictional immunity" enjoyed by "diplomatic agents". However, the United Kingdom Government accorded to senior officials all diplomatic facilities and courtesies including registration numbers for their cars comprising the letter "D".

In 1983 the Government changed its policy on the issue of diplomatic registration number in view of the abuse of diplomatic privileges. Under the new policy, diplomatic registration plates would only be granted to persons who enjoy full diplomatic immunity. As the IMO senior officials did not have such immunity, they would be granted "X" registration plates(1).

This issue was placed on the agenda of the fifty-fourth session of the Council, which decided to request the Secretary-General to continue with his consultations on it with the United Kingdom authorities(2).

### (ii) RELATIONS WITH OTHER ORGANIZATIONS

Many United Nations bodies(3) and non-governmental organizations are involved in one aspect or another of shipping with the possibility that their work will overlap with the IMO. Furthermore, confusion to the shipping industry will arise when an issue is dealt with by two organizations. This situation could be avoided by defining the kind of work to be undertaken by each organization. Therefore, co-ordination of the programme of work between the organizations concerned with shipping is essential.

---

(1) Under the present arrangements, full diplomatic status is accorded only to three officials, whereas before December,1983, 65 senior officials were entitled to the letter "D" on their car registration plates.
(2) Council - 54th session, 13 May,1985, C54/12.
(3) Fifteen UN bodies and ten specialized agencies are concerned with one sector or another of shipping.

1. Relationships with United Nations bodies

The IMO has established a close working relationship with a number of international organizations and United Nations bodies such as the United Nations Development Programme (UNDP)[1]; the United Nations Environment Programme (UNEP)[2]; the United Nations Industrial Development Organization (UNIDO)[3]; the International Telecommunications Union (ITU)[4] and

---

(1) The UNDP is the principal source of finance for the Technical Co-operation Programme. In 1980 its share amounted to 73.3 per cent of the funds and in 1981 it reached 75.6 per cent.
(2) A memorandum of understanding between the UNEP and the IMO concerning their roles and responsibilities was signed in November, 1976 in Nairobi. It recognized the co-ordinating role of the UNEP in relation to matters concerning the environment. At the same time it emphasized the responsibility of the IMO for implementing specific programmes relating to the prevention and control of pollution of the marine environment from ships and also its responsibility for developing standards and projects through joint action plans sponsored by the UNEP.
(3) The relationship between the two bodies is governed by a memorandum of understanding of 23 January, 1978. Under the terms of this memorandum, the two organizations agreed to co-ordinate their programmes of technical co-operation and assistance in the following areas: (a) establishment and development of port equipment, services and facilities such as mechanical, electrical, maintenance, etc. workshops; (b) establishment and development of shipbuilding and ship repairing facilities including associated supporting industries; (c) the development of a joint programme of assistance and co-operation, particularly where this is considered necessary or useful to integrate assistance in the field of shipping with programmes that are related to or dependent upon shipping; (d) development of human capacity through jointly developed fellowship or other training programmes.
(4) The IMO is concerned with the use of telecommunications in shipping. Therefore, constant contacts are maintained between the IMO Sub-Committee on Radiocommunications and the ITU.

the International Civil Aviation Organization[1] (ICAO)[2]. A few words are necessary to describe the relationship with the International Labour Organization (ILO) and the United Nations Conference on Trade and Development (UNCTAD).

ILO: Since its establishment in 1919[3], the ILO has considered several issues in the maritime social and labour areas. It adopted what is known as the

---

(1) The IMO is co-operating with ICAO in two main areas: (a) safety of helicopter operations to and from ships and other marine vehicles; and (b) aeronautical and maritime search and rescue services. A Draft Memorandum of Understanding between the Secretariats of the two organizations on these two issues was endorsed by the Maritime Safety Committee in June,1983 at its forty-eighth session. It provides for demarcation of responsibilities between the two organizations for collaboration when respective areas cannot be clearly defined and for the exchange of information and documentation.

(2) The IMO co-operates with a number of specialized agencies of the United Nations, in particular FAO, UNESCO, WHO and IAEA, through its sponsorship of the Joint Group of Experts on Scientific Aspects of Marine Pollution (GESAMP) which was established in 1969. This body provides advice on marine pollution problems, including the development of standards for evaluating the hazards from harmful substances carried in ships, the development of criteria determining the harmful materials and the formulation of guidelines for identifying substances that may be harmful. The IMO also co-operated with the United Nations Conference on the Law of the Sea (UNCLOS). See, for example, article 197 of the UN Convention on the Law of the Sea.
Again the IMO issued a joint appeal with the UN High Commissioner for Refugees concerning the rescue of refugees in distress at sea, called the 'boat people'. See the draft resolution proposed by the United Nations High Commissioner for Refugees to the IMO Council, C53/15/(e), 12 October,1984.

(3) The ILO is tripartite in structure, employers' and workers' representatives taking part with government delegates with the right to vote independently. However, maritime labour

"International Seafarers' Code" covering a set of minimum standards on all aspects of seafarers' employment conditions[1]. In 1958 an agreement between the secretariats of the IMO and the ILO provided for the establishment of joint committees.

---

questions are considered in the first instance by a bipartite body, the Joint Maritime Commission, composed of representatives of shipowners and seafarers, which advises the Governing Body of the ILO on the action to be taken.

(1) Conventions:

No. 7 Minimum Age (Sea), 1920.
8 Unemployment Indemnity (Shipwreck), 1920.
9 Placing of Seamen, 1920.
15 Minimum Age (Trimmers and Stokers), 1921.
16 Medical Examination of Young Persons (Sea), 1921.
22 Seamen's Articles of Agreement, 1926.
23 Repatriation of Seamen, 1926.
53 Officers' Competency Certificates, 1936.
54 Holidays with Pay (Sea), 1936.
55 Shipowners' Liability (Sick and Injured Seamen), 1936.
56 Sickness Insurance (Sea), 1936.
57 Hours of Work and Manning (Sea), 1936.
58 Minimum Age (Sea) (Revised), 1936.
68 Food and Catering (Ships' Crews), 1946.
69 Certification of Ships' Cooks, 1946.
70 Social Security (Seafarers), 1946.
71 Seafarers' Pensions, 1946.
72 Paid Vacations (Seafarers), 1946.
73 Medical Examinations (Seafarers), 1946.
74 Certification of Able Seamen, 1946.
75 Accommodation of Crews, 1946.
76 Wages, Hours of Work and Manning (Sea), 1946.
91 Paid Vacations (Seafarers) (Revised), 1949.
92 Accommodation of Crews (Revised), 1949.
93 Wages, Hours of Work and Manning (Sea) (Revised), 1949.
108 Seafarers' Identity Documents, 1958.
109 Wages, Hours of Work and Manning (Sea) (Revised), 1958.
133 Crew Accommodation on Board Ship (Supplementary Provisions), 1970.
134 Prevention of Occupational Accidents to Seafarers, 1970.

This agreement was followed by three other understandings: in 1972 on training of sea-going personnel, in 1974 concerning the terms of reference, responsibilities and working arrangements of

---

145 Continuity of Employment of Seafarers, 1976.
146 Annual Leave with Pay for Seafarers, 1976.
147 Minimum Standards in Merchant Ships, 1976.

Recommendations

No.9 National Seamen's Codes, 1920.
10 Unemployment Insurance (Seamen), 1920.
26 Migration (Protection of Females at Sea), 1926.
27 Repatriation (Ships Masters and Apprentices), 1926.
28 Labour Inspection (Seamen), 1926.
48 Seamen's Welfare in Ports, 1936.
49 Hours of Work and Manning (Sea), 1936.
75 Seafarers' Social Security (Agreements), 1946.
76 Seafarers (Medical Care for Dependants), 1946.
77 Vocational Training (Seafarers), 1946.
78 Bedding, Mess Utensils and Miscellaneous Provisions (Ships' Crews), 1946.
105 Ships' Medicine Chests, 1958.
106 Medical Advice at Sea, 1958.
107 Seafarers' Engagement (Foreign Vessels), 1958.
108 Social Conditions and Safety (Seafarers), 1958.
109 Wages, Hours of Work and Manning (Sea), 1958.
137 Vocational Training of Seafarers, 1970.
138 Seafarers' Welfare at Sea and in Port, 1970.
139 Employment Problems Arising from Technical Developments on Board Ship, 1970.
140 Air Conditioning of Crew Accommodation and certain other Spaces on Board Ship, 1970.
141 Control of Harmful Noise in Crew Accommodation and Working Spaces on Board Ship, 1970.
142 Prevention of Occupational Accidents to Seafarers, 1970.
153 The Protection of Young Seafarers, 1976.
154 Continuity of Employment of Seafarers, 1976.
155 Improvement of Standards in Merchant Ships, 1976.

See also IMCO/ILO Guidelines for Training in the Packing of Cargo in Freight Containers, 1978, Sales No. 78.13.E.

the joint IMCO/ILO committee on training; and a third in 1975 on the convening of a conference on training, qualifications or certification of mariners[1]. The Committee undertook preparatory work which led to the adoption of the Standards of Training, Certification and Watchkeeping for Seafarers (STCW) Convention, 1978. Recently[2], the Joint Maritime Commission adopted the following resolutions which were communicated to the IMO:

(a) Resolution concerning carrying radioactive nuclear cargoes[3];

(b) Resolution on the unlawful detention of seafarers abroad[4]; and

(c) Resolution concerning occupational safety and working conditions on board mobile offshore units.

<u>UNCTAD</u>: UNCTAD was set up in 1965 as an organ of the United Nations and started its activities in 1967. Through its Committee of Shipping and with assistance from the United Nations Commission on International Trade Law (UNCITRAL), it formulated

---

(1) The ILO co-operates also with UNCTAD in various fields, one of which is the open registry. UNCTAD aims to phase-out the system while the ILO is seeking to ensure that minimum labour standards are applied on board the ship whatever the flag of registration may be.

(2) 20-28 September, 1984.

(3) This Resolution is relevant to the work of the Sub-Committee on the Carriage of Dangerous Goods. See Maritime Safety Committee (MSC) 51 session, 25 February, 1985 - MSC 51/16/1. See also MSC/Circ.360 on Guidelines for Reporting Incidents Involving Packaged Dangerous Goods.

(4) It must be noted that SOLAS, Load Line and MARPOL Conventions prescribe the procedures to be followed when foreign ships are detained in ports including the obligation to inform immediately the flag State, its diplomatic representative in the port State, the classification society concerned and the IMO. No similar provision with respect to the detention of the crews or passengers of ships are at present contained in the Convention on Facilitation of International Traffic, 1965.

the Hamburg Rules, 1978[1] and the Convention on Multimodal Transport of Goods, 1980[2]. It also adopted a Code of Conduct for Liner Conferences which came into effect on October 6, 1983. In its work, UNCTAD has to protect the interests of the developing countries[3].

---

(1) See the Author, The Hamburg Rules on the Carriage of Goods by Sea, published by Sijthoff, 1978.
(2) See the Author, the Multimodal Transport of Goods Convention, published in the International and Comparative Law Quarterly, Vol.32, January, 1983, pp. 120-140.
(3) See, for example, UNCTAD Report "Action on the Question of Open Registry", 3 March, 1980, TD/B/C.4/220, where it stated:
There are ten basic reasons why non-observance of standards is likely to be greater under an open registry flag than under the flag of a country with a normal registry and a responsible maritime administration.
1. Real owners are not readily identifiable (partly because of difficulties in identifying, partly because of lack of incentive to identify) and are therefore in a good position to take risks by comparison with owners in normal registries who are living under the eyes of a maritime administration.
2. Real owners can change their identities by manipulating brass plate companies and consequently avoid being identified as repeated substandard operators or risk-takers.
3. Since the master and other key shipboard personnel are not nationals of the flag state, they have no need or incentive to visit the flag state and can avoid legal action.
4. Owners who reside outside the jurisdiction of the flag state can defy the flag state by requiring to testify at an inquiry by the flag state and avoid prosecution.
5. Since open registry owners do not have the same interests in preserving good relations with the flag state, they do not feel the need to co-operate with inspectors of the flag state.
6. Open registry shipping lacks the union structure which is so essential to the application of safety and social standards in countries of normal registries, namely a national trade union of the flag state

The line of demarcation of the work of both the IMO and UNCTAD was, and is still not clear. A possible duplication of work is evident in the following three topics: maritime liens and mortgages; arrest of vessels and other sanctions; and registration of rights in respect of ships under construction.

During the tenth session of the UNCTAD Committee on Shipping held on 24 June, 1982, the Secretary-General of the IMO said: "... the fact that IMO had considered the problem did not necessarily mean that other organizations could not consider the problem in areas appropriate to their field of competence." This point was taken by the Director of the Shipping Division of UNCTAD when he stated that wherever "foreseeable overlapping of subjects in their treatment appeared likely, it behoved both Organizations, and particularly their secretariats, to co-operate with each other to prevent unnecessary friction and waste of resources, while keeping in mind the distinctive concerns of Member States of each Organization"(1).

After several meetings between the IMO and UNCTAD, an understanding was reached in an Agreement dated 2 March, 1983. The understanding provided that, if the issues were agreed to be essentially technical or ship-related, IMO would be the body to deal with them, with UNCTAD co-operating as necessary If on the other hand, the issues were agreed to be essentially commercial or trade-related, then the reverse arrangement would be adopted. Furthermore, if the issues were found to involve significant

---

representing seamen on vessels owned by owners who have economic links with the flag state.

7. Open registry owners are in a better position to put pressure on masters and officers to take risks, since there is no really appropriate government to which shipboard personnel can complain.

8. Port state control is weaker because the port state can only report substandard vessels and practice to a flag state which has no real control over the owner.

9. Owners can suppress any signs of militancy among crews by virtue of their freedom to change nationalities of crews at whim.

10. Enforcement of standards is basically inconsistent with the operation of a registry with the sole aim of making a profit.

(1) TD/B/C.4 (X)/MISC.4, p.76.

technical as well as commercial elements then the joint or co-operative approach would be adopted, with IMO or UNCTAD acting as the "lead agency" as may be considered appropriate[(1)].

Following this understanding, an agreement[(2)] was reached on the arrangements and procedures to be followed by the two secretariats in further consultation as well as on the preparation of a list of principal issues for in-depth examination[(3)].

Accordingly, a list containing the issues of concern to both organizations was drawn up[(4)] and

---

(1) Council - 52nd session - C52/17(c), 20 March, 1984.

(2) The text of agreement was published in Council - 53rd session - C53/15(d)/Add.1, 8 November, 1984.

(3) In the list of issues agreed by the secretariats of UNCTAD and IMO, a number of major objectives were identified as deserving priority consideration in any investigations regarding possible international action on maritime liens and mortgages. These were:
   (a) to encourage ship financing by affording appropriate protection to persons providing finance;
   (b) to afford protection in respect of selected claims;
   (c) to encourage the provision of services to ships;
   (d) to protect the ship against multiple actions; and
   (e) to minimise the potential encumbrances to the operation of the ship.

   See *ibid* document C53/15(d)/Add.1, Annex pp.1-4.

(4) In other areas of maritime transport, it was noted that it was difficult to limit the advice and assistance provided by IMO and UNCTAD experts to the technical and economic fields, respectively. This is because governments do not always find it convenient to separate the technical from the non-technical aspects of any project. It was therefore agreed to offer the advice on a comprehensive basis by experts of the two organizations. In this respect, the following areas were regarded as suitable: (a) development and harmonization of maritime legislation; (b) development, modernization and rationalization of ports and port operations; and (c) problems of containerization and multi-modal transport. See C52/17(c), 20 March, 1984.

the Council at its fifty-second session (10-14 September,1984) took note of the list. The Council expressed the view that while "agreement was reached on a basic approach to be followed in this regard, a number of important points of detail have yet to be clarified to the satisfaction of both secretariats"(1).

2. Relationships with non-governmental organizations (NGO)

Various non-governmental organizations such as the International Chamber of Shipping (ICS)(2), the International Association of Independent Tanker Owners (INTERTANKO)(3), the International Association of Lighthouse Authorities (IALA) and the Comité Maritime International (CMI)(4) were established to

---

(1) C53/15(d), 17 September, 1984, p.3. See also the following documents published by UNCTAD. Maritime fraud: preliminary report on the feasibility of a bank super-service (TD/B/C.4/AC.4/7); Maritime fraud, preliminary study on ship-related information (TD/B/C.4/AC.4/5); Maritime liens and mortgages: analysis of progress in the existing international regime of maritime liens and mortgages and a possible methodology of approach to future work (TD/B/C.4/ISL/52); Draft revision of the International Convention for the unification of Certain Rules relating to Maritime Liens and Mortgages (TD/B/C.4/ISL/L.77); and draft revision of the International Convention for the Unification of Certain Rules relating to the Arrest of Sea-Going Ships (TD/B/C.4/ISL/L.78).

(2) The ICS works closely with the IMO on several matters and in particular tanker safety, such as Crude Oil Washing (COW) and Inert Gas Systems (IGS).

(3) INTERTANKO has a Safety and Technical Committee consisting of twelve members representing major international shipping companies.

(4) The CMI aims to unify international maritime and commercial law. It is composed of several national associations meeting periodically at international conferences. Draft conventions prepared by the CMI were submitted to the Belgian Government to convene a diplomatic conference.
In 1961, at the eleventh session of the Dip-

deal with certain activities of the shipping and related industries. Their expertise is valuable to the work of the IMO. On the other hand, these organizations and their members would be affected by any rules or measures taken by the IMO in their respective sphere of activities. Therefore, the IMO since its inception has had special arrangements to grant non-governmental organisations "consultative status".

The principles governing "consultative status" were adopted by the Assembly on April 13, 1961, under the title: "Rules Governing Relationship with Non-Governmental International Organizations". These rules were amended on various occasions and

---

lomatic Conference on Maritime Law held in Brussels, a proposal was made to set up a permanent secretariat. The IMO felt that this secretariat, if set up, would tend to divide at international level the responsibilities for maritime affairs assumed by a single government and to encourage duplication of work. For this reason, the Secretary-General of the IMO tried in 1963 to establish a close relationship and stated in a letter to the CMI that the IMO did not wish to interfere with its work in the maritime legal field. See Distr. General A111/30, 26 July, 1963, IMO Assembly, 3rd session Agenda item 13/6. However in recent years, the CMI started to submit the draft conventions to the IMO for approval. Recent drafts relate to (1) draft convention on salvage; (2) draft convention on offshore mobile craft; and (3) draft convention on the unification of certain rules concerning civil jurisdiction, choice of law and recognition and enforcement of judgments in matters of collision.
In 1985, the CMI approved a new draft convention on the arrest of ships to go for debate by IMO and UNCTAD. The draft favoured requiring an owner or bareboat charterer of a vessel to be personally liable for a claim before a ship could be arrested unless there was another specified factor involved. The draft eliminated an alternative proposal which could have allowed the arrest of a ship as security against the liabilities of its time or voyage charterer. At present, the CMI is working on a draft convention on maritime liens and mortgages.

the latest amendments were approved in September, 1984[1].

Under the rules, the Council, subject to the approval of the Assembly, may grant consultative status to any non-governmental international organization if it can reasonably be expected "to make a substantial contribution to the work of the IMO" (Rule 1). The purposes of consultative status are: (a) to enable the IMO to obtain information or expert advice from non-governmental organizations with special knowledge in a particular sector; and (b) to enable such "non-governmental organizations representing large groups whose activities have an important and direct bearing on the work of the IMO, to express their points of view to the Organization" (Rule 2).

In determining whether an organization can make such a contribution, the following considerations are taken into account: (a) the activities of the organization and whether they are related directly to the purposes of the IMO; (b) the objectives of the organization and whether they are in harmony with the spirit and functions of the IMO; and (c) the programmes or projects of the organization which can show the relevance of its work and interests to those of the IMO (Rule 3).

The granting of consultative status confers upon the organization the following rights:

(a) to receive the provisional agenda for sessions of the Assembly, the Council and the Committees;

(b) to submit written statements on items of the agenda provided that such submission does not impede the smooth functioning of the IMO or the organ involved;

(c) to be represented by an observer at plenary sessions of the Assembly and, on the invitation of the Secretary-General, of the meetings during sessions of the Council and the Committees at which matters of special interest to it are to be considered; and

(d) to receive the texts of resolutions adopted by the Assembly and, at the discretion of the Secretary-General, recommendations made by the Council and the Committees (Rule 6).

---

(1) See Council - 53rd session - C53/20, 3 September, 1984.

Normally one observer from each organization is admitted to any session or meeting. He has no voting rights but may, on the invitation of the Chairman and with the approval of the body concerned, speak on any item on the agenda of special interest to his organization.

The Secretariat maintains a record of NGOs' activities including their attendance at the IMO's meetings and their contributions to the work of the Council and the Committees(1). On the basis of this information, the Council from time to time reviews the list of NGO's(2).

(iii) TECHNICAL ASSISTANCE

Many developing countries were and are still in need of assistance in the selection, acquisition and effective use of technologies which would be appropriate to them. Such assistance was needed in all economic sectors. For this reason in 1974, the General Assembly of the United Nations at its sixth special session, adopted a Programme of Action on the Establishment of a New Economic Order. The Assembly invited its agencies and Member States to take effective measures to assist developing countries.

In shipping the problems facing developing countries were numerous and complex. The most important ones were the need for financial resources and the shortage or lack of trained and experienced personnel. Many countries started to look to the IMO and other United Nations bodies(3) for

---

(1) See Council - 54th session - 26 March, 1985, C54/20(b).

(2) As of 26 March, 1985, forty-two non-governmental organizations enjoy consultative status. See the list of these organizations, appendix II.

(3) UNCTAD offers technical assistance in the following areas: port operations; port administration; port development; planning; economics and management of shipping; freight rates and conference practices; consultation machinery; trade organisation and shipping; private maritime law, multimodal transport; containerization and training courses.
ILO offers assistance in the fields of: labour legislation, administration and conditions of employment; maritime manpower; vocational

assistance. In fact, the IMO entered the field of technical assistance in 1975 in order to strengthen the scientific and technological capabilities of some of its Member States. Through various measures, it offered assistance to certain countries in an effort to accelerate their development in the field of shipping and other related areas. In 1975, the Committee on Technical Co-operation was institutionalized(1). It:

(a) considers programmes relating to the implementation of technical co-operation projects for which the IMO acts as the executing or co-operating agency;

(b) considers any other matters relating to the IMO's functions in the technical co-operation field; and

---

training and certificates; recruitment and placement; occupational safety and health; welfare; social security and labour management co-operation.
The ILO, UNCTAD and IMO have jointly put out a booklet entitled "Technical Co-operation in Maritime Transport", informing potential recipients of technical co-operation available from each body.

(1) The IMO has eight inter-regional advisers to provide technical advice on problems such as setting up effective maritime administration and ship inspection, organizing and improving training of nationals, and taking measures to formulate the necessary legislation affecting their merchant fleets. It has also seven regional advisers in Africa and Latin America. The IMO is responsible for assisting a number of training schools such as the one in Abidjan and in Accra.
See also MEPC 21/13/1, 20 February,1985, on Technical Assistance Programmes, Regional Seas Programme of the United Nations Environment Programme. It covers at present eleven regions; (1) Mediterranean Region; (2) Kuwait Action Plan Region; (3) Wider Caribbean Region; (4) West and Central African Region; (5) East African Region; (6) East Asian Region; (7) Red Sea and Gulf of Aden Region; (8) South-West Pacific Region; (9) South-East Pacific Region; (10) South-West Atlantic Region; and (11) South Asian Region.

(c) keeps under review the work of the Secretariat concerning technical co-operation.

In order to give a proper conception of technical assistance, it would be necessary to say a brief word on the bodies entrusted with providing finance, the forms and the fields of assistance.

Financing of Technical Assistance Projects

Resolution A.400 (X) (1977) states the various sources from which finance could be obtained. It provides that:

> "(a) The Technical Co-operation Committee shall consider, as appropriate, any matter within the scope of the Organization concerned with the implementation of technical co-operation projects funded by the relevant United Nations programme for which the Organization acts as the executing or co-operating agency or by funds-in-trust voluntarily provided to the Organization, and any other matters related to the Organization's activities in the technical co-operation field.
>
> (b) The Technical Co-operation Committee shall keep under review the work of the Secretariat concerning technical co-operation."

In fact, funds for financing projects could be obtained from the UNDP, UNEP, developing countries and industrialist countries.

The United Nations Development Programme (UNDP): The UNDP is the principal body(1) by which the United Nations provides technical assistance to developing countries. The activities of the UNDP are financed by voluntary contributions which come from both developed and developing countries. The UNDP may use these resources or participate with the host country in financing the project on an agreed percentage.

---

(1) IMO together with UNCTAD and ILO are participating and executing agencies of UNDP and as such are represented on the Inter-Agency Consultative Board.

The United Nations Environment Programme (UNEP): The UNEP is concerned with the protection of the environment and therefore it works with the IMO in matters related to the protection of the marine environment.

Funds from Developing Countries

Several developing countries have their own financial resources but are in need of the know-how. Without this scientific progress, the gap will be widened between developed and developing countries.

Funds from Industrialist Countries

Some of the more advanced nations offer technical advice, equipment or other forms of assistance to certain projects in developing countries either directly or through the Organization(1).

Forms of Assistance

Assistance may take various forms, vary in its size and duration. The most popular form of assistance is the provision of experts and consultants who may be assigned individually or as a team.

Training will be provided through fellowships to nationals of developing countries, seminars or special courses.

The most spectacular form is the setting up of the World Maritime University (WMU)(2) at Malmo (Sweden) which started on 4 July, 1983. The

---

(1) The IMO has set up a special fund for financing technical assistance projects concerned with maritime training. It will be financed not from the Organization's ordinary budget but by voluntary contributions from Member States.

(2) The charter of the University states that: "The World Maritime University shall be the international maritime training institution for the training of senior specialist maritime personnel in various aspects of shipping and related fields concerning the improvement of maritime safety, the protection of the marine environment and the efficiency of international shipping, in furtherance of the purposes and objectives of the International Maritime Organization as a specialized agency of the United Nations."

University provides a two-year course in General Maritime Administration; Maritime Safety Administration; Maritime Education; and Technical Management of Shipping Companies.

Another form of assistance is the supply of equipment necessary for the project, such as the supply of radar or a simulator.

Fields of Assistance

The last few years have seen an expansion in the fields of technical assistance. The IMO is involved in various projects around the World. A great emphasis is placed on the promotion of maritime training to agreed standards. Technical assistance has been provided to a number of developing countries in their effort to establish new maritime facilities in conformity with future global standards(1). However, the various fields of assistance could be grouped under three headings: shipping; ports and harbours; and maritime pollution.

Shipping

The principal aim is the development of national and merchant mariners and this could be achieved in the following areas: training; legislation; safety; cargoes; communication and shipbuilding and ship repairs.

---

(1) The report of the Committee on Technical Co-operation shows that IMO is assisting more than thirty countries. Among the projects are: the establishment of a maritime training institute at Lobito in Angola; the National Nautical School of Argentina; the inter-related projects in Bangladesh; the training of merchant marine personnel at Belem in Brazil; the regional maritime training academy, Accra, Ghana; the regional maritime training academy, Abidjan, Ivory Coast; assistance to the Higher Institute for Maritime Studies at Casablanca, Morocco; the development of a maritime training institute in Mozambigue, the establishment of an integrated maritime training institute in Nigeria; the development of the Panama National Nautical School and the development of maritime transport in Peru. See IMO News, No.4, 1982, p.14. See also the survey of the Committee's work in the leaflet published by the IMO in 1981, entitled Technical Assistance Programme.

Maritime training: The IMO has been active in supporting the setting up of maritime training schools at all levels. In addition, the establishment of the Maritime World University at Malmo would serve as a centre for maritime education and a valuable source of exchange of information.

Maritime legislation: Although Maritime Law is international in its character, a great deal of harmonization is needed. Some technical rules are required to be introduced into national law. Organization of ships' registration could be the prime purpose of the legal rules in certain countries.

Maritime safety: Safety measures are of paramount importance and the assistance to national administration as well as national organizations would be crucial.

Dangerous goods: Many countries require assistance on the safe transport and handling of dangerous goods in ports, stowage procedures on board, procedures for arrival of dangerous goods and the adoption of the dangerous goods Code.

Radio communication: Communication is going through a revolutionary phase. Yet, some countries need assistance in this field and in particular in the establishment of position-fixing systems and navigation safety lanes.

Shipbuilding and ship repairs: This area covers shipyard development, design and construction of new vessels, ship repair facilities, towing tank operations and welding and steel fabrication.

## Ports and Harbours

The IMO is involved in advisory services in regard to port reception facilities in the Mediterranean. The assistance of the IMO in this field may extend to cover port re-organisation, containers, harbour piloting, navigation and related services, port operation, radio aids, dredging, hydrographic surveys and harbour administration.

## Marine Pollution

The two main areas of work of the IMO are in safety

and the protection of the marine environment. Therefore, the technical assistance can be directed towards marine pollution control,the establishment of regional combating centres, co-operation in the event of pollution emergencies and open sea oil transfer operations.

## (iv) LONG-TERM WORK PLAN OF THE ORGANIZATION

By Resolution A.554 (13) the Assembly approved the current long-term work plan for the period up to 1990 and requested the Council and the various committees to keep it under review. The following is a list of the subjects to be dealt with by each committee. It must be noted that this list is not exhaustive and the subjects are not listed in any order or priority.

### Maritime Safety Committee

- Implementation, technical interpretation and improvement of conventions, codes, recommendations and guidelines.
- Procedures for the control of ships including deficiency reports.
- Casualty statistics and investigations into serious casualties.
- Implementation of harmonized survey and certification requirements and additional guidelines for survey and certification.
- Training, watchkeeping and operational procedures for maritime personnel, including seafarers, fishermen, maritime pilots and those responsible for maritime safety in mobile offshore units.
- Measures to improve navigational safety, including ships' routeing, requirements and standards for navigation aids and ship reporting systems.
- The global maritime distress and safety system and other maritime radiocommunication matters including navigational warning services, shipborne radio equipment and operational procedure.
- Survival in case of maritime casualties and distress, and the provision of maritime search and rescue services.
- Safe carriage of solid bulk cargoes, timber, grain

and other cargoes by sea, including containers and vehicles.

- Carriage of dangerous goods in packaged form, portable tanks, unit loads, other transport units, shipborne barges and intermediate bulk containers (IBCs).
- Emergency procedures and safety measures for ships carrying dangerous goods, medical first aid in case of accidents involving dangerous goods and the safe use of pesticides in ships.
- Safe handling and storage of dangerous goods in port areas.
- Intact stability, subdivision, damage stability and load lines for all types of ships.
- Tonnage measurement of ships.
- Safety considerations for machinery and electrical installations.
- Manoeuvrability of intact and disabled ships.
- Control of noise and related vibration levels on board ships.
- Matters pertaining to fire safety in all types of ships.
- Safety aspects of the design, construction, equipment and operation of all types of ships, such as fishing vessels, oil tankers, chemical tankers, gas carriers, dynamically supported craft, mobile offshore drilling units, special purpose ships, offshore supply vessels, nuclear merchant ships, roll-on/roll-off ships, barge carriers, dry cargo ships carrying dangerous chemicals in cargo tanks, barges carrying dangerous chemicals in bulk and diving systems.
- Co-operation with the United Nations and other international bodies on matters of mutual interest.
- A possible single (unified) international instrument (i.e. one comprehensive convention concerning safety of life at sea and marine environment protection) incorporating and superseding relevant conventions and instruments currently applicable, which might include:

  1974 SOLAS Convention
  1978 SOLAS Protocol
  1966 Load Line Convention
  MARPOL 73/78
  International Bulk Chemical Code
  International Gas Carrier Code

Legal Committee

- The question of salvage, in particular the possible revision of the existing legal regime to take account of salvage in connection with maritime casualties posing hazards of environmental pollution.
- Revision of the 1969 Intervention Convention to deal with the reporting of incidents posing serious threats of maritime pollution.
- Draft convention on civil jurisdiction, choice of law, recognition and enforcement of judgments in matters of collision at sea.
- Draft convention on offshore mobile craft.
- Consideration of the legal status of novel types of craft, such as air-cushion vehicles, operating in the marine environment.
- A possible convention on wreck removal and related issues.
- A possible convention on the regime of vessels in foreign ports.
- Arrest of seagoing ships.
- Legal status of Ocean Data Acquisition Systems (ODAS).
- Possible review of the CMI Brussels Conventions with a view to their being replaced by updated conventions under the auspices of the IMO.

Marine Environment Protection Committee

- Uniform interpretation and application of the provisions of MARPOL 73/78 and possible amendments thereto.
- Reception facilities for residues.
- Oil discharge monitoring and control systems, including those for light refined oils.
- Procedures for the control of ships and certificates and the control of discharges from ships.
- Surveys and certification of ships under MARPOL 73/78.
- Penalties for infringement of convention provisions.
- Casualty investigations in relation to marine pollution.

- Promotion of regional arrangements for combating marine pollution.
- Development and updating of anti-pollution manual.
- Identification of particularly sensitive sea areas.
- Development of manual on intervention under the 1969 Convention Relating to Intervention on the High Seas in Cases of Oil Pollution Casualties and the 1973 Protocol Relating to Intervention on the High Seas in Cases of Marine Pollution by Substances other than Oil.
- Categorization of liquid substances.
- Prevention of pollution by noxious solid substances in bulk.

Technical Co-operation Committee

- Advice and assistance to governments of developing countries for the development of well co-ordinated and more efficient maritime transport systems.
- Promotion of adequate infrastructure in the shipping and ports sectors.
- Promotion of appropriate self-reliance at national level.
- Encouragement of sub-regional and regional co-operation, particularly technical co-operation among developing countries.
- Advice and assistance to governments of developing countries in taking appropriate measures to rectify important conventions and instruments of the IMO and to implement their provisions.
- The planning and organization of regional workshops and seminars as and when the occasion arises to emphasize the importance of maritime training, maritime safety and prevention of marine pollution from ships.

Facilitation Committee

- The implementation, technical interpretation and improvement of the Convention on Facilitation of International Maritime Traffic, 1965, and its Annex.
- Facilitation activities within the Organization including:
  (i) promotional activities carried out in co-operation with Member Governments, Contracting

Governments and organizations concerned;
(ii) facilitation aspects of forms and certificates emanating from other activities of the Organization.

- IMO policy on automatic data processing of shipping documents and documents used for the clearance of ships.
- Examination and possible adaptation of elements of conventions, codes and recommendations of a facilitative nature elaborated by other organizations.
- Consideration and formulation of proposals for amending the Convention or its Annex including harmonization with other UN FAL Conventions.
- Formalities connected with the arrival, stay and departure of ships, persons and cargo.

References

Harvey B. Silverstein, Superships and Nation-States: the Transnational Politics of the Inter-Governmental Maritime Consultative Organization, published by Westview Press.

IMCO's Technical Assistance Programme, published by the IMO in 1981.

Kamil A. Bekiashev/Vitali V. Serebriakov, International Marine Organizations, published by Kluwer.

Technical Co-operation in Maritime Transport; a booklet prepared for actual or potential recipients of technical co-operation from IMO, UNCTAD and ILO, published in 1981.

- The Activities of the Inter-Governmental Maritime Consultative Organization - International Economic Co-operation - Environmental Marine Pollution, UN Document A/36/237, June,1981.

# CHAPTER II

# RULES ON SHIP CONSTRUCTION, DESIGN AND EQUIPMENT

Ship Construction

In the past, governments were not involved in the design, equipment and the materials used for the construction of the ship[(1)]. These matters were left to the parties and were carried out in accordance with the standards adopted by the shipyard under the supervision of a classification society[(2)]. It was not until the second half of the nineteenth century[(3)] when it became clear that the construction of the ship should not be treated as a private matter and that safety at sea[(4)] requires governmental control to ensure the physical fitness of the

---

(1) In the early part of the nineteenth century, many vessels sank with loss of lives and very little was known about the conditions of these vessels.

(2) Classification is a device which has now been in use for over two hundred years to inform interested parties that a particular ship and its equipment has complied with accepted standards of structural and mechanical reliability. The two main activities of classification societies are: inspection and certification. The first activity is carried out through a survey of the hull and machinery, and if satisfactory the ship would be classed appropriately for the type and service intended. In case the surveyor detects any defect, he should notify the shipowner, and failing to remedy the defect the ship would lose its class.
The second type of activity is to certify a ship when the classification society is officially approved as certifying authority. Many governments have delegated to classification societies, work on their behalf to varying degrees in connection with survey and certification.

(3) In 1889, the first maritime conference was held in Washington. Various matters such as regulations for preventing collisions, safety of life, shipwreck, lanes for steamers, etc., were discussed. In 1897, the International Maritime Committee was established to deal with the legal aspect of merchant shipping. The Committee assisted in the work of several international conventions including the 1914 Convention for the Safety of Life at Sea.

(4) An analysis of 80 deficiency reports submitted to the IMO between November,1977 and April,1978 by fourteen countries shows that 47.5 per cent

ship. It is necessary during the construction of the ship that materials and workmanship are carefully inspected, checked and tested so that defects can be remedied. However, no real strategy on the various requirements, their scope and inspection existed.

This situation has changed radically since World War II and gradually a body of rules on ship construction, design and equipment started to emerge. Rules on cargo ships, equipment to be carried on board including liferafts (and on passenger ships) were adopted. Rules on subdivision of passenger ships were also approved. The work of the IMO on these rules has been accelerated through the assistance of certain maritime countries and has culminated in the adoption of the Safety of Life at Sea (SOLAS) Convention. Several amendments to various provisions of the Convention were made in order to bring it up-to-date.

The IMO adopted another important Convention, i.e. the Load Line, 1966, which brought limitations on the draught to which a ship may be loaded, in the form of free boards.

All the important requirements of the SOLAS Convention and its amendments are not applicable to fishing vessels. A fishing vessel is quite different from an ordinary dry cargo vessel in its construction and field operations. The former operates in the open sea while the latter loads and

---

of deficiencies related to ships of between 20 and 30 years of age, while a further 10 per cent related to vessels aged more than 40 years. The list of the type of deficiencies is as follows:

| | |
|---|---|
| Life-saving equipment | % 77.50 |
| Fire-fighting equipment | 47.50 |
| Machinery installation | 15.00 |
| Electrical installation | 2.50 |
| Machinery and electrical installations | 15.00 |
| Watertight integrity | 17.50 |
| Navigation equipment and related matters (including distress signals, radar, muster roll) | 8.75 |
| Radio equipment | 11.25 |
| Lifeboats, radio | 5.00 |
| Hatches, opening/closing appliance, load line mark | 5.00 |
| Certificates' validity | 18.75 |

See IMO News, No.1, 1979, p.6.

discharges the cargo in port. A special convention on Fishing Vessels was adopted in 1977.

Although SOLAS and the Load Lines Convention were major steps, the high rate of technological change, as evidenced by the introduction of sophisticated chemical and gas tankers, created the need for the adoption of higher standards. To this end, the IMO adopted a number of Codes which provide for rules on the design, construction and, to a limited extent, the operation of these vessels.

Thus, this chapter covers:

(i) the SOLAS Convention with its Amendments;

(ii) the Load Line Convention, 1966;

(iii) the rules on Safety of Fishing Vessels; and

(iv) the IMO Codes.

## (i) THE SAFETY OF LIFE AT SEA (SOLAS) CONVENTION AND ITS AMENDMENTS

Background: The SOLAS Convention 1974 is the latest edition of safety of life at sea conventions which started in 1914 after the *Titanic*(1) incident. The outbreak of World War I prevented it from coming into force. The 1914 Convention, which was revised in 1928, came into force in 1933. A further revision took place in 1948 and this edition came into force in 1952. Again in 1960, SOLAS was updated.

The 1960 Convention was amended on several occasions: in 1966, 1967, 1968, 1969, 1971 and 1973. But these amendments did not come into force because they all required ratification by two-thirds of the Contracting Parties. The steady increase in the membership of the Organization meant that a higher number of ratifications was required for the amendments.

In the meantime, the IMO established the "tacit acceptance" procedure which is considered as a prescription and a way to solve the delay in bringing the amendments into force. Thus, in order to bring the above numerous amendments into effect and to introduce the magic procedure of "tacit acceptance"(2), the IMO decided in 1974 to adopt a "new" version. In essence, SOLAS 1974(3) is not new as it simply consolidated the changes. It is an improved version of the 1960 Convention.

---

(1) The *Titanic* sank on her maiden voyage in April, 1912 with the loss of more than 1,500 passengers and crew.

(2) Amendments adopted by the Maritime Safety Committee (MSC) come into force two years after being communicated to the Contracting States unless they are rejected by one-third of the Contracting States or by Contracting States owning 50 per cent of the World's gross tonnage of merchant shipping. Amendments to the articles of the Convention and to Chapter 1 of the Annex come into force six months after being accepted by two-thirds of the Contracting States.

(3) The Convention came into force on May 25, 1980. Some of its requirements were deferred for two years, and so they became effective on May 1, 1983.

## 1. Objectives and brief outline

The main objective of SOLAS is to specify minimum standards for the construction, equipment and operation of ships. It deals with stability requirements, watertight compartments, maintenance of machinery and electrical installations under various emergency conditions, fire protection and extinction, life-saving appliances, radio equipment, etc. Contracting States issue a number of certificates in order to show that the requirements are met. They are also responsible for setting up a control system for ships flying their flags.

As mentioned above, SOLAS covers a wide range of subjects. The comprehensive Annex to Attachment 1 of the Convention is divided into eight chapters, each of which consists of a number of regulations.

Chapter I, which is entitled "General Provisions", states that the Regulations apply only to ships engaged on international voyages (Reg.1). War ships, ships of less than 500 tons, ships not propelled by mechanical means, wooden ships of primitive build, pleasure yachts not engaged in trade and fishing vessels are not made subject to the Regulations (Reg.2). Regulation 3 provides for the case where a ship engaged on international

---

(1) In 1988, a conference will be held to consider amendments to Chapter I of SOLAS. A draft was prepared by the Secretariat which includes the proposed amendments. Part A covers: (1) Application. (2) Definitions. (3) Exceptions. (4) Exemptions. (5) Equivalents. Part B covers: (6) Definitions. (7) Survey procedure. (8) Surveys of passenger ships. (9) Surveys of hull, machinery and equipment of cargo ships. (10) Surveys of safety equipment of cargo ships. (11) Surveys of radio installations of cargo ships. (12) Additional surveys of chemical tankers. (13) Additional surveys of gas carriers. (14) Surveys of nuclear ships. (15) Maintenance of condition after survey. (16) Issue of certificates. (17) Issue or endorsement of certificates by another government. (18) Duration and validity of certificates. (19) Form of certificates. (20) Acceptance of certificates. (21) Qualification of certificates. (22) Control. Part C is on Casualties to which Regulation 23 is devoted. See MSC 50/3, June 25, 1984, and IMO News, No.3, 1985, p.20.

voyages is exempted from the Regulations by the Administration in exceptional circumstances. The life-saving appliances and other equipment of cargo ships are subject to surveys at intervals not exceeding 24 months (Reg.8). The radio installations and motor life-boats or portable radio apparatus for survival craft are subject to surveys at intervals not exceeding 12 months (Reg.9). Regulation 10 of this chapter requires that the hull, machinery, equipment, steering gear, electrical installations are to be surveyed at intervals not exceeding 5 years.

Chapter II, which consists of 85 Regulations, provides for the rules required on subdivision and stability[1], machinery and electrical installations; and fire protection.

---

(1) For a cargo ship, see the Merchant Shipping (Cargo Ship Construction and Survey) Regulations, 1984 (S.I.1217/1984) which came into force on September 1, 1984. These Regulations were made under the Merchant Shipping Act, 1979. The Regulations define a "cargo ship" as "a mechanically propelled ship which is not a passenger ship, troop-ship, pleasure craft or fishing vessel". Part II A states:

Structural strength.
2. The structural strength of every ship and the number and disposition of transverse watertight bulkheads shall be adequate for the service for which the ship is intended. The hull, superstructure, structural bulkheads, deck and deckhouses shall be constructed of steel or other equivalent material except that the crowns and casings of machinery spaces of Category A shall be constructed only of steel.

Collision bulkheads.
3. (1) Every ship shall be fitted with a collision bulkhead which shall be watertight up to the freeboard deck. This bulkhead shall be located at a distance from the forward perpendicular of not less than 5 per cent of the length of the ship or 10 metres, whichever is the least, and except as may be permitted by the Secretary of State not more than 8 per cent of the length of the ship.
See also The Merchant Shipping (Cargo Ship Construction and Survey) Regulations (Amendment), 1984 (S.I.1219/1984) which came into operation on September 1, 1984.

Subdivision and stability: The subdivision of a passenger ship[1] into watertight[2] compartments

---

(1) See The Merchant Shipping (Passenger Ship Construction and Survey) Regulations, 1984 (S.I. 1216/1984) made under the Merchant Shipping Act, 1979. The Regulations which came into force on September 1, 1984, provide for the following classes of passenger ships:

Ships engaged on international voyages.
Class I. Ships engaged on voyages (not being short international voyages) any of which are long international voyages.
Class II. Ships engaged on voyages (not being long international voyages) any of which are short international voyages.

Ships not engaged on international voyages.
Class II(A). Ships engaged on voyages of any kind other than international voyages.
Class III. Ships engaged only on voyages in the course of which they are at no time more than 70 miles by sea from their point of departure and not more than 18 miles from the coast of the United Kingdom, and which are at sea only in favourable weather and during restricted periods.
Class IV. Ships engaged only on voyages in partially smooth waters, or voyages in smooth and partially smooth waters.
Class V. Ships engaged only on voyages in smooth waters.
Class VI. Ships engaged only on voyages with not more than 250 passengers on board, to sea, or in smooth or in partially smooth waters, in all cases in favourable weather and during restricted periods, in the course of which the ships are at no time more than 15 miles, exclusive of any smooth waters, from their point of departure nor more than 3 miles from land.
Class VI(A). Ships carrying not more than 50 passengers for a distance of not more than 6 miles on voyages to or from isolated communities on the islands or coast of the United Kingdom and which do not proceed for a distance of more than 3 miles from land; subject to any conditions which the Secretary of State may impose.

(2) The above Regulations state in Part IIA: watertight subdivision
6. Every ship shall be subdivided by bulkheads, which shall be watertight up to the bulkhead

is done in order that it will remain afloat and in a stable condition after any damage to her hull. The degree of subdivision varies with the ship's length and the type of service or trade in which it is engaged.

Machinery and electrical installations:[1] The rules in this respect are designed to ensure that the installations will continue to operate under the various emergency conditions.

---

deck, into compartments the maximum length of which shall be calculated in accordance with such of the provisions of Schedule 1 to these Regulations as apply to that ship. Every other portion of the internal structure which affects the efficiency of the subdivision of the ship shall be watertight, and shall be of a design which will maintain the integrity of the subdivision.

See also The Merchant Shipping (Means of Access) Regulations, 1981 (S.I.1729/1981). The Regulations require United Kingdom merchant ships of 30 metres or more registered length to carry a gangway, and of 120 metres or more registered length to carry an accommodation ladder, and require all ships to carry safety nets and, where necessary, bulwark ladders. The Regulations stipulate the minimum sizes and specifications required for these items and for any portable ladder which a ship may carry. Bulwark handholds and guardrails are required in specified circumstances. The Regulations also include provisions about the maintenance, deployment, safe rigging and use of access equipment, safety nets and ancilliary equipment. A ship not carrying the necessary access equipment may be detained, and owners (including the employers of masters) may be fined. Owners (including employers of masters) and masters may be fined for failing to maintain the specified access equipment or for failing to deploy safe access equipment as required under the Regulations. Any person who does not board or leave any merchant ship by the access equipment provided, or who damages or interferes without authority the access equipment, will be liable to a fine.

(1) See The Merchant Shipping (Cargo Ship Construction and Survey) Regulations, 1984 (S.I.1217/1984).

Fire protection: The main objective of the fire safety regulations is to ensure a uniformly minimum standard of safety for the protection of life and property(1). As these regulations set minimum standards, any Member State can adopt a higher standard for its own ships(2).

---

Where electrical equipment for use in potentially explosive atmospheres is required to be certified to indicate compliance with a specific standard type of electrical protection against ignition of potentially explosive atmospheres, such equipment may be constructed, inspected, tested, marked and certified in accordance with the corresponding type of protection specified in The European Economic Communities Council Directive 79/196/EEC of 6 February, 1979 and 76/117/EEC of 18 December, 1975.

(1) The provisions of the 1974 version are similar to those of the 1960 with the exception that steam is excluded as a fire extinguishing medium in new ships and may only be permitted in restricted areas. Under Resolution A.327 (IX), the conditions for exemption from the fitting of a fixed extinguishing system are much more severe.
Ships engaged in the carriage of dangerous goods must be provided with a fixed gas fire extinguishing system. For tankers, the Convention makes a distinction between tankers carrying crude oil and petroleum products having a flashpoint not exceeding 60°C (140°F) and other tankers carrying cargoes having flashpoints above this temperature. Part E contains the requirements of Resolution A.271 (VIII) requiring fire protection and constructional features which take account of a fire originating in the cargo or cargo pumping spaces. For tankers less than 100,000 tons deadweight, Resolution A.326 (IX) prescribes deck foam fire fighting systems to cover the deck area and the surfaces of tanks which have been ruptured.
See also the Revised Regulation 62 of Chapter 11-2 of SOLAS on Inert Gas Systems adopted by the Assembly at its eleventh session. The MSC also adopted guidelines for inert gas systems which are designed to assist governments to implement the requirements. These are included in the 1981 amendments to the Convention.

(2) See The Merchant Shipping (Fire Protection) Regulations, 1985 (S.I.1218/1985) which came

Chapter III, which deals with life-saving[(1)] appliances, is divided into three parts. Part A applies to all ships and describes the appliances required and the procedures for emergency and routine practice[(2)]. Both parts B and C contain

---

into operation on August 12, 1985. See also the International Safety Guide issued by the International Chamber of Shipping (ICS). In fact, the ICS prepared the following documents: Tanker Safety Guide (Chemicals), Tanker Safety Guide (Liquefied Gas), Safety in Oil Tankers, Misuse of VHF Channel 16, Steering Gear, and Guide to Helicopter/Ship Operations.

(1) The existing life-saving system can be divided into two categories: primary and secondary systems. Primary systems are conventional lifeboats, either open or covered, with totally enclosed boats predominating through improved design and development as well as regulations. Secondary systems consist of all liferafts, with inflatable types in the forefront.
Two mainstream thoughts have been evident. First the gradual development of the conventional lifeboat from the early wooden craft to today's totally enclosed survival craft (TESC). Second is the concept of totally integrated life-support systems rather than individual items of life-saving equipment and the emphasis placed on functional requirements of new designs of life-saving appliances.

(2) Life-saving systems would be hampered by outdated regulations. In the United Kingdom, the regulations have been revised to reflect the recent developments. See S.I. No.538 of 1980 of The Merchant Shipping (Life-Saving Appliances) Regulations, 1980, as amended by The Merchant Shipping (Life-Saving Appliances) (Amendment) Regulations, 1981, which states: (1) In every ship of Class I, II or II(A), an electric lighting system shall be provided throughout the ship and in particular upon the docks from which lifeboats and liferafts are embarked. Provision shall also be made in every such ship for the electric lighting of the launching gear and of the lifeboats, and of the liferaft launching appliances where provided and the liferafts which they serve, during the preparation for and process of

additional requirements for passenger and cargo ships(1).

Chapter IV is on radiotelegraphy and radiotelephony. It is divided into four parts. Part A prescribes the type of facility to be carried, while part B deals with the operational requirements for watchkeeping and listening. Part C includes technical provisions and the last part is concerned with the radio officer's obligations towards entries into the log-book. The requirements of this chapter are

---

launching and also for illuminating the water into which the lifeboats and liferafts served by launching appliances are launched until the process of launching is completed, and for lighting the stowage position of liferafts for which launching appliances are not provided. The lighting shall be operated from the ship's main generating plant and shall be so arranged that power may be supplied from the emergency source of power referred to in Regulation 43 of The Merchant Shipping (Passenger Ship Construction) Regulations,1980.
The Regulations require all ships between 500 and 1,600 tons gross to carry liferafts of sufficient aggregate capacity to accommodate at least the total number of persons on board. See also Survey of life-saving appliances - Instructions for the guidance of surveyors, issued by the Department of Trade.

(1) The Brazilian delegation proposed (MSC 47/5/7) that the MSC when requiring new equipment should give information on their manufacture and operational specification, instructions on their assembly and other relevant data. This kind of information would enable developing countries to manufacture such equipment. The proposal was refused as the MSC is only concerned with the operational requirement leaving the plans and specifications to Member States. See MSC 49/19 of April 11, 1984, p.14.
The ICS put forward a proposal to the effect that when a ship changes flag, the new administration should accept the navigational equipment currently fitted, provided that the equipment conforms to the relevant IMO specifications. This proposal was referred to the Sub-Committee on Safety of Navigation for further study. *Ibid*, p.15.

closely linked with those of the Radio Regulations of the International Telecommunication Union.

Chapter V, which is on safety of navigation, deals with matters of an operational nature for all ships such as the maintenance of meteorological services; the ice patrol service; and the maintenance of search and rescue operations[1].

Chapter VI is on the Grain Rules: "The 1969 Equivalent Grain Arrangement" (often referred to as IMO Resolution A.184 (VI)) was recommended at the beginning to operators in the United Kingdom and other countries. As these arrangements proved

---

(1) See also Resolution A.321 (IX) concerning the guidelines which will help control officers to find out the deficiencies. Under these guidelines, complaints alleging that a ship is sub-standard should be made in writing to port state authorities. It is advisable that the information should be submitted by more than one crew member.
In addition, while the port state is obliged to pass on such complaints to flag states, this does not relieve the former of its responsibility for taking appropriate action. If there is no opportunity to remedy the situation, port states are expected to pass on the information to the government of the next country the ship visits. In every case of a ship sailing with known deficiencies, advance warning should be sent to the next port of call, and a report made to the IMO.
The guidelines stress the need to check that the ship is sufficiently and efficiently manned. Prior to boarding a vessel, the guidelines say that the inspector should "gain, from the appearance in the water, an impression of its standard of maintenance, from items such as conditions of paintwork, corrosion or pitting, and unrepaired damage".
The next step should involve ascertaining the year of build - in order to determine which conventions apply - and then to check certificates. If the certificates are valid, and the ship looks to be of a good standard, the surveyor should limit his inspection to investigation of any reported deficiencies. More detailed inspection may take place if there are grounds for suspecting that the ship is deficient in some way.

satisfactory, the IMO agreed to revise the whole of Chapter VI of the 1960 Safety of Life at Sea (SOLAS) Convention which dealt with the carriage of grain in bulk. In this revision "The 1969 Equivalent Grain Arrangements", amended in the light of operational experience, were accepted *in toto* to form the basis of new international requirements for the carriage of grain in bulk. To be known as "The IMO Grain Rules", these new requirements were initially adopted by the IMO General Assembly on 20 November, 1973 by Resolution A.264 (VIII) and were subsequently incorporated into Chapter VI of the 1974 SOLAS Convention(1).

---

(1) See The Merchant Shipping (Grain) Regulations, 1980 (S.I.536/1980) as amended by S.I.576/1981. These Regulations apply to all United Kingdom registered sea-going ships when loaded with grain and to all foreign registered ships so loaded when in United Kingdom ports or territorial waters. There is no lower limit on the size of ship to which these regulations apply. Under the Regulations, every ship which is to carry grain must fulfil two requirements:
(a) it has been issued with, and carries on board, a Document of Authorisation, and
(b) the grain is properly loaded in accordance with the Regulations as described in the Document of Authorisation.
The Document of Authorisation takes the form of a booklet of stability information which includes grain loading conditions and other information indicating that the ship is capable of meeting the relevant provisions of the SOLAS Convention pertaining to the carriage of grain in bulk. If the Document of Authorisation cannot be produced, on demand to a Surveyor of the Department of Trade, the ship will be refused permission to load grain, or to depart, until it can be demonstrated to the satisfaction of the Survey that the ship, in the loading conditions and throughout the voyage, complies with the Regulations in terms of both cargo stowage and stability.
The Regulations allow exemptions to visiting UK ships employed in the Near Continental Trading Area. Exemptions granted to foreign ships by their Administrations, and entered in each case on a Document of Authorisation, will be recognised by the Surveyor for ships employed

The IMO Grain Rules are the result of international studies which established that in a compartment nominally filled with grain there existed a void space between the surface of the grain and the crown or deckhead of the loaded compartment. The basis of the Rules is to demonstrate by calculation that at all times during a voyage the ship will have sufficient intact stability after taking into account the adverse heeling effects caused by an assumed pattern of grain movement within and amongst the void spaces lying directly above the grain surfaces. Provision of temporary grain fittings to reduce the effects of grain shift, e.g. shifting boards, bagged grain, etc., depends entirely upon achieving the correct relationship between the intact stability characteristics of the ship and the heeling effects of a possible grain shift within the various compartments of the ship. The IMO Grain Rules stipulate the minimum level of acceptable stability for the carriage of grain in terms of initial metacentric height, angle of heel due to assumed grain shift and residual dynamic stability[(1)].

Chapter VII is devoted to the carriage of dangerous goods. It contains provisions for the classification, packing, marking and stowage of dangerous substances in packaged form. This chapter does not apply to substances carried in bulk in purpose-built ships.

Chapter VIII is concerned with nuclear ships. To ensure compliance with the SOLAS requirements, the following certificates are required:

1. Cargo Ship Safety Construction Certificate;
2. Cargo Ship Safety Equipment Certificate; and
3. Radio or Telegraph Certificate.

---

in the Near Continental Trading Area provided they are broadly in line with those allowed for UK ships.

(1) See a Note entitled IMO and the Carriage of Cargoes in Bulk, prepared by the IMO in July, 1984. The Sub-Committee on Containers and Cargoes in its 26th session, agreed to develop guidance on the carriage of grain and a preliminary example was submitted to the MSC. The aim is to develop harmonized interpretations of current circulars, including those on trimming and the IMO Grain Rules. See IMO News No.2, 1985, p.4.

It is clear that a ship is subject to inspection at various dates in order to conform with the requirements of the different conventions. The intervals of these inspections, which include periodic and intermediate surveys, vary considerably. For this reason, Resolution 10 of the Conference on Tanker Safety and Pollution Prevention, 1978, recommends that the IMO will "take early action to develop Guidelines for Administrations as to the extent, particulars and frequency of such surveys and inspections of ships having due regard to their construction, machinery, equipment and age".

## 2. The 1978 Protocol to the SOLAS Convention

Several accidents involving oil tankers occurred during the winter of 1976-77 and the investigations(1) revealed that further requirements need to be introduced to SOLAS. The difficulty, however, was that SOLAS itself was not in force and therefore it was not possible to make any changes to it. For this reason, the Conference on Tanker Safety and Pollution Prevention (TSPP) decided to include the amendments into a Protocol which was adopted in 1978.

Under the original SOLAS Convention, the inert gas system (IGS)(2) was only required for new oil

---

(1) From investigation of explosions which occurred in 1969, it was found that the probable cause of these was the build up of a static electric charge during the operation of fixed tank washing machines when water washing. It was found that with a mixture of 95 per cent water and 5 per cent crude oil, a charge in excess of 40,000 volts could be generated. That is, a charge capable of producing an incendiary spark. There are three ways in which control can be exercised in this respect and these are:
  (a) By making the atmosphere too lean to burn by removing the fuel source.
  (b) My making the atmosphere too rich to burn by saturating the atmosphere with fuel.
  (c) By making the atmosphere oxygen deficient. This could be achieved by using Inert Gas (IG).

  See the Revised Regulation 62 of Chapter 11-2 of SOLAS adopted by the IMO Assembly at its eleventh session.

(2) The normal method is to fill the tanks with

tankers over 100,000 dwt, and new combination carriers over 50,000. The Protocol brought changes to these requirements and it provides that:

(1) New[1] crude oil and product tankers of 20,000 tons deadweight and above to be fitted with an Inert Gas System (IGS).

(2) Existing crude oil tankers of 70,000 tons deadweight and above to be fitted with IGS as from May 1, 1983. Crude oil tankers of 20,000-70,000 tons deadweight to be so fitted as from May 1, 1985.

(3) Exisisting product carriers of 70,000 tons deadweight and above to be fitted with IGS as from May 1, 1983. Product carriers of 40,000-70,000 tons deadweight and tankers of 20,000-40,000 tons deadweight where fitted with high capacity washing machines to be fitted with IGS as from May 1, 1985.

(4) All tankers of 10,000 gross tons and above should have two remote steering gear control systems, each operable separately from the navigating bridge.

(5) The main steering gear of new tankers of 10,000 grt and above should comprise two or more identical power units, and be capable of operating the rudder whilst operating with one or more power units. Ships so equipped must also have an alarm on the navigating bridge to warn of system failure and an alternative power supply that will start to operate automatically within 45 seconds of a failure.

As for radar and collision avoidance aids, it was agreed that all ships between 1,600 and 10,000 grt be fitted with radar. All ships of 10,000 grt and above must have two radars, each capable of

---

inert gas, that is, a gas which is non-explosive. This is done by using the gas from the ship's boiler flue; it is cleaned and then pumped into the entry tanks, or into the spaces left above the oil in loaded tanks.

(1) New oil tanker means an oil tanker to which any of the following dates apply:
(a) contract placed after June 1, 1979;
(b) keel laid after January 1, 1980; or
(c) delivery after June 1, 1982.

operating independently of the other on the date the Protocol enters into force.

The Protocol contains provisions relating to the periodical surveys[1] required by the SOLAS Convention[2] to the tanker and its equipment such as the cargo pumping, piping and venting arrangements and to reporting accidents and deficiencies.

3. The 1981 Amendments

A further set of amendments[3] to SOLAS were adopted in 1981[4].

---

(1) The inert gas equipment now forms part of an annual survey of safety equipment, see M Notice M.964. See also Resolution A.413 (XI) adopted on November 15, 1979, on Guidelines on surveys and inspections under the two Protocols of 1978. In 1984, the MSC approved draft amendments to Resolution A.413 (XI) to cover the annual and intermediate surveys of chemical tankers and gas carriers under the IBC and IGC Codes and amendments relating to the annual survey of the inert gas system as set out in Annex 7. MSC 49/19, p.22.

(2) The annual survey covers an examination of the ship's certificates (SOLAS, LL Convention and the Classification Society) and a visual examination together with certain tests of the ship's safety equipment in order to make sure that they are being properly maintained. The equipment in this respect covers the life-saving appliances, fire appliances and navigational equipment. Additional survey is required for tankers.

(3) No objections to the Amendments had been received by March 1, 1984, and therefore they entered into force on September 1, 1984. The MSC is preparing a circular which will specify the SOLAS requirements in the light of the various amendments.

(4) The 1981 Amendments have made necessary the enactment of the following Regulations and Rules:

A. Merchant Shipping (Passenger Ship Construction and Survey) Regulations, 1984 (S.I.1216/1984.

B. Merchant Shipping (Cargo Ship Construction & Survey) Regulations, 1984 (S.I.1217/1984).

C. Merchant Shipping (Fire Protection) Regulat-

In Chapter II-1, the changes incorporated Resolution A.325 (IX) on machinery and electrical requirements and amendments to Regulations 29 and 30 of the 1978 SOLAS Protocol on steering gear. Under the 1981 Amendments, the concept of duplication of steering gear control systems in tankers was introduced.

Other amendments to Chapter II-1 related to collision bulkheads in cargo ships, passenger ships designed for the carriage of goods vehicles and accompanying personnel(1), bilge pumping arrangements for cargo ships.

---

ions, 1985 (S.I.1218/1985).

D. Merchant Shipping (Navigational Equipment) Regulations, 1984 (S.I.1203/1984).

E. Merchant Shipping (Radio Installations) (Amendment No.2) Regulations, 1984 (S.I.1223/1984).

F. Merchant Shipping (Passenger Ship Construction) (Amendment) Regulations, 1984 (S.I.1220/1984).

G. Merchant Shipping (Cargo Ship Construction and Survey) Regulations, 1981 (Amendment) Regulations, 1984 (S.I.1219/1984).

H. Merchant Shipping (Fire Appliances) (Amendment) Regulations, 1985 (S.I.1194/1985).

J. The Merchant Shipping (Fire Protection) Regulations, 1985 (S.I.1218/1985).

(1) On conventional ships, the hull is divided into a number of separate holds by means of transverse bulkheads, many of which may be watertight. In the case of the hull being holed, the bulkheads will limit or delay the in-rush of water, resulting in the ship sinking slowly enough for the evacuation of those on board or even preventing the ship from sinking. But in ro-ro ships, the installation of unpierced transverse bulkheads is a major obstacle, at least on the upper "through" decks. The huge vehicle decks make it possible for water to enter very rapidly and fire can also spread very quickly. Furthermore, the movement of cargo on the vehicle deck can affect the intact stability of the ship, causing it to list.

The safety of ro-ro ships was considered by the Assembly in 1975 which adopted Resolution A.323 (IX). The Resolution permitted in passenger ships the fitting of bulkheads below the bulkhead deck with watertight doors designed to

The amendments to Chapter II-2 brought about the requirements of Resolutions A.327 (IX) and A.372 (X), for halogenated hydrocarbon extinguishing systems and Regulation 62 on inert gas systems.

Chapter III (Life-saving Appliances) was amended in order to provide a cross-reference to the amendments to Chapter II-1.

Seven regulations in Chapter IV (Radiotelegraphy and Radiotelephony) were replaced or amended and important changes were made to Chapter V on Safety of Navigation. In particular, new requirements were added concerning the carriage of navigational equipment(1). The revised requirements

---

permit the movent of vehicles, on condition that other more stringent safety requirements were met. These stipulations were then embodied in the 1981 Amendments.
More recently, the Sub-Committee on Stability and Load Lines and on Fishing Vessels Safety agreed, at its 29th session in January, 1984, to a proposal concerning a draft probabilistic method for testing subdivision and stability requirements for ro-ro ships. Members were invited to perform sample calculations on various types and sizes of ships and Norway undertook to summarize and analyse the calculations. The idea of this exercise is to assist the sub-committee to determine a preferred level of survival capability. See IMO note of November 1984 on IMO and Ro-Ro Safety.

(1) See The Merchant Shipping (Navigational Equipment) Regulations, 1984 (S.I.1023/1984), which came into force on September 1, 1984. The Regulations have been made in connection with the implementation of the 1981 Amendments to SOLAS. They state:
3. (1) Every ship shall be fitted with a magnetic compass installation and comply with Part I of these Regulations.
(2) Every ship of 500 tons or over but less than 1600 tons constructed on or after 1st September 1984 shall:
(a) be fitted with a gyro compass installation and comply with Part II of these Regulations;
(b) be fitted with a radar installation and comply with Part III of these Regulations;
(c) be fitted with indicators showing the rudder angle, the rate of revolution and

cover such matters as gyro and magnetic compasses; the mandatory carriage of two radars and of automatic radar plotting aids to ships of 10,000 grt and above; echo-sounders; devices to indicate speed and distance; rudder angle indicators; propeller revolution indicators; rate of turn indicators; radio direction finding apparatus; and equipment for homing on the radiotelephone distress frequency.

---

direction of thrust of each propeller and, if fitted with variable pitch propellers or lateral thrust propellers, the pitch and operational mode of such propellers. All these indicators shall be readable from the normal navigation control position.

(3) Every ship of 500 tons or over but less than 1600 tons when engaged on an international voyage shall:

(a) if constructed on or after 25th May, 1980 be fitted with an echo sounder installation and comply with Part IV of these Regulations;

(b) if constructed on or after 1st September 1984 be fitted with a speed and distance measuring installation and comply with Part V of these Regulations.

(4) Every ship of 1600 tons or over, whenever constructed, shall:

(a) be fitted with a gyro compass installation and comply with Part II of these Regulations. Provided that this requirement shall apply to ships constructed before 1st September, 1984, only when engaged on international voyages;

(b) be fitted with a radar installation (or, if the ship is of 10,000 tons or over, two radar installations), and comply with Part III of these Regulations;

(c) be fitted with indicators showing the rudder angle, the rate of revolution and direction of thrust of each propeller and, if fitted with variable pitch propellers or lateral thrust propellers, the pitch and operational mode of such propellers. All these indicators shall be readable from the normal navigation control position.

(5) Every ship of 1600 tons or over when engaged on an international voyage shall:

As for Chapter VI on the Carriage of Grain, its application was extended to cover ships of less than 500 grt engaged in international voyages.

4. The 1983 Amendments to SOLAS

A second set of amendments were adopted in November, 1983[(1)]. They include minor changes to Chapter II-1

---

(a) whenever constructed, be fitted with an echo sounder installation and comply with Part IV of these Regulations;
(b) if constructed on or after 1st September, 1984 be fitted with a speed and distance measuring installation and comply with Part V of these Regulations;
(c) Whenever constructed, be fitted with a direction finder installation and comply with Part VI of these Regulations;
(d) if constructed on or after 25th May, 1980 be fitted with an installation for homing on the radiotelephone distress frequency (2182 kHz) and comply with Part VII of these Regulations.

(6) (a) Every ship of 10,000 tons or over constructed on or after 1st September, 1984 shall be fitted with an automatic radar plotting aid and comply with Part VIII of these Regulations.
(b) Ships constructed before 1st September, 1984 shall be fitted with an automatic radar plotting aid and comply with Part VIII of these Regulations as follows:
(i) tankers of 40,000 tons or over by 1st January 1985;
(ii) tankers of 10,000 tons or over but less than 40,000 tons by 1st January, 1986;
(iii) ships, other than tankers, of 40,000 tons or over by 1st September, 1986;
(iv) ships, other than tankers, of 20,000 tons or over but less than 40,000 tons by 1st September, 1987;
(v) ships, other than tankers, of 15,000 tons or over but less than 20,000 tons by 1st September, 1988.

(7) Every ship of 100,000 tons or over constructed on or after 1st September, 1984 shall be fitted with a rate of turn indicator and comply with Part IX of these Regulations.

(1) Under the tacit acceptance procedure, the Amend-

on Subdivision and Stability, Machinery and Electrical installations. These changes were made because of the interrelationship between subdivision requirements and those for survival craft for passenger ships.

Although Chapter II-2 on Construction, Fire Protection, Fire Detection and Fire Extinction was revised in the 1981 Amendments, a number of changes were made to it in the 1983 Amendments. The changes aimed to improve the provisions on fire, safety of passenger ships and combination carriers.

Chapter III on Life Saving Appliances was rewritten. It is divided into three parts[1].

---

ments will enter into force on July 1, 1986. Further amendments are planned for 1988 as the IMO is studying a system on the Future Global Maritime Distress and Safety System (FGMDSS) to make use of satellite communications.

(1) The revised Chapter requires that all partially or totally enclosed lifeboats be equipped with an engine (Regulation 41). All totally enclosed boats must be self-righting. Cargo ships must carry sufficient totally enclosed lifeboats or, in certain instances, self-righting partially enclosed lifeboats on each side to accommodate all on board. Cargo ships must also carry liferafts for launching on each side which will accommodate all on board. Chemical and oil tankers must carry totally enclosed lifeboats equipped with a self-contained air support system (if the cargo emits toxic gases). In addition, these lifeboats must afford protection against fire for at least eight minutes (where the cargo is flammable).
A specified number of the boats carried on board ships should also be rescue boats - that is, boats which are designed to rescue persons in distress and to marshal survival craft.
On most passenger ships, partially or totally enclosed lifeboats are required on each side able to accommodate not less than 50 per cent of all persons on board.
The requirements for inflatable and rigid liferafts have also been rewritten and expanded.
The new Chapter incorporates several regulations which are designed to ensure that all lifesaving appliances are kept in good condition and can be used promptly in the event of an emergency.

Part A deals with general matters such as application, exemptions, definitions, evaluation and testing and production tests. Part B is concerned with ship requirements and contains three sections: Section I (Regulations 6 to 19) deals with passenger ships and cargo ships; Section II (Regulations 20-25) contains additional requirements for passenger ships, and Section III, additional requirements for cargo ships (Regulations 26-29). Part C of the new Chapter deals with life-saving appliance requirements. It contains 24 Regulations divided into eight sections.

The revised Chapter requires compulsory fittings or satellite emergency position-indicating radio beacons (EPIRBs) from the date the satellite EPIRB alerting system becomes operational. One survival craft EPIRB would be required on each side of the ship.

It was decided to retain the requirement that cargo ships carry sufficient liferafts for all on board. Also that lifejackets on passenger ships would be fitted with lights and that ships on short international voyages would be exempted. The requirement that survival craft be capable of being launched from a ship against a list of 20 degrees, instead of 15 degrees under the original chapter.

The new Chapter also includes (Regulation 28) a requirement that lifeboats on cargo ships of 20,000 tons gross tonnage and above be capable of being launched when the ship is making headway at speeds of up to 5 knots. This is a new requirement and is in response to the fact that ships have increased greatly in size since the original Chapter was drafted and take much longer to stop.

Changes to Chapter IV on Radiotelegraphy and Radiotelephony were made as a result of the amendments to Chapter III.

Chapter VII on the Carriage of Dangerous Goods was made applicable to chemical tankers and liquefied gas carriers. Consequently, the provisions of the International Bulk Chemicals Code and the International Gas Carrier Code were made compulsory. These Codes relate to ships built on or after July 1, 1986.

## 5. Proposed Amendment to be adopted in 1988

In 1984, the MSC considered the merits of harmonizing the survey and certification requirements under SOLAS, LL Convention and MARPOL. The idea of harmonization is attractive but it is difficult to achieve. One of the difficulties is that Chapter I of SOLAS, which contains the survey and certification requirements, and the Load Line Convention are not subject to the tacit acceptance procedure which covers the remainder of SOLAS.

The MSC considered a composite document which includes the following proposals:

(a) A draft SOLAS protocol including amendments to Chapter I which would retain the explicit acceptance procedure for future amendments to that Chapter.

(b) A draft SOLAS protocol including amendments to Chapter I which would allow application of the tacit acceptance procedure to future amendments to regulations relating to survey items.

(c) A draft amendment to Chapter I in which survey items would be transferred to an appendix which would be subject to the tacit acceptance procedure.

(d) A draft protocol to the Load Line Convention, including amendments to articles relating to survey and certification amendments previously adopted by the Assembly.

(e) An outline of a new Load Line Convention[(1)].

---

(1) MEPC 21/12 of February 7, 1985, p.4. The Japanese delegation, in presenting document MSC 50/3/2, expressed that when the Future Global Maritime Distress and Safety System (FGMDSS) is introduced, this would require further amendments. They added that frequent amendments to conventions will bring not only a heavy burden to administrations but will affect the stability of the Conventions. See MSC 49/WP.10.

References

IMO Resolution A.422 (XI) 15.11.1979, Performance Standards for Automatic Radar Plotting Aids (ARPA).

IMO Resolution A.424 (XI) 15.11.1979, Performance Standard for Gyro Compasses.

IMO Resolution A.281 (VIII) 20.11.1973, General requirement for electronic navigational aids.

IMO Resolution A.224 (VII) including Resolution A.281 (VIII). General requirements for electronic navigational aids.

IMO Resolution A.478 (XII) 19.11.1981, Performance Standards for Devices to indicate Speed and Distance, adopted as amendment to Regulation 12, Chapter V of the 1974 SOLAS Convention.

International Electrotechnical Commission (IEC), Recommendation Standard for Gyro Compasses, September, 1981; Recommendation Standard for Speed and Distance Measuring Equipment, September, 1981.

## (ii) THE INTERNATIONAL CONVENTION ON LOAD LINES, 1966

The ship's sides must be marked with lines to indicate its safe carrying capacity and the position of these lines is determined by the watertight integrity and geometric properties of the ship. In 1930, the Load Lines Convention which dealt with these matters was adopted. However, as a result of many technical developments, the Convention was revised and replaced by the 1966 'Load Lines Convention'(1).

The main objective of the Convention(2) is to ensure structural strength and stability of ships by establishing minimum freeboards and by setting up "uniform principles and rules with respect to the limits to which ships on international voyages may be loaded"(3). It allows for a smaller freeboard for ships but requires more stringent protection of openings in decks and superstructures(4).

---

(1) See the text of the Convention. Sales No. 1972 6. See also Resolution A.411 (XI) adopted on November 15, 1979, on Amendment to the Convention concerning the seasonal tropical area of the north-west Coast of Australia.
(2) The Convention came into force on July 21, 1968.
(3) See the preamble to the Convention.
(4) The stability of a ship might be described as a quantitative measure of its ability to remain afloat without capsizing in the worst conditions of wind and wave to which it is likely to be exposed at sea.
The basic principle of ship stability is to treat the ship as a free floating rigid body subjected to two resultant forces: the weight of the ship (W) assumed to be acting through the centre of gravity and the hydrostatic pressure distribution of buoyancy force assumed to be acting through the geometric centre of buoyancy (B).
These two forces are equal in magnitude but opposite in direction and when a stable ship is heeled transversely, a righting moment W.GZ is set up. Calculations and inclining experiments will establish righting moments and the ship's range of stability, or, in other words, the maximum angle to which it may safely heel.

1. The Merchant Shipping (Load Lines) Act, 1967: The provisions of the Convention were incorporated into the Merchant Shipping (Load Lines) Act, 1967[1]. Part I of Schedule 4 of the Merchant Shipping (Load Lines) Rules, 1968[2] states:

"Structural Strength and Stability

2. (1) The construction of the ship shall be such that her general structural strength will be sufficient for the freeboards to be assigned to her.

(2) The design and construction of the ship shall be such as to ensure that her stability in all probable loading conditions will be sufficient for the freeboards to be assigned to her, and for this purpose regard shall be had, in addition to the intended service of the ship and to any relevant requirements of Rules made under the Merchant Shipping (Safety Convention) Act, 1949 (a) and the Merchant Shipping Act 1964, (b), to the following criteria:-

(a) The area under the curve of Righting Levers (GZ curve) shall not be less than:

(i) 0.055 metre-radians up to an angle of 30 degrees;

(ii) 0.09 metre-radians up to an angle of either 40 degrees or the angle at which the lower edges of any openings in the hull, superstructures or deck-houses being openings which cannot be closed weathertight, are immersed if that angle be less;

(iii) 0.03 metre-radians between the angles of heel of 30 degrees and 40 degrees or such lesser angle as is referred to in (i).

(b) The Righting Lever (GZ) shall be at least 0.20 metres at an angle of heel equal to or greater than 30 degrees.

---

(1) The Act came into effect on July 21, 1968.
(2) S.I. No.1053/1968. See also the following statutory instruments: No. 1072/1968 (Length of Ship); No. 1003/1970 (Amendment); No. 1841/1972 (Particulars of Depth of Loading); No. 595/1975 (Amendment); No. 1269/1979 (Amendment); and No. 641/1980 (Amendment).

(c) The maximum Righting Lever (GZ) shall occur at an angle of heel not less than 30 degrees.

(d) The initial transverse metacentric height shall not be less than 0.15 metres. In the case of a ship carrying a timber deck cargo which complies with sub-paragraph (a) by taking into account the volume of timber deck cargo, the initial transverse metacentric height shall not be less than 0.05 metres.

(3) To determine whether the ship complies with the requirements of sub-paragraph (2) the ship shall, unless the Board otherwise permit, be subjected to an inclining test carried out in the presence of a surveyor appointed by the Board, and the Board shall notify the Assigning Authority whether or not they are satisfied that the ship complies with those requirements."[1]

---

(1) Following the loss of *The Lairdsfield*, the Court of Inquiry recommended that simplified stability information be provided. This eliminates the need to use cross curves of stability and develop righting lever GZ curves for varying loading conditions by enabling a ship's stability to be quickly assessed, to show whether or not all statutory criteria are complied with, by means of a single diagram or table. Considerable experience has now been gained and three methods of presentation are in common use. These are:
(a) The Maximum Deadweight Moment Diagram or Table;
(b) The Minimum Permissible GM Diagram or Table;
(c) The Maximum Permissible KG Diagram or Table.
In all three methods the limiting values are related to salt water displacement or draught. Free surface allowances for slack tanks are however applied slightly differently.
The IMO Sub-Committee on Subdivision, Stability and Loadlines has recently initiated an in-depth investigation into the watertight sub-division and damage stability of dry cargo ships including ro-ro ships.
In addition, a Code of Practice is currently being formulated by IMO for special purpose ships, those vessels carrying a number of personnel who are not strictly crew, such as

2. A brief outline of the Convention

Scope of Application: The rules of Load Lines apply "to all ships engaged on international voyages"[1]. The exceptions[2] are:

(a) ships of war;

(b) ships solely engaged in fishing;

(c) pleasure yachts not engaged in trade; and

---

drivers in ro-ro ships and other workers in whale factory ships.

(1) See art. 4(2) of the Convention.

(2) The Exemption Order, S.I.1053/1968. The Rules grant exemption to ships of the following classes provided they are under 80 tons register, engaged solely in the coasting trade and not carrying cargo:
 (a) tugs and salvage ships;
 (b) ships engaged in the surveying of harbours or the approaches thereto;
 (c) hopper barges and dredgers;
 (d) ships which are pilot boats within the meaning of Section 38 of the Pilotage Act,1913;
 (e) ships used by or on behalf of:
  (i) a general or local lighthouse authority for the purpose of the authority's functions as such;
  (ii) a Government department for fishery protection purposes, or a local fishery committee for the regulation of sea fisheries within its district;
  (iii) a Government department for fishery or scientific research;
  (iv) the Secretary of State for Defence for the purpose of ensuring safety in the use of firing ranges or weapons at sea;
 (f) sailing ships;
 (g) ships in respect of which passenger steamer certificates are in force specifying limits beyond which the ship must not ply, and which operate solely within those limits;
 (h) ships carrying not more than 12 passengers on voyages in the course of which they are at no time more than 15 miles (exclusive of any smooth waters) from the point of departure or more than 3 miles from land.

(d) ships solely navigating the Great Lakes of North America and the River St.Lawrence as far east as a rhumb line drawn from Cap des Rosiers to West Point, Anticosti Island, and, on the north side of Anticosti Island, the meridian of longitude 63°W; the Caspian Sea; and the Plate, Panama and Uruguay Rivers as far east as a rhumb line drawn between Punta Norte, Argentina, and Punta de Este, Uruguay[1].

Paragraph 2 of article 6 of the Convention gives the Contracting States the right to exempt ships which embody features of a novel kind. Accordingly, section 19 of the Merchant Shipping (Load Lines) Act,1967, gives the Department of Trade powers to exempt ships registered in the United Kingdom of the following descriptions from all or specified provisions of the Act:

(a) novel ships;

(b) ships required to undertake a single international voyage, e.g. for delivery or scrapping; and

(c) an existing ship of less than 150 tons gross, a new ship of less than 24 metres in length, or any ship which does not ply on international voyages.

Submersion: Article 12, paragraph 1, of the Convention states that the "appropriate load lines on the sides of the ship corresponding to the season of the year and the zone or area in which the ship may be, shall not be submerged at any time when the ship puts to sea, during the voyage or on arrival".

Survey, Inspection and Marking: The surveyors[2] inspect all ships to which the Convention applies

---

(1) See Resolution A.411 (XI) adopted on November 15, 1979, concerning the seasonal tropical area off the north-west Coast of Australia. See also the amendments adopted by MSC in its 47th session to extend the summer and tropical zones southwards on the south-west Coast of South America.

(2) Sections 11 and 17 of the Merchant Shipping (Load Lines) Act, 1967, confer the power in this field to the surveyors of the Department of

to see that its rules are complied with[(1)].

In the United Kingdom, the powers of the surveyors in relation to foreign ships are limited to seeing that:

(a) the ship is not overloaded;

(b) the lines marked on the ship accord with the certificates;

(c) no material alterations have been made to the ship which affect the position in which any of the lines ought to be marked; and

(d) the fittings and appliances for the protection of openings, the guard rails, the freeing ports and the means of access to the crew's quarters have been maintained in a condition as effective as when the certificate was issued (the relevant details will be shown on the 'Record of Particulars' or equivalent document).

<u>Issue of Certificates</u>: Once the survey is carried out a Load Line Certificate or an Exemption Certificate will be issued. The Load Line Certificate must meet the following conditions:

(a) the certificate must show that it was issued by or on behalf of the Government of the country to which the ship belongs, which must be a party to the 1966 Convention (see paragraph 1.28);

---

Transport. In addition, the following classification societies (known as Certifying Authorities) are authorised to carry out load line surveys, assign freeboards and issue load line certificates: Lloyd's Register of Shipping; The British Committee of Bureau Veritas; The British Technical Committee of the American Bureau of Shipping; The British Committee of Det norske Veritas; The British Committee of Germanischer Lloyd.
This leaves smaller ships which are not classed and which apply to the Department of Transport for load line assignment.

(1) An infringement of the requirements for a ship registered in the United Kingdom renders an owner or master liable on summary conviction to a fine not exceeding £200.

(b) the certificate must be in the official language of the country of issue and if this is neither English nor French must include a translation into one of those languages;

(c) the certificate must be in the form prescribed by the Convention and contain all the required particulars

(d) the certificate must be currently in force and must be applicable to the voyage being undertaken;

(e) the period for which the certificate is expressed to be valid must not exceed 5 years from the date of issue;

(f) any extension of the period for which the certificate is expressed to be valid must have been duly endorsed on the certificate by the issuing authority and must not exceed 5 months;

(g) the required periodical inspections must have been carried out and the appropriate endorsements made on the certificate by the issuing authority.

The maximum period of validity of a load line certificate or load line exemption certificate is 5 years from the date of completion of survey, i.e. the final date of inspecting the ship in drydock or out of water. Subject to this maximum, the period of validity shall be determined by the Assigning Authority.

Cancellation of Certificates: The grounds for cancellation include the following:

(a) the ship to which the certificate relates does not comply with the conditions of assignment;

(b) the structural strength of the ship is lowered to such an extent that the ship is unsafe;

(c) information on the basis of which freeboards were assigned to the ship was incorrect in a material particular.

Periodical Inspections: A periodical inspection is to be carried out not more than three months before or three months after each anniversary of the date of completion of the survey on the basis of which the certificate was issued. Thus inspection shall in no case be more than 15 months from the date of the previous inspection.

Overloading: Overloading occurs:

(a) if the ship is in salt water and has no list, the appropriate load line on each side of the ship is submerged; or

(b) in any other case, the appropriate load line on each side of the ship would be submerged if the ship were in salt water and had no list.

Freight will still be due even though the ship has been overloaded in breach of the Convention[(1)]. A ship registered in the United Kingdom which commits the offence of overloading and proceeds or attempts to proceed to sea may be detained until it ceases to be overloaded. The master or owner is liable to a fine not exceeding £400 and also such additional fine as the Court thinks fit to impose having regard to the increased earning capacity of the ship. This latter fine is subject to a maximum of £400 per inch (25.4 mm) of overloading.

A Convention ship[(2)] must not be detained nor must proceedings be instituted unless the ship has been inspected by a ship surveyor or an engineer surveyor[(3)].

---

(1) See *St. John Shipping Corporation* v. *Joseph Rank Ltd*. (1957) 1 Q.B. 267; (1956) 3 All E.R. 683.
(2) Section 28(3) of the Merchant Shipping (Load Lines) Act,1967 provides for the making of an Order enabling non-Convention load line certificates issued by any other country to be recognised as equivalent to United Kingdom load line certificates provided that country has requirements for the marking of ships with load lines which are equally effective as those contained in or made under the Act, and grants reciprocal recognition to United Kingdom load line certificates under its own legislation.
(3) See section 17 of the Merchant Shipping (Load Lines) Act,1967.

Proposed amendments to be considered in 1988

The Sub-Committee on Stability, Load Lines and Fishing Vessel Safety prepared amendments to the Convention covering several issues such as intact stability of pontoons, of passenger and cargo ships over 24 metres long. It did not accept a proposal that freeboard be determined in relation to compliance with stability criteria since this is only one of several factors which should be taken into account.

At its 30th session, the Sub-Committee recommended ship motions in seaway studies using recent oceanographic wave studies as being the most desirable and promising method of evaluating freeboard and sheer. It was recognized that such studies will cover several sessions before sufficient data could be collected.

It has been announced that a conference will be convened in 1988 to consider amendments to both SOLAS and the LL Convention[1].

3. Carriage of Timber

Timber may be either:

(a) loose timber, i.e. individual planks of sawn timber, logs or pit-props; or

(b) packaged timber, i.e. bundles of sawn timber, consisting of either

(i) similar sized planks forming a regular cuboid - ("regular packaged timber") or

(ii) random sized planks which do not form a regular shape - ("irregular packaged timber"). The stowage factor for "irregular packaged timber" is usually much higher than for other types of timber.

The most obvious hazard to a ship carrying a cargo of timber is a transverse shift of the stowed timber but this is seldom the sole cause of a dangerous list. More often the effects of a transverse shift are aggravated either by an inadequate

(1) IMO News, No.3, 1985, p.20

standard of stability, imprudent stowage or unsecured deck openings which permit the ingress of seawater, or even by all three.

In 1973, the IMO adopted the Code of Safe Practice for Ships Carrying Timber Deck Cargoes which was amended in 1978(1). The Code is not mandatory and gives guidance to governments which can implement it if they desire, either in whole or in part.

The Code is intended to apply to ships of 24 metres (79 feet) in length and over. Timber deck cargoes are defined as cargoes of timber, including logs, and sawn timber whether loose or packaged, which are carried on an uncovered part of a freeboard or superstructure deck. It lists requirements on stowage, lashings, stability, protection of the crew and other matters. An Annex gives information on the calculation of stability curves and rolling period tests.

The Merchant Shipping (Load Lines) (Deck Cargo) Regulations, 1968(2) distinguish between:

---

(1) The amendments include an Annex on Stowage and Securing of Deck Cargoes of CANTS. These are logs which are "slab cut"; that is, they are ripped lengthwise so that the resulting thick pieces have two opposing parallel flat sides and in some cases a third side which is sawn flat. The irregularities caused by varying thicknesses and curved sides of the timber pieces make it difficult to achieve a compact bundle. As such cargo is vulnerable to shifting in bad weather, it was necessary to lay down special provisions in the Annex. See IMO News, No.1, 1979, p.5.
Recently a draft circular reminding masters of the heavy loads which can be imposed on timber deck cargo lashings under certain circumstances was submitted to the MSC. The draft circular is primarily concerned with dangers resulting from the rapid and violent ship motions associated with an excessive metacentric height, the hazards of not moderating speed when the ship encounters heavy weather and the dangers associated with ballasting or transferring ballast to reduce the list caused by shift of cargo. The move behind the preparation of this circular came from the Canadian delegation. See IMO News, No.2, 1985, p.4.

(2) S.I.1089/1968.

(a) ships which carry timber deck cargoes and are not marked with timber load lines; and

(b) ships which carry timber deck cargoes and which are marked with timber load lines[1].

Ships of the second category are permitted to load more deeply by virtue of their timber deck cargo being stowed and secured in the manner specified in the Regulations[2].

## References

Code of Practice for Ships Bridge Design - 1977, prepared by the Department of Industry.

Merchant Vessel Bridge Layout - 1979, prepared by the Netherland Institute of Perception and the Netherland Maritime Institute.

---

(1) The Department of Trade has published a booklet entitled "Load Line - Loading of Ships" which gives notes on the chart of zones, areas and seasonal periods.

(2) See M.Notice 1051 on the Carriage of Wood Pulp, of January,1983. It referred to an accident where the timber deck cargo of a vessel shifted in heavy weather and sheared the air pipe to the deep tank in which wood pulp was stowed in the lower ten feet, with bales of plywood, assorted timber and cedarwood shingles above it, reaching to within six inches of the crown of the deep tank structure.

## (iii) THE RULES ON SAFETY OF FISHING VESSELS

The construction, design, size and equipment of fishing vessels are quite different from dry cargo vessels. Furthermore, in the case of an ordinary ship, after loading or discharging her cargo in the port, the hatches are closed watertight and they continue to be closed during the voyage. When the ship arrives at her destination or at a port of call, the hatches will be opened. But fishing vessels carry out their operations at sea with open hatches. The crew of a fishing vessel may even work without shelter on open deck. A fishing vessel is restricted in her ability to manoeuvre since she has to pull heavy gear. All these features, and others were the reason for excluding fishing vessels from both the SOLAS and Load Line Conventions. A separate convention was needed to meet these special requirements and the Convention of Fishing Vessels, 1977, was passed to fill this gap.

### 1. A brief outline of the 1977 Convention

The provisions of the Convention[1] apply to new[2] fishing vessels of 24 metres in length and over[3]. The Convention spells out various stipulations on the construction of the hull and superstructure. The watertight integrity is subject to certain requirements. All openings through which water can enter must be provided with suitable closing devices. Calculations are given for static stability. Other requirements deal with matters such as fire protection, detection, extinction, and fire fighting, life-saving appliances, emergency procedures, musters and drills; radiotelegraphy and

---

(1) The Convention was adopted at a conference held in Torremolinos, Spain. It will come into force one year after fifteen States with 50 per cent of the world's fishing fleet of vessels of 24 metres in length have ratified it. As from January 1, 1985, twelve States have ratified the Convention.
(2) Existing vessels are covered only in respect of radio equipment.
(3) The reason for excluding fishing vessels less than 24 metres in length was the lack of information on these vessels. See Hjalmar R. Bardarson, Safety of Fishing Vessels and Their Crew, IMO News, No.4, 1984, p.2.

radiotelephony; and shipborne[1] navigational equipment[2].

Recent work: The Sub-Committee on Stability, Load Lines and Fishing Vessel Safety approved at its 30th session a recommendation relating to the protection of the crew on the fishing deck. It covers guidance on a method of calculation of the

---

(1) See Resolution A.484 (XII) on "Basic Principles to be observed in keeping a Navigational Watch on Board Fishing Vessels" to ensure that a safe navigation watch is maintained. See also M.Notice 997 of November 1981, where it was stated that:
"The investigation of groundings and collisions involving fishing vessels continues to reveal that one or more of the following were important contributory factors:
(a) an unqualified man in charge of the watch;
(b) only one man on watch;
(c) a poor lookout being kept;
(d) divided command.
...
There have also been a number of casualties involving fishing vessels where a crew member employed by virtue of his experience in fishing techniques has been in virtual command of the vessel notwithstanding the presence on board of a certificated Skipper. Attention is drawn to the need to ensure that an appropriately qualified Skipper is in command of the vessel and that experts in fishing techniques do not go beyond their role as advisers, thereby giving rise to a divided command with its attendant hazards."
The IMO, with the co-operation of the ILO and FAO, is studying the matter of training of fishermen. The three organizations may issue a document in 1986 for guidance on fishermen's training and certification.

(2) Among the EEC fishing policy are the restructuring of the fishing fleet of Member States by the withdrawal and partial modernization of the deep sea fleet and the modernization and renewal of the inshore fleet.

minimum distance from the deepest operating waterline to the lowest point of the top of the bulwark or to the edge of the working deck.

## 2. The Fishing Vessels (Safety Provisions) Rules, 1975

In the United Kingdom, the Fishing Vessels (Safety Provisions) Rules, 1975[(1)] set out requirements for hull construction, stability[(2)], structural fire protection and fire detection, means of escape, watertight integrity, boilers and machinery, pumping[(3)] arrangements, electrical equipment and installations, miscellaneous plant and equipment, crew protection (bulwarks, guard rails etc.), the carriage of charts and publications and survey and certification arrangements for UK fishing vessels of 12 metres[(4)] registered length and over. These

---

(1) The Rules came into force on May 1, 1975.

(2) Rule 15 stipulates criteria for freeboard which take into account stability criteria, safe working on deck and watertight integrity of the vessel. Draught of water marks are required by Rule 15(2). Rule 15(1) states:
"Every vessel of 12 metres in length and over to which these Rules apply shall be so designed, constructed and operated as to ensure that in all foreseeable operating conditions the freeboard will be adequate to provide:
  (a) compliance with the stability criteria set out in Rule 16 of these Rules;
  (b) reasonable safety for men working on deck;
  (c) reasonable safety to the vessel from the entry of water into enclosed spaces having regard to the closing appliances fitted."

(3) Several cases of flooded fish holds of fishing vessels had occurred. In some cases the vessels were lost due to the inability of the bilge pumping systems to clear the flooded fish holds after discovery by the crew.

(4) Fishing vessels of less than 12 metres in length are required to carry the life-saving equipment prescribed by Rule 81 of the Fishing Vessel (Safety Provisions) Rules,1975, namely at least two lifebuoys (one with buoyant line) and six red star distress signals.
Experience of casualties to small fishing vessels has shown, however, that liferafts have

requirements come into force for different vessels at different times over a six year period commencing on 1 July 1975.

The Rules also incorporate the requirements applying to all fishing vessels in respect of life-saving appliances, fire appliances and muster and drills(1).

---

been effective in providing essential out of water support in a cold climate for crews and many small fishing vessels now carry liferafts.

(1) Surveys are required for the construction, etc. of life-saving, fire appliances and radio equipment carried by fishing vessels of 12 metres registered length and over.
Vessels which are satisfactory in all these respects will be issued with a United Kingdom Fishing Vessel Certificate valid for a period not exceeding four years subject to an intermediate survey of safety equipment at two years. General inspections of safety equipment will also be carried out on all fishing vessels. See also the "Report of the Working Group on the Occupational Safety of Fishermen" which was published on 5 March, 1979. The Working Group, which included representatives of all parts of the industry together with representatives of the interested Government Departments, also prepared new and extensively revised editions of the "Recommended Code of Safety for Fishermen" and the personal safety booklet "Fisherman and Safety". These were also published on 5 March, 1979.
Provision is also made for the surveys of vessels classed with Lloyd's Register of Shipping or subject to survey by the White Fish authority or the Herring Industry Board under their grant and loan schemes and in such cases a declaration from the appropriate body stating that the vessel complies with the Rules as far as the particular "class" requirements are concerned in respect of hull construction, machinery and closing appliances, will be accepted as meeting the requirements of the Rules in these respects. This is so as to avoid duplication of surveys.

(iv) THE CODES

A physically safe or seaworthy ship must be built to a high standard regarding her hull structural strength, machinery, electrical equipment and design qualities. This is quite evident for the sophisticated ships such as chemical and gas tankers. Therefore, in developing standards for these types of ship, the effect of the hazards on the cargo, the crew and the environment must be taken into account. The design of the ship must be suitable to withstand its special characteristics on matters such as gravity, pressure and temperature.

As mentioned earlier, the 1960 SOLAS Convention in Chapter VII dealt with the safety issues associated with the carriage of dangerous goods in packages. But at that time, the chemical and the gas industries were in their infancy and the carriage of their products did not call for special requirements.

The picture has changed with the rapid increase in the carriage of chemicals, liquefied natural gas (LNG) and liquefied petroleum gas (LPG). The need, thus, has emerged for international standards on the design, construction and to a limited extent, the operation of these ships[1] to ensure a high level of safety. Codes were thought by the IMO to be the most suitable instrument for providing a regulatory framework.

By observing the IMO Codes, a ship will fulfil stability requirements and will ensure, to a certain extent, its safe employment. Thus, it is necessary during the construction of the ship that materials and workmanship are carefully inspected, checked and tested so that defects can be remedied. It is also necessary from time to time to see that she is seaworthy.

In fact, the requirements of the IMO Codes form the basis of national rules for safety equipment and most manufacturers base their design on these rules because they govern the largest part of the market. While the IMO rules form the basis of an international standard, there is nothing to prevent States from having higher or additional requirements. A difficulty, however, arises from States adopting

---

(1) The Load Lines Convention brought limitations on the draught to which the ship may be loaded in the form of free boards.

different testing procedures(1). As science advances and new knowledge and methods of checking are available, the IMO is continually revising the Codes.

Several Codes(2) were adopted and the most important ones are:

1 - the Code for the Construction and Equipment of Ships Carrying Dangerous Chemicals in Bulk, known as the Bulk Chemical (BCH) Code, revised by the International Bulk Chemical (IBC) Code;

2 - the Code for the Construction and Equipment of Ships Carrying Liquefied Gases in Bulk (this is applicable to ships contracted for after 31 October,1976 or delivered after 30 June,1978; and the Code for Existing Ships Carrying Liquefied Gases in Bulk (this is applicable to ships delivered before 31 October, 1976 or before the entry into of the above Code) revised by the International Gas Carrier (IGC) Code; and

3 - the Code for the Construction and Equipment of Mobile Offshore Drilling Units (MODU).

## 1. THE INTERNATIONAL BULK CHEMICAL CODE (IBC)

In October,1971, the IMO Assembly adopted(3) a Code

---

(1) The IMO is working on a Code of practice for testing the equipment.

(2) See the list of the Codes in Appendix III. Recently the IMO adopted a Code of Safety for Nuclear Merchant Ships. It has two main objectives:
(a) protecting people and the environment against unacceptable hazards due to the emission of ionising radiation at sea and in ports;
(b) safeguarding the ship in respect of nuclear hazards and any others due to interactions between the nuclear propulsion plant and the remainder of the ship and cargo, the sea, and the environment.
To meet these objectives, the Code sets out design criteria and requirements on construction, equipment, the nuclear steam supply system, machinery and electrical installations, radiation, safety, operation, and surveys. Explicit rules are also given on assessing safety.

(3) Resolution A.212 (VII), the Assembly invited all

for the Construction and Equipment of Ships Carrying Dangerous Chemicals in Bulk (BCH). The Code was developed to provide an agreed international standard for the safe carriage of dangerous chemicals in bulk by prescribing the constructional features of ships involved and the equipment they carry. It has since been amended several times. In 1983, a revised version of the Code, known as the International Bulk Chemical (IBC) Code, was approved[(1)]. The BCH Code applies to chemical tankers constructed before July 1, 1986, and the IBC Code applies to chemical tankers constructed on or after the entry into force of the 1983 Amendments to the 1974 SOLAS Convention which has been set for July 1, 1986[(2)]. In other words, tbe BCH applies to all chemical tankers built before the date at which the IBC Code comes into force, and the IBC Code will cover all ships built after that date. The provisions of the IBC will become mandatory as from July 1, 1986.

Chapter I - General: This chapter contains information concerning the application and scope of the

---

governments to give effect to the Code as soon as possible.

(1) Resolution MSC.4(48).

(2) The Amendments to SOLAS involve the replacement of the existing Chapter VII (Carriage of Dangerous Goods) with a new text. This is divided into three sections. Section A covers the present contents of Chapter VII related to dangerous goods carried in packages and also solid dangerous goods in bulk. Section B deals with chemical tankers and contains three regulations, the third of which states: "A chemical tanker shall comply with the requirements of the International Bulk Chemical Code ... For the purpose of this regulation, the requirements of the Code will be treated as mandatory."

Code[1]. It applies[2] to tankships which transport bulk cargoes of dangerous chemical substances. These are defined as products which have significant fire hazards in excess of petroleum products, and products which have significant hazards in addition to or other than flammability. Cargoes which are liquids at normal temperature are governed by the Code.

---

(1) The Code is only concerned with safety aspects. However, amendments to both the BCH and IBC Codes are in sight to cover requirements designed to prevent marine pollution. Two problems had to be solved. The first is that in Annex II of MARPOL 73/78, noxious substances are evaluated for their hazards to the environment and grouped into categories A, B, C and D. Different discharge criteria apply to those categories according to the hazard they present to the marine environment.
A list of substances in the Codes are different from those in the Annex. Therefore, the IMO has agreed that the BCH and IBC Codes should be extended to cover pollution aspects and work, at present, is carried out to ensure that the substances in the Codes are the same as in Annex II of MARPOL. Before this could be achieved, the safety requirements for each product listed in Chapter VI of the BCH Code and Chapter 17 of the IBC Code have to be reviewed and reassessed.
The second problem is the assignment of ship types. The Marine Environment Protection Committee (MEPC) has already agreed on the rationale for the assignment of ship types for the carriage of noxious liquid substances according to the hazards they present to the marine environment. Thus, ship types will be assessed from the points of view of both safety and pollution hazards of a noxious liquid substances and whichever type is more stringent will be assigned.

(2) At its 13th session, the Sub-Committee on Bulk Chemicals agreed on draft interpretation of both the IBC and IGC Codes. See IMO News, No.3, 1984, p.19.

Chapter II - Cargo Containment: This chapter contains the features of the design of ships. Measures to prevent the cargo from release were incorporated into ship design standards. Recognising the probability that damage resulting from collision or grounding could lead to uncontrolled release of the cargo, three degrees of protection for the cargoes were developed. The degrees of physical protection, or 'ship types', define the location of the cargo with respect to the ship's side and bottom and the extent to which a ship should be capable of remaining afloat after damage. The assignment of ship types to the various cargoes takes into account the nature and severity of the product's hazard to the environment should it be released. The more severe requirements are imposed against the more hazardous substances.

The highest standard of physical protection, Type I ship, is required for those substances considered to have the greatest environment hazard, i.e. if released, the cargo would have wide reaching effects beyond the immediate neighbourhood of the ship. Tanks containing Type I products are required to be located inboard from the ship's side a distance equivalent to 1/5 the ship's beam. The tank's bottom must also be located above the ship's bottom a distance equal to 1/15 the ship's beam. Further, a Type I ship must be able to survive certain defined damage anywhere in its length, including the engineroom, and remain in an upright stable condition.

A Type II ship is required to transport those cargoes which would present a significant hazard to the ship and crew if released. The release of a Type II cargo would not have the same far-reaching effects as a Type I product. Type II tanks must be located at least 760mm from the ship's side and above the bottom of the ship a distance equivalent to 1/15 the ship's beam. This tank location provides cargo protection against low energy collisions and groundings which often occur to ships in port. The survivability requirement for a Type II ship is based upon ship length. A Type II ship over 150 metres in length must meet the same survival requirements as a Type I ship. Type II ships less than 150 metres in length must be able to withstand the defined damage anywhere in the cargo area and, separately, withstand flooding of the engineroom.

Type III ships are required for the remaining products covered by the Code. Type III ships are very similar to the petroleum product tanker, i.e., a single skin tanker, although it is significant to note that they are required to meet a higher standard survivability than is required for an oil tanker.

Cargo Segregation: Many of the chemicals which are transported on chemical tankers will react violently if accidentally mixed with other chemicals. Therefore, the Code requires that incompatible cargoes be physically separated on the ship by a cofferdam, void space, or mutually compatible cargo. Similarly, the piping and tank vent systems for incompatible cargoes must be completely separate. The Code does not specify which products are reactive; however, this information is available from other sources, e.g., the US Coast Guard.

Chapter II also develops in detail additional requirements on the location and arrangement of the accommodation space, machinery spaces, cargo pump-room, cargo piping and hose, tank vent systems, tank gauging systems, etc.

Chapter III - Safety Equipment and Related Considerations: One of the major objectives of the Code is to make each chemical ship a safe working environment for its operating personnel. A chemical ship is alive with various operations, such as transferring cargo, cleaning tanks and other similar operations, each of which presents hazards to the vessel's personnel. Within Chapter III are the following major sections:

1. Requirements for ventilation of cargo handling spaces.
2. Standards for electrical equipment.
3. Standards for the gauging of cargo tanks.
4. Standards for fire protection.
5. Standards for personnel protection.

Chapter IV - Special Requirements: Chapter IV contains special requirements which extend the Code's more general parts. This is to recognise the unusual hazards or properties of certain products.

The subsequent chapters deal with matters such as the operating and minimum requirements. The Code also contains a list of the dangerous liquid chemicals.

It must be recalled that the IBC Code covers the same requirements as the BCH Code. However, the former contains a chapter on ships engaged in the incineration of liquid chemical waste at sea. The text of the IBC Code has been harmonized to bring it into alignment with the IGC Code.

## 2. THE INTERNATIONAL GAS CARRIER (IGC) CODE

In 1975, the IMO Assembly adopted[(1)]:

(a) the Code for the Construction and Equipment of Ships Carrying Liquefied Gases in Bulk; and

(b) the Code for Existing Ships Carrying Liquefied Gases in Bulk.

Four sets of amendments to each of the Codes have been adopted. In 1983, a revised version of the Codes, known as the International Gas Carrier (IGC) Code, was approved[(2)]. As with the chemical Code, the purpose of the Code is to provide international safety standards for the design, construction and operation of ships carrying liquefied gases in bulk. The IMO recognized the need to develop such a Code because of the hazards associated with the carriage of liquefied gases and to put an end to unilateral control systems such as the one called the Letter of Compliance, introduced by the United States. The provisions of the IGC Code will become compulsory on July 1, 1986. The Code contains detailed requirements governing the design and equipment. The various provisions of the Code are of complex and technical nature. However, it is useful to say a brief word on its important chapters.

Chapter I - General: This chapter contains the administrative details of the Gas Code including application, definitions, scope, certification, surveys, etc. During the drafting of the Code it was discovered that certain commonly used terms in the gas tanker industry had very different meanings

---

(1) Resolution A.328 (IX).
(2) Resolution MSC.5(48).

in different parts of the world. Therefore, major emphasis was given to the development of an agreed set of definitions.

Chapter I concludes with provisions for certification and inspection of the ship. A model certificate is included. The model Certificate has been designed especially from the point of view of providing important information on the design of the vessel, e.g., ship type, cargo tank design information, and exceptions.

Chapter II - Ship survival capability and cargo tank location: In developing the Code, a major concern has been the possibility of a cargo release posing a hazard over a wide area. While most cases do not present a water pollution hazard, other potential hazards such as flammability, toxicity, and low temperature call for special attention to cargo containment under both normal and emergency conditions. The Code specifies design criteria which provide a level of protection commensurate with these hazards both for personnel on the ship and in the ports.

The subsequent Chapters of the Code deal with: ship arrangements; cargo containment(1); process pressure piping systems; materials of construction; cargo pressure temperature control; cargo vent systems; environmental control for cargo containment systems; electrical arrangements; fire protection and fire extinguishing; mechanical ventilation in cargo area; instrumentation (gauging gas detection); personnel protection; filling limits for cargo tanks; use of cargo as fuel; special requirements; operating requirements(2); and summary of minimum requirements.

## 3. THE MOBILE OFFSHORE DRILLING UNITS (MODU) CODE, 1979

In 1979 the IMO Assembly adopted a Code for the Construction and Equipment of Mobile Offshore

---

(1) The following types are defined: (a) Integral tanks from a structural part of the ship's hull; (b) Membrane tanks which are non-self-supporting tanks; (c) Semi-membrane tanks which are self-supporting tanks when empty; and (d) Independent tanks which are self-supporting.

(2) See also the Tanker Safety Guide (Liquefied Gas Tankers) prepared by the ICS.

Drilling Units (MODU). The Code provides for standards for mobile offshore drilling units of new construction. Its objectives are to facilitate the movement and operation of offshore units and to ensure a level of safety for both the units and the men on board.

The Code deals, among other matters, with subdivision, stability and free board. It does not prohibit the use of an existing unit simply because its design, construction and equipment does not conform to its requirements. Many existing mobile offshore drilling units have operated successfully and safely and their operating history should be considered in evaluating their suitability to conduct international operations[(1)]. Therefore, the coastal State may permit any unit designed to a lesser standard than that of the Code to engage in operations having taken account of the local environmental conditions. Any such unit should, however, comply with safety requirements which in the opinion of the coastal State are adequate for the intended operation and ensure the overall safety of the unit and the personnel on board.

The Code (Resolution A.414 (XI)) and the Recommendation on Maritime Safety Training Personnel of Mobile Offshore Units (Resolution A.538(13)) contain definitions of mobile offshore units and personnel on board, but no definition is provided for the category of offshore units which are classified as ships.

Resolution A.414 (XI) states:

"Mobile offshore drilling unit is a vessel capable of engaging in drilling operations for the exploration for or exploitation of resources beneath the sea-bed such as liquid or gaseous hydrocarbons, sulphur or salt.

Surface unit is a unit with a ship or barge-type displacement hull of single or multiple hull construction intended for operation in the floating condition.

Self-elevating unit is a unit with moveable legs capable of raising its hull above the surface of the sea.

---

(1) Requirements for the drilling operations or the procedures for the control of a well are outside the scope of the Code.

Column stabilized unit is a unit with the main deck connected to the underwater hull or footings by columns or caissons."

Resolution A.538 (13) provides:

"Mobile offshore units means vessels which can be readily relocated and can perform an industrial function involving offshore operations other than those traditionally provided by vessels covered by Chapter I of the 1974 SOLAS Convention. Such units could include at least the following:

Mobile offshore drilling units capable of engaging in drilling operations for the exploration for or exploitation of resources beneath the sea-bed such as liquid or gaseous hydrocarbons, sulphur or salt.

Mobile offshore accommodation units the primary purpose of which is to accommodate personnel working offshore.

Other mobile offshore units involved in activities such as:

- construction
- maintenance
- lifting operations
- pipe laying
- fire fighting.

Special personnel means all persons carried on board a mobile offshore unit in connection with the special purpose of the unit or with special work being carried out on the unit and who are neither seafarers nor directly or indirectly paying passengers.

Personnel on mobile offshore units are for practical reasons divided into four categories:

1. visitors and special personnel not regularly assigned;
2. regularly assigned special personnel without designated responsibility for the survival of others;
3. regularly assigned special personnel with designated responsibility for the survival of others; and
4. seafarers on self-propelled mobile offshore units or, where required, on other units."

It was clear when the Code was drafted that its requirements are based on the design engineering principles and experience gained from current offshore activities. As technology is rapidly evolving in this area, the Code is under review(1).

Amendments to the MODU Code are in sight: At the 46th session of the Maritime Safety Convention (MSC), the Norwegian delegation proposed a review of the stability and subdivision requirements of the MODU Code. The MSC accepted the proposal and decided that periodic review would be appropriate to update the Code in the light of the experience gained and having regard to the lessons learned from the *Alexander Kielland* and *Ocean Ranger* rig disasters(2).

At the 28th session of the Sub-Committee on Ship Design and Equipment, it was agreed that some chapters of the Code should be reviewed. A number of changes to the preamble and Chapter 1 (general) were tentatively agreed. Chapter 4 (machinery installations) and Chapter 5 (electrical installations) were referred to an *ad hoc* working group for further studies. The Sub-Committee agreed that Chapter 10 (life-saving appliances and equipment) was urgently in need of revision to take account of experience gained from recent disasters, research studies on evacuation procedures and Chapter III of the 1974 SOLAS Convention. Similarly Chapter 14 (operating requirements) was badly in need of extensive review. The Sub-Committee is waiting for

---

(1) Eleven States have notified the IMO that they apply the Code to units under their flag and three more States informed the Secretariat that they intend to do so in the near future. See IMO News, No.1, 1985, p.11.

(2) Norway submitted two documents: one dealing with a research project on the safety of mobile offshore; and the other on the safety of mobile offshore structure. The latter paper dealt with what might happen to mobile units involved in various hypothetical incidents, such as a collision between a semi-submersible unit and a fixed installation, a drifting supply vessel, a cruising supply vessel and a drifting tanker. The conclusion was that the damage in each case would far exceed what is covered by the Code. See IMO News, No.1, 1984, p.4.

further studies by working groups and information from Member States (1) before approving the amendments to the Code.

## References

Chemical/Parcel Tankers: their cargoes, markets and design, 3rd ed., 1984.

Design and Construction Specification for Marine Loading Arms, 1981, prepared by OCIMF.

Disabled Tankers - Report of Studies on Ship Drift and Tonnage, 1981, prepared by OCIMF.

Ewart, W.D., Bulk Carriers, 1984.

Ffooks, R., Gas Carriers, 1984.

General Guide to Tank Container Operations, prepared by Sea Containers, 1984.

International Chamber of Shipping, Tanker Safety Guide (Liquefied Gases), 1978.

International Safety Guide for Oil Tankers and Terminals (ISGOTT), Revised ed. 1984, prepared by ICS/OCIMF/IAPH.

Lakey, R.J., The IMCO Code for Gas Tankers, a review of the finalized Code, Gastech Conference, 1975.

Safety Guide for Terminals Handling Ships Carrying Liquefied Gases in Bulk, 1982, prepared by OCIMF.

Scott, R., Standard Ship Design, Vol.3 and Vol.4.

Ship to Ship Transfer Guide (Petroleum), 1978, prepared by ICS/OCIMF.

Tanker Safety Guide (Chemicals), prepared by ICS.

Tanker Safety Guide (Liquefied Gas), prepared by ICS.

---

(1) The possible inclusion of anchoring systems in the Code was discussed but the Sub-Committee concluded that more information was needed before a decision could be taken.
See the Report of the MSC, DE 28/10 of Jan. 17, 1984, pp. 4,5,6.

# CHAPTER III

# RULES ON CARGOES

# AND CONTAINERS

While the adoption of several rules on ship construction, design and equipment was essential to ensure safety at sea, it was necessary for the IMO at the same time to set up rules on cargoes and containers. In fact, the carriage of dangerous goods has been one of the main preoccupations of the Organization since its establishment. After an assessment of hundreds of dangerous substances, they were compiled in the International Maritime Dangerous Goods (IMDG) Code. The Code is constantly reviewed so as to bring it up to date with any new development in this field.

A further move was made by the IMO when it adopted the Safe Practice for Solid Bulk Cargoes (BC) Code. It gives, among other things, valuable information on cargoes which may oxidize, emit toxic fumes and describes the procedures to be followed in the carriage of such substances.

Other measures[1] taken to supplement the above Codes are:

- the Medical First Aid Guide (MFAG) for use in accidents involving dangerous goods
- the recommendation on the Safe Use of Pesticides in Ships; and
- the recommendation on the Safe Transport, Handling and Storage of Dangerous Substances in Port Areas.

These measures and others are considered as an extension to the IMDG Code.

Another problem arose from the substantial increase in the quantities of dangerous goods carried by sea, and the potential hazards to the ships' personnel. To this end the IMO, with the co-operation of the International Labour Organization (ILO) prepared Guidelines for Packing of Cargo in Freight Containers and Guidelines on Training and Qualifications of Officers and Crew on Ships Carrying Hazardous Cargoes in Bulk[2].

---

(1) It must be noted that many rules mentioned in Chapter II on Ship Construction, Design and Equipment, such as the Grain rules, are established with the objective not only to ensure the safety of the ship but also the cargo.

(2) See DE VII/2/2, August 25, 1971.

Although radioactive materials are covered by the term "dangerous goods", the work on them was entrusted to the International Atomic Energy Agency (IAEA). The IAEA, with the cooperation of the IMO, adopted Regulations for the Safe Transport of Radioactive Materials and as a result of the revision of the IAEA Regulations, Chapter VIII of the SOLAS Convention 1974 and Class 7 of the IMDG Code were revised.

Though the above measures were excellent in their own way, it was necessary to establish, in view of the wide use of containers, rules to ensure the structural safety of the containers. To this end, the International Convention for Safe Containers (CSC), 1972 was adopted.

Furthermore, the Assembly adopted in 1981(1) and 1983, resolutions which recommended that governments should issue guidelines(2) on the safe stowage and securing of cargo units on ships other than cellular container ships(3). It also recommended the carriage of a Cargo Securing Manual.

---

(1) A.459/XII.

(2) The Guidelines cover minimum requirements for lashing and securing road vehicles on ro-ro ships. They apply to ro-ro ships which can carry commercial road vehicles on both long and short international voyages which are not in sheltered water, but will not apply to passenger cars, buses and special vehicles. Two sections of the guidelines are directed to shipowners and builders. These are concerned with securing points on ships' decks and lashings. Two others are intended primarily for manufacturers and operators of vehicles. They deal with securing points on road vehicles and stowage of cargo in the vehicles.
See also M. Notice 849 on the Carriage and Securement of Vehicles and Cargo Units in Roll-on/Roll-off ships. The Notice opens with the reports of damage caused by the shifting of vehicles and cargo units within the vehicle/cargo space of ro-ro ships. After stating the sources of trouble, it spells out the duties of the shippers, shipowners and masters, and gives general advice on securement.

(3) The Sub-Committee prepared general guidelines for other types of cargo in the form of a Code of Safe Practice which covers general cargo, heavy items of cargo, metals and containers on

Accordingly, the Sub-Committee on Containers and Cargoes formulated a set of rules to provide a uniform approach to the layout and content of these Manuals. The approved rules cover such matters as details of fixed cargo securing arrangements, portable cargo securing arrangements, portable cargo securing gear and its correct application, and an indication of the magnitude of forces expected to act on cargo units(1).

This brief introduction points to three main areas for consideration.

(i) the carriage of dangerous goods;

(ii) the carriage of radioactive materials; and

(iii) the Convention for Safe Containers (CSC), 1972.

---

conventional cargo ships not specifically equipped or built for that purpose. The purpose of the Code is to advise masters on the specific hazards and difficulties associated with the transport of certain cargoes, cargo securing techniques and stowage, and associated ship-handling measures. The Code applies to non-standardised cargoes on all ships and to standardised cargoes on board ships that have not been built and equipped specifically for the transport of such cargoes.

(1) Many delegates submitted proposals for developing safer criteria for cargoes which may shift or liquefy. As a result of the study carried out on this issue by a Working Group, a resolution was adopted in 1985 to improve the safety of ro-ro ships.

## (i) THE CARRIAGE OF DANGEROUS GOODS

The movement of dangerous goods, some of which are combustible, toxic or chemically reactive, across the sea has increased[1] substantially owing to the rapid growth in their production and use. Goods are considered to be dangerous because of their physical nature, improper packing or both[2]. The extent of the risks in the carriage of dangerous goods largely depends on:

(a) the way in which the goods are packed;

(b) the means of transport; and

(c) the methods of stowage.

These factors are taken into account in the regulations governing the duties and the liabilities of the parties involved in the carriage of dangerous goods[3]. The regulations are framed in a way which would not impede unnecessarily their movement.

Historical developments: In many countries[4], the

---

(1) Every year, over 1000 million tonnes of dangerous goods such as oil, gases and chemicals are carried by sea. The scale of the increase is striking. Emphasis, therefore, should be given to the Law on the Carriage of Dangerous Goods by Sea.

(2) *Accinanto Ltd. and Others* v. *A/S J. Ludwig Mowinckels and Another* (1953) 1 Lloyd's Rep. 38 (the damage was caused by the reaction between the content and the packing materials). See also the definition of s.(1)(2) of the Merchant Shipping (Dangerous Goods) Regulations, 1981.

(3) See for example sections 3, 4 and 5 of the Merchant Shipping (Dangerous Goods) Regulations, 1981.

(4) The first reference to dangerous goods was made in the Merchant Shipping Act, 1894. It stated under the heading Dangerous Goods and Carriage of Cattle "that an emigrant ship shall not proceed to sea if she carries an explosive.... or any vitriol, lucifer matches, guano or green hides or any article which by reasons of the nature, quantity or mode of stowage is likely to endanger the health or lives of the passengers or the safety of the ship."

acts or regulations on dangerous goods differ widely in their framework, the label or marking to be used or the methods of stowage and packing. As these differences created serious practical difficulties, the SOLAS Conference 1929[1] recommended that the rules on dangerous goods should be unified.

In 1948, the SOLAS Conference was held and by that time the carriage of dangerous goods had grown considerably. With new development, it was inevitable for the Conference to deal with the matter and the result was the introduction of Chapter VI which was devoted to the "Carriage of Grain and Dangerous Goods". However, it was recognised by many delegations that the new SOLAS requirements were far from being adequate. This view was reflected in Recommendation 22[2] adopted by the Conference to emphasise the importance of international uniformity in the safety precautions applicable to the carriage of dangerous goods by sea.

Further progress towards unification was achieved when in 1956, a Committee of Experts on the Transport of Dangerous Goods[3] completed a report which stipulated the minimum requirements. This report, known as the United Nations Recommendations (Orange Book) offered a general framework within which national regulations could be developed.

---

(1) The SOLAS Convention,1914, expressed the rule that the carriage of dangerous goods was forbidden. It contained a definition stating that goods were dangerous by reason "of their nature, quantity and mode of stowage". The Convention left to each State the right to lay down the conditions of packing, the mode of stowage and other precautions to be taken. When meeting these conditions, the carriage of goods was regarded as safe and consequently was permitted under the provisions of the Convention.

(2) Recommendation 22 widened the definition of dangerous goods so as to cover goods which are "dangerous on the basis of their properties". It called for setting up a labelling system which would use distinctive symbols indicating the kind of danger of each class of substances or articles and to develop international regulations on this subject.

(3) This Committee was established by the United Nations Economic and Social Council.

When the SOLAS Convention came again for revision in 1960, it offered the IMO an opportunity to deal in more detail with dangerous goods. Chapter VII [1] (Regulation 1) prohibited the carriage of dangerous goods unless it was made in accordance with its provisions. Regulation 2 outlined the various classes of dangerous goods (e.g. explosives, gases, inflammable liquids and solids, oxidising substances, organic peroxides, poisonous, infectious and radioactive substances and corrosives). Other regulations dealt with packing, marking and labelling; documents; stowage requirements; and explosives on board passenger ships.

Resolution 56 was passed in order to strengthen the provisions of Chapter VII. It recommended that governments should adopt a uniform international code for the carriage of dangerous goods by sea and that the IMO, in co-operation with the UN Committee of Experts, should "pursue its studies on such an international code, especially in respect of the classification, description, labelling and the list of dangerous goods and shipping documents...". Resolution 56 further recommended that this Code should cover such matters as packing; container traffic and stowage, with particular reference to the segregation of incompatible substances.

In response to the above recommendation the IMO set up a Working Group made up of countries which had considerable experience in the carriage of dangerous goods. Preliminary drafts on each class were compiled by individial national delegations. They were then considered by the Working Group, which took into account the practices and procedures of a number of maritime countries in order to make the Code as widely acceptable as possible.

After a vigorous assessment of hundreds of substances, a document called the International Maritime Dangerous Goods (IMDG) Code [2] was formulated and approved by the IMO Assembly in 1965.

---

(1) The provisions of this Chapter applied to all ships of 500 gross tonnage or more engaged on international voyages.

(2) The Code is designed primarily for mariners. However, its provisions may affect industries and services from manufacturer to consumer. Manufacturers, packers and shippers are guided by the advice given for terminology, packing and labelling. Feeder services, such as road,

The Code has undergone many changes. It was published in five loose-leaf volumes[(1)] so that amendments could be easily inserted[(2)]. All substances and articles of the Code are listed in the General Index which gives the product's UN number; its Emergency Schedule Number (EmS No.); and the IMDG Code-page number of the individual schedule.

It must be noted that the legal issues of liability, burden of proof and offences are not mentioned in the Code as they are left to national law. In the United Kingdom, the Merchant Shipping (Dangerous Goods) Regulations,1981 is the piece of legislation[(3)] concerned with dangerous goods.

---

rail and harbour craft use the Code in respect of labelling and classification. Port authorities also use the Code to effect suitable segregation within loading, discharge and storage areas. Although the Code only applies to the ships covered by the SOLAS Convention, the IMO takes the view that it is highly desirable that its requirements should be extended to other ships.

(1) The Code is published in three languages: English, French and Spanish.

(2) In 1965, the Assembly agreed that amendments "which do not affect the principles upon which the Code is based" could be adopted by the Maritime Safety Committee (MSC) alone. In practice, the Sub-Committee on the Carriage of Dangerous Goods meets once a year. Its main objective is to keep the Code up-to-date. A set of amendments comprising some 400-500 replacement pages is the normal result of each meeting. After the amendments have been adopted by the Maritime Safety Committee (MSC), it takes approximately a year to prepare them for publication. For this reason the MSC has agreed that the amendments to the Code should be implemented six months after their publication.

(3) See also the Merchant Shipping (Safety Officials and Reporting of Accidents and Dangerous Occurrences) Regulations, 1982 (SI 1982/876) as amended by 1984 Regulations (SI 1984/93). Part I of the Regulations describes the appointment and election of safety officials and of safety committees on board ships. It gives to those officials and committees, and to the

Thus, in order to give a proper conception of the carriage of dangerous goods, it would be necessary to consider:

(1) an outline of the IMDG Code, its Annexes and Supplements;

(2) the codes, guides and recommendations supplementing the provisions of the IMDG Code; and

(3) a brief analysis of the Merchant Shipping (Dangerous Goods) Regulations, 1981.

(1) AN OUTLINE OF THE IMDG CODE, ITS ANNEXES AND SUPPLEMENTS

The first part of the Code consists of a general introduction. Chapter VII of the 1974 SOLAS Convention and Resolution 56 of the 1960 SOLAS Conference are both reprinted, followed by the classification of dangerous goods used in the Code and a description of standardisation of methods for establishing the flashpoint of substances (the flash-point is the lowest temperature of a liquid at which its vapour forms an ignitable mixture with air and consequently gives a measure of the risk of formation of explosive or ignitable mixtures when the liquid or its vapour escapes from its package).

The introduction goes on to describe methods of marking, identification, labelling, documentation and packing. It also contains sections on the special requirements for freight containers, portable tanks and road tank vehicles; stowage and segregation; fire prevention and fire-fighting. The final sections deal with the carriage of dangerous goods on roll-on/roll-off (ro-ro) ships; and in shipborne barges on barge-carrying ships.

Annex I to the Code gives recommendations on the packing of dangerous goods and on the construction and testing of packagings[1]. The recommendations take into account the mandatory requirements

---

master and employer, certain duties or powers. The Regulations apply to all UK ships in which a crew of more than five are employed. The exceptions are non-sea-going ships, fishing vessels, pleasure-craft and offshore installations whilst on their working stations.

(1) Annex I was adopted by the Maritime Safety Committee (MSC) in 1984 and is included in

on packing provided for in Regulation 3 of Chapter VII of the 1974 SOLAS Convention(1).

The Code was adopted by forty-one States(2). Some of them gave its provisions a statutory effect(3) while in others they are regarded as

---

Volume I of the Code. It follows the Recommendations of the UN Committee of Experts on the Transport of Dangerous Goods which divides the goods, other than those covered by classes 1, 2 and 7, into three packing groups: packaging group I covers goods presenting great danger; packaging group II for goods presenting medium danger; and packaging group III is for goods presenting minor danger.
See MSC 49/19 of April 1, 1984, p.7.

(1) Regulation 3 requires packages containing dangerous goods to be capable of withstanding the ordinary risks of handling and carriage by sea and lays down other specifications.

(2) As from February,1985, the following States have adopted the Code: Argentina; Australia; Bahamas; Belgium; Brazil; Bulgaria; Canada; Chile; China; Denmark; Finland; France; German Democratic Republic; Germany, Federal Republic; Greece; Hong Kong; India; Ireland; Israel; Italy; Japan; Liberia; Netherlands; New Zealand; Norway; Pakistan; Peru; Philippines; Poland; Republic of Korea; Saudi Arabia; Singapore; Spain; Sweden; Switzerland; USSR; United Kingdom; United States. See Focus on IMO, February,1985, p.7. In 1984, the MSC invited Member States to provide:

(a) additional or updated information on their adoption of the International Maritime Dangerous Goods (IMDG) Code (MSC/Circ.343, MSC/Circ.343/Add.1, MSC/Circ.343/Add.2, MSC/Circ.343/Add.3, MSC/Circ.343/Add.4 and MSC/Circ.343/Add.5);

(b) contact names and addresses of the offices of designated national competent authorities; and

(c) information on their experience in applying the IMDG Code.
See MSC 49/19, April 1, 1984, p.8.

(3) In the United Kingdom, the Merchant Shipping (Dangerous Goods) Regulations,1981, which came into operation on January 1, 1982, gave

recommendations[1].

Following the general introduction, the Code provides a list[2] of dangerous goods divided into the following nine classes:

Class 1 - Explosives

Class 2 - Gases: compressed, liquefied or dissolved under pressure

Class 3 - Inflammable liquids

Class 4 - Inflammable solids, substances liable to spontaneous combustion, and substances emitting inflammable gases when wet

Class 5 - Oxidising substances and organic peroxides

Class 6 - Poisonous (toxic) and infectious substances

Class 7 - Radioactive substances

Class 8 - Corrosives

Class 9 - Miscellaneous dangerous substances

---

statutory effect to the IMDG Code and its Annexes. The detailed rules were included in a Code of Practice (the Report of the Department of Transport's Standing Advisory Committee) simply called the Blue Book.
The latest edition of the Blue Book was published on March 1, 1985. It contains variations from the IMDG Code as they are necessary for the sake of clarity, ease of implementation or to meet appropriate standards of safety. It takes precedence over the IMDG Code.

(1) It must be noted that in countries where the provisions of the IMDG Code are considered as recommendations, the requirements and undertakings provided by the SOLAS Convention are not affected.

(2) Some chemicals may escape from being shipped in accordance with the provisions of the IMDG Code; the reasons are:
(a) they are new;
(b) they have not been shipped before in significant quantities;
(c) they are mixtures; or
(d) the manufacturer wants to use a new form of packing.

Each class is preceded by an introduction which describes the properties and definitions of the goods and gives details of stowage and segregation (i.e. the degree to which goods should be kept separate from other dangerous substances carried on a ship). The class introduction also gives information concerning procedure which should be followed during loading and unloading.

---

The Sub-Committee on the Carriage of Dangerous Goods (DG) considered the "not otherwise specified" (NOS) entries. The question was how best to ensure that appropriate action is taken for a consignment whose contents for one reason or another have not been listed in the Code and are thus covered by an NOS number whose entry and UN number do not provide sufficient information for the emergency services.
The Sub-Committee took the view that NOS entries should be supplemented by additional information in the shape of a recognised chemical name currently used in readily available scientific and technical books. The use of trade names is not recommended. Not more than two constituents, in a mixture of dangerous goods, need to be shown. Should a package containing a mixture bear subsidiary label(s), one of the two chemical names shown in the parenthesis should represent the name of the constituent compelling the use of the subsidiary label.
In the United Kingdom, the Marine Safety Branch of the Department of Trade is often approached by manufacturers and shippers asking for a ruling on the classification, packing and storage of various dangerous goods. When necessary they approach their scientific advisers, mainly the Laboratory of the Government Chemist. This body acts as scientific advisers on the hazards of dangerous goods with the exception of explosives, compressed gases, radioactive materials and infectious substances.
The information that is required is, first, the chemical composition, the nature of packages, the approximate size of cargo and, in some instances, the duration of the voyage and the route to be taken. Chemical composition is not always easy to ascertain and the names given by shippers are sometimes difficult to identify.

Each class is identified by a distinctive label - some of which will be familiar to road users since they often appear on commercial vehicles which carry dangerous goods, such as petrol tank vehicles. Where appropriate, each schedule in the Code shows the label which should be affixed to a package.

Classification is not an easy task. For instance, some silicone type products spontaneously evolve hydrogen. In case the pressure is high, they must be treated as class 2, otherwise they can be declared as class 9 with a suitable warning(1).

## Class 1 - Explosives

These are among the most dangerous(2) of all goods(3) carried by sea and the precautions outlined

---

(1) Other substances cannot be adequately dealt with by reference to the IMDG Code, owing to the fact that reducing agents are not listed as dangerous goods unless they possess another hazardous property. Incidents have occurred when a considerable amount of heat was generated after the accidental mixing of sodium perborate (not now in class 5.1) and sodium thiosulphate. If a strong oxidising agent had been involved, the consequences would have been much more serious. This hazard would be taken care of by including in the IMDG Code a list of reducing substances that must not be stowed near class 5 substances.

(2) Usually a series of accidents are cited to show that the non-adherence to the IMDG Code led to such catastrophic accidents. However, the investigation carried out on each accident is crucial in pointing to the direct or mixed cause, the party to blame and the person or persons to bear the liability. The Halifax incident of 1917 is a good illustration. The ship *Mont Blanc* was overloaded with more than 2,600 tons of explosives when she entered Halifax harbour. She collided with another ship and caught fire. Shortly afterwards, the ship exploded in the biggest man-made explosion until the advent of the atomic bomb. 3,000 persons were killed, 9,000 were injured and 6,000 homes were destroyed.

(3) Military Explosives are shipped in accordance with the requirements and classifications of Class 1. Military Explosive is defined as one

in this class of the Code are particularly stringent.

The Class is divided into five divisions which present different hazards. The divisions are as follows:

| | |
|---|---|
| Division 1.1 | Substances and articles which have a mass explosion hazard. |
| Division 1.2 | Substances and articles which have a projection hazard but not a mass explosion hazard. |
| Division 1.3 | Substances and articles which have a fire hazard and either a minor blast hazard or both, but not a mass explosion hazard. |
| Division 1.4 | Substances and articles which present no significant hazard. |
| Division 1.5 | Very insensitive substances which have a mass explosion hazard: the substances in this division are so insensitive that there is very little probability of initiation or of transition from burning to detonation under normal conditions of transport. |

---

which is exempt from the provisions of the Explosives Act,1875, and derived legislation by virtue of:
(a) the provisions of Section 97 of the Explosives Act,1875; or
(b) The Visiting Forces and International Headquarters (Application of Law) Order,1965, which is executed by the terms of S.I. 1536 of 1965.

This means that a Military Explosive is either:
(a) under the control of HM Government or a Visiting Force; or
(b) not under the control of HM Government or of a Visiting Force, but otherwise held for the service of the Crown or of a Visiting Force; or
(c) an explosive, the conveyance of which is certified by HM Government to be in connection with the execution of a contract with HM Government or a Visiting Force.
See M.Notice 806.

Class 1 is unique in that the type of packaging has a decisive effect on the hazard and therefore on the assignment of the particular division.

Goods in this class are also assigned to various Stowage Categories. Stowage Category I (Ordinary) covers goods which present relatively little hazard. Category II involves the provision of a magazine for stowage of such goods, and is itself divided into three groups. Stowage Category III is for pyrotechnics and Category IV for special items, mainly goods which contain both explosive and chemical agents which can evolve tear-producing or toxic gases.

Although the safety of goods in Class I can best be assured by stowing them separately, in practice this can rarely be done. To ensure that they are stowed as safely as possible, the substances in the class are arranged in twelve compatibility groups. These are lettered from A to L (the I is missing) and the letter S.

In addition to the name and UN number, the individual schedules in Class 1 also give the substance's or article's division and compatibility group. This information must also be shown on the label which goes on the package. The schedule also shows the substance's or article's stowage category.

Class 2 - Gases

Gases carried on board ships have very varied properties and come in different forms. They may be compressed liquefied at ambient temperature under high pressures; dissolved under pressure in a solvent, which is then absorbed in a porous material; or liquefied by refrigeration. They may be for example poisonous, corrosive, inflammable, supporters of combustion (oxygen), or a combination of all or some of these. Some are much lighter than air (hydrogen) while others are much heavier (carbon dioxide). Lighter gases will tend to disperse more quickly should a leak occur, while the heavier gases will tend to accumulate close to the ground(1).

---

(1) The schedules include the UN number, the chemical formula, and for inflammable gases, their explosive limits. The latter refers to the amount of gas required to make a quantity of air explosive. The wider the explosive limit range, the more hazardous the gas, as there is the

The Code gives general information concerning the properties of gases, packing, stowage, segregation and fire precautions[(1)].

---

possibility of an explosion over a large range of concentrations. An example of such a gas is acetylene whose lower explosive limit (LEL) is 2.1% and upper explosive limit (UEL) is 80%. This means that a mixture of acetylene in air can become explosive when quite dilute up to high concentrations.
The schedule goes on to describe the gas's properties, any special observations, and details of packing and stowage.
There are three sub-classes: inflammable gas (2.1), non-flammable compressed gas (2.2), and poisonous gas (2.3).

(1) Several accidents involving goods of Class 2 have occurred. On November 9, 1974, the Japanese LPG tanker *Yuyo Maru No.10* was carrying LPG in her cargo tanks, Naptha in her wing tanks and oil in the forward reserve tank. As a result of a collision in Tokyo Bay with the *Pacific Area*, a large amount of Naptha leaked onto the *Pacific Area* and the water. It caught fire which in turn caused the loss of thirty-two persons.
Another incident occurred in 1974 off the south coast of England. The crew of the container ship *Asia Freighter* began to feel ill. The situation became so bad that the ship was abandoned. It was eventually discovered that a cylinder of arsine gas (class 2.3) was rolling about freely inside a freight container and was leaking from the valve. The container did not bear the required "Poison" placards and apparently was not included on the dangerous cargo manifest.
In July 1978, in Los Alfraque, a lorry tanker carrying liquefied propylene, sprang a leak and the fumes quickly gathered forming a cloud. This incident happened near a camp site in Los Alfraque, Spain. The cloud was immediately ignited from a stove or lighting a cigarette. The ignition was followed by an explosion and fire, with the terrible tragedy of more than 150 persons in the camp burnt to death.
In Port Kelang (Malaysia) 1980, a fire which started in the port was followed by a series of explosions. The fire destroyed almost every

## Class 3 - Inflammable liquids

This class(1) deals with liquids which give off an inflammable vapour at or below 61°C (141°F); some liquids may be included in other classes because of other dangerous characteristics(2).

The class is divided into three sub-classes according to flashpoint. Class 3.1 consists of liquids with a low flashpoint of below -18°C (0°F); class 3.2 consists of liquids with an intermediate flashpoint of -18°C up to but not including 23°C (73°F); and class 3.3 consists of liquids with a high flashpoint of 23°C and above up to 61°C (141°F).

---

building and caused the loss of thirteen lives. The incident highlights the importance of port planning to ensure adequate separation of areas processing, storing, loading and discharging dangerous goods.

(1) The introduction to the class includes information on packing, stowage, segregation and fire precautions.
Individual schedules are arranged in the three sub-classes referred to above starting with class 3.1. The schedule includes the substance's name, UN number, chemical formula, explosive limits and flashpoint.
Other information comes under similar headings to those which appear in other classes of the Code, i.e. properties, (special) observations, packing and stowage.
Substances in this group are also assigned to a packaging group which is determined by the degree of danger presented. Packing Group I includes liquids presenting great danger, Group II medium danger and Group III minor danger.
A similar system of assigning goods to one of three packaging groups is used in other classes of the Code, with the exception of Classes 1, 2 and 7.

(2) In 1974, the ship *Ocean Liberty* caught fire in the harbour of Brest. Steam was used to put out the fire but the firemen were not equipped with breathing apparatus. Their attempts failed and an explosion occurred killing twenty-one persons.
Another incident in 1970 involved the *Tacoma*, a tank barge used to carry pyrolysis gasoline. Gas was leaked and suddenly ignited, causing considerable damage.

The Code refers to the various methods which can be used to establish the flashpoint of liquids. Liquids with low flashpoints are more hazardous than those with higher ones, and thus the requirements for low flashpoint liquids are more stringent.

Generally speaking, water[(1)] is unsuitable for fighting inflammable liquid fires. The Code recommends either the use of water as a fine spray or the use of foam which forms a scum on the burning liquid surface, making the access of oxygen difficult.

<u>Class 4 - Inflammable solids</u>
Substances liable to spontaneous combustion
Substances emitting inflammable gases when wet

This class is divided into three sub-classes which are very different in their properties. The classes include some common products, many of which seem harmless enough but which can be very dangerous unless properly handled[(2)].

<u>Class 4.1: Inflammable solids</u>

The substances in this class are easily combustible and can be ignited by external sources, such as sparks or flames.

Individual schedules give the substance's name, UN number and chemical formula. The schedules are often detailed, since properties vary considerably.

Some common substances which come in this class are lighter flints; dried vegetable fibres

---

(1) The ship *Grandcamp* was loaded in April 1949, in the port of Texas, with a quantity of ammonium nitrate. A fire broke out and the water used to put it out failed to quell the blaze. An explosion occurred, with the loss of 468 persons.

(2) The ship *Fort Sikine* was carrying 1,400 tons of explosives when she entered Bombay Harbour. She had also on board a large quantity of cotton. Fire broke out, probably through spontaneous combustion.
Another incident happened in 1957, where fire broke out on the ship *Seistan* when she approached Bahrain. Her cargo was toe puff, a mixture of cotton or wool with cellulose. The ship blew up, killing 57 persons.

such as flax and hemp; film; hay and straw; matches; and toe puffs.

Class 4.2: Spontaneously combustible

The substances in this class are all liable to heat and to ignite spontaneously(1). Some are more likely to do so when wetted by water or in contact with moist air. Others may also give off toxic gases when involved in a fire.

The degree of spontaneity of combustion ranges from those substances which immediately catch alight from exposure to air, such as pyrophoric liquids, which are difficult to extinguish and are better jettisoned, to those substances such as fish meal which can take days to heat up(2).

Class 4.3: Dangerous when wet

Substances in this class usually give off gases when wet which sometimes ignite spontaneously (e.g. hydrogen gas from sodium metal). Therefore, fire-fighting is essential. The use of water, steam or water-foam extinguishers will only aggravate the situation, and carbon dioxide must not be used with some substances(3

## Class 5 - Oxidising agents
## - Organic peroxides

The class is divided into two sub-classes. Class 5.1 deals with oxidising substances which, although not necessarily combustible themselves, have the potential to increase the intensity of a fire by

---

(1) In view of these properties, packing and stowage requirements are important. A pyrophoric liquid such as Butyl Lithium in a solvent which is transported in cylinders with an inert gas nitrogen in the top, should be stowed upright with the valve protected. The location on the ship should permit access for jettisoning should a leak occur.

(2) Some common substances which appear in this class are charcoal; celluloid; iron oxide; carbon paper; some plastics; and seed cakes.

(3) Some common substances in this group include powder derivatives of aluminium and calcium; ferro-silicon; lithium; magnesium-based products; potassium-based products; rubidium; and sodium and zinc in powder.

giving off oxygen (a supporter of combustion) which is present in the structure of all oxidising agents. Therefore, the use of fire extinguishers which act by excluding oxygen from the fire, will not work with these materials. Class 5.2 includes organic peroxides, most of which are combustible.

Class 5.1: Oxidising agents

The fact that all substances in this class[(1)] give off oxygen when involved in a fire creates obvious fire-fighting difficulties. Some substances may also be sensitive to impact, friction or a rise in temperature. Others may react vigorously with moisture, increasing the risk of fire[(2)].

Class 5.2: Organic peroxides

In addition to being oxidising agents, most substances in this class are also liable to explosive decomposition. Most will burn rapidly and are sensitive to heat[(3)]. Some are also

---

(1) This class includes ammonium nitrate fertilizers, hydrogen peroxide, copper chlorate and lead nitrate.

(2) Oxidising substances should be kept away from combustible materials, e.g. spilt oil, oily rags, sawdust, which may catch fire and burn explosively. The use of sawdust on ships for absorbing spillages must not be used for Class 5 substances and, in fact, it is better replaced with an inert absorbent such as vermiculite. Most oxidising substances react vigorously and sometimes explosively, with strong mineral acids. For example, sodium chlorate reacts violently with sulphuric acid, giving off a toxic gas.
Since the use of a fire extinguisher such as carbon dioxide may be ineffective with oxidising materials because they give off oxygen, the Code recommends the prompt use of large quantities of water as being the best means of controlling this type of fire.

(3) Organic peroxides can be particularly dangerous to the eyes. Immediate medical attention is necessary following contact.
Packages containing organic peroxides should be moved away from the seat of a fire or jettisoned otherwise an explosion may result. If this is

sensitive to impact or friction. To reduce this sensitivity to a safe level they are carried in a solution, as a paste, wetted with water or with an inert solid. Violent decomposition may be caused by traces of impurities such as acids, metallic oxides or amines. This decomposition may give rise to toxic or inflammable gases.

The introduction to the class contains information concerning temperature control, and the schedule gives specific temperature requirements.

## Class 6 - Poisonous (toxic) and infectious substances

The Class is divided into two sub-classes. These are Class 6.1 - Poisonous (toxic) substances and Class 6.2 - Infectious substances. Substances in Class 6.1 may cause death or serious injury if swallowed, inhaled or absorbed by skin contact. They are arranged into three packaging groups, in descending order of risk. The introduction to the class shows how this grouping is determined(1).

Class 6.2 includes substances containing disease-producing micro-organisms. These substances contain micro-organisms or their toxins which are known or suspected to cause disease in animals or humans(2).

---

not possible, packages should be sprayed with large quantities of water from a safe distance. Even when the fire has been extinguished, packages containing organic peroxides should be treated with great care as they may explode violently at any time.
Some organic peroxides require subsidiary hazard labels such as Class 1 (explosives) or Class 3 (inflammable liquid).

(1) Fire-fighting precautions are basically the same as those given for Class 3 (inflammable liquids) but because of the high risk of poisoning through fumes, the Code states that ships carrying poisonous substances should always carry protective clothing and self-contained breathing apparatus.
If a spillage occurs involving toxic substances - such as liquid pesticides - decontamination should be carried out by trained staff wearing suitable clothing and equipment.

(2) The labels required for the various substances

## Class 7 - Radioactive substances (materials)

The provisions of this class are based upon the principles of the International Atomic Energy Agency's Regulations for the Safe Transport of Radioactive Materials, 1973 (as amended). They offer guidance to shipowners and others handling packages in ports and on ships without necessarily consulting IAEA regulations.

Basically, there are two types of packings for radioactive materials, A and B. The former used for substances of lower radioactivity, the latter for high levels of activity. Type B packing has to undergo very stringent tests which include a drop test, fire engulfment at 850°C for half an hour, and total water immersion, without suffering significant radiation leakage. A substances is regarded as being radioactive if it emits more than 0.002 microcuries of radiation per gram of material(1).

---

in the class vary according to the substance's properties. Most are required to carry the 'poison' label, but some carry a label indicating that the substance is harmful to foodstuffs. In addition, further labels may be required, depending upon the substance's properties.

(1) The practical unit of measurement of radioactivity for transportation purposes is the Transport Index, which simply described is that amount of radiation measured at 1 metre from a package. On a ship the maximum quantity of radioactive material permitted in any one location is determined by its transport index, which must not exceed 50, separated by 6 metres from any other radioactive material. The total for a ship must not exceed 200.
The chemical hazards associated with some radioactive materials far exceed those due to the radioactivity. For example, uranium hexafluoride, ($UF_6$), has little radiation hazard, but if a spillage occurs will evolve a highly corrosive and toxic gas (hydrogen fluoride). Apart from bearing a radioactive hazard label, uranium hexafluoride must also bear subsidiary labels of 'Corrosive' and 'Poison'.
Packing, labelling and placarding, segregation and other requirements vary according to the radioactivity of the material as indicated above. Radioactive substances are divided into three categories, depending upon radiation

## Class 8 - Corrosives

Substances in this class can damage living tissue and materials, in some cases very severely. Some of them give off irritating or harmful vapours and others are toxic or give off toxic gases. Some are inflmammable or give off inflammable gases under certain conditions.

In view of the differing properties, packing and stowage are extremely important. The substances are divided into three packaging groups (group I being the most dangerous). The introduction to the class gives detailed information on the types of packaging to be used.

## Class 9 - Miscellaneous dangerous substances

This class includes substances which, for various reasons, do not come within any of the other classes. Since their properties are so varied, the individual schedules usually include detailed information on stowage, labelling, packaging and other information.

Substances in this class include aerosol dispensers, some ammonium nitrate fertilizers, asbestos and safety matches.

## Evaluation of the IMDG Code

As mentioned earlier, the IMDG has been amended several times(1) and the numerous cross-references contained in it, make it difficult for those using it. Therefore, the Sub-Committee on the Carriage of Dangerous Goods, at its 37th session, supported the views expressed by the delegation of the German

---

levels, category I white being the least dangerous. Category II and III labels are printed in yellow and white for additional emphasis. Category I white label has the wording 'Principal Radioactive Content' and 'Activity of Contents ... Curies' across the front. In addition to this, category II and III labels have the wording 'Transport Index this Package'.

(1) For example, in 1984, the Sub-Committee on the Carriage of Dangerous Goods adopted a number of changes to the Code. They included:
- a revised Annex I (packing recommendations);
- amendments to the Medical First Aid Guide (MFAG) for use in Accidents involving Dangerous Goods; and

Democratic Republic which include the following[1]:

1. Countries with national languages other than English, French or Spanish, have to translate the Code and its amendments. As a result, national variations from the official Codes are of a considerable proportion[2].

---

- MFAG Table 851 for Castor Beans.

It was agreed that in accordance with the established procedures, the amendments to the IMDG Code and MFAG would be implemented six months after their publication in English. IMO News, No.2, 1984, p.6.

Amendments to Annex III of MARPOL, see *infra* Chapter VII, were agreed and submitted to the Maritime Safety Committee (MSC) for adoption in 1986.

Amendments to the Emergency Procedures for Ships Carrying Dangerous Goods (EmS) and Medical First Aid Guide for Use in Accidents Involving Dangerous Goods (MFAG) were also submitted to the MSC. See IMO News, No.3, 1985, p.15.

Amendments numbered 21-84 and 22-84 were adopted. The first amendments came into force on January 1, 1985, and the second is scheduled to enter into force on July 1, 1986. See C 5/22(c), p.2.

(1) See IMO News, No.3, 1985, p.16.

(2) See M.Notice 926 of April,1980 which states that the Department of Trade is frequently asked to provide page numbers of schedules in the IMDG Code for annotation on shipping documentation. Furthermore, it has been noted internationally that not only are page numbers not necessary on shipping documents, but it is distinctly a dangerous practice to provide such information, e.g.

(a) there is an additional risk of a clerical error in transposition;

(b) IMDG page numbers differ from one language edition to another; and

(c) the "re-use" by IMO of page numbers first allotted to entries which have subsequently been transferred from one Class to another or removed from the Code. The use of the UN serial numbers on shipping documents is strongly supported as an additional element of the description of the goods and hazard class required under the Merchant Shipping (Dangerous Goods) Rules.

2. The increasing number of N.O.S. (not otherwise specified[1]) entries has led to uncertainty regarding the properties of such substances and the precautionary measures to be taken.

3. National interpretations with regard to new transport technologies vary considerably. This can lead to uncertainty and delays at ports.

4. For multimodal transport[2], lack of harmonization between the IMDG Code and other regulations creates problems.

5. The existence of two separate publications for emergency measures (the Emergency Schedules and the Medical First Aid Guide) for use in connection with incidents involving dangerous goods increases the effort of planning safe stowage and segregation[3].

The delegates to the Sub-Committee agreed that the Code has led to higher standards of safety. In order to strengthen this standard, the following steps were approved:

(1) the concept of having as much information as possible on individual substances in the schedules should be maintained;

(2) efforts should be made to align the General Introduction and the introductions to the various classes so as to minimize the need for any subsequent amendment;

(3) amendments consequential to decisions taken by the UN Committee of Experts should only be taken up by the Sub-Committee after the amended UN recommendations have been communicated to the IMO; and

(4) the UN Committee of Experts should be invited to consider the need for providing guidance to the modal transport organizations with regard to target dates for multilateral implementation of their recommendations, similar to the action taken by the

---

(1) See *supra*, p.108.
(2) See the Author, The Multimodal Transport of Goods Convention: A Challenge to Unimodal Transport Convention, International and Comparative Law Quarterly, January,1983, pp. 120-140.
(3) See *infra*, p.125.

International Atomic Energy Agency (IAEA) in their 1985 Edition of the Regulations for the Safe Transport of Radioactive Materials.

## (2) THE CODES, GUIDELINES AND RECOMMENDATIONS SUPPLEMENTING THE IMDG CODE

The provisions of the IMDG Code are supplemented by a number of other Codes, guidelines[1] and recommendations.

### (A) THE SAFE PRACTICE FOR SOLID BULK CARGOES (BC) CODE

The problems and hazards[2] involved in the carriage of solid bulk cargoes were recognized by the SOLAS Conference of 1960 when the rules on the carriage of grain were adopted. The Conference recommended the formulation of a Code on the Safe Practice for Solid Bulk Cargoes. This was achieved and the Code was adopted in 1965. Its main objectives are to:

---

(1) See for example the Guidelines for Reporting Incidents Involving Dangerous Goods in Packaged Form, prepared by the Marine Environment Protection Committee, MSC/Circ.360. See also the Code for Portable Tanks and Road Tank Vehicles for the Carriage of Liquid Dangerous Goods in Ships, prepared by the Department of Trade. The Code sets out the provisions pertinent to the carriage by sea of dangerous substances in portable tanks and road tank vehicles. It is mainly addressed to those engaged in the design and construction of tanks, or is of equal importance to consignors since their responsibility to provide a suitable tank for transport is imposed by the Merchant Shipping Act.

(2) The hazards may be considered as falling into these categories:
- (a) structural damage due to improper distribution of the cargo;
- (b) loss or reduction of stability during the voyage usually as a result of a shift of cargo in heavy weather; and
- (c) chemical reactions, e.g. emission of toxic or explosive gases, spontaneous combustion or severe corrosive effects.

(a) highlight the dangers[1] associated with the shipment of certain types of bulk cargoes[2];

(b) give guidance on the procedures to be adopted when the shipment of such bulk cargoes is contemplated;

(c) list typical materials currently shipped in bulk together with advice on their properties and handling; and

(d) describe test procedures to be employed to determine various characteristics of the bulk cargo materials.

The BC Code is kept under review and has been revised four times since 1965. The latest edition was published in 1984. Generally speaking, it consists of three main parts:

(a) general practical advice on the shipment of bulk cargoes which is of particular importance to ship masters;

(b) recommended test procedure to determine the "flow moisture point" of a concentrate which is intended primarily for scientists and chemists; and

(c) a list of products shipped in bulk together with approximate details of their physical properties.

---

(1) Many substances are dangerous to load in bulk no matter how they are secured against movement, either because of their chemical content or their inherently dangerous properties.

(2) All grades of coal will emit methane, an odourless flammable gas which is less dense than air. A methane/air mixture containing between 5 per cent and 15 per cent methane constitutes an atmosphere which can be readily ignited by sparks or naked flames to produce a highly dangerous and potentially lethal explosion. In recent years, such explosions have resulted in a number of deaths and serious injuries. M.Notice 970 describes the precautions considered necessary to reduce this danger when carrying the following types of cargoes: coal slurry; coal drift; coal drift containing particles greater than 50mm; small coal; and coke.

The BC Code deals with three basic types of cargo:

(a) those cargoes which may liquefy (Appendix A);

(b) materials possessing chemical hazards (Appendix B)[(1)]; and

(c) other materials not falling within these two categories (Appendix C)[(2)].

Failure to observe the advice given in the Code has on a number of occasions led to the loss of both ship and lives. Therefore, the recommendations are directed to governments, ship operators, masters and others concerned with safety of bulk cargoes shipments. Thus, before loading any bulk cargo it is important for the shipper to know the physical and chemical properties of the cargo. The master should be provided with sufficient information to enable him to plan the loading of the ship so as not to overstress the structure and to calculate the stability in bad weather conditions.

The BC Code gives details of precautions for cargoes which may oxidize, emit toxic fumes or become wet, and for health hazards arising from dust or fumes

---

(1) Appendix B contains a list of materials currently known to be carried in bulk which, because of their chemical nature or properties, can present a hazard during transport. The list is not exhaustive. Consequently, whenever the shipment of bulk cargo is contemplated, it is essential to obtain valid information on its physical characteristics and chemical properties prior to loading. The essential information covers the United Nations number and the IMO class or the MHB (materials hazardous in bulk) classification and a BC number; the relevent MFAG (Medical First Aid Guide) table number; approximate angle of repose and stowage factor; separation and stowage requirements and properties, observations and special requirements.

| UN No. | IMO Class | MFAG Table No. | Approximate Angle of Repose | Approximate Stowage Factor, $m^3/t$ |
|---|---|---|---|---|
| | | | | |

(2) Examples of cargoes in this category are clay, cement, iron ore, pig iron, sand and sugar.

which may create a danger of explosion. In its twenty-fifth session (13-17 February, 1984), the Sub-Committee on Containers and Cargoes proposed that the Code should be made mandatory(1).

## (B) MEDICAL FIRST AID GUIDE (MFAG) FOR USE IN ACCIDENTS INVOLVING DANGEROUS GOODS 1982

The MFAG was developed in close co-operation with the World Health Organisation (WHO) and the International Labour Organisation (ILO). It is intended as a supplement to the International Medical Guide for Ships (IMGS) although issued as a separate publication.

The Guide was first adopted by the Maritime Safety Committee in 1972. In December 1981, the Sub-Committee on the Carriage of Dangerous Goods completed what virtually amounts to a complete revision of the Guide. The new version was adopted by the MSC at its forty-sixth session in April, 1982(2).

The advice in the MFAG refers not only to the substances listed in the IMDG Code but also to those in Appendix B of the Code of Safe Practice for Solid Bulk Cargoes.

It is intended to provide the advice necessary if chemical poisoning is to be diagnosed and treated within the limits of the facilities available on board ships.

It covers such matters as diagnosis of poisoning; first aid; the complications of poisoning; general toxic hazards; emergency treatment; chemical tables(3) including indexes; and a list of medicines.

Closely connected with the Guide is the Emergency Procedures for Ships Carrying Dangerous Goods (Emergency Schedules - EmS) which are contained in a supplement to the Code(4).

---

(1) MSC 50/11, August 24, 1984.

(2) The MSC adopted in 1984 amendments to the Guide, see MSC 49/19 of April 1, 1984, p.7. See also the Ship Captain's Guide, 21st ed., published by HMSO.

(3) Within the MFAG, chemicals are grouped into tables according to their chemical properties.

(4) The Emergency Procedures were adopted by the Maritime Safety Committee at its 43rd and 44th sessions and published by the IMO in 1981. See also the supplement published in 1984 covering Amendments Nos. 20 and 21 of the IMDG Code.

The Emergency Schedules divide the various substances and articles contained in each of the nine classes into groups and advise on any special emergency equipment which should be carried. They also include the emergency procedures which should be followed and the action to be taken in case of spillage or fire.

## (C) RECOMMENDATION ON THE SAFE USE OF PESTICIDES IN SHIPS

Insects and rodents on ships are objectionable for various reasons. Some species may only annoy persons aboard without really doing harm. Some are able to spread disease and infection. Some may contaminate food during its stowage and preparation in galleys and food stores. Others may cause actual damage to cargoes or result in commercial or other losses due to their presence.

Insect and mite pests of plant and animal products may be carried into the holds with goods (introduced infestation); may move from one kind of produce to another (cross infestation) and may remain to attack subsequent cargoes (residual infestation). Their control may be required to comply with phytosanitary requirements to prevent spread of pests and for commercial purposes to prevent infestation and contamination of or damage to cargoes of human and animal food.

Rodents should be controlled not only because of the damage they may do to cargo, but also as required by the International Sanitary Regulations, to prevent the spread of disease(1).

In order to assist masters, fumigators and competent authorities in this field, the IMO issued a circular entitled Recommendation on safe use of pesticides in ships, 1971. In 1980(2), a revised document was published. It incorporates substantial revisions, with particular regard to fumigation practice(3).

---

(1) MSC/Circ. 108.
(2) Sales No. 267.81.08.E.
(3) In the United Kingdom, see The Prevention of Damage by Pests Act, 1949, 12 and 13 GEO 6, CH55; The Prevention of Damage by Pests (Application to Shipping) Order,1951 - Pests: Infestation. Statutory Instrument,1951 No.967; The Hydrogen Cyanide (Fumigation) Act,1937.I Edw

## (D) IMO/ILO GUIDELINES FOR PACKING OF CARGO IN FREIGHT CONTAINERS OR VEHICLES

The Guidelines open with this introduction: "Whilst the use of freight containers and other transport units substantially reduces the physical hazard to which goods are exposed, improper or careless packing of goods into a container may be the cause of injury to personnel when the container is handled or transported. In addition, serious and costly damage may occur to the goods inside or to other equipment. The person who packs and secures goods in the container for export may be the last person to look inside the container until it is opened at its final destination. Consequently, a great many persons will rely on his skill: road vehicle drivers and other highway users when the container is carried by road; railway; personnel and others when the container is lifted on or off a ship; crew members of the ship which may be taking the container through very difficult conditions; and shippers, forwarders and consignees, etc. All may be at risk from a poorly packed container, in particular one which is packed with dangerous goods."(1).

Therefore, the IMO in co-operation with the ILO, prepared a set of guidelines for the packing and securing of cargo in freight containers or vehicles. They do not cover the filling or emptying of bulk containers or tanks, the transport of bulk cargo in dry freight containers or refrigerated cargo.

---

and 1 GEO 6, CH45; The Hydrogen Cyanide (Fumigation of Ships) Regulations. Statutory Instrument,1951,No.1760; Memorandum of Arrangements agreed between the Ministry of Agriculture and Fisheries and the Department of Agriculture for Scotland (in consultation with the Ministry of Transport) and the Chamber of Shipping of the United Kingdom and the Liverpool Steamship Owners' Association. June,1951; Ministry of Agriculture, Fisheries and Food - Safe and Efficient Fumigation Practice - Code of Practice for the Fumigation of Commodities in Craft with Methyl Bromide; Guidance Note from the Health and Safety Executive: Fumigation using methyl bromide (bromomethane); Advisory Leaflet by the Health and Safety Executive: Safe Handling of Fumigated Freight Containers.

(1) Sales No.78.13.E.

The advice given in the guidelines[1] refers to the packing of goods in containers but much of the advice applies equally to vehicles which are to make a ro-ro international voyage.

The guidelines were revised in 1984 and the new version states that the variety of weather conditions gives rise to pitching, rolling, heaving, surging, yawing or swaying forces or a combination of two or more. Such movements can exert forces on the cargo greater than those usually found ashore and may exert them over a prolonged period. It adds that: "packing and securing of cargo inside a container or vehicle should be carried out with this in mind. It should never be assumed that the weather will be kind and the sea smooth ... improper or careless loading of goods into such units, or lack of proper blocking and bracing, may be the cause of personal injury when they are handled or transported; in addition, serious and costly damage may occur to the goods inside or to the equipment. The person who packs and secures goods into the container or vehicle for export may be the last person to look inside the unit until it is opened by the consignee at its final destination. Consequently, a great many persons will rely on his skill."[2].

---

(1) The Guidelines deal with:

1. Visual examination of the container
   - 1.1 Interior
   - 1.2 Exterior
2. Advice on the stowage planning, packing and securing of goods in containers
   - 2.1 Before Packing
   - 2.2 Packing and Securing
3. Special advice on the packing, stowage and securing of dangerous goods in containers
   - 3.1 Before Packing
   - 3.2 Packing and Securing
4. On completion of packing of dangerous goods
   - 4.1 Marking and labelling of the Container
   - 4.2 Packing Certificates
5. General advice on receipt of containers containing dangerous goods.

(2) IMO News, No.2, 1984, p.5.

## (E) RECOMMENDATION ON SAFE TRANSPORT, HANDLING AND STORAGE OF DANGEROUS SUBSTANCES IN PORT AREAS

The risks associated with the carriage of dangerous goods by sea are not limited to the crew but could extend to those working or living adjacent to the port area. In fact the hazards could cause a series of losses to the ship, cargo on board, cargo on shore, and to human lives. For all these reasons, the IMO Assembly in 1973 adopted resolution A.289 (VIII) on Safe Practice on Dangerous Goods in Ports and Harbours.

The recommendation contained in the above resolution provided a standard framework within which port authorities or other organizations can formulate regulations to ensure the safe storage and handling of dangerous goods(1). It defines the duties of the port authority in this respect and refers to the emergency procedures to be followed in cases of accidents.

Subsequent development in cargo handling and ship operations, as well as the desirability of extending the recommendation to cover dangerous goods in packaged form, liquid substances and solid dangerous materials and gases carried in bulk, made it necessary to revise the 1973 resolution. So, new recommendations were adopted by the MSC in 1980(2). The revised recommendations are concerned only with operational matters(3) and not with the

---

(1) The prime safety concern is to ensure adequate separation of the areas processing, storing, discharging or loading dangerous goods from other vulnerable areas of the port. The separation distances are determined by the criteria required, e.g. for crew to be able to take remedial action on a vessel if the land storage tanks are ablaze, and for one blazing tank not to threaten another.

(2) Resolution A.435 (XI), MSC/Circ.299 and MSC/Circ. 299/Add.1. A revised edition was adopted by the MSC at its 48th session in June, 1983.

(3) See P.R. Lyon, Port Planning and Management Aspects of the Safe Shipment of LNG and LPG, a paper presented to the Gastech Conference, 1981, at Hamburg. See also the Port of London Export Schedule, effective Jan.1, 1972, which refers to the Dangerous, Hazardous and Poisonous Goods - Classified Lists, Conditions and Regulations.

construction or equipment in the terminals[1]. They spell out the duties of the master and berth-operator with regard to fire precautions, ship handling and the reporting of incidents.

Under the heading of Dangerous Goods, the recommendations give guidance on various aspects concerned with goods in packaged form including those which may be carried in portable tanks or transport units. There are four appendices to the recommendations covering advance notification, transport and handling of explosives, segregation of radioactive substances on shore, and a ship/shore check list.

## (3) A BRIEF ANALYSIS OF THE MERCHANT SHIPPING (DANGEROUS GOODS) REGULATIONS, 1981

The Regulations, which came into operation on 1 January,1982, re-enact those provisions giving effect to Chapter VII of the 1974 SOLAS Convention and its Protocol of 1978. The Regulations are made under Sections 21 and 22 of the Merchant Shipping Act, 1979 in addition to those under Section 23 of the Merchant Shipping (Safety Convention) Act, 1949.

Definition of "dangerous goods": Dangerous goods are defined as meaning "goods classified in the Blue Book, the IMDG Code or any other IMO publication, and any other substance or goods the properties of which might be dangerous if that substance or those goods were carried by sea, and includes empty receptacles[2], residues in empty tanks or cargo

---

They require that the contents are to be properly and fully described in the shipping note or loading order and that they are to be packed according to the Blue Book.

(1) As for handling dangerous goods in the ports of the United Kingdom, each port has its own bye-laws because ports are not controlled by the Government. These bye-laws contain provisions for handling dangerous goods. The Department of the Environment, in consultation with the Port and Harbours Association, produced a Code of Practice in 1967 for the handling of dangerous goods and the various bye-laws are based upon this Code.

(2) Empty uncleaned receptacles which have been used previously for the carriage of dangerous goods,

holds which have been used previously for the carriage of dangerous goods unless such receptacles, empty tanks or cargo holds have been cleared and dried or ventilated as appropriate."

Accordingly, dangerous goods are those goods which are dangerous by nature, classed in the Blue Book or the IMDG Code. The definition is restrictive as goods could be dangerous because of defective packaging. This cause is frequently mentioned in definitions in many international conventions[1].

Scope of application: The Regulations apply to:

(a) United Kingdom ships;

(b) other ships while they are loading or discharging cargo or embarking or disembarking passengers or bunkering or discharging fuel within the United Kingdom or its territorial waters; and

(c) any ship flying the flag of a country party to both SOLAS 1974 and its Protocol of 1978 provided the loading or discharging have been carried out in accordance with the law of that country.

Duties of the shipper or the person responsible for packing the goods into a container or vehicle: The shipper is required to provide specific written information about the goods and to sign a declaration to the effect that the consignment has been correctly

---

are, therefore, subject to the same provisions as filled receptacles unless adequate measures have been taken to nullify any hazard. Recent incidents involving empty gas cylinders, including some which still contained a residue of Chlorine, have highlighted the dangers of uncleaned receptacles during sea voyages. It is considered essential that gas cylinders which are nominally empty, but which may contain a residue of their former contents, should be subjected to the same provisions as those which are filled, i.e. treated as hazardous cargo.

(1) See art.12 of the International Convention Concerning the Carriage of Goods by Rail (CIM) and also the European Agreement Concerning the International Carriage of Goods by Road (CMR) 1967, which came into force in the United Kingdom on July 9, 1968. Cmnd. 3769.

described, classified, packaged, marked, labelled and is otherwise in proper condition for the carriage by sea[1]. The Regulations specify the duties of the shipper in respect of packaged goods; goods packed into a freight container; and goods carried in bulk.

In the case of packaged dangerous goods, the shipper must furnish the shipowner or master with a dangerous goods declaration (s.7)[2]. It indicates, among other things, the technical name, the identity of the goods, the United Nations number and the class. The absence of a declaration or the act of providing a false declaration with the actual or false knowledge of the real fact, is considered as an offence (s.7, b). The shipper must also provide the shipowner or master with the following information in writing where appropriate:

(a) the number and type of packages;

(b) the total quantity of dangerous goods carried by the declaration (gross weight);

(c) the net weight of explosive content of class 1; and

(d) the closed cup flash point if 61°C or below.

Failure to comply with the above requirements is an offence (s.7, 3a)[3].

---

(1) The Simplification of International Trades Procedures Board (SITPRO) provides exporters with a standard document called the Dangerous Goods Note (DGN). It combines the documentary functions of an application for stowage space, a dangerous goods declaration, a special stowage order, a container/trailer packing certificate and a standard shipping note.

(2) "Dangerous goods declaration" means a certificate or declaration in writing that the shipment offered for carriage is properly marked or labelled in accordance with the Regulations. See s.1 (2).

(3) The shipper can nevertheless escape liability if he can show that he neither knew nor ought to have known that there would be non-compliance with the Regulations.

For goods packed into a freight container(1) or vehicle, the person responsible for packing the goods has to furnish the shipowner or master with a packing certificate which indicates that:

(a) the freight container or vehicle was clean, dry and appeared fit to receive the goods;

(b) no incompatible substances have been packed within the freight container or vehicle;

(c) the packages inside the container or vehicle are in a sound condition; and

(d) labelling or other appropriate marking is made(2).

As for dangerous goods loaded in bulk, the shipper must furnish the shipowner or the master with a notification in writing indicating the nature of the goods and stating the flashpoint of those liquids with a flashpoint at or below 60°C (closed cup) (s.13)(3).

<u>Duties of the shipowners</u>: The Regulations provide for a statutory duty to care for the cargo(4) during

---

(1) Freight container means an article of transport equipment used for the containment of cargo which is:
  (a) strong enough for repeated use;
  (b) capable of facilitating the transport of goods, by one or more modes of transport, without intermediate reloading; and
  (c) capable of being readily handled, and of being secured during carriage, and having fittings for these purposes.

(2) Failure of the person responsible for packing the goods to furnish the certificate is an offence (s.7 (4)).

(3) Failure to comply with the above requirements is an offence under the Regulations (s.13 (2)).

(4) Under Common Law the shipowner is under a duty to care for the cargo. Failure to carry out this duty would give rise to his liability for the loss or damage to the cargo. However, failure to comply with the statutory duty under the Regulations would give rise not only to questions of compensation but also constitute a criminal offence. The shipowner will be guilty of an offence and liable on summary conviction to a fine not exceeding £1,000 (s.3 (3)).

the voyage. The cargo must be stowed properly with adequate ventilation where appropriate, having regard to its identity and its dangerous properties (s.10). The objectives of this undertaking are to:

(a) ensure the health, safety and welfare aboard ship of all employees;

(b) maintain the ship's equipment used for the handling, stowage and transport, safe and without risk to health; and

(c) provide information, instruction, training and supervision to ensure the fulfilment of the above duty (s.3 (2)).

The Regulations spell out in more detail the duties in respect of packaged dangerous goods; dangerous goods packed in a freight container or vehicle; dangerous goods carried in bulk, and dangerous goods on passenger ships.

In the case of packaged goods, they must be packed and marked with distinctive labels in accordance with the Code. It is an offence for the shipowner or the master to accept the goods if he knew or ought to have known that they are not properly packed and marked with the correct technical name (s.9). Further, the master is under a duty to prepare a list, manifest, or stowage plan covering the details on the dangerous goods carried on his ship. The information in such a list is obtained from the shipping documents presented by the shipper (s.7 (5))[1].

For goods packed in a freight container or vehicle, the goods shall be packed in a manner which is safe and proper, having regard to their identity and dangerous properties (s.10 (2))[2]. Section 14 states that dangerous goods shall not be loaded in bulk into any ship if the owner of the ship or any of his servants or agents knows or ought to know that

---

(1) Failure to prepare a specific list, manifest or stowage plan, record of location of goods or additional special document to be carried, is an offence. Furthermore, the ship will be liable to be detained.

(2) It is a good defence that before the freight container or vehicle was taken on board the ship, the person responsible for packing the goods into the container or vehicle had furnished the shipowner or master with a packing certificate that the goods had been properly packed.

the goods cannot safely be carried in bulk to the destination to which they are consigned. Bulk cargoes should be carried in accordance with the provisions of the Bulk Cargoes Code.

The Regulations give concentration limits as large quantities of dangerous goods would represent an added hazard to passenger ships. Accordingly, Section 12 states that

(1) No explosives shall be taken on board or carried in any ship which is carrying more than 12 passengers except: safety explosives and explosives the net weight of which does not exceed 10 kilogrammes;

(2) No dangerous goods shall be taken on board or carried in any ship which is carrying more than 25 passengers or more than one passenger per three metres of overall length, whichever is the greater number.

Standard of care and defences: The standard of care is to be decided according to what is reasonably practicable[1]. The burden of proof is on the accused. He can escape liability if he could prove that it was not reasonably practicable to do more than was in fact done to satisfy the duty or requirements.

The Regulations point to two main defences:

(a) proof that the requirements of the Blue Book or the IMDG Code were observed; or

(b) proof that the accused did not know nor ought to have known nor had reasonable grounds to suspect the goods to be dangerous goods.

---

(1) For cases decided before the Regulations, see *Brass* v. *Maitland* (1865) 6 E & B 470; *Barfield* v. *Goole and Sheffield Transport Co. Ltd.* (1910) 2 K.B. 94 (the shipper was held liable although unknown to both the shipper and the carrier the substance underwent a change during the sea voyage). *Great Northern Railway Company* v. *L.E.P. Transport and Depository Ltd.* (1922) 2 K.B. 472 (the argument that the defendants acting as forwarding agent with no previous knowledge that the goods were dangerous, was not accepted).

## References

Bo Bengtsson, Sea Transport of Liquid Chemicals in Bulk. Code of Federal Regulations, published by the Office of the Federal Register, Washington, D.C.

Conference on Hazardous Cargoes: Proceedings held at U.S. Coast Guard Academy, 1970, published by the Committee on Hazardous Materials of the National Research Council, Washington, D.C.

Greg S. Marton, Tanker Operations: A Handbook for the Ship's Officer, published by Cornell Maritime Press.

Handling Chemicals Safely (1980 ed.) published by Dutch Chemical Industry Association.

Hazardous Cargo Bulletin.

International Safety Guide for Oil Tankers and Terminals (ISGOTT) (Revised edition, 1984), prepared by ICS/OCIMF/IAPH.

Merchant Shipping (Dangerous Goods) Regulations, 1981.

Merchant Shipping (Code of Safe Working Practices) Regulations, 1980.

Minerals Transportation - Proceedings of the First International Symposium on Transport and Handling of Minerals, Vancouver, 1971, published by Miller Freeman Publications Inc.

Recommendations on Equipment for the Towing of Disabled Tankers (September 1981), published by OCIMF.

Safety Guide for Terminals Handling Ships Carrying Liquefied Gases in Bulk (1982), prepared by OCIMF.

Tanker Safety Guide (Chemicals), prepared by ICS.

Tanker Safety Guide (Liquefied Gas), prepared by ICS.

## (ii) THE CARRIAGE OF RADIOACTIVE MATERIALS

The carriage of radioactive materials is governed by a number of international conventions(1), bilateral agreements(2), national law(3), licensing arrangements(4) and codes of practice for the safe handling and transport of nuclear materials. The complexity of the subject is mainly due to the following reasons:

(a) the production of nuclear material is controlled by the State;

(b) radioactive materials play a significant role in the development of nuclear energy; and

(c) the great demand for nuclear power.

Before shipment of nuclear materials the competent authority in the State from which the materials are being shipped must ensure that:

(a) treaty obligations are observed;

(b) safety requirements are followed; and

(c) insurance covers are effected.

These assurances are embodied in Nuclear Law, a branch of law which aims, among other things, at providing a deterrent to national diversion for the use of radioactive materials for non-peaceful purposes and reducing any hazards which may arise from the operation of nuclear installations.

---

(1) See *infra* the Conventions on Liability, p.144.

(2) See, for example, the agreement between Australia and the United Kingdom concerning Nuclear Transfers signed in London on July 24, 1979.

(3) In the United Kingdom, see the following Acts:
- The Atomic Energy Act, 1946;
- The Radioactive Substances Act, 1960;
- The Nuclear Installations Acts, 1965 to 1969;
- The Factories Act, 1961;
- The Social Security Act, 1975; and see also *infra* National Rules in the United Kingdom, p.147.

(4) Apart from the health and safety requirements, the operator of a nuclear installation must comply with cartel and anti-trust legislation, obtain site and operating licences from competent authorities.

## (1) SAFETY AND POLITICAL RULES AND CONVENTIONS

### (A) The International Atomic Energy Agency (IAEA) Regulations, 1985

On December 8, 1953, President Eisenhower addressed the United Nations on "Atoms for Peace". The President, in recognising the spread of nuclear know-how beyond the United States and the Soviet Union, called for the establishment of an international Atomic Energy Agency under the auspices of the United Nations to exercise strict control on the movement of nuclear materials.

In 1957 the International Atomic Energy Agency (IAEA) was set up with the aims of establishing and administering safeguards on nuclear materials and facilities, ensuring that they will not be used for military purposes. One of the first tasks of the IAEA was to draft regulations on the transport of radioactive materials. The first set of these Regulations was published in 1961. They provided for certain "standards" to be followed in transport operations and they were recommended to Member States and also to organisations interested in this field. The Regulations were revised in 1964, 1967[1] and 1973[2] in the light of extensive operating experience that had accumulated to the IAEA and to clarify and simplify them in so far as this could be done without any reduction in the standard of safety. Further changes were made in 1975, 1977 and 1979, and as a result an amended version of the Regulations was issued in 1985[3].

---

(1) The revised editions differ from the original version mainly in the areas of package design and test requirements.

(2) See the text IAEA Safety Series No.6. With the 1973 Regulations there was also a companion document providing supplementary information and advisory material on how best to achieve the necessary level of protection. See IAEA Safety Series No.37.

(3) A Standing Advisory Group on the Safe Transport of Radioactive Materials was set up in 1978 to advise the Agency on the interpretation and revision of the IAEA Regulations. A comprehensive revision of the Regulations took place in 1985.

The main objectives of the Regulations are to protect the public, transport workers and property from radiation in the shipment of radioactive material. The Regulations contain provisions for:

(1) small quantities of radioactive materials which can be exempted from the packaging and labelling requirements;

(2) simple packing requirements for low specific activity material;

(3) design criteria and performance tests for packaging for normal and special form radioactive and fissile materials;

(4) labelling and placarding;

(5) storage of packages, and their carriage; and

(6) administrative controls, including competent authority approval of package design and shipment, transport documents, information for carriers and notification of any necessary authorities.

The Regulations only apply to materials and facilities in which the IAEA plays a role in the transferral or where the supplier and recipient request the IAEA to participate or where a State asks for the IAEA involvement(1). As the IAEA does not impose such safeguards on its Member States, there was a need for strong political backing and this was achieved by the adoption of the Non-Proliferation Treaty.

(B) The Non-Proliferation Treaty (NPT), 1968

The NPT(2) is based on the assumption that some degree of separation is possible between peaceful

---

(1) The Regulations are observed by Members of the Council for Mutual Economic Assistance (COMECON) and are applied to the transport of nuclear materials for use in 24 research reactors and three nuclear power plants. In fact, the Regulations are considered as a "model" recommended to Member States and international organisations.

(2) The Treaty came into force on March 5, 1970. France, Israel and India did not sign the Treaty.

and warlike nuclear technologies[1]. Its objective is to limit the spread of nuclear weapons by imposing tight control on the re-processing of nuclear fuels, which produces the materials for nuclear weapons[2].

Article I of the Treaty[3] prohibits nuclear weapon States transferring weapons or technology to anyone else. Article II prohibits the non-weapon States acquiring or making weapons[4]. Article III obliges the non-weapon States to accept the safeguards of the International Atomic Energy Agency (IAEA)[5]. Under article IV, countries with the

---

(1) The division between peaceful and military use of nuclear weapons seems to be illusory. India exploded a small nuclear device. West Germany agreed to sell Brazil a full nuclear fuel cycle capability. France agreed to sell Pakistan, South Korea and Iraq a reprocessing plant.

(2) In 1978, a treaty banning nuclear weapons in Latin America was signed. Again, in 1967, the Outer Space Treaty which prohibited orbital nuclear weapons came into existence. Members of the EEC have to comply with the Euratom requirements.

(3) Article I states: Each nuclear-weapon State Party to the Treaty undertakes not to transfer to any recipient whatsoever nuclear weapons or other nuclear explosive devices or control over such weapons or explosive devices directly, or indirectly; and not in any way to assist, encourage, or induce any non-nuclear-weapon State to manufacture or otherwise acquire nuclear weapons or other nuclear explosive devices, or control over such weapons or explosive devices.

(4) Article II provides: Each non-nuclear-weapon State Party to the Treaty undertakes not to receive the transfer from any transferor whatsoever of nuclear weapons or other nuclear explosive devices or of control over such weapons or explosive devices directly, or indirectly; not to manufacture or otherwise acquire nuclear weapons or other nuclear explosive devices; and not to seek or receive any assistance in the manufacture of nuclear weapons or other nuclear explosive devices.

(5) Article III provides:
1. Each non-nuclear-weapon State Party to the Treaty undertakes to accept safeguards, as set

necessary technology promise to help others to develop nuclear energy programmes. They also pledge themselves in article V to do much the same in

---

forth in an agreement to be negotiated and concluded with the International Atomic Energy Agency in accordance with the Statute of the International Atomic Energy Agency and the Agency's safeguards system, for the exclusive purpose of verification of the fulfilment of its obligations assumed under this Treaty with a view to preventing diversion of nuclear energy from peaceful uses to nuclear weapons or other nuclear explosive devices. Procedures for the safeguards required by this Article shall be followed with respect to sources or special fissionable material whether it is being produced, processed or used in any principal nuclear facility or is outside any such facility. The safeguards required by this Article shall be applied to all source or special fissionable material in all peaceful nuclear activities within the territory of such State, under its jurisdiction, or carried out under its control anywhere.

2. Each State Party to the Treaty undertakes not to provide: (a) source or special fissionable material, or (b) equipment or material especially designed or prepared for the processing, use or production of special fissionable material, to any non-nuclear-weapon State for peaceful purposes, unless the source or special fissionable material shall be subject to the safeguards required by this Article.

3. The safeguards required by this Article shall be implemented in a manner designed to comply with Article IV of this Treaty, and to avoid hampering the economic or technological development of the Parties or international co-operation in the field of peaceful nuclear activities, including the international exchange of nuclear material and equipment for the processing, use or production of nuclear material for peaceful purposes in accordance with the provisions of this Article and the principle of safeguarding set forth in the Preamble of the Treaty.

respect of nuclear explosives for peaceful purposes(1). Article VI commits everyone to negotiate a speedy end to the arms race and ultimately a treaty on general disarmament(2).

---

4. Non-nuclear-weapon States Party to the Treaty shall conclude agreements with the International Atomic Energy Agency to meet the requirements of this Article either individually or together with other States in accordance with the Statute of the International Atomic Energy Agency. Negotiations of such agreements shall commence within 180 days from the original entry into force on this Treaty. For States depositing their instruments of ratification or accession after the 180-day period, negotiation of such agreements shall enter into force not later than eighteen months after the date of initiation of negotiation.

(1) Seven countries supplying nuclear materials used to meet in London in what became known as the "London Nuclear Suppliers' Conference". In May, 1975, this group of countries made a declaration to strengthen the IAEA safeguards on exports of material, equipment and technology and replicated technology to preclude their use in nuclear explosive devices, including those for peaceful purposes. They also agreed to apply restraint in the transfer of sensitive technologies and accept special conditions governing the use or transfer of sensitive material, equipment and technologies. The number of the group has been increased to fifteen countries.

(2) One of the weaknesses is that while about two-thirds of the international community has agreed to abide by its terms, the remaining one-third contains a significant number of potential proliferators. Furthermore, the negotiation between the nuclear weapon powers towards stopping the nuclear arms race progressed very slowly. The second Strategic Arms Limitation Agreement (Salt-2) has been signed but not ratified. Talks have also opened on a Comprehensive Test Ban Treaty (CTBT) and have made substantial progress, although a treaty has not yet been agreed.
There is no agreement among the States on the parts of the NPT which deal with the transfer of technology, nuclear materials and the safeguards. Supplier countries would like to see

Whatever the view taken on the NPT, it is clear that together with the IAEA Regulations, they serve as a deterrent to national diversion for the use of radioactive materials for non-peaceful purposes.

(C) The 1974 SOLAS Convention and the IMDG Code

The IAEA Regulations were further strengthened by the adoption of Chapter VIII of the 1974 SOLAS Convention(1) which contains rules designed to provide for the control of the safety of nuclear ships. Similarly, class 7 of the IMDG Code is based on the IAEA Regulations(2).

(2) The legal framework of the carriage of radioactive materials

As mentioned earlier, the carriage of radioactive materials is governed by certain international conventions(3) on liability(4) and a number of

---

the safeguards tightened so that the IAEA can monitor the country's entire nuclear programme instead of the individual parts supplied. On the other hand, a number of countries want to see a greater liberalization in the transfer of nuclear technology.
The most fundamental weakness of the NPT is that it confers no clear benefit on those non-nuclear weapon powers who sign it. Similarly, there are no obvious disadvantages suffered by those who do not.

(1) See p.57.
(2) See p.118.
(3) Physical protection against theft or unauthorised diversion of nuclear material is a matter of great concern to many countries. Therefore, the IAEA published in 1972 "Recommendations for the Physical Protection of Nuclear Material". These recommendations were revised in 1975 and 1977. See INFCIRC/225/Rev.1, 1977.
The IAEA also prepared a draft Convention on the Physical Protection of Nuclear Material.
(4) See also the Convention on the Liability of Operators of Nuclear Ships, 1962, which sets up uniform rules concerning the liability of operators of nuclear ships for damage caused by nuclear incidents involving the nuclear fuel,

national acts and regulations. It is suggested that English Law will be taken as an example in this respect. Thus, the following points call for examination:

A - conventions on liability;
B - national rules in the United Kingdom; and
C - the application of nuclear and other conventions to maritime transport.

## A. CONVENTIONS ON LIABILITY

There are three conventions in this respect: the Paris Convention, 1960; the Vienna Convention, 1963 and the Brussels Convention, 1971.

### The Paris Convention on Third Party Liability in the Field of Nuclear Energy, 1960

This Convention[1] provides that the operator of a nuclear installation is the person exclusively liable for damage - other than damage to the means of transport - caused by a nuclear incident occurring in the course of maritime carriage of nuclear material[2]. Liability is limited to 5 million European Monetary Agreement units of account. If national legislation specifies that the operator shall compensate for damage to the means of transport, it must be on condition that the right of other victims to the minimum amount of 5 million units of account is not reduced by this extension of liability.

This Convention was amended by an Additional Protocol signed on 28 January,1964[3], the purpose of which was to bring the Convention into line with the IAEA Regulations.

---

or radioactive products or waste produced in such ships. The Convention is not yet in force and has not been ratified by the United Kingdom. See also the Code of Safety for Nuclear Merchant Ships prepared by IMO in 1982, Resolution A.491 (XII). Sales No. 851 82.10.E.

(1) This OECD Convention was signed in Paris in July 1960 and came into force on April 1, 1968. See Cmnd. 1211.
(2) See art.III.
(3) This Protocol came into force on April 1, 1968, and has been ratified by the same countries.

In 1963, a Supplementary Convention on Third Party Liability in the Field of Nuclear Energy was signed(1). It provides for the payment of additional compensation out of public funds beyond the maximum amount laid down in the Paris Convention. For damages exceeding the maximum amount which the operator of a nuclear installation must have available under the Paris Convention (a) payment up to 70 million units of account is guaranteed by the State on whose territory the plant involved is situated; and (b) payment between 70 million and 120 million units of account is guaranteed by the Contracting States together.

This Supplementary Convention was amended by an Additional Protocol in 1964(2) which became necessary as a result of the Additional Protocol to the Paris Convention, 1960.

<u>The Vienna International Atomic Energy Agency Convention on Civil Liability for Nuclear Damage, 1963</u>

Although the aims of the Convention(3) are similar to the Paris Convention, 1960, it was intended to have a wider application through the world rather than to be limited to the OECD countries.

It must be recalled that the purposes of both the Paris and Vienna Conventions are to make the operator liable irrespective of fault, to simplify the procedures for obtaining redress and to set a ceiling for the maximum amount of compensation to which the operator is liable.

In the event of a nuclear incident, the identity of the operator could be easily determined by reference to the transport certificate which will be delivered to the carrier. Such a certificate is issued by the insurer as approved by national authority. Thus, the operator is required to maintain an insurance policy or a financial security for the full amount of his liability. In order to simplify the insurance arrangements, the Standing Committee on Atomic Risk of the European Insurance Committee has formulated a draft model bilateral agreement between the insurers concerned and a draft

---

(1) The Convention was signed in Brussels on January 31, 1963, and came into force on December 4, 1974.
(2) The Protocol was signed on January 28, 1964.
(3) The Convention was signed on May 21, 1963.

model certificate of financial security to be issued by them.

The Brussels Convention relating to Civil Liability in the Field of Maritime Carriage of Nuclear Material, 1971

Under both the Paris Convention (art. 6,b) and the Vienna Convention (art. II,5), shipowners were still liable, beside the operator of a nuclear installation, when their vessels were involved in a nuclear incident. As a result, it has been difficult for shipowners to obtain insurance for the carriage of nuclear material. This position has been remedied by the Brussels Convention, 1971(1).

The basic principle of the Convention is to ensure that third party liability for accidents arising out of the maritime carriage of nuclear material is channelled exclusively onto the operator of the nuclear installation. Thus Article I provides that "any person who by virtue of an international convention or national law in the field of maritime transport might be held liable for damage caused by a nuclear incident shall be exonerated from such liability" if the operator of a nuclear installation is liable for such damage under the Paris or Vienna Conventions or under national law (provided that such law is as favourable to persons suffering damage as the Paris or Vienna Conventions). Such persons are also exonerated from liability where damage is done to the nuclear installation or the ship carrying the nuclear material and for which the operator of the nuclear installation is not liable under the Paris or Vienna Conventions. However, in these cases the liability of any person

---

(1) This Convention is the work of a conference held in Brussels from November 29 to December 2, 1971, under the joint auspices of IMO, IAEA and ENEA. The Convention was signed by nine States in Brussels on December 17, 1971. It requires five ratifications in order to enter into force. The only reservations a State may make are those corresponding to the reservations it has made to the Paris or Vienna Conventions. The Convention may be denounced on giving one year's notice; it continues to apply to any damage caused by a nuclear incident occurring before the denunciation takes effect. See the text of the Convention. Sales No. 1972. 11.

who has caused the damage by an act or omission done with intent to cause damage is not affected. The Convention on the Liability of Operators of Nuclear Ships, 1962 and certain other special regimes govern or are intended to govern the liability of operators of nuclear ships. The present Convention provides that such operators shall not be exonerated by the new Convention from liability "in respect of damage caused by a nuclear incident involving the nuclear fuel or radioactive products of waste produced in" a nuclear ship.

The present Convention supersedes any international conventions in the field of maritime transport to the extent that such conventions are in conflict with it. This, of course, will only apply to those States which are parties to the present Convention. As regards States which are not parties to the present Convention, the obligations of States Parties to the present Convention under the earlier maritime conventions remain unaffected.

## B. NATIONAL RULES IN THE UNITED KINGDOM[1]

At Common Law, there is a duty on the person who possesses cargo which he knows to be dangerous, to exercise reasonable care to make it as safe as possible and to disclose any hidden dangers before parting with it. Furthermore, under *Rylands* v. *Fletcher*[2] a person who for his own purposes brings on his property or collects and keeps there anything likely to do mischief if it escapes, must keep it in at his peril and, if he does not do so, is *prima facie* answerable for the damage which is the natural consequence of its escape.

In addition, the employer is liable towards his employees for injuries caused by his negligence, such as the case of his failure to provide a safe system of working or safe equipment. Finally, the employer is vicariously liable for any tort which his servant commits in the course of his employment.

---

(1) In the United States, see the Nuclear Non-Proliferation Act, 1978, which provides the criteria governing the American international nuclear commerce and the procedures for exports.
(2) (1868) L R 3, H L, 330.

## Various Acts and Regulations

With the increase in the activities in the nuclear field, it became apparent that the few rules of common law are not adequate. Therefore, a number of acts and regulations were passed. The most important are the following:

- The Atomic Energy Act, 1946, which empowers the Secretary of State for Energy to promote and control the development of atomic energy(1).
- The Radioactive Substances Act, 1948, which provides for the control of radioactive substances and certain apparatus producing radiation, in the interests of safety and health(2).
- The Atomic Energy Authority Act, 1954, set up the United Kingdom Atomic Energy Authority (UKAEA) as a statutory corporation with the responsibility for day to day details of the production and use of atomic energy. The Secretary of State for Energy has the general duty of securing that the Authority attach proper degrees of importance to various applications of atomic energy, and has power to give directions to the Authority(3).
- The Nuclear Installations Acts 1965 and 1969 provide that no person other than the United Kingdom Atomic Energy Agency (UKAEA) may use a site for installing or operating a nuclear reactor or other installation covered by the Act except under licence. The Acts also provide that the UKAEA and licensees are under a duty to ensure that no personal injury or damage to property caused by the operation of such

---

(1) See also the Atomic Energy (Disclosure of Information) (No.1) Order 1947, Statutory Rules and Orders 1947, No.100.
(2) Radioactive substance is defined as any substance consisting of or containing radioactive chemical elements whether natural or artificial.
(3) See also the Atomic Energy Authority Act 1971, which transferred to British Nuclear Fuels Limited and the Radiochemical Centre Limited, parts of the UKAEA's undertakings and most of the property, rights and liabilities appertaining to those parts.

installations or by the radioactive properties of the materials used. The liability of any persons to pay damages under the Act is limited to £5million for any one occurrence. Parliament is responsible for providing money up to an aggregate £50million[1].

- The Radioactive Substances Act, 1960, regulates the keeping and use of radioactive material and makes provisions as to the disposal and accumulation of radioactive waste. It makes provisions for registration of users of radioactive material and mobile radioactive apparatus and prohibits the disposal or accumulation of radioactive waste except with an authorisation.
- The Factories Act, 1961[2] provides for the protection of employees against ionising radiation. Under it, regulations were made to:
  - require the notification to the appropriate Authorities of the use of sources of ionising radiation;
  - require that certain employees be designated as "classified workers" and that special medical records are kept of these people;
  - govern arrangement of premises and plant in order to minimise the exposure of employees to radiation; and to
  - lay down procedures to be followed for monitoring radiation levels and exposure of employees to radiation.
- The Social Security Act, 1975, includes regulations allowing the payment of benefits in respect of diseases caused by electro-magnetic or ionising radiation, to people whose employment involves exposure to such radiation.
- The Merchant Shipping (Dangerous Goods) Rules,

---

(1) See also the Nuclear Installations (Insurance Certificate) Regulations 1965, as amended by the Nuclear Installations (Insurance Certificate) (Amendment) Regulations, 1969.

(2) See also the Radiological Protection Act, 1970, as amended by the Health and Safety at Work etc. Act, 1974, which provides for the setting up of a National Radiological Protection Board and an Advisory Committee, with functions and powers concerning the protection of people from the dangers of ionising radiation.

1981, contains rules on labelling, packaging and stowage of radioactive materials.

## C. THE APPLICATION OF NUCLEAR AND OTHER CONVENTIONS TO MARITIME TRANSPORT

The nuclear conventions were drafted on the assumption that liability for nuclear damage will not be covered by the provisions of any conventions in the field of transport. Therefore, art.6(b) of the Paris Convention states: "This provision shall not affect the application of any international agreement in the field of transport in force or open for signature, ratification or accession at the date of this Convention." The Vienna Convention contains a similar provision - Article II C(5) states: "..this, however, shall not affect the application of any international convention in the field of transport in force or open for signature, ratification or accession at the date on which this Convention is opened for signature."

Thus, a person who has paid compensation for nuclear damage under any transport convention will have a recourse action against the operator of the nuclear installation, in conformity with the Paris or the Vienna Conventions[1].

Conventions in the field of Maritime transport are the only ones which are not affected by either the Paris or the Vienna Conventions. Examples of these conventions are: the Hague Rules, 1924, on bills of lading, and the Athens Convention on the Carriage of Passengers and their Luggage on board Ships, 1974. The position of other conventions which are not concerned with transport but are closely connected with nuclear conventions such as the Collision Convention, 1972[2], and the Convention

---

(1) There is, however, a difference between the two conventions. Under the Paris Convention, the right of recourse action can be exercised by any person regardless of his nationality or domicile, while under the Vienna Convention, only nationals of the Contracting States are entitled to this right.

(2) The Exposé des Motifs of the Paris Convention lists three categories of such agreements:
1) international agreements dealing with third party liability for damage involving a means of transport;
2) international agreements dealing with

on the Arrest of Sea-Going Vessels, 1952[1] is open for discussion.

It is clear that while the Paris and the Vienna Conventions expressly preserved the application of conventions in the field of maritime transport, the Brussels Convention states that it shall supersede such agreements.

## Damage to the Means of Transport

The Paris and the Vienna Conventions provide that the operator shall not be liable for nuclear damage caused to the means of transport[2] on which the nuclear materials were carried at the time of the nuclear incident[3]. The two conventions also add that national law where the nuclear installation of the operator is situated, may provide that the operator shall be liable for nuclear damage to the means of transport. If national law makes use of this option, the minimum amount of 5 million dollars shall be available for compensation for nuclear damage other than damage to the means of transport[4].

## Damage to the Goods

The operator is liable for any damage caused to the goods. He is also liable for damage to non-nuclear cargo caused by nuclear incident involving nuclear material carried on board the same ship. In such a case, the cargo owner has the choice between claiming under the traditional maritime law or under nuclear law, since these two laws apply concurrently. Thus, the cargo owner may present his claim against the shipowner and such a claim would be governed by the Hague Rules in case a bill of lading is issued, or by the terms of the charter party in case the cargo is carried under a charter party. Or, he may

---

collisions involving a means of transport; and

3) international agreements dealing with bills of lading.

(1) The arrest of a ship carrying nuclear substances could be dangerous because of contamination.

(2) Art.3a II 2 and art.IV 5 b respectively.

(3) The only possible source of compensation for such damage would come from the insurance cover.

(4) All States which have ratified the Paris Convention have made use of this option.

prefer to claim from the operator of the nuclear installation[1] under the Paris or the Vienna Conventions[2]. These Conventions require that the nuclear material emanated from or was destined to a nuclear installation in a State party to the Paris or the Vienna Conventions and the incident occurred within the territory of such State or on the high seas[3].

Where the shipowner is found liable for any damage or loss under the traditional maritime law, the Paris Convention (art.6,d) gives him the right to recourse action against the operator of the nuclear installation.

As mentioned earlier, the purpose of the Brussels Convention, 1971, is to eliminate the dual liability of the maritime carrier and the operator of the nuclear installation. The liability of the maritime carrier is extinguished as he will be in the same position as other suppliers of goods and services to nuclear installations. The main principle of this Convention is that no person shall be liable under maritime law if the operator of a nuclear installation is liable for the damage under either the Paris or the Vienna Conventions or under

---

(1) Usually the operator of the nuclear installation is the owner of the nuclear cargo.

(2) The amount of limitation under the nuclear conventions is higher than the one under the Hague Rules. However, the cargo owner, if he elects to bring an action under the nuclear conventions, must bring it only before the courts of the Contracting State in whose territory the nuclear incident occurred, or if the incident occurred outside the territory of the Contracting States, before the courts of the Installation State.

(3) Although the Paris Convention applies neither to incidents occurring in the territory of a non-contracting State, nor to damages suffered in such territory, it, nevertheless, protects all persons suffering loss even if they are nationals of a non-contracting State. This is the result of art.14 which states that national law of the competent court shall be applied without any discrimination based upon nationality, domicile or residence.

a national law having equivalent effect(1).

## References

Clingan, Thomas A. and Alexander, Lewis (editors) Hazards of Maritime Transport, Cambridge, Mass., Ballinger Publishing Co., 1973.

Fairbairn, A. The IAEA Transport Regulations: A Review of their Development. IAEA Bulletin, Vol.21, No.6, pp. 2-12.

Ho Vinh Phuong, Legal Aspects of the International Transport of Radioactive Materials. IAEA Bulletin, Vol.21, No.6, pp. 13-18.

International Atomic Energy Bulletin, published six times a year by the IAEA. Address: Wagramer-strasse 5, P.O. Box 100, A-1400, Vienna.

Maritime Carriage of Nuclear Materials (edited), International Atomic Agency's editorial staff, Vienna, 1973.

Swindell, International Regulatory Control of the Transport of Radioactive Materials. IAEA Bulletin, Vol.21, No.6, pp. 19-23.

---

(1) It must be remembered that the provisions of this Convention are binding only as between States which ratified it. Moreover, its application depends on whether the Paris or the Vienna Convention or an equivalent national law, is applicable.

## (iii) THE INTERNATIONAL CONVENTION FOR SAFE CONTAINERS (CSC)

### Efforts for Standardisation and the Preparation of the CSC

In 1961, the International Standards Organisation (ISO) set up the Freight Container Committee TC 104 to consider the formulation of uniform rules on matters such as dimensions, corner fittings and strength(1) of containers, in consultation with governmental agencies and interested bodies. After a long debate, the TC 104 was able to recommend a set of uniform rules(2). The various sizes of containers were reduced to one series: 10 ft., 20 ft. and 40 ft. At the present time, only 20 ft. and 40 ft. containers are used. Recommendations were also made regarding the height and the one approved was the 8 ft. 6 in. height(3).

Despite the valuable work done by the ISO, some countries, in particular the United Kingdom and Australia, were planning to introduce compulsory rules in view of the large number of containers in circulation(4).

Unilateral action by States could well have led to the adoption of different or even conflicting standards on containers. This would have affected the activities of container operators trading in different countries. Furthermore, there was a strong opinion in the transport industry that the ISO requirements were costly and a new "standard", cheaper than the ISO, might be introduced.

---

(1) In 1972, TC 104 added racking strength requirements to the list of strength standards for containers.

(2) The standards for containers are ISO 668 dimensions and ratings, ISO 1161 requirements for corner fittings, ISO 1494 which deals with the specification and testing of the various types of containers, ISO 1894 covering internal dimensions, mainly for general purpose containers, ISO 6359 requirements for a consolidated date plate, DIS 830 definition of terminology and ISO 3874 guidelines on the handling and securing of containers.

(3) Up to 2% of all containers in circulation have non-standard heights of 9 ft. or 9 ft. 6 in.

(4) It is estimated that at present more than 3 million containers are in use.

Therefore, the IMO took the initiative and prepared, in co-operation with the Economic Commission for Europe, a draft convention which was submitted to a conference jointly convened by the United Nations and the IMO. The Conference adopted(1) in 1972 the International Convention for Safe Containers (CSC) which came into force on September 6, 1977(2).

Objectives of the CSC

The CSC has two main objectives. The first is to secure the safety of dockers, seamen and other transport workers(3) by requiring all freight containers used in international transport, other than those specially designed for air transport, to be approved and plated. To achieve this status, the container must comply with prescribed standards of structural safety and be regularly examined and maintained to ensure that these standards are constant.

The second objective is that the container will be assured free passage by recognition of its prescribed safety plates, unless there are obvious defaults, in which case it may be stopped for repairs to be undertaken. In this way, proliferation of divergent national safety regulations could be avoided.

Scope of Application

The Convention applies to new and existing containers(4) used in international transport, excluding

---

(1) The structural safety requirements and tests are largely based on the ISO recommendations.
(2) See the text of the Convention - IMO Sales No. 74.10.E. The United Kingdom ratified the CSC in 1978. In fact the ratification of both the UK and the USA were crucial as 60% of the container fleet belongs to both countries.
(3) See the IMO/ILO Guidelines for Training in the Packing of Cargo in Freight Containers, IMO Sales No. 78.13.E. The Guidelines dated 1978 provide *inter alia* for visual examination of the container and state general advice on receipt of containers containing dangerous goods.
(4) Article II of the Convention defines "container" as "an article of transport equipment:
 (a) of a permanent character and accordingly strong enough to be suitable for repeated

containers specially designed for air transport (art.III, r.1). New containers do not have to be examined until five years after plating at the time of delivery, but after this period the container must be examined at intervals not exceeding 24 months.

Various anomalies have arisen with regard to the early plating of existing containers and "phasing" dates have been agreed upon to alleviate the burden on owners for existing containers. By September 6, 1982, all containers operated by owners resident in countries which have ratified the Convention, or trading with such countries, must carry a CSC plate on which is indicated the country of approval, date of manufacture, maximum operating gross weight, stacking weight, racking value and the date by which the container must be examined to ensure that it still complies with the Convention's requirements. From this point forward, each container must be re-examined as indicated by the date on the plate, repairs as necessary carried out, and the new date for re-examination indicated on the container.

Structural Safety Requirements and Tests

The requirements of Annex II of the Convention are more flexible than the ISO recommendations as the Convention is designed to apply to all containers with corner fittings, including containers for international and captive trade(1). Only containers

---

use;
(b) specially designed to facilitate the transport of goods, by one or more modes of transport, without intermediate reloading;
(c) designed to be secured and/or readily handled, having corner fittings for these purposes;
(d) of a size such that the area enclosed by the four outer bottom corners is either
 (i) at least 14 sq.m (150 sq.ft) or
 (ii) at least 7 sq.m (75 sq.ft) if it is fitted with top corner fittings."

The term "container" includes neither vehicles nor packaging, however, containers when carried on chassis are included.

(1) As, for example, the type of container adopted by many European railways, which can only be stacked two-high.

especially designed for air transport are excluded. Annex II states: "...it is implicit that in all phases of the operation of containers the forces as a result of motion, location, stacking and weight of the loaded container and external forces will not exceed the design strength of the container. In particular, the following assumptions have been made:

(a) the container will so be restrained that it is not subjected to forces in excess of those for which it has been designed;

(b) the container will have its cargo stowed in accordance with the recommended practices of the trade so that the cargo does not impose upon the container forces in excess of those for which it has been designed."

The instigation of the CSC means that most categories of containers must display a CSC approval plate(1) bearing a date, structural date and maximum weight. Containers older than five years will have to undergo visual examination at least every two years. All new container types must have their type approved by the government or the body to which the government delegates this task(2).

---

(1) The plate gives date of manufacture, identification number, maximum gross weight and various strength data. The standard dimensions adopted for the plate were based on a 100 mm × 200 mm rectangle, with the CSC title lettering 8 mm high. The specification and age details lettering selected is 5 mm high.

(2) The sub-committee on containers and cargo called attention to the fact that containers exist with weight markings on them which differ from the maximum gross weight information on the CSC safety approval plate. It urged member governments of IMO to advise container handlers to consider either the maximum gross weight information on the CSC safety approval plate or, where a container is not yet plated, the actual weight of the loaded container given in the shipping manifest. See IMO document BC24 WP/8 (Annex 3) to the draft sub-committee on container and cargoes to the MSC.

## Duties Under the CSC

There are three distinct duties[1] on the part of the owner of the container. These are:

(a) the initial approval and plating of existing and new containers via documentary procedures;

(b) the examination[2] and re-examination of containers; and

(c) the maintenance of the containers in a safe condition.

## Control Procedures

Under article VI of the Convention, the contracting governments should retain control of the whole system through authorised government officials with the power to detain any container showing signs of being a safety risk. Those containers with lapsed approval plates should be distinguished from those considered unsafe by an appropriate identification so it will denote that the container should be examined at the first practical opportunity. One country's containers may be approved by an authorised body from another signatory country. This is encouraged in order that less developed nations may benefit from the expertise of the leaders in the container field, such as the United States and Western Europe.

---

(1) In the United Kingdom, implementation of the requirements of CSC has been assigned to the Government's Health and Safety Executive (HSE). The HSE is responsible for providing for the approval of new and existing containers; prescribing or approving examination schemes for container owners. They exercise control to ensure that no container is a safety risk and that the examination is properly conducted. The HSE has instructed a number of classification societies and other bodies to act on its behalf as approval authorities.

(2) The owner of the container is responsible for in-service examination under CSC. It is the examination procedure which must be approved, not the examiner, which is chosen by the container owner.

## The 1981 and 1983 Amendments

As mentioned earlier according to Chapter IV, Annex I, a safety plate must be affixed to existing containers (that is those built before September, 1977) and within five years (ending September,1982) to new containers. The safety plate can be affixed only when an administration is satisfied that the container meets the requirements.

By April,1981, it became clear to the IMO that owners and operators were unable to complete plating and approval by the deadline. Therefore, the Maritime Safety Committee approved an Amendment which came into force on December 1, 1981. The Amendments allow owners to postpone fixing the CSC safety approval plates to containers until a new deadline of January 1, 1985. In addition, the Amendments defer for another two years the requirement for the marking of containers for their next examination. The new date is January 1, 1987. The extension of the periods were necessary in order to give owners more time in planning examination and plating schedules and also to even out the re-examination work load. However, IMO in agreeing to this extension, maintained the distinction between fixing the plates and their approval.

In June,1983 a second Amendment was approved which came into force on January 1, 1984. The Amendments extend the interval between re-examination to thirty months and permit a choice of container re-examination procedures between the original periodic examination scheme or a new continuous examination programme(1).

---

(1) In 1983, the MSC agreed that:
1. on the dissemination of MSC/Circ.361 urging Member Governments to ensure that containers owned by their national operators display the same markings for maximum gross weight, such as the ISO and other marks on the container, as on the CSC plate and that container handlers should ensure that any handling equipment used is adequate for lifting loaded containers;
2. that the benefits which might accrue from the ISO proposal for a consolidated data plate are not sufficient to justify the required changes to the CSC and other conventions; and
3. that air-mode containers, within the scope

Proposed Amendments

Certain amendments to CSC Annex 1 are being considered by the Maritime Safety Committee. The sub-committee on Containers and Cargoes, in the course of its work on a harmonized interpretation and implementation of CSC and the removal of obsolete requirements of the technical annexes, has recommended the amendment of Regulation 2 of Annex I. The proposed amendment will introduce the concept of a continuous examination programme as an alternative to the periodic examination scheme(1).

The sub-committee also suggested deleting paragraph 3 of Annex II under the heading "Construction". Instead it proposed that all maximum gross weight markings on containers should be consistent with the information on the CSC safety approval plate(2).

---

of Article III, would not come under the CSC and, if within the definition of Article II, air/surface (intermodal) containers would be covered by CSC and therefore require plating. See MSC 48/25, July 12, 1983, pp. 51,52.

(1) The MSC authorized the Sub-Committee on Containers and Cargoes to consider the problem of the continued occurrence of accidents involving overloaded containers. See MSC 51/10 of March 20, 1985.

(2) In 1984, a Working Group met to consider the problems encountered in repatriation, examination and plating existing containers. This Group recommended the following circular: "Contracting Parties to the International Convention for Safe Containers, 1972, will be aware that in accordance with Annex I, regulation 9 of the Convention, all existing containers should have a Safety Approval Plate affixed not later than 1 January, 1985.
At the Maritime Safety Committee's fiftieth session (19-30 November, 1984), concern was expressed by a number of delegations over the problems they were experiencing in meeting this target date owing to the difficulties as to the repatriation, examination and plating of containers in accordance with the provisions of the Convention. Concern was also expressed at the present restriction, in 9.3.1. of the Harmonized Interpretation (CSC/Circ.67) placed on the repatriation of loaded containers for

## Settlement of Disputes

The CSC contained rare and probably controversial provisions on the settlement of disputes between Contracting Parties. Article XIII states:

> "1. Any dispute between two or more Contracting Parties concerning the interpretation or application of the present Convention which cannot be settled by negotiation or other means of settlement shall, at the request of one of them, be referred to an arbitration tribunal composed as follows..."

Although reservations to the Convention are permitted as a general rule under Article XIV, no reservation is allowed to Articles I-VI and XIII Article XIII has not yet been put to the test. However, it would raise a number of questions:

1. What is the nature of the arbitration conducted under Article XIII - is it commercial arbitration or otherwise?
2. A dispute might be referred to arbitration if it is not possible to settle it by negotiation or *other means of settlement*. What is meant by other means of settlement? And how can an arbitration tribunal find that such means have been exhausted before ascertaining its jurisdiction?
3. Problems of enforcement will arise in case the disputes to the tribunal are considered to be of a non-commercial nature.

## Evaluation of the Convention

The CSC Convention generated a heated debate both within and outside IMO on the ways in which unsafe containers (which can be stopped under the CSC) may be distinguished from those which may simply have

---

plating. The Committee, after having given the matter careful consideration, invited Administrations, notwithstanding their national laws and regulations, to exercise flexibility in interpreting paragraphs 9.3.1 and 9.3.4 of the Harmonized Interpretations during the initial stages with regard to these concerns." See MSC 50/WP.12 of November 27, 1984.

missing or time-expired plates.

Delegates to IMO have reviewed several options such as labelling containers which in some way fall short of the requirements but which might still be allowed to proceed. However, there was a marked lack of experience in such systems of control and experts have decided that the time was not suitable for such a step. In fact, there are four main categories in this respect:

(a) those which are clearly unsafe and therefore liable to be stopped;

(b) those which are undamaged but which have a missing plate or have somehow never been plated;

(c) those with time-expired plates; and

(d) those which are damaged, but not so badly as to pose a risk to safety.

One can argue that containers in the last three categories should be allowed to proceed to their destinations, provided they are not re-stuffed until the requirements are complied with.

The CSC is also criticised with regard to the delegation of responsibility to classification societies and other inspection agencies. Some Contracting States have urged IMO to recommend that governments should only delegate the responsibilities to the leading classification societies, i.e. members of the International Association of Classification Societies.

The issue of delegation has been a controversial one for some time. Few classification societies have attempted, for commercial reasons, to accept slightly fewer tests on the containers. For this reason, voices were heard at the IMO that guidelines should be introduced on quality control - that is checking of production methods, the skills of the welders and the qualities of the materials used - as distinct from the testing of finished containers. On the other hand, it was argued that any guidelines would lead to a rigid system.

The enormous problems facing port authorities, governmental bodies and the transport industry, could only find solution in the light of the practical experience and within the framework of the IMO, and the CSC should be considered the first step in ensuring a safe container.

References

Agnew & Hunter, Container Stowage: A Practical Approach.

Containerization International, a monthly journal.

Containerization: a bibliography, published by Hatrics, Southampton.

Containerization: published by Journal de la Marine Marchande.

Customs Conventions on Containers, 1972.

Journal of ICHCA Cargo Systems: a monthly journal.

Maritime Transportation of Containerized Cargo, published by Netherlands Ship Research Centre.

# CHAPTER IV

# RULES ON SEAFARERS

For many years, the International Labour Organization (ILO)[1] has been active in formulating rules[2] for the employment, safety and welfare of seafarers[3]. The body of law in this area has grown considerably as it is constantly reviewed. In addition to the valuable work of the ILO, many non-governmental organizations such as the International Chamber of Shipping (ICS) have prepared a number of operational manuals[4] and safety

---

(1) The ILO was established by the Peace Treaty of 1919 and under the United Nations system it became a specialized agency of the UN. Its principal organs are: the International Labour Office; the Governing body; and the International Labour Conference.
(2) See Nagendra Singh, British Shipping Laws, Vol.8 on International Conventions of Merchant Shipping, pp.1131-1329.
(3) See the following conventions and recommendations:
- Convention for establishing Facilities for Finding Employment for Seamen (No.9 of 1920), *ibid*, p.1136-1139.
- Recommendations concerning the engagement of seafarers for service in vessels registered in a foreign country (No.107 of 1959), *ibid*, pp.1139-1140.
- Convention concerning Seamen's Article of Agreement (No.107 of 1958), *ibid*, pp.1140-1144.
- Recommendation concerning employment problems arising from technical developments on board ship (No.139 of 1970), *ibid*, pp.1144-1146.
- Recommendation concerning the Organization of Training for Sea Service (No.77 of 1946), pp.1146-1148.
- Recommendation concerning Vocational Training of Seafarers (No.137 of 1970), pp.1148-1153.
- Convention fixing the minimum age for admission of children to employment at Sea (No.7 of 1920), pp.1153-1155.
- Convention fixing the minimum age for the admission of children to employment at Sea (Revised 1936, No.58), *ibid*, pp.1155-1157.

(4) Operating manuals fall into two categories:
(a) operating and maintenance instructions provided by the manufacturers of specific equipment; and
(b) ship cargo operating manuals compiled by the shipbuilder or shipowner and related to a

guides[1].

In the early days, the IMO was content with a modest role of co-operation with the ILO and non-governmental organizations. However, the technical assistance programmes provided by the IMO revealed that seafarers in many developing countries are in need of proper training. Too often accidents are caused by human error of the personnel on board the ship and therefore it is necessary to make them fully competent in their work, acquire skills[2] and learn how to face unfamiliar situations. For these reasons, it was inevitable that the IMO would turn its attention to training and education. In 1978,

---

particular ship, its specific systems and flexibility.

Manufacturers' instructions are generally available to the ship and in most cases are in tune with the particular application of the equipment in a marine environment.

(1) See the ICS Tanker Safety Guide (Chemicals) which is a sister document to its Tanker Safety Guide (Petroleum). See also the ICS Tanker Safety Guide (Liquefied Gas).

(2) In *The "Farrandoc"* (1967) 2 Lloyd's Rep. 276, the Canadian Exch. Court found that the second engineer was not competent to be in charge of the engine-room and that there was no plan of the engine-room piping. Therefore, the *Farrandoc* was regarded as not properly manned and equipped and was to that extent unseaworthy. In this case, Thurslow, J., said (at p.282): "To my mind a person taking reasonable care for his own ship or cargo or seeking to discharge this obligation even when told that the person to be employed in a position involving responsibility held a qualifying certificate would scarcely fail to make further inquiries as to his ability and experience. Even after making such inquiries he would, in my opinion, inquire how far the man's experience fitted him for service in the particular ship and take steps to see that the man was adequately instructed with respect to any features of the particular ship with which it was necessary for him to be familiar to properly discharge the duties of his position and to avoid damage to the ship and her cargo. Here it was not established that any such inquiries were made or that any sufficient steps were taken to ensure that Humble (the second engineer) would

it adopted the Convention on Standards of Training and Watchkeeping for Seafarers (STCW) and established the World Maritime University (WMU)(1) at Malmo (Sweden). The STCW Convention serves as a framework for national regulations but it is too early to assess the contribution of the WMU to the shipping community.

It would be beyond the scope of this work to cover fully the rules on seafarers and only the issues in which the IMO were involved mainly

---

be adequately instructed."
Noel, J., in the same case, took a different view when he stated (at p.287): "Humble (the second engineer), being 38 years of age, and holding the above certificate from a public body, could be engaged without any question on the strength of this certificate and although I would see no harm in questioning him further with regard to his past experience or conduct, I do not think that the fact he was not questioned would, in the particular circumstances of the present case, constitute a want of due diligence on the part of the owner of the vessel or even that any questioning or investigating would have disclosed anything useful in determining whether he would be adequate to fulfil the not too exacting duties of a second engineer on board the vessel."
See also *The Makedonia* (1962) 1 Lloyd's Rep. 316 which dealt with the inadequacy of inquiries to discover the record and competence of a chief engineer and the duty of the shipowner to exercise proper care in the appointment of both the chief and the second engineer.

(1) The University is concerned with training teachers, surveyors and administrators for developing countries. Therefore, it is difficult to accept the argument that the WMU will ensure the implementation of the IMO Conventions and Protocols. When the University becomes a centre of research, this would be an important factor in developing the international rules on shipping adopted by the IMO.

manning[1] and training[2] will be considered.

(1) For the ILO manning rules, see the Convention concerning the Hours of Work on Board Ship and Manning (57 of 1936). Singh, British Shipping Laws, Vol.8, p.1176; Recommendation concerning Hours of Work on Board Ship and Manning (49 of 1936) *ibid*, p.1183; Conventions concerning Wages, Hours of Work on Board Ship and Manning (76 of 1946) (93 of 1949) (109 of 1949), *ibid*, pp.1185-1203.

(2) For ILO rules on training, see Recommendation concerning the Organisation of Training for Sea Service (77 of 1946) *ibid*, p.1146; Recommendation concerning Vocational Training of Seafarers (137 of 1970) *ibid*, p.1148; Convention concerning the Certification of Able Seamen (74 of 1946) *ibid*, p.1167; Convention concerning Certification of Ships' Cooks (69 of 1946) *ibid*, p.1173.

(i) RULES ON MANNING

At common law[1], any person sending a ship to sea is required to ensure that it is seaworthy, i.e. fit in all respects and capable of completing her voyage. The physical fitness of the ship includes the existence of the required equipment, proper stowage[2] and safe manning. Whether the ship is safely manned depends on the trading area and the nature of the service for which the ship is intended[3]. In fact, the safe manning means that the ship has sufficient officers and ratings with appropriate skills and experience to ensure the performance of the ten following duties (the so-called ten commandments)[4].

---

(1) Under American Law, the concept of seaworthiness is very wide and it has been described as "a child of 20th century Federal Jurisprudence". It has grown far beyond the one adopted by English Law. It is not limited to physical fitness of the vessel but includes non-physical matters, i.e. financial difficulties of the shipowner. Some American commentators proposed the application of the rules on negligence to determine whether the ship is seaworthy or not. See note on Risk Distribution and Unseaworthiness, 75 Yale L.J. (1966), p.1174.

(2) Bad stowage may affect the safety of the vessel or it may damage the cargo stowed or other cargoes. Only in the first case where bad stowage endangers the vessel, it amounts to unseaworthiness. See *Canadian Transport Co. Ltd.* v. *Court Line Ltd.* (1940) 3 All E.R. 112; *The "Aga"* (1968) 1 Lloyd's Rep. 431; *The "Anthony II"* (1966) 2 Lloyd's Rep. 437.
Closely connected with this point is the issue of cargo-unworthiness which arises when the cargo already in the vessel's hold is of such a nature that it will readily damage the cargo which is subsequently loaded therein. But bad stowage which affects nothing but the cargo damaged, is just bad stowage and nothing more. In such a case the vessel is still considered to be seaworthy.

(3) See sections 458-459 of the Merchant Shipping Acts 1894; section 45 of the Merchant Shipping Act 1970; and section 44 of the Merchant Shipping Act 1979.

(4) See the IMO Resolution A.481 (XII). See also the Guidelines for the Application of Principles

1. maintaining a safe bridge watch in accordance with Regulation II/I of the 1978 STCW Convention(1);
2. mooring and unmooring the vessel effectively and safely;
3. maintaining all watertight closing arrangements;
4. operating all fire equipment and life saving appliances;
5. managing the safety functions of the ship when it is not under way;
6. maintaining a safe engineering watch at sea in accordance with Regulation III/I of the 1978 STCW Convention;
7. operating in a safe condition the main propulsion and auxiliary machinery;
8. keeping machinery spaces clean to minimise the risk of fire;
9. providing medical care; and
10. maintaining a safe radio watch in accordance with 1974 SOLAS and the ITU Regulations as amended.

---

of Safe Manning; M.Notice 1178, 1985. The introduction states: "These guidelines should be used in applying the basic principles of safe manning to ensure the safe operation of ships covered by Article III of the 1978 STCW Convention. This application may differ depending upon such factors as:
1. voyage description including trade or trades in which the ship is involved, length and nature of voyage, and waters;
2. number, size (kW) and type of main propulsion units and auxiliaries;
3. size of ship;
4. construction and technical equipment of ship."

(1) A bridge watch must consist of one officer and at least one deck rating and, when appropriate, a helmsman. In clear waters and by day the rating need not be present on the bridge, provided he is on duty in the immediate vicinity of the bridge and on immediate call. In all other circumstances, such as by night, or when the vessel is in congested waters, or in poor

The Safe Manning Scheme: In order to minimize the risk of delays and difficulties for UK ships in foreign ports, the Department of Trade has operated since 1977 a voluntary Safe Manning Scheme. The scheme includes engineer officers and engine-room ratings, radio officers, ships' doctors(1) and cooks(2). After an individual assessment of each ship, a Safe Manning Certificate is issued.

The Merchant Shipping (Certification of Deck Officers) Regulations, 1983(3) states in section 4 (1): "Every ship to which the Regulations apply shall carry such number of qualified deck officers as is required by Part II of these Regulations."

For manning purposes, the trading areas fall into three categories: Near Continental trading area; Middle trading area; and unlimited trading area(4). The following tables show the minimum required number.

---

visibility, or when in the proximity of navigational hazards, the rating must be present on the bridge to assist the officer of the watch.

(1) See the Merchant Shipping (Ships' Doctors) Regulations, 1981 (S.I.1065/81).

(2) The Merchant Shipping (Certification of Ships' Cooks) Regulations, 1981 (S.I.1076/81).

(3) S.I.1306/85.

(4) Near Continental trading area: any location within the area bounded by a line from a point on the Norwegian coast in latitude $62^{\circ}$ North to a point $62^{\circ}$N $02^{\circ}$W, thence to a point $58^{\circ}$N $10^{\circ}$W, thence to a point $51^{\circ}$N $12^{\circ}$W, thence to Brest, but excluding all waters which lie to the eastward of a line drawn between Kristiansand, Norway, and Hanstholm Lighthouse on the North Danish Coast.
Middle trading area: any location not within the Near Continental trading area but within an area (which includes places in the Baltic Sea) bounded by the northern shore of Vest Fjord (Norway) and a line joining Skomvaer Lighthouse (latitude $67^{\circ}$ 25IN, longitude $11^{\circ}$ 53IE) to a point $62^{\circ}$N $02^{\circ}$W, thence to a point $58^{\circ}$N $10^{\circ}$W, thence to a point $51^{\circ}$N $12^{\circ}$W, thence to a point $41^{\circ}9'$N $10^{\circ}$W, thence to Oporto. This includes UK oil concessions on the continental shelf.
Unlimited trading area: any location not within the Middle Trade or Near Continental trading area.

PASSENGER SHIPS

| Column 1 | Column 2 | Column 3 | | | | |
|---|---|---|---|---|---|---|
| | Description of passenger ships | Minimum number of certificated officers to be carried | | | | |
| | | Class 1 Cert | Class 2 Cert | Class 3 Cert | Class 4 Cert | Class 5 Cert |
| Unlimited or Middle Trade | Any tonnage | 1 | 1 | 1 | 1 | - |
| Near Continental | 2,000 GRT and over | 1 | 1 | - | 1 | - |
| | 1,000 GRT but under 2,000 GRT | 1 | - | - | 1 | - |
| | 200 GRT but under 1,000 GRT | | - | - | 1 | 1 |
| | Under 200 GRT | - | - | - | - | 1 |

SHIPS OTHER THAN PASSENGER SHIPS AND TUGS

| Column 1 | Column 2 | Column 3 | | | | |
|---|---|---|---|---|---|---|
| Trading Area | Descriptions of ships | Minimum number of certificated Officers to be carried | | | | |
| | | Class 1 Cert | Class 2 Cert | Class 3 Cert | Class 4 Cert | Class 5 Cert |
| Unlimited | 1,600GRT and over | 1 | 1 | 1 | 1 | - |
| | under 1,600 GRT | 1 | 1 | 1 | - | - |
| Middle Trade | 5,000 GRT and over | 1 | 1 | 1 | 1 | - |
| | 1,600 GRT but under 5,000 GRT | - | - | 1 | 1 | 1 |
| | under 1,600 GRT | - | - | - | 2 | 1 |
| Near Continental | 10,000 GRT and over | 1 | 1 | 1 | - | - |
| | 5,000 GRT but under 10,000 GRT | 1 | - | 1 | 1 | - |
| | 1,600 GRT but under 5,000 GRT | - | - | - | 2 | 1 |
| | 800 GRT but under 1,600 GRT | - | - | - | - | 3 |
| | 200 GRT but under 800 GRT | - | - | - | - | 2 |
| | under 200 GRT | - | - | - | - | 1 |

## MINIMUM CERTIFICATION REQUIREMENTS OF ENGINEER OFFICERS

| Column 1 | Column 2 | Column 3 | |
|---|---|---|---|
| Area | Registered power (kilowatts) of ships including sail training ships | Required classes of certification | |
| | | Chief Engineer Officer | Second Engineer Officer |
| Unlimited or Middle Trade | 3,000 and over | 1 | 2 |
| | 750 or more but under 3,000 | 2(e) | 3 |
| | 350 or more but under 750 | 3(e) | 4 |
| Near Continental | 6,000 and over | 1 | 2 |
| | 3,000 or more but under 6,000 | 2(e) | 3 |
| | 750 or more but under 3,000 | 3(e) | - |
| | 350 or more but under 750 | 4(e) | - |

(ii) RULES ON TRAINING AND CERTIFICATION

The importance of training was recognised by the IMO from its early days. Its recommendation No.39 called for practicable steps to ensure that the education and training of seafarers in the use of aids to navigation, ship's equipment and devices was comprehensive.

In 1964, a committee on training was established by the IMO/ILO. It published a document called Code for Guidance which contained information on the education and training of masters, officers and seamen in the use and operation of aids to navigation, life-saving appliances, devices for the prevention, detection and extinction of fires and other ship's equipment contributing to safety at sea. The Code was subsequently amended in 1970(1), 1975 and 1977.

Despite the valuable work done by the ILO, IMO and indeed many non-governmental organizations, there were still further measures needed to strengthen and improve standards of training and qualifications. Shipping is the scene of intense change. Specialized ships and new technology are among the forces driving change on and is now faster than ever before. The revolution in information technology has led to the disappearance of many traditional jobs and to far-reaching changes in the structure and content of others. New patterns of work are also emerging. In fact, the direction and pace of change places great emphasis on competence and adaptability of the officers and crew. All these considerations highlight the connection between training, safety, business performance and organizational effectiveness. The IMO realised that there must be a policy for the development and use of human resources. A policy that recognizes that if seafarers are to make a contribution to safety and at the same time make a company succeed or fail,

---

(1) The Sub-Committee on Ship Design and Equipment stated in view of the substantial increase in the quantities of hazardous cargoes in bulk carried by sea and the potential hazards to ships' personnel and to the environment, the personnel manning such ships should possess appropriate specialist knowledge. It prepared a programme of training and recommended that it would be added as a new section to the Code of Guidance 1970. See DE VII/3/2, August 25, 1971.

spending on their training is an investment. To meet all these aspirations, the IMO Assembly decided in 1971 to convene a conference to adopt a Convention on this subject. The preparation of the Convention took seven years and in 1978, the Convention on Standards of Training, Certification and Watchkeeping for Seafarers (STCW) was adopted.

To the Convention, an Annex and a number of resolutions were attached. The question is: how do these arrangements match up to the increasing demands being placed upon seafarers? The answer is that the Convention is the framework and more work will follow[(1)]. However, one of the problems is that training has generally been seen as a technical matter and overwhelmingly about technical skills within restricted occupational ranges.

## 1. THE CONVENTION

The Convention deals with various issues usually to be found in every international convention such as the promotion of technical co-operation (a matter of a political aspiration rather than a legal duty), signature, ratification, coming into force[(2)], amendments[(3)], denunciation and the official language. The articles on these issues are clear and will not give rise to any difficulties. However, the main features of the Convention could be illustrated by considering the scope of application;

---

(1) The IMO/ILO Committee on Training held a meeting in December 1985 to consider the proposed revised Document for Guidance 1975. The Sub-Committee on Standards of Training and Watch-keeping approved in 1984 the terms of reference for the development of detailed teaching syllabuses, frameworks of model courses and specimen examination papers. MSC 50/12, July 20, 1984. See also C54/22(c) of April 12, 1985, p.15.

(2) The Convention came into force on April 28, 1984.

(3) The Convention incorporates in article XII a tacit acceptance procedure. Amendments to the Annex will enter into force two and a half years after being communicated to all Parties unless in the meantime they are rejected by one-third of the Parties or by Parties whose combined fleets represent 50 per cent of World tonnage.

certificate of competency; dispensation and the control measures.

The scope of application: The provisions of the Convention apply to ships of non-party States when visiting ports of States which are Parties to the Convention. Article X requires Parties to the Convention to apply the control measures to ships of all flags to the extent necessary to ensure that no more favourable treatment is given to ships entitled to fly the flag of a State which is not Party than is given to ships entitled to fly the flag of a State that is a Party.

It must be noted that International Law empowers the coastal State to apply the provisions of the Convention to a ship of a non-party State when visiting its port or being within its territorial waters not as a STCW Convention but as part of its national law.

The certificates of competency: Every officer of a sea-going ship shall hold an appropriate certificate of competency. Article VI states that the certificates "shall be issued to those candidates who, to the satisfaction of the administration, meet the requirements for service, age, medical fitness, training, qualification and examinations in accordance with the appropriate provisions of the Annex."

Article VI goes on to state that the certificates for master and officers must be endorsed by the issuing administration in the form prescribed by Regulation I/2. This regulation specifies that the certificates shall be in the official language of the issuing country but if the language used is not English, the text shall include a translation into that language.

Closely connected with this issue is Resolution 21 which invites the IMO to develop a standard form and title for an international certificate of competence, in the same manner in which the International Telecommunications Convention specifies the title of Radio Officers' certificates.

Dispensation: Article VIII defines the conditions in which an administration may issue a dispensation permitting a seafarer to serve in a specified ship for a certain period in a capacity for which he does not hold the appropriate certificate. Dispensations can only be issued "in circumstances of exceptional necessity" and their effective period must not exceed six months. In the case of Masters and Chief

Engineers, these dispensations may only be issued in circumstances of "force majeure" such as a sudden illness. The philosophy behind granting dispensations is to make their use for the shortest possible period.

<u>The control measure</u>: In order to ensure strict adherence to the provisions of the Convention, limited power of control was given to the authorised port officers. The inspection is limited to two issues mainly to:

(a) verify that all seafarers serving on board are so certificated or hold an appropriate dispensation; and

(b) assess the ability of seafarers to maintain the required watchkeeping standards if believing that such standards are not being maintained[1].

Even within this limited area of inspection, Regulation I/4 spells out the grounds upon which the standards were not adhered to; these being:

1. The ship has been involved in a collision, grounding or stranding.

2. There has been a discharge of substances from the ship when underway, at anchor or at berth which is illegal under international conventions.

3. The ship has been manoeuvred in an erratic or unsafe manner or navigational course markers or traffic separation schemes have not been followed.

These grounds are exhaustive. Any deficiencies have to be reported to the master and the authorities of the flag State. Paragraph 3 of Regulation I/4 provides that the only cases for which a ship could be detained are:

---

(1) The US Coast Guards frequently ask an officer who holds a certificate showing that he is qualified in the operational use of ARPA, to demonstrate before them his ability to do so.

1. Failure of the master, chief engineer officers, officers in charge of navigational and engineering watches and, where relevant, the radio officer to have an appropriate valid certificate or valid dispensation.
2. Failure of navigational or engineering watch arrangements to conform to the requirements specified for the ship by the flag State.

The power of control is even further weakened by paragraph 4 of article X which states that all possible efforts shall be made to avoid a ship being unduly detained or delayed and that if a ship is so detained it shall be entitled to compensation for any loss or damage resulting therefrom(1).

## 2. THE ANNEX

Six chapters of the Annex spell out the detailed requirements of the Convention. They carry the following titles: I. General provisions; II. Master-deck department; III. Engine department; IV. Radio department; V. Special requirements for tankers; and VI. Proficiency in survival craft.

Chapter I - General Provisions: This chapter opens with a list of definitions of the terms used in the Annex. The purpose of these definitions is to assist the Contracting States in reaching a harmonized interpretation of the various requirements(2). However, the Sub-Committee on Standards of Training and Watchkeeping felt that there is still a need for approving a harmonized interpretation of certain

(1) The MSC considered a harmonized interpretation of certain provisions of the Convention and circulated its views for the advice of Member Governments. See C54/22(c), p.15. Also a joint FAO/ILO/IMO working group commenced developing a document for guidance on fishermen's training and certification. *Ibid*, at p.15.

(2) One of the disadvantages of these definitions is that some of them may soon appear to be inadequate in view of the developments in technology.

provisions of the Convention[1].

Regulation I/2 deals with the content of certificate and the endorsement form. All certificates must have a translation into English.

The requirements of the Annex may be waived for seafarers on ships engaged on "near-coastal voyages" which are defined in Regulation I/1 as "voyages in the vicinity of a Party as defined by that Party". This is hardly a definition as the matter is left entirely to the Coastal State. In fact, the reason for introducing the term "near-coastal voyages" was to provide some relaxation from the compulsory requirements. It was left to Regulation I/3 to provide for the applicable rules to be followed in this respect. They are intended to secure equal treatment for all ships trading on similar voyages and to prevent applying the exclusion to ships going beyond the near-coastal voyages.

The equal treatment duty towards all ships implies that no Party is allowed to impose training, experience or certification requirements to seafarers serving on board ships entitled to fly the flag of another State and engaged on near-coastal voyages in a manner resulting in a more stringent way for such seafarers than for seafarers serving on board a ship entitled to fly their own flag. At any rate, the requirements in respect of seafarers serving on board ships engaged in near-coastal voyages shall not exceed the requirements of the Convention in respect of ships engaged on longer voyages.

Regulation I/4 deals with control procedures and elaborates on article X. Control is limited to checking the certificates of personnel and assessing the ability of seafarers to maintain convention standards in certain eventualities, such as the ship's involvement in a collision or grounding, the discharge of an illegal substance or erratic or unsafe manoeuvring.

Certificates issued by another contracting State must be recognized[2] unless these are fraudulently obtained for the purpose of seeking

---

(1) See MSC 50/12, July 20, 1984.

(2) See M.Notice 1129 which states that certain certificates of competency issued by a number of Commonwealth countries and the Republic of Ireland are recognised as valid for service on UK ships in capacities for which there is a statutory requirement for certificated officers.

employment[1]. The officer carrying out the control is also required to give a written notification of the grounds on which the ship has been detained, and to specify the deficiencies which may cause hazards to persons, property or the environment.

Chapter II - The Deck Department: This chapter stipulates the basic principles to be observed in keeping a navigational watch and covers matters such as watch arrangements, fitness for duty, navigational equipment, duties and liabilities.

Regulations II/2, II/3 and II/4 prescribe the mandatory minimum requirements for certification of Masters, Chief Mates and officers in charge of navigational watches on ships of various sizes engaged on near-coastal voyages or on unrestricted voyages. The steps of the sub-division which take account of the size of the ship are stipulated at 200 and 1600 gross tons. In addition, further sub-division is made of ships of "limited size" engaged on near-coastal voyages without defining any numerical limits for the tonnage of such ships. In fact the Convention does not impose any pattern of certification on the Parties and leaves each country the freedom to adopt a suitable system with regard to the number of certificates and the sizes of the ships on near-coastal voyages.

The appendices to the regulations give the minimum knowledge for the certification of Masters, Chief Mates and officers but the level and the depth of knowledge required under the different headings of each appendix is left to the administration[2].

---

(1) See M.Notice 1067 concerning a seaman who has been convicted at Liverpool Magistrates Court under s.16 of the Theft Act, 1968, for fraudulently obtaining employment. He had claimed to be the holder of a Certificate of Competency of Master (Foreign-Going) when, in fact, his only qualification was that of Efficient Deck Hand. He had gained employment as Master on two ships and attempted to gain employment on a third ship.

(2) See The Merchant Shipping (Navigational Watch Ratings) Regulations,1984 (S.I.96/1984). The Regulations provide that only ratings who are qualified in accordance with these Regulations may form part of a navigational watch on certain sea-going United Kingdom ships of 200 GRT or over. Other ratings may participate in navigat-

Regulation II/5 defines the mandatory minimum requirements to ensure the continued Proficiency and Updating of Knowledge for Masters and Deck Officers(1). Requirements for deck ratings forming part of a navigational watch, form the subject of Regulation II/6. Ratings who comply with this regulation must be not less than 16 years old. They should have completed at least six months of service at sea or undergone special training.

---

ional watchkeeping duties only as part of their training under the supervision of a qualified deck officer or navigational watch rating.
The necessary qualification is to have a valid certificate certifying that the holder has complied with the specified requirements.
See, for the detailed requirements, M.Notice 1096.

It is an offence for an employer to fail to ensure that sufficient qualified ratings are carried to enable the master to perform his duties. It is also an offence for the master to permit an unqualified rating to form part of a navigational watch or to perform duties for which he is not qualified.

(1) M.Notice 1107 states:
A certificate of competency or service held by a master or deck officer will remain valid for sea-going service in any capacity appropriate to the certificate, on any ship to which the Decks Officer Regulations apply, for a period of 5 years from 28 April, 1984, or from its date of issue if later, subject to the holder being medically fit for such service. Thereafter, the certificate will only remain valid for sea-going service as a master or deck officer, as the case may be, for a further 5 year period if the holder has either:
(a) served as a master or deck officer in sea-going ships of any flag, other than pleasure craft of less than 80 GRT and fishing vessels, for at least 12 months (which need not be continuous) during the preceding 5 years; or
(b) satisfactorily completed either:
  (i) an approved shore-based updating course in accordance with the outline syllabus at Annex I to this Notice; or
  (ii) not less than 3 months sea-going service as a supernumary deck officer

The last two regulations are devoted to the basic principles to be observed in keeping watch in port(1) and mandatory minimum requirements for a watch in port on ships carrying hazardous cargo.

Chapter III - Engine Department: This chapter follows the format of Chapter II and opens with a regulation which outlines the basic principles to be observed in keeping an engineering watch.

While requirements for deck officers vary according to the tonnage of the ship, for engineer officers the determining factor is the size of the engine. Regulation III/2 deals with mandatory minimum requirements for certification of chief engineer officers and second engineer officers of ships powered by main propulsion machinery of 3,000 kW propulsion power or more. Candidates for certification as second engineers must have not less than 12 months' sea-going experience as engineer officers or assistants. Candidates as chief engineers must have at least 36 months' sea-going experience, including at least 12 months as an engineer officer in a position of responsibility while qualified to serve as second engineer officer. They must have attended an approved fire-fighting course and have passed an examination covering subjects listed in an appendix.

Regulation III/3 contains similar requirements for ships with main propulsion machinery between 750 kW and 3,000 kW. The main difference between this and the previous regulation is that the requirement for previous service for candidates as chief engineers is reduced from 36 months to 24. Officers

---

immediately prior to sea-going employment in a capacity in respect of which a certificate is required; provided that sea-going service of not less than 3 months in any deck officer capacity performed immediately prior to the expiry of validity of a certificate for sea-going service will be accepted in lieu of the supernumerary service specified.

The Refresher/Up-dating Training Syllabus for Shore-based Courses covers: Safe navigation and anti-collision; the carriage and handling of cargo; operation of ships; and ship personnel matters.

(1) See M.Notice 1016.

qualified to serve as second engineers on ships of 3,000 kW or more may serve as chief engineers of ships of lesser power, provided that not less than 12 months' approved sea-going service shall have been served as an engineer officer in a position of responsibility.

Regulation III/4 contains mandatory minimum requirements for certification of engineer officers in charge of a watch in a traditionally manned engine room or designated duty officers in a periodically unmanned engine room. The minimum age requirement is 18 and candidates must also have not less than three years' approved training or education and have completed an adequate period of sea-going service. Candidates must have knowledge of the operation and maintenance of marine machinery, together with a knowledge of watchkeeping routines; main and auxiliary machinery; pumping systems; generating plant safety and emergency procedures; anti-pollution procedures; and first aid.

Other regulations cover the proficiency and updating of knowledge[1] and that the minimum age of

---

(1) See M.Notice 1106 which states:
A certificate of competency or service held by an engineer officer will remain valid for sea service in any capacity appropriate to that certificate, on any ship to which the Engineer Officers Regulations apply for a period of 5 years from 28 April 1984, or from its date of issue if later, subject to the holder being medically fit for such service. Thereafter the certificate wll only remain valid for services in the highest rank appropriate to that certificate if the holder has served as an engineer officer on a sea-going ship of any flag for at least 12 months (which need not be continuous) during the preceding 5 years.
Where a certificate holder has not served sufficient time on board sea-going vessels to satisfy the requirements of the above paragraph, he will be able to serve on ships to which these Regulations apply in ranks below that to which his certificate is appropriate (i.e. Chief Engineer Officers may sail as Second Engineer Officers, Second Engineer Officers as Senior Engineer Watchkeepers, and Senior Engineer Watchkeepers as second in charge of a watch). After 3 months sea service at this lower rank his certificate will automatically become valid for any appropriate rank.

a rating forming part of an engine room watch is 16[1].

Chapter IV - Radio Department: Training of radio officers and operators is subject not only to the STCW and SOLAS Conventions but it is also governed by the rules laid down by the International Telecommunications Union (ITU).

Regulation IV/1 (mandatory minimum requirements for certification of radio officers) states that radio officers must hold a certificate issued under the provisions of the Radio Regulations and have adequate qualifying service[2]. Radio officers must

---

(1) See The Merchant Shipping (Engine Room Watch Ratings) Regulations, 1984 (S.I.95/1984). The Regulations provide that only ratings who are qualified in accordance with these Regulations, or ratings whose duties while on watch are of an unskilled nature, may form part of an engine room watch on certain sea-going United Kingdom ships having registered power of 750 kW or more. Other ratings may participate in engine room watchkeeping duties only as part of their training under the supervision of a qualified engineer officer or engine room watch rating. It is an offence for an employer to fail to ensure that sufficient qualified ratings are carried to enable the master and chief engineer officer to perform their duties. It is also an offence for the master and chief engineer officer to permit an unqualified rating to form part of an engine room watch, other than those whose duties while on watch are of an unskilled nature.

(2) The Merchant Shipping (Radio Installations) (Amendment) Regulations,1984 came into operation on 28 April,1984 (S.I.346/1984). These Regulations provide that holders of a valid certificate of competency as a radio officer or radiotelephone operator issued on or after 28 April 1984 (and a valid Authority to Operate) shall, in order to be qualified to serve in a capacity in UK ships which requires such a certificate, also hold a certificate (here called a Convention certificate) confirming that the holder satisfies the additional knowledge and training requirements of the Convention. These are set out in a schedule to the Regulations.
See also The Merchant Shipping (Radio Installat-

also be over 18 and have passed an examination which shall take into account subjects listed in an appendix, particularly concerned with safety and emergencies. Other regulations deal with the proficiency and updating of knowledge of radio officers and establish minimum requirements for certification of radiotelephone operators.

Chapter V - Special Requirements for Tankers: The employment of chemical, gas and oil tankers is associated with certain hazards such as pollution, explosion and fire. Accidents on these specialized ships may be due to a variety of causes, one of which could be the lack of knowledge and ability of personnel to take the right action. Therefore,

---

ions( (Amendment No.2) Regulations, 1984 (S.I. 1223/1984).

M.Notice 1123 requires additional knowledge on the following topics:

(a) The provision of radio services in emergencies including:
  (i) abandon ship;
  (ii) fire aboard ship;
  (iii) partial or full breakdown of the radio station.

(b) The operation of lifeboats, liferafts, buoyant apparatus and their equipment, with special reference to portable and fixed lifeboat radio apparatus and emergency position-indicating radio beacons.

(c) Survival at sea.

(d) First aid.

(e) Fire prevention and fire-fighting with particular reference to the radio installation.

(f) Preventative measures for the safety of ship and personnel in connection with hazards related to radio equipment including electrical, radiation, chemical and mechanical hazards.

(g) The use of the IMO Merchant Ship Search and Rescue Manual (MERSAR) with particular reference to radiocommunications.

(h) Ship position-reporting systems and procedures.

(i) The use of the International Code of Signals and the IMO Standard Marine Navigational Vocabulary.

(j) Radio medical systems and procedures.

special training is necessary to reduce human error. It must be noted that good basic design and strict adherence to the Codes of Practice could be controlled by legislation whereas training, even at the highest standard, must always be subject to more intangible factors.

Thus, the aim of the special training is to equip the personnel concerned with the knowledge, skills and experience in order to operate the ship efficiently and safely.

All crew members should receive a basic safety introduction to the hazards and precautions associated with the vessel. The topics to be covered are, broadly:

- Health hazard and precautions;
- Safety equipment and its use;
- Familiarisation with emergency procedures;
- General description of ship type and its cargo handling equipment; and
- Fire fighting.

Preferably this training would be given prior to joining the ship or, if this is impracticable, at least as soon as possible after joining the ship.

Those officers, and ratings, if any who are involved in the cargo handling processes or otherwise concerned with the associated equipment, should receive further operational safety training covering the following topics:

- Introduction to the properties of the cargo;
- The types of cargo to be carried and their main properties;
- The types of ships and their containment systems;
- The safety implications of the ship and its cargo;
- An outline of operation cycles and procedures;
- The importance of ship/terminal liaison; and
- Emergency procedures.

It is impossible to predict the nature of all types of potential emergency, but it is possible to make the personnel familiar with certain situations to:

- Locate the incident;
- Raise the alarm;

- Assess the nature, magnitude and implications of the incident;
- Organise and implement a plan of attack which employs the full manpower and equipment resources available on board;
- Decide whether the stopping of all or some cargo operations is prudent; and
- Take action to protect all personnel whether involved or not in the procedures being implemented.

Chapter V contains three regulations dealing with oil tankers, chemical tankers and liquefied gas tankers(1).

<u>Chapter VI - Proficiency in Survival Craft</u>: This chapter establishes requirements governing the issuing of certificates of proficiency in survival

---

(1) See The Merchant Shipping (Tankers - Officers and Ratings) Regulations, 1984 (S.I.94/1984) (came into operation on April 28, 1984). The Regulations provide that only officers and ratings who are qualified in accordance with these Regulations and those officers whose certificates of competency or of service are endorsed with an appropriate dangerous cargo endorsement may perform duties in connection with the cargo and cargo equipment of sea-going United Kingdom tankers. The necessary qualifications are to have served for at least six months in the period of five years up to April 28, 1984, in a tanker of the type concerned as part of the regular crew complement or to have completed specified training and periods of supervised service. Other officers and ratings under training may participate in these duties only under supervision of qualified personnel. It is an offence under the Regulations for the master to permit an unqualified officer or rating to perform duties in connection with the cargo and cargo equipment of tankers, and for the employer to fail to ensure that sufficient qualified officers and ratings are carried to perform such duties.
See also M.Notice 1091 on Training of Crews of Petroleum, Liquid Chemical and Liquefied Gas Tankers, dated January, 1984.

craft. These include approved sea-going service of not less than 12 months, or nine months if the candidate has attended an approved training course. There is provision for testing 'by examination or continuous assessment during an approved training course'. An appendix lists the minimum knowledge required for the issue of certificates of proficiency(1).

## 3. THE RESOLUTIONS

Since some of the provisions of the Chapters in the Annex are expressed in a fairly general language, it was necessary for the Conference to attach to the Convention a number of resolutions to indicate the work to follow and to ensure that training and retraining will keep pace with technological change.

Resolution 1 is related to Regulation II/1 on basic principles to be observed in keeping a navigational watch. An annex contains a recommendation on operational guidance for officers in charge of a navigational watch.

Resolution 2 is on Operational guidance for engineer officers in charge of an engineering watch. It relates to Regulation III/1. The Annex deals with engineering watch underway and at an unsheltered anchorage(2).

---

(1) See The Merchant Shipping (Certificates of Proficiency in Survival Craft) Regulations, 1984 (S.I.97/1984). These Regulations prescribe requirements for the issue of certificates of proficiency in survival craft. More detailed requirements are specified in M.Notice 1092.

(2) Regulation 5 of The Merchant Shipping (Certification and Watchkeeping) Regulations, 1982 (S.I.1699/1982), which came into operation on April 28, 1984, requires Chief Engineers when deciding the composition of the watch to take into account the principles set out in Schedule 2 of the Regulations and the operational guidance specified by the Secretary of State. The operational guidance specified by the Secretary of State is set out in the Appendix to M.Notice 1103.

Resolution 3 is concerned with Principles and operational guidance for deck officers in charge of a watch in port [(1)].

Resolution 4 is on Principles and operational guidance for engineer officers in charge of an engineering watch in port. It relates to Regulation III/1, with recommendations in an annex.

Resolution 5 deals with Basic guidelines and operational guidance relating to safety radio watchkeeping and maintenance for radio officers. The comprehensive annex is divided into basic guidelines and safety radio watchkeeping and maintenance.

Resolution 6 is on Basic guidelines and operational guidance relating to safety radio watchkeeping for radio telephone operators. It follows the same format as Resolution 5.

Resolution 7 is on Radio operators. Four recommendations are annexed to this resolution dealing with (i) minimum requirements for certification of radio officers; (ii) minimum requirements to ensure the continued proficiency and updating of knowledge for radio operators; (iii) basic guidelines and operational guidance relating to safety radio watchkeeping and maintenance for radio operators; and (iv) training for radio operators.

Resolution 8 is concerned with Additional training for ratings forming part of a navigational watch. It relates to Regulation II/6 and recommends that such ratings be trained in use and operation of appropriate bridge equipment and basic requirements for the prevention of pollution.

Resolution 9 is on Minimum requirements for a rating nominated as the assistant to the engineer officer in charge of the watch. It recognizes that suitable training arrangements are not widely available. Detailed requirements are contained in an annex.

Resolution 10 is on Training and qualifications of officers and ratings of oil tankers. It refers to Resolution 8 adopted by the International Conference on Tanker Safety and Pollution Prevention, 1978,

---

(1) M.Notice 1016 contains recommendations on principles and operational guidance for deck

which deals with the improvement of standards of crews on tankers[1].

<u>Resolution 11</u> is on Training and qualifications of officers and ratings of chemical tankers. It refers to Resolution 286 (VIII) adopted by the IMO Assembly which deals with training. Recommendations are contained in an annex.

<u>Resolution 12</u> is on Training and qualification of masters, officers and ratings of liquefied gas tankers[2].

---

officers in charge of a watch in port. The Recommendation applies to ships which are safely moored or safely at anchor under normal circumstances in port and where the master has decided in the prevailing conditions that a navigational watch need not be kept.

Watch Arrangement:

1. Arrangements for keeping a watch when the ship is in port should:
   (a) ensure the safety of life, ship, cargo and port;
   (b) observe international, national and local rules;
   (c) maintain order and the normal routine of the ship.
2. The ship's master should decide the composition and duration of the watch depending on the conditions of mooring, type of ship and character of duties.
3. A qualified deck officer should be in charge of the watch, except in ships under 500 gross register tons not carrying dangerous cargo, in which case the master may appoint whoever has appropriate qualifications to keep the watch in port.
4. The necessary equipment should be so arranged as to provide for efficient watchkeeping.

(1) See Training Bulletin No. 3-75 of the Merchant Navy Training Board which advises companies of the Board's recommendations for the training of crews of oil tankers and similar vessels carrying hazardous cargoes in bulk.

(2) See also M.Notice 771 in which it is stated that the Department of Trade considers that all personnel should receive a basic safety induction to the main hazards associated with the transport of oil, chemicals and liquefied

Resolution 13 is on Training and qualifications of officers and ratings of ships carrying dangerous and hazardous cargo other than in bulk. It recognizes that there is an urgent need for establishing such training requirements and invited the IMO to study this problem as a matter of urgency.

Resolution 14 is on Training for radio officers. It recognizes that despite adoption of Regulation IV/1, additional training requirements are still needed.

Resolution 15 is on Training for radio-telephone operators. It is similar to Resolution 14, but refers to Regulation IV/3.

Resolution 16 deals with Technical assistance for the training and qualification of masters and other responsible personnel of oil, chemical and liquefied gas tankers. It refers to requirements in several convention regulations and recognizes that training facilities may be limited in some countries. It urges governments which can provide assistance to do so.

Resolution 17 is on Additional training for masters and chief mates of large ships and of ships with unusual manoeuvring characteristics. It is designed to assist those moving to ships of this type from smaller vessels, where characteristics are very different(1).

---

gas in ships before joining ships carrying such cargoes or, alternatively, on joining these ships. The Department also endorses the Merchant Navy Training Board Recommendations.

(1) See M.Notice 1015 which states:
"Manoeuvring and handling of a ship in all conditions, including:
(a) manoeuvres when approaching pilot vessels or stations with due regard to weather, tide, headreach and stopping distances;
(b) handling a ship in rivers, estuaries, etc., having regard to the effects of current, wind and restricted water on the response to the helm;
(c) manoeuvring in shallow water, including the reduction in keel clearance due to the effect of squat, rolling and pitching;
(d) interaction between passing ships and between own ship and nearby banks (canal

Resolution 18 is on Radar simulator training. It recommends that such training be given to all masters and deck officers(1).

Resolution 19 is on Training of seafarers in personal survival techniques. A recommendation is annexed(2).

Resolution 20 is on Training in the use of collision avoidance aids. It refers to Resolution 13 adopted by the TSPP Conference requesting the IMO to develop requirements for such equipment(3).

---

effect);
- (e) berthing and unberthing under various conditions of wind and tide with and without tugs;
- (f) choice of anchorage; anchoring with one or two anchors in limited anchorages and factors involved in determining the length of anchor cable to be used;
- (g) management and handling of ships in heavy weather, including assisting a ship or aircraft in distress, towing operations, means of keeping an unmanageable ship out of a sea trough, lessening drift and use of oil;
- (h) precautions in manoeuvring for launching boats or liferafts in bad weather."

(1) See M.Notice 1159 which gives information about courses of training in the use of radar and electronic navigation equipment which have replaced, from September 1, 1984, the former Radar Observer, Radar Simulator and Electronic Navigation Aids (Operation) courses. See also M.Notice 1191 on training courses to provide the knowledge and skill necessary to maintain the Electronic Navigational Equipment (known as the ENEM Certificate). Among the topics to be covered are fault finding techniques, test instruments, digital techniques and the maintenance of the equipment.

(2) See The Merchant Shipping (Certificate of Proficiency in Survival Craft) Regulations, 1984 (S.I.97/1984). See also M.Notice 1092.

(3) See M.Notice 1005 which outlines new courses of training in the use of radar and electronic navigation equipment. See also M.Notice 1006 which states that mandatory carriage of ARPA equipment will be phased-in from September 1, 1984. Furthermore, the USA Port and Tanker

Resolution 21 deals with the International Certificate of Competency. It invites the IMO to develop a standard form and title for this certificate.

Resolution 22 is on Human relationships. It emphasizes the importance of good human relationships between seafarers on board.

Resolution 23 is on Promotion of technical cooperation. It records appreciation of the IMO's work in assisting developing countries to establish maritime training facilities in conformity with global standards of training, and invites the Organization to intensify its efforts with a view to promoting universal acceptance and implementation of the STCW Convention.

---

Safety Act, 1978, requires bulk hazardous goods carriers of 10,000 gross tons and upwards entering US waters to be fitted with ARPA equipment from July 1, 1982. See also Resolution A.482 (XII) which recommends that all masters, chief mates and officers in charge of a navigational watch on ships fitted with ARPA be trained in the proper use of the equipment.

Under English law, the legal requirement on training for the use of ARPA derives from The Merchant Shipping (Navigational Equipment) Regulations, 1984 (S.I.1203/1984) which states in section 41: "when at any time on or after 1st September, 1985, a ship required to be fitted with an automatic radar plotting aid is at sea and a radar watch is being kept on the automatic radar plotting aid, the installation shall be under the control of a person qualified in the operational use of automatic radar plotting aids, who may be assisted by unqualified personnel."

References

British Shipping Federation: Fleet and Manpower Inquiry 1972-76 (1972).

G. Bonwick, Automation on Shipboard, Macmillan, 1967.

P.B. Buck, Technological Change and the Merchant Seaman, International Labour Review, Vol.92, No.9, October, 1965.

Conference on Education and Training of Seafarers for the 1990s organized by the Institute of Marine Engineers and the Nautical Institute held in London, 9-10 February, 1984.

J.M.M. Hill, The Seafaring Career, Tavistock Institute of Human Relations, 1972.

J.S. Kitchen, The Employment of Merchant Seamen, Croom Helm, 1980.

J. McConville, Changing Patterns of Manpower and Management in the UK Shipping Industry, Maritime Policy and Management, Vol.6, 1979.

E.E. Mitropoulos, The implementation of the International Convention on Standards of Training, Certification and Watchkeeping for Seafarers, 1978, Odessa Seminar on Maritime Training, 8-19 June, 1979.

D.H. Moreby, Personnel Management in Merchant Ships, Pergamon, 1968.

A.S. Ruchlin, Manpower Resources of the US Maritime Industry: A Definitional and Descriptive Analysis of the Maritime Labour Force, Washington, 1968.

A. Sadek, The STCW 1978 Convention, Journal of the Arab Maritime Transport Academy, 1979.

S.G. Sturmey, British Shipping and World Competition, Athlone Press, 1962.

# CHAPTER V

# RULES ON TRAFFIC AND TRANSPORT

The IMO has been working in co-operation with other organizations on a number of issues concerning the simplification of documents, namely:

(a) standardisation of documentation on the carriage of dangerous goods;

(b) automatic data processing (ADP) of shipping documents and documents used for clearance of ships;

(c) collection and dissemination of information on shipping documentation required by and available in different countries; and

(d) documentary requirements for ships carrying nuclear (radioactive) and other noxious cargoes during "innocent passage".

However, the main concern of the IMO(1) was to reduce and standardize the documents and to simplify the formalities connected with the arrival and departure of ships engaged in international trade, their passengers, crews, cargoes and stores. To

---

(1) The IMO was also concerned with sub-standard ships and barratry. Resolution A.441 (XI) adopted on November 15, 1979, states: "...Recognizing that in certain circumstances the registered owner of a ship may contract or otherwise entrust to another person the discharge of his responsibilities for the ship in respect of matters relating to maritime safety and the protection of the marine environment ... Invites every State to take the necessary steps to ensure that the owner of a ship which flies the flag of that State provides such State with the current information necessary to enable it to identify and contact the person contracted or otherwise entrusted by the owner to discharge his responsibilities for that ship in regard to matters relating to maritime safety and the protection of the marine environment."
Sub-standard ships refer to those of unsound structure, badly equipped, badly operated or have incompetent crews.
As for barratry, see the resolution adopted on November 15, 1979, and the resolution of November, 1983 which recalls the great concern for the increasing number of incidents involving piracy and armed robbery. See also the Report

this end, the Convention on Facilitation of International Maritime Traffic, 1965, was adopted. Several amendments to the Convention failed to attract sufficient acceptance within the stipulated period. Therefore, special attention was given to amend the provisions of article VII dealing with the amendment procedure. This was achieved and the amendments entered into force on June 2, 1984. As a result of the new provisions, a better and more adaptable machinery has been introduced to develop the procedures which would ensure the fulfilment of the objectives of the Convention.

Another issue closely related to traffic and trade is the Tonnage Measurement of Ships Convention 1969. It has already made its contribution to safety but more important it introduced a universal system which the shipping community badly needed.

Equally important to shipowners, underwriters and others is the Convention on Limitation of Liability for Maritime Claims, 1976.

Turning from measures to facilitate traffic to the carriage of passengers, one is confronted with two conventions: the Athens Convention on the Carriage of Passengers and their Luggage by Sea, 1974, and the Special Trade Passenger Ships Agreement, 1971.

Thus, this chapter considers the following topics:

(i) the Convention on Facilitation of International Maritime Traffic;

(ii) the Tonnage Measurement of Ship Convention, 1969;

(iii) the limitation of liability;

(iv) the carriage of passengers and their luggage; and

(v) the Special Trade Passenger Ships Agreement, 1971.

---

prepared by the International Chamber of Commerce, International Maritime Bureau, MSC 50/INF.2 of July 10, 1984, which covers the nature and frequency of attacks; proposed measures on board ship; attacks on refugees in South East Asian Waters. See IMO News, No.3, 1983, p.1.

## (i) THE CONVENTION ON FACILITATION OF INTERNATIONAL MARITIME TRAFFIC (FAL), 1965

In most seafaring countries, there is a national body of rules which govern the formalities and procedures for ships entering and departing from ports and the documents required by the authorities. Some of these rules have not been changed since the days of sailing ships. The diversity of the national laws is remarkable. The result is delay at various ports which would increase the burden on shipowners and shippers. This would, in turn, damage international trade which depends upon a system of information handling. Such a system operates by means of interchange of paper documents to control the movement of the goods and their clearance through customs and other frontiers. Therefore, a uniform system of facilitation to minimise the formalities and procedures is crucial for shipping and international trade.

The IMO[1] gave this matter[2] special attention and in 1962 the IMO set up a group of experts

---

(1) Other bodies have been active in the field of simplification such as the Simplification of International Trade Procedures Board (SITPRO), the International Chamber of Commerce (ICC) and the International Association of Ports and Harbours and the Customs Co-operation Council. See, for example, the International Convention on the Simplfication and Harmonization of Customs Procedures (Treaty Series No.36, 1975) which states in its preamble: "...divergences between national Customs procedures can hamper international trade ... simplification and harmonization of their Customs procedures can effectively contribute to the development of international trade and of other international exchanges."

(2) The International Sanitary Regulations adopted by the Fourth World Health Assembly on 25th May, 1951, revised and consolidated the provisions of thirteen International Sanitary Conventions and similar arrangements. Their essential aim is to ensure the maximum security against the international spread of diseases with the minimum interference with world traffic. The Eighth and Ninth World Health Assemblies, in 1955 and 1956, amended the Regulations as regards the Yellow-fever provisions, the sanitary control of

to examine a draft convention(1) prepared by the Secretariat and to study the facilitation under the headings of customs, immigration and health(2). Three sub-groups studied each of these problems

---

pilgrim traffic, and the International Certificate of Vaccination or Revaccination against Smallpox. See International Sanitary Regulations, WHO, 1957. In the United Kingdom, see the Public Health (Ships) Regulations, 1970 (No. 1881) as amended by S.I.287/1978.

(1) The first step, at regional level, was taken by the Organization of American States (OAS). In 1956, the Inter-American Port and Harbour Conference met at San Jose (Costa Rica) and issued a declaration according to which the OAS established a permanent technical committee on ports. This committee drafted the Inter-American Convention on Facilitation of International Waterhouse Transportation in the Western Hemisphere. The second Inter-American Port and Harbour Conference met in 1963 in Mar del Plata and adopted a Convention on Facilitation. The first three articles (I-III) deal with facilitation in general, stating the objectives of the Contracting Parties. The adoption and amendment of standards and recommended practices being entrusted to the Inter-American Port and Harbour Organization of OAS, whilst a group of experts will carry out the relevant studies (Art.IV). The procedure of adoption and amendment of standards and recommended practices is laid down in articles X and XI. Notification by dissenting governments is made to the Secretary-General of OAS. Articles VII-XII deal with the signature of the Convention, adherence, ratification, amendment and denunciation. Article X provides for the establishment of a permanent technical committee, whose function will be to review the standards and recommended practices which will direct the work of the group of experts.

(2) The sub-group on customs considered the results of the Conference of Mar Del Plata as well as the United Nations Conference on International Travel and Tourism (Rome 1963). A questionnaire was distributed to governments concerning formalities and documents required by port authorities for customs in respect of entry and departure of ships, persons and cargo. While

separately[1]. In April 1964, the group of experts reached agreement on the text of a draft convention and an Annex. In May 1964, the Council of the IMO approved the draft and sent it to member governments to obtain their opinions. In accordance with Resolution A.63 (III) adopted by the IMO Assembly in 1963, the special conference for the adoption of the Convention was held in March,1965 in London. It approved the draft convention subject to changes and opened it for signature on April 9, 1965[2].

---

the sub-group on immigration gave particular attention to the International Civil Aviation Organization (ICAO) and OAS precedents, the sub-group on health inquired into the relevant regulations and procedures adopted by the World Health Organization (WHO), particularly the International Sanitary Regulations. For the purpose of sanitary control, the sub-group defined two categories of persons: (a) immigrants, seasonal workers and pilgrims over whom control should be extensive; and (b) other travellers over whom control might be relaxed and simplified. The expert group also had at its disposal a report on the work of the Economic Commission of Europe (ECE) in the field of simplification and standardisation of export documents, and it was able to ascertain the views of shipowners and business circles on facilitation by consultation with the International Chamber of Shipping, the International Shipping Federation, the International Chamber of Commerce and other non-governmental organizations.

(1) All three sub-groups considered the similarities of air transport and transport by sea to ascertain the extent to which ICAO patterns of facilitation could be followed. It was felt that problems relating to transport of persons by sea could be solved in a similar way to those arising in the field of air transport. However, some of the problems of ships and cargo are not completely similar and thus certain procedures peculiar to air traffic were found not to be applicable to maritime transport. See FAL/EG I/SR 2, 14/1 1963; FAL/EG II/2, 3/4 1963, IMO.

(2) The Convention came into force on March 5, 1967.

## 1. THE CONVENTION IN OUTLINE

The Convention is concerned with documentation and other procedures and is designed to minimise delays and inconvenience. Thus, its purpose is to "facilitate maritime traffic by simplifying and reducing to a minimum the formalities, documentary requirements and procedures on the arrival, stay and departure of ships engaged in international voyages"(1). In order to achieve these purposes, the Contracting States "undertake to co-operate ... in the formulation and application of measures for the facilitation of the arrival, stay and departure of ships"(2). They also(3) undertake to co-operate in securing the highest practicable degree of uniformity in formalities, documentary requirements and procedures in all matters in which such uniformity will facilitate and improve international maritime traffic and keep to a minimum any alterations in formalities, documentary requirements and procedures necessary to meet special requirements of a domestic nature(4). For this purpose the Convention and its Annex contain "Standards" and "Recommended Practices". Article VI defines:

> "Standards" as those "measures the uniform application of which by Contacting Governments in accordance with the Convention is necessary and practicable in order to facilitate international maritime traffic."
>
> "Recommended Practices" as those "measures the application of which by Contracting Governments

---

(1) See the preamble to the Convention.
(2) Article II.
(3) Article III.
(4) This calls for an adjustment of national laws on the Contracting Parties to international standards and thus a duty arises on their part to pass legislation which would bring about uniformity of standards relating to facilitation. On the other hand, "all matters that are not expressly provided for in the Convention remain subject to the legislation of the Contracting Governments", (Art. V(3)). However, any Contracting Country is allowed to maintain its own national standard if they offer wider facilities than those stipulated in the Convention (Art. V(1)).

is desirable in order to facilitate international maritime traffic."

With the Convention and the Annex, six Resolutions were approved:

Resolution 1 is on Encouragement of acceptance of and accessions to the Convention.

Resolution 2 is on Acceptance of Standards. It invites Contracting Governments to bring, whenever practicable, their own formalities, documentary requirements and procedures into full accord with the Standards.

Resolution 3 relates to the creation of national and regional committees.

Resolution 4 deals with the establishment of an *ad hoc* Working Group to examine, when needed, any amendments to the Annex to the Convention.

Resolution 5 is on Future work on Facilitation.

Resolution 6 is devoted to Facilitation of International Travel and Tourism.

## 2. THE ANNEX

The Annex follows Annex IX of the International Civil Aviation Organization (ICAO) Convention[1]. It is divided into five sections and contains a list of definitions. Certain words such as cargo, mail, passenger in transit[2], shipowner, ship's equipment are defined. These definitions are useful as they

---

(1) The Annex to the ICAO Convention is divided into several chapters dealing with definitions and applicability, entry and departure of aircraft, entry and departure of persons, and with special problems peculiar to civil aviation such as cargo, traffic and airports.

(2) The definition of "passenger in transit" was not acceptable to the United Kingdom. An acceptable definition would be "a passenger in transit is a person who arrived by ship from a foreign country and who continues his journey on the same voyage in the same ship from the same port to a foreign country". See Supplement Relating to the Annex to the Convention, IMO Sales No. 360, 82.20.E, p.7.

would eliminate any dispute as to their meanings. An attempt to define the term "international voyage" which determines the scope of application of the Convention, failed to gain approval(1).

A strict distinction is made between standards and recommended practices. No other documents except those mentioned in the Annex should be required from a ship. Thus, what is required is:- the General Declaration, the Cargo Declaration, the Ship's Stores Declaration, the Crew's Effects Declaration, the Crew List, the Passenger List, the Document required under the Universal Postal Convention for Mail, and the Maritime Declaration of Health (Sect. 2(a)).

The purpose and contents of these documents are defined in Section 2(b) and a duty is imposed on the receiving harbour authorities (public authorities) to accept the documents, as evidence of the facts stated in them. The special provisions included in the Annex with respect to the arrival and departure of persons (Sect. 3) refer *inter alia* to passports and identity cards, certificates required by the International Sanitary Regulations and Customs inspection.

It must be noted that some of the standards and recommended practices are in a negative form and some in a positive form. The first require States not to impose more on ships and persons than certain maximum requirements in respect of documents, restrictions and control. On the other hand, the positive provisions require States to provide certain minimum facilities for traffic and for the convenience of passengers and crews. Whenever a

---

(1) The Sub-Group on Health had prior to the adoption of the Convention considered the meaning of the term "international voyage" and explained the term as covering: (a) in the case of a ship, a voyage between ports in the territories of more than one State, or a voyage between ports in the territory or territories of the same State if the ship has relations with the territory of any other State on its voyage but only as regards those relations; (b) in the case of a person, a voyage involving entry into the territory of a State other than the territory of the State in which that person commences his voyage. The Conference discussed the possibility of defining the term "international voyage" but finally dropped it.

question arises under a negative provision, it must be assumed that States will relax their requirements below the maximum stipulated in the standards and recommended practices. On the other hand, in the case of a positive provision, it must be assumed that States will, wherever possible, furnish more than the minimum stipulated in the Annex. This distinction is in so far significant that while in both cases the interpretation of provisions must be extensive in favour of ships (passengers, crews) engaged in international voyages, it is only in the case of negative provisions that the jurisdiction of the State receiving ships in its ports tends to be restricted. In practice the whole problem of facilitation is predominantly a negative one. Its most important purpose is to reduce documentation, restrictions and control and this could only be done by defining a maximum for requirements beyond which a Contracting State should not go.

## 3. MEASURES OF FACILITATIONS

The Convention following the pattern of ICAO and the World Health Organization (WHO) distinguished among the measures(1) between "standards" and "recommended practices". They are defined in article VI in the same way as ICAO standards and recommended practices. While the first are "necessary and practicable in order to facilitate international maritime traffic", the second are only "desirable" to achieve the above effect. Article VIII states that any Contracting State which finds it impracticable to comply with any standard included in the Annex or which deems it necessary for special reasons(2) to adopt formalities, documentary

---

(1) Art. II(1) introduces what may be called an international most-favoured-transport clause; in particular the Contracting Governments undertake that measures for facilitation of maritime transport shall be "not less favourable than measures applied in respect of other means of international transport" such as, for instance, air transport. However, art. II(1) states that "these measures may differ according to particular requirements".

(2) Provision is made for special circumstances and thus the contracting parties have the right to pass temporary measures (even inconsistent with

requirements or procedures differing from the standard, must inform the Secretary-General of the IMO and notify him of the differences between the two. Such notification should be made as soon as possible after the Convention comes into force in the State concerned, or after the adoption of differing national standards(1).

The provisions of article VIII show that the Convention has followed the ICAO procedure. Standards are measures which become immediately operative after they are adopted by the Contracting Parties. They do not call for ratification. A Contracting Government which is unable to adjust its national law to international standards must make this clear to the Secretary-General of the IMO, who acts in this case on behalf of the Contracting Parties. If the government fails to notify the Secretary-General, it is presumed that it will comply with the international standards. The weakness of this procedure lies in the fact that a Contracting Government can submit a notification not only in the case of impossibility of adjusting its municipal standards to international standards but also when it takes positive action and passes, at any time, municipal standards which differ from international standards.

On the other hand, though the standards come into force without ratification, any Contracting State which finds it impracticable to comply with a standard in the Annex or which adopts differing municipal standards, shall inform the Secretary-General of the IMO of the difference between its own practice and international standards. Thus, a Contracting State may at any time deviate from the standards in the Annex and insist on the validity of its own municipal law which would usually grant fewer concessions to ships engaged in international

---

international standards) in order "to preserve public morality, order and security, or to prevent the introduction or spread of diseases or pests affecting public health, animals or plants" (Art. V(2)).

(1) The text of notifications received from Contracting Governments in compliance with article XIII is reported in a special publication entitled "Supplement to the Annex - Notifications by Contracting Governments under article XIII of the Convention'.

voyages and those stipulated in the Annex(1).

It seems, from the records of the Conference and the construction of article XIII, that the standards in the Annex are not mandatory(2). The view held by the Participating States was to establish flexible rules of general acceptance in the field of maritime facilitation without making their operation dependent on a binding force or legal provisions to avoid any excessive pressure on the adjustment of national laws.

## 4. AMENDMENTS TO THE ANNEX

Article VII of the Convention provided for two methods of amendment, initiated either by a proposal from one of the Contracting Governments or by a conference convened for that purpose(3). These two

---

(1) If a State does not submit a notification, it is presumed that it will comply with the standards and other Contracting States must expect it to grant all the stipulated facilities to ships on an international voyage. However, if a Contracting State neither complies nor notifies, it will be guilty of breach of the duty to submit notification and not of non-compliance with international standards. Any State suffering damage because of non-notification has legal redress against the law-breaking State. However, the injured State cannot take advantage of the IMO machinery for settling disputes.

(2) The chairman of one of the Conference committees expressed the majority view when he stated that standards in the Annex are not mandatory though they "carried more weight" than recommended practices.

(3) If the first method is followed, the proposing government must forward a draft amendment to the Secretary-General of the IMO. At the request of the proposing State the Secretary-General may communicate with the other Contracting States, or in the absence of such request he may proceed to consultations before communicating the proposal to the above States. The latter may inform the Secretary-General of their acceptance (or rejection) of the proposal and the amendment will come into force six months after the date on which it is accepted by a majority of the Contracting Governments (Art.

methods proved to be so inhibiting that it was difficult to bring widely accepted amendments into force within a reasonable period of time. In fact, the difficulty[1] brought about by article VII paralysed the work on facilitation as many Member Governments took the view that there was little point in bringing the modern methods[2], such as the use of automatic data processing and other techniques[3] before solving the amendment procedure.

---

VII(2)(d). The alternative method of passing an amendment is laid down in Article VII(3). It starts with the request of at least one-third of the Contracting Governments. Every amendment adopted by a two-thirds majority of the Contracting Governments present and voting at the conference will come into force six months after the date on which the Secretary-General of the IMO notifies the Contracting Governments of the amendment adopted.

(1) Since the FAL Convention has been ratified by 53 countries, amendments to the Annex had to be accepted by 27 Contracting Parties before entering into force.

(2) See Resolution A.452 (XI) passed on November 15, 1969, which approved the "Application of Automatic Data Processing" (ADP) following the definition of the term "document" as referring to "data carrier with data entries", and to the addition to Standard 2.15 of Section 26 of the following:
"Documents produced by electronic and other automatic data processing techniques, in legible and understandable form, shall be accepted."
The Resolution recommends that in applying Standard 2.15:
"(a) the possibility of accepting, for certain documents, non-paper media, subject to prior agreement (including the method of authentication) between the parties concerned, should be explored;
(b) the presentation of data in any automatic data processing (ADP output) document should follow the layout of the Standardised Model Forms;
(c) any substantial deviation from that layout should require prior agreement between the parties concerned."

(3) Confidentiality of information is crucial to the development of sophisticated computerised hand-

For this reason, an amendment to article VII was adopted in 1973 to give effect to the "tacit acceptance" procedure(1). It provides that amendments(2) adopted by a two-thirds majority of the Facilitation Committee(3) will enter into force within 15 months unless they are rejected by one-third of the Contracting Parties. Thus, the onus will be on governments to reject amendments within one year.

Amendments to the Convention are in sight

In October, 1984, the Facilitation Committee, which was established to assist in the application and further development of the Convention and which has served as a most suitable forum for discussing issues and problems arising in connection with it, held a meeting to consider its future work. It reviewed its outstanding amendments and agreed on a package of measures, including provisions to permit the increased use of automatic data processing (ADP).

---

ling of documentation at the ports. The exchange of information among operators may be different from those submitted to the Customs or other administrations.

(1) The 1973 amendments to article VII came into force on June 2, 1984.

(2) As a result, a better and more adaptable machinery has been introduced to develop meaningful procedures to assist the smooth movement of international trade.

(3) See the Report of the Facilitation Committee to invite the Council (C53/9/Add.1 of October 11, 1984) to approve:
- the publication of a pamphlet on "Facilitation - what it is, what it does" to replace the one on Facilitation in Maritime Travel and Transport.
- a study of ways in which the Standard Model Forms 1-6 can be improved to enhance their implementation and the publication by the IMO of directly usable Forms for sale to operators and authorities.
- to authorise the Committee to compare the IMO and ICAO Facilitation Convention with a view to strengthening the provisions of the IMO Convention by including provisions covered by the ICAO Convention.

It requested the Council to convene a conference in 1986 to consider the proposed amendments[1].

References

The SITPRO Report, 1970.

The SITPRO progress report, 1974/75.

The United Nations Conference on International Travel and Tourism, 1963.

---

(1) The Conference is to be held in conjunction with the 16th session of the Facilitation Committee, and the amendments proposed for consideration are intended to enhance the employment of automatic data processing by removing provisions which may impede their use. See C54/22(c), p.29.

## (ii) THE TONNAGE MEASUREMENT OF SHIPS CONVENTION, 1969

Tonnage(1) is used for various reasons such as the assessment of port and harbour dues, pilotage fees, canal dues, insurance premiums, manning levels, shipping statistics and the application of international conventions.

Most countries base the measurement of their ships' capacity on the British system developed by George Moorsom in 1854(2), where tonnage is calculated in volume - 100 cubic feet to the ton.

The purpose of measuring the volume rather than the weight was to establish the amount of cargo a ship could carry and hence how much it could earn. However, this method led to shipbuilders constructing vessels which could hold more cargo than the tonnage indicated, saving owners on port dues and canal tolls.

Various systems for measuring the tonnage of the ship were used and the issue has become more complex with the Suez and Panama canals using their own methods of calculating tonnage. Among the most well known systems are: registered tonnage(3), gross tonnage(4), net registered tonnage(5),

---

(1) The word tonnage comes from earlier days when harbour dues were collected on vessels carrying cargo in "tuns". A "tun" is still a recognised wine measure of 252 gallons, but over the years the words tons and tonnage have come into use as a means of indicating the size of ships both in respect of capacity and weight.

(2) Under the Moorsom system, tonnage came to represent cargo-carrying capacity, with 100 cu. ft representing one gross registered ton. But net tonnage calculations exempted non-revenue areas such as engine room and crew accommodation for the purposes of assessing tolls and other charges.

(3) The registered tonnage is the internal capacity of a ship, and denotes the cubical capacity of the vessel under the tonnage deck - a registered ton being 100 cubic feet of internal measurement.

(4) The gross tonnage is the registered tonnage to which has been added "over deck" tonnage, that is the space covered by poop, bridge, deckhouse, etc.

(5) When non-earning capacities of the ship, such as engine room, tanks, peak tanks, etc., are

displacement tonnage[1], deadweight tonnage[2], freight tonnage[3] and Thames measurement tonnage[4]. This situation gives rise to many difficulties, the most important is to find out the areas which should be exempted or deducted when calculating net tonnage for computing tolls and dues. As a result, a ship may have its tonnage calculated in several ways to conform with differing national requirements. Two sister ships may be allocated different tonnages because they sail under different flags.

The IMO began work in this area by looking at the problems posed by shelter-deck, wells between poop, bridge and forecastle used for carrying cargo, protected by awnings, but exempted from tonnage measurement. Problems arose when the awnings disappeared to be replaced by more permanent protection for the shelter-deck, posing safety hazards. The IMO thought the problem could be solved by the introduction of the tonnage mark scheme. The idea was to enable owners to abolish the shelter-deck without losing valuable exemption, provided the prescribed tonnage draught mark was not submerged. However, port authorities were not happy with this idea as their revenue depends on whether or not the tonnage mark is submerged. So, the approach taken by the IMO was unsuccessful and it was clear that a comprehensive overhaul of the whole tonnage measurement system was needed.

To overcome these difficulties, the 1969 Convention[5] adopted a new and unified system of

---

deducted from gross tonnage, one gets the net registered tonnage.

(1) This is the actual weight of the ship and corresponds to the weight of water displaced by her. It is regarded as light displacement when only the ship, equipment and machinery weight, are concerned, and loaded displacement when she carries water, cargo, fuel, stores, passengers, etc.

(2) It denotes the difference between light displacement and loaded displacement.

(3) Freight rates for cargo carrying may be assessed on weight or volume. If a given cargo occupies more than 40 cubic feet per ton or 1 cu.m per tonne, then the shipper pays on volume.

(4) It is intended as a means of accurately comparing the size of one yacht and another.

(5) The Convention came into force on July 18, 1982. For English Law, see S.I. No.841 of 1982 on The

measurement by which the tonnage of ships of all nations is determined. The new system is relatively simple to apply and has none of the anomalies which existed under the previous systems.

The Convention provides for gross and net tonnages, both of which are calculated independently. The gross tonnage is a realistic indication of the ship's size. It is based upon the moulded volume of the entire ship (hull plus erections and all enclosed spaces) and there are no deductions, exemptions or special allowance therefrom. The net tonnage is a general indication of the ship's earning capacity. It is produced by a formula which is a function of the moulded volume of the cargo spaces, the number of passengers carried, the moulded depth of the ship and the summer draught. The net tonnage should not be taken as less than 30% of the gross tonnage.

The provisions of the Convention apply to ships of 24 metres(1) in length or over, which are:

"New" ships, i.e. ships whose keels are laid or are at a similar stage of construction on 18 July, 1982(2) or after;

Existing ships, which undergo alterations or modifications which result in a substantial variation in their existing gross tonnage;

Existing ships, if the owner so requests; and

All ships with effect from 18 July, 1994.

---

Merchant Shipping (Tonnage) Regulations, 1982 which came into force on July 18, 1982.

(1) Pleasure yachts not exceeding 15 tons burden (net) are exempt from registry under the Merchant Shipping Acts if they are employed solely in navigation on the rivers or coasts of the United Kingdom. However, many pleasure yachts within that tonnage limit are in fact so registered and include those which are voluntarily registered to facilitate mortgage or to assist the owner to obtain an "Admiralty Warrant" to wear a privileged ensign.
In case a pleasure yacht is registered, the Registrar will require a Certificate of Survey (Tonnage Measurement).

(2) Ships when measured are issued with a form of tonnage certificate known as the "International Tonnage Certificate (1969)".

The new system stipulated by the Convention would result in the elimination of the shelter-deck vessel and the tonnage mark scheme. There is only one net tonnage and its change is allowed only once a year. It will apply to new ships which are defined as those whose keels have been laid or which are at a similar stage of construction on the agreed date, i.e. July 18, 1982. Owners of existing ships will be able to switch to the new system if they wish. However, they are allowed to carry on as before for a period of 12 years in order to avoid undue problems to shipowners.

The rules of the Convention(1) will ensure that gross and net tonnages calculated under it will not differ too widely from those arrived at under present methods. As far as gross tonnages are concerned, this has been generally achieved, although some ships which now have large exempted spaces such as ro-ro ships, will end up with much greater tonnages. As far as net tonnages are concerned, it seems likely that some ships designed for carriage of high density cargoes, such as ore carriers, will have their tonnages significantly reduced. This will also be the case with small ships of under 500 tons gross, while tankers and general purpose dry cargo ships will see little change.

The new system has the advantages of simplicity and speed. As far as net tonnage is concerned, only the cargo spaces will need to be measured. For gross tonnages, the spaces will be measured collectively without the nature or location of individual spaces being taken into account. Speed of measurement is another factor and it has been estimated that it will take only half the time now needed to assess the tonnage of a ship.

For some time it was felt that the types of ship which would show a big increase in gross tonnage under the new system could be faced with increased requirements resulting from the application of other IMO Conventions. This would cause these "new" ships to be treated differently from similar existing ships. For this reason, an interim scheme(2) was adopted to allow "new" ships to be

---

(1) At its forty-sixth session, the Maritime Safety Committee agreed on interpretations of the terms used in the Convention.

(2) In 1977, Resolution A.389 was passed for the benefit of certain ships, notably shelter-deck vessels, whose tonnage will be significantly

measured for gross tonnage in accordance with national measurement systems previously in force and to use this figure for SOLAS(1).

In order to encourage the design of segregated ballast tankers of all sizes in accordance with MARPOL 1973, an entry may be made on the remarks section of the International Tonnage Certificate indicating the tonnage of segregated ballast tanks dedicated exclusively to that purpose(2). Harbour

---

higher when measured under the Convention. It provides for ships which would be subject to the 1969 Convention to be measured also in accordance with present national rules. The latter tonnage can then be used for the application of SOLAS. This scheme was terminated at the end of 1985.

This Resolution was revised by Resolution A.495 (XII) in 1981 which states that as far as the requirements of Regulation 3 of Chapter IV of SOLAS are concerned, the interim solution may continue to apply until July,1994. In respect of requirements for cargo vessels of less than 1,600 gross tonnage under the present national tonnage system, the interim solution may also continue until July,1994.

The MSC issued two circulars. The first deals with the interpretation of the technical terms used in the Convention. The second states that ships which regularly alter their load line and tonnage marks in order to change from higher to lower tonnage and vice versa, without any modification to the ship itself, will not constitute a "substantial variation" as far as the Convention is concerned. The higher tonnage will be used for the application of SOLAS.

(1) The MSC considered the question of replacement of tonnage parameters in various conventions. After a long discussion it reached agreement that a complete adherence to the principles of the 1969 Convention and the interim tonnage schemes would be the most equitable solution, but the substitution of tonnage figures by other parameters could cause more problems than may be solved. See C54/22(c), p.24.

(2) Resolution A.388 enables the tonnage of segregated ballast tanks which are required to be fitted to oil tankers under MARPOL 73/78, to be deducted from the overall tonnage of the ship, thus resulting in lower dues.

authorities may reduce dues by this amount.

In 1984, the Maritime Safety Committee (MSC) invited[(1)] the governments concerned to:

(a) urge the appropriate authorities of the Panama and Suez Canals[(2)] to complete their studies and to provide an adequate transitional period for new tonnage schemes introduced by them; and

(b) limit mutual agreements for recognition of tonnage certificates for existing ships with States not parties to the Tonnage Measurements Convention.

References

Corkhill, The Tonnage Measurement of Ships: A Guide to the New Convention, published by Fairplay ISBN:090 50 45 033.

---

(1) MSC 49/19 of April 11, 1984, p.4. See also Resolution A.492 (XII).

(2) The Facilitation Committee was informed that the authorities of the Panama Canal were considering adopting the universal tonnage measurement system. No information was received on action taken by the Suez Canal authority. MSC 50/2/1, October 19, 1984.

(iii) THE LIMITATION OF LIABILITY

Historical background: The concept of limitation of the shipowner's liability existed in the maritime laws of Europe for a long time(1). In some continental countries, shipowners were entitled to put a ceiling on their liabilities. In others, they were given the right of extinction of their liabilities by abandoning the ship or what was left of it, i.e. wreck, and the freight, to the creditors. The abandonment was, in fact, a type of limitation which historically was based on two grounds: (a) the ship represented the extent of the owner's investment; and (b) the ship possessed an independent personality as a wrongdoer.

International conventions on limitation: Over the years, the rules on the limitation of the shipowner's liability were developed by extending them to persons other than the shipowner and to cover loss of life and personal injury. However, there was no agreement on the basis of limitation. In some legal systems, the maximum limitation was determined by reference to the value of the ship and her pending freight, while in others it was calculated on the tonnage of the ship. This difference of approach was the main reason for the formulation of the 1924 Brussels Convention for the Unification of Certain Rules Relating to the Limitation of the Liability of Owners of Sea-Going Vessels. The Convention did not, however, solve the issue and its provisions were based on a compromise. The 1954 Convention was revised in 1957 which adopted the tonnage system for the purpose of the limitation amount.

It must be noted that the United States did not accept either the 1954 nor the 1957 Conventions and the Limitation Act of 1851 (municipal act) is still applicable. Severe criticisms have been directed to the concept of limitation. In *Maryland Casualty Co. v. Cushing*(2), Black, J. said: "Judicial expansion

(1) In the past, maritime law has recognised the right of the shipowner to limit his liability in case of collision to the value of the ship and anticipated freight. The limitation of the shipowner's liability, which is a kind of statutory insolvency, was introduced into English law in 1733, see *Boucher* v. *Lawson*, Cas. temp Hard. 85.

(2) 347 U.S. 409 (1954).

of the Limited Liability Act at this date seems especially inappropriate. Many of the conditions of the shipping industry which induced the 1851 Congress to pass the Act no longer prevail. And later Congresses, when they wished to aid shipping, provided subsidies paid out of the public treasury rather than subsidies paid by injured persons"(1).

Despite the force in these arguments, the abolition of limitation would lead to an increase in the insurance premium which might throw many shipowners out of business. So, the general view in shipping circles was not to abolish the concept of limitation but to reform the 1957 Convention. This task was undertaken by the IMO and a new convention on Limitation of Liability for Maritime Claims (LLMC) was agreed(2).

Thus, on the international level, we have four different situations. Countries which still apply the 1924 Convention; countries which apply the 1957 Convention, the United States which has never adopted any of these conventions; and countries which adopted the LLMC Convention(3).

---

(1) "Limitation is merely a subsidy to the maritime industry ... If the matter were an open question unhindered by a hundred years of history, few could deny the injustice of subsidising a segment of the transportation industry at the expense of those killed or injured by its operations." See Eyer, Shipowners' Limitation of Liability - New Directions for an Old Doctrine, 16 Stan. L. Rev. 307,371, 1964.

(2) See the text of the Convention, IMO, No.77.04.E. The Convention will come into force on December 1, 1986. It has been ratified by the following countries: Bahamas, Benin, Denmark, Finland, France, Japan, Liberia, Norway, Spain, Sweden, Yemen and the United Kingdom.
The necessary legislation is already on the statute book; the Merchant Shipping Act, 1979, Section 17(1) and Schedule IV. Consequently on December 1, 1985, the LLMC became part of English law.

(3) This is inevitable during a transitional period and it is hoped that more States will ratify the LLMC Convention.

## 1. The 1924 Convention

Article 1 of the Convention states that: "the liability of the owner of a seagoing vessel is limited ... in respect of: (1) compensation due to third parties by reason of damage caused, whether on land or on water, by the acts or faults of the master, crew, pilot, or any other person in the service of the vessel ..."

Accordingly, the owner, in case of oil pollution damage, can limit his liability. Article 10 extends the right of limitation to other persons such as a bareboat charterer. All that is required under Article 2 is the absence of fault on the part of the person claiming the limitation. Fault was explained in *Lord* v. *Goodall S.S. Co.*[1] as: "... a personal participation of the owner in some fault, or act of negligence, causing or contributing to the loss, or some personal knowledge or means of knowledge, of which he is bound to avail himself of a contemplated loss, or a condition of things likely to produce or contribute to the loss, without appropriate means to prevent it."

The amount of limitation is determined by reference to the value of the vessel, the freight and the accessories of the vessel provided that it shall not exceed an aggregate sum equal to 8 pounds sterling per ton of the vessel's tonnage. The value of the vessel is assessed at the termination of the voyage. The owner's liability insurance and the hull insurance are not included in the limitation fund because insurance is a personal contract.

## 2. The 1957 Convention

The 1924 Convention was revised in 1957 and a new Convention was adopted[2]. Under it: "the owner, charterer, manager and operator of the ship, and ... the master, members of the crew and other servants of the owner, charterer, manager or operator acting in the course of their employment, may limit their liability for loss of life of, or personal injury to, or damage to any other property or infringement of any rights ..." Obviously this covers the case of

---

(1) 15 Fed. Cas. 884, No.8506, C.C. Cal. 1877.
(2) The provisions of the Convention were incorporated into the Merchant Shipping (Liability of Shipowners and Others) Act, 1958.

an oil pollution damage(1).

The limits of liability in case of property claims are 1,000 francs for each ton; 3,100 francs for personal claims, and in both personal and property claims is 3,100 francs of which 2.100 francs will be for the payment of personal claims and 1,000 francs for property claims(2).

## 3. The 1976 Limitation Convention

The amount of limitation fixed by the 1957 Convention was adequate at that time, but over the years and in view of inflation it became far from being sufficient. What really was needed was the introduction of a machinery to review such an amount from time to time(3). There were other reasons for updating the Convention, for example, the various decisions of the courts where limitation was denied to the shipowner because of the term "actual fault or privity"(4) and the need to replace the franc with the SDR.

---

(1) For claims for oil pollution damage, see Chapter VII.

(2) A Protocol was adopted on December 21, 1979, to substitute SDRs for gold francs.

(3) Article 21 provides that a special conference may be called by the IMO in order to adjust the limitation amounts. One-fourth of the Parties must request this Conference and a decision to alter the amounts or to substitute the unit of account must be taken by a two-thirds majority of those present and voting at the Conference.

(4) See *Paterson Steamships* v. *Robin Hood Mills* (1937) 59 Ll.L.R.33; *The Lady Gwendolen* (1965) P. 294.In this latter case the Court held that the shipowner had delegated the navigation to professional persons and should have arranged some degree of supervision over the way they discharged their duties. In fact, there was no system of supervision at all. See also *The Truculent* (1952) P.1.
In the fairly recent case, *The Garden City*, (1982) 2 Lloyd's Rep. 382, Mr. Justice Staughton found that the system of inspections introduced by the shipowner was adequate, although not perfect. The shipowner had appreciated the problems of radar navigation in fog, impressed upon his master the need for

Although the 1976 Convention preserved the distinction between property claims, personal claims and personal and property claims, it is based on a quite different philosophy. Under the new Convention, it is expected that the owner would insure his liability risks to the extent known in the insurance practice as "commercial insurability"[1].

The amount of limitation: the amount[2] is calculated on a sliding scale.

(a) in respect of claims for loss of life or personal injury[3]:

  (i) for a ship with a tonnage not exceeding 500 tons, 333,000 SDRs (about $369,630);

  (ii) for a ship with a tonnage in excess of 500 tons, the following amounts must be added to the above figure:

---

care and instigated an adequate system of supervision. In the event, the system failed, but the shipowner was held to have done all that could be reasonably expected from him. See also *The Marion* (1984) 2 Lloyd's Rep.1.

(1) The International Union of Marine Insurance (IUMI) stated that the maximum available capacity (excluding the cover for oil pollution and nuclear risks) for an insurance cover was about $100m. Such a cover could be obtained at an economically acceptable premium.

(2) The limitation amounts are expressed in terms of units of account. These are equivalent in value to the Special Drawing Rights (SDRs) as defined by the International Monetary Fund (IMF). However, States which are not members of the IMF and whose law does not allow the use of SDRs, may continue to use the old gold franc (referred to as 'monetary unit').

(3) Under the LLMC Convention the limitation fund of a ship will be increased compared with the system under the 1957 Convention. For example, the limitation of an 8,000 tons ship under the 1957 Convention is approximately £720,000 ($1.05m) whereas under the LLMC it will be approximately £2.3m ($3.35m). The sliding scale is one reason for the increase and the other is the application of measurement under the Tonnage Measurement of Ships Convention, 1969.

for each ton from 501 to 3,000 tons, 500 SDRs (about $555)

for each ton from 3,001 to 30,000 tons, 333 SDRs (about $370)

for each ton from 30,001 to 70,000 tons, 250 SDRs (about $277), and

for each ton in excess of 70,000 tons, 167 SDRs (about $185).

(b) in respect of other claims,

(i) for a ship with a tonnage not exceeding 500 tons, 167,000 SDRs (about $185,370);

(ii) for a ship with a tonnage in excess thereof, the following amount to be added:

for each ton from 501 to 30,000 tons, 167 SDRs (about $185)

for each ton from 30,001 to 70,000 tons, 125 SDRs (about $139), and

for each ton in excess of 70,000 tons, 83 SDRs (about $92)[1].

<u>Loss of the right of limitation</u>: Under article 4: "A person liable shall not be entitled to limit his liability if it is proved that the loss resulted from his personal act or omission, committed with the intent to cause such loss, or recklessly and with knowledge that such loss would probably result".

This article is important in two respects. Firstly, it reverses the burden of proof. Under the existing law the burden of proof is upon the party seeking to limit his liability whereas under

---

(1) The Merchant Shipping (Sterling Equivalents) (Various Enactments) Order, 1985 (S.I.230/1985) does not specify sterling equivalents for references to gold francs for the purpose of the Merchant Shipping (Liability of Shipowners and Others) Act 1958 (c.62). This is no longer required as a result of the entry into force of the Protocol of December 21, 1979, which amends the International Convention of 1957 by substituting SDRs for gold francs. The Protocol is implemented by sections 1 and 3 of the Merchant Shipping Act, 1981 (c.10), which were brought into force by the No.3 Commencement Order for that Act (S.I.1695/1984) on November 29, 1984.

article 4 it is for the person seeking to bar limitation to prove one or more of the matters referred to in it. Secondly, the language of this article is different from the term "actual fault or privity" used in the 1957 Convention and under which the limitation was denied to shipowners in many cases. Under article 4(1), the person liable loses the right of limitation in cases of intention to cause the loss or if act or omission is recklessly(2) and with knowledge that such loss would probably result, is done. This case is perhaps similar to wilful misconduct(3).

References

Coghlin, Terence, The Convention on Limitation of Liability for Maritime Claims, 1976, IMO 1st ed., pp. 234-251.

Pineus & Rohreke - Limited Liability in Collision Cases, published by Lloyd's of London Press, 1984.

---

(1) Article 4 states: "A person liable shall not be entitled to limit his liability if it is proved that the loss resulted from his personal act or omission, committed with intent to cause such loss or recklessly and with knowledge that such loss would probably result."

(2) The word "reckless" indicates a high level of carelessness, something more than negligence. In the words of Lord Devlin, it means deliberately running an unjustifiable risk", see *Reed* v. *London and Rochester Trading Co.* (1954) 2 Lloyd's Rep. 463.

(3) For claims for oil pollution damage, see Chapter VII. As for collision, article 5 of the Convention provides that where there is a claim and a counterclaim, these shall be set off against each other and the right to limit liability will apply to the resulting net balance.

## (iv) THE CARRIAGE OF PASSENGERS AND THEIR LUGGAGE

For many years, the international community showed concern for the carriage of passengers by air. Legal rules were established and developed by the adoption of the Warsaw Convention, 1929, as amended by the Hague Protocol, 1955, the Guadalajara Convention, 1961, the Guatemala Protocol, 1971, and the Montreal Protocols, 1975. By contrast, no international attention was given to the carriage of passengers by sea until 1961 when the Brussels Convention for the Unification of Certain Rules Relating to the Carriage of Passengers by Sea was adopted(1). However, this latecomer was ineffective due to lack of ratifications and thus the way was paved for action by the IMO.

### THE CONVENTION ON THE CARRIAGE OF PASSENGERS AND THEIR LUGGAGE ON BOARD SHIPS, 1974

The IMO took the Brussels Convention of 1961 as the basis for formulating a new convention which would take into account the development in this area. Its work resulted in the adoption in 1974 of the Athens Convention on the Carriage of Passengers and their Luggage on Board Ships. Under article 24, the Convention will enter into force on the ninetieth day following the date on which ten States have become Contracting States(2). This condition has not yet been met and therefore the Convention is not yet in force. In 1976, a Protocol was adopted with regard to the unit of account in order to replace the franc by the Special Drawing Rights (SDR)(3).

---

(1) Another Convention for the Unification of Certain Rules Relating to the Carriage of Passenger Luggage by Sea was adopted in 1967.

(2) As to March 31, 1985, nine Contracting States have ratified the Convention and one more instrument is required. See C54/5 of April 1, 1985.

(3) The provisions of the Convention were incorporated into English Law by the Merchant Shipping Act, 1979. The Convention was set out in a schedule to the Act. Section 16 states that Orders in Council will specify when parts of the Act will come into force.
The Principal Order in Council is the Carriage of Passengers and their Luggage by Sea (Interim

Definitions

Article 1 contains a list of definitions of the most important terms and expressions in the Convention.

"Carrier" and "performing carrier": Frequently, the passenger buys a ticket which allows him to travel by the ship of another carrier (the performing carrier). The carrier may not even own any ship. Again, when a ship is under a charter-party, it is sometimes difficult to establish who is the carrier as the name of the carrier may appear on the ticket. Therefore, it was necessary to define the terms "carrier" and "performing" or "*de facto*" carrier. "Carrier" means a person by or on behalf of whom a contract of carriage has been concluded. "Performing carrier" means the person who actually performs the whole or part of the carriage.

It must be noted that under articles 3 and 4, the Contracting carrier is the person primarily

---

Provisions) Order, 1980 (S.I.1092/1980). It provides for a modification to article 2 on the scope of the application of the Convention. It also states that section 28 of the Unfair Contract Terms Act, 1977 (which made temporary provisions for contracts for the carriage of passengers and their luggage by sea, pending the provisions of the Athens Convention having the force of law in the United Kingdom) ceases, upon the date of the coming into operation of this Order, to apply to any contract to which this Order applies, but it continues to apply to any contract made before that date. The Order came into operation on January 1, 1981.
The Carriage of Passengers and their Luggage by Sea (Interim Provisions) (Notice) Order, 1980 (S.I.1125/1980) (came into force on January 1, 1981) requires a carrier in relation to any contract of carriage to which the Order applies, to give to passengers notice of specified provisions of the Convention. Those provisions relate to valuables, the limit of the carrier's liability for death or personal injury and for loss of or damage to luggage (including a vehicle), and the notice to be given by the passenger in respect of loss or damage to luggage. Notice must be given by the carrier before departure and where practicable, on the ticket itself.

liable for the damage, loss, injury or death and he could not escape his liability by arranging for the passenger to be carried by a ship of another carrier. However, the passenger or his executors or administrators can bring their claim against the performing carrier if the incident which caused the damage occurred while the carriage was performed by him.

Contract of carriage: This expression means a contract made by or on behalf of a carrier for the carriage by sea of a passenger or of a passenger and his luggage. This contract is not negotiable. It could be argued that the use of the words "by sea" would exclude from the Convention, carriage of passengers and their luggage on ships plying on inland rivers, canals, estuaries and lakes(1).

Ship: means a seagoing vessel, excluding an air-cushion vehicle(2).

Passenger: In ordinary language, a passenger is the person who travels in a private or public conveyance as opposed to the one who drives or operates the mode of transport. The Convention defines passenger as any person carried in a ship:

(a) under a contract of carriage; or

(b) who, with the consent of the carrier, is accompanying a vehicle or live animals which are covered by a contract for the carriage of goods not governed by this Convention.

This definition links the status of a passenger to the existence of a contract of carriage or his

---

(1) But safety rules will still apply to those ships if they carry more than twelve passengers on board. See M.Notice 913. See also Section 26(1), Merchant Shipping (Safety Convention) Act, 1949; Section 281 Merchant Shipping Act, 1894 (which revised penalties under Section 25, Merchant Shipping (Load Lines) Act, 1967, and paragraph 7 of Part VI of Schedule 6, Merchant Shipping Act, 1979); and Section 17(1), Merchant Shipping Act, 1964.

(2) See the Hovercraft (Civil Liability) Order, 1971 (S.I.720/1971).

presence on a ship with the consent of the carrier[1]. A better definition could be found in Section 26(1) of the Merchant Shipping (Safety Convention) Act, 1949, where the expression "passenger" means any person carried on a ship except:

(a) a person employed or engaged in any capacity on board the ship on the business of the ship;

(b) a person on board the ship either in pursuance of the obligation laid upon the master to carry shipwrecked, distressed or other persons, or by reason of any circumstances that neither the master nor the owner nor the charterer (if any) could have prevented or forestalled; and

(c) a child under one year of age.

The distinction between "persons engaged on the business of the ship" and "passengers" was raised in *The "Biche"*[2]. In this case, the owner of *The Biche* had made his vessel available for various maritime activities including excursions. On two occasions, a party of young people together with adult supervisors, boarded the vessel for an excursion. It was their intention to take part in sailing the vessel, which could not have operated under sail without their participation. The Department of Trade charged the owner with contravening s.271 of the Merchant Shipping Act,1894, as amended by s.17 of the Merchant Shipping Act,1964, and Schedule 6 of the Merchant Shipping Act,1979, in that he proceeded to sea on a voyage or excursion on a vessel carrying more than 12 passengers without a certificate of survey. The dispute centred on the word "engaged" in exception (a) above. Lord Justice Kerr said[3] that the word engaged "has a technical meaning relating to the terms of the engagement of the person in question to render services on board in some capacity, and it cannot properly be interpreted to refer merely to his activities while on board and to the question whether or not these happen to have been carried out 'on the business of the ship'. For instance, if a person comes on board as a fare-paying passenger, but renders assistance

(1) A stowaway is not a passenger.
(2) (1984) 1 Lloyd's Rep. 26.
(3) *Ibid*, at p.30.

to the crew during the voyage, he does not thereby cease to be a passenger or to become 'engaged on the business of the ship' for the purposes of this provision.

Construed in this way, the youngsters on board on these two occasions were clearly not "engaged"... In our view, ... the persons in question are to be treated as passengers"[1].

Another interesting case came before the High Court[2] as an appeal from the Magistrates sitting at North Shields. The case was concerned with the common practice for drivers of commercial vehicles to travel with their vehicles aboard the ship for the cross-channel voyage. On several occasions, the vessel *Somerset* was carrying lorry drivers with their vehicles. No fare was paid by the drivers and they were provided with meals free of charge. They did not perform any work or duty in connection with the ship as such but they did carry out routine maintenance of their lorries. The drivers were accommodated in one cabin but if the vessel did carry a fare-paying passenger, as she sometimes did, then that passenger would occupy the owner's cabin and eat with the master and officers. The drivers ate in their own mess but had the same food as the crew.

The master failed to engage a licensed pilot when entering into a compulsory area. Therefore, the Tyne Pilotage Authority charged the master with contravening section 11 of the Pilotage Act,1913, in that he was carrying passengers and failed to engage

---

(1) See M.Notice 1194 in which it was stated that as a result of this decision, it has been decided to give the following guidance regarding the status of persons when carried on board United Kingdom ships.
The only persons who can be considered as being lawfully "employed or engaged on the business of the ship" are those over the minimum school leaving age (about 16 years) who:
 (i) have a contractually binding agreement to serve on the ship in some defined capacity and which could include carrying out such duties under training, or are
 (ii) duly signed on members of the crew.

(2) Journal of Commerce, January 24, 1983. The High Court consisted of Mr. Justice Melford Stevenson, Mr. Justice Browne and Mr. Justice Milmo.

a licensed pilot. The Magistrates dismissed the summonse.

The question before the High Court was whether the lorry drivers were or were not passengers. Mr. Justice Stevenson, after referring to section 267 of the Merchant Shipping Act,1894, said that it was a fair inference that drivers were expected to be and were in fact accommodated for the purpose of driving the lorries on and off the ship and were permitted to be on the ship for that purpose. These matters brought these drivers within the concept of "passenger".

Mr. Justice Milmo agreed and said that the drivers took no part whatsoever in the navigation of the ship and did nothing in connection with the vessel herself. They were being carried on the vessel for one purpose only, namely to take them from the point where they had driven their lorry on to the vessel to the point from which they were going to drive it off. It was, therefore, inescapable that the drivers were passengers.

Luggage: means any article or vehicle carried by the carrier under a contract of carriage, excluding:

(a) articles and vehicles carried under a charter-party, bill of lading or other contract primarily concerned with the carriage of goods; and

(b) live animals.

Cabin luggage: means luggage which the passenger has in his cabin or otherwise in his possession, custody or control. This will cover luggage in the vehicle. However, for the purpose of limitation of liability, the damage to the vehicle includes all luggage carried in or on the vehicle.

Carriage: Paragraph 8 of article 1 defines carriage for the purposes of the commencement of the application of the rules of the Convention. It states that "with regard to the passenger and his cabin luggage, the period during which the passenger and/or his cabin luggage are on board the ship or in the course of embarkation or disembarkation, and the period during which the passenger and his cabin luggage are transported by water from land to the ship or vice versa". The words "in the course of embarkation or disembarkation"(1) may give rise to

(1) For air transport, a court of the Federal

various meanings. For instance, it is not clear that injury to a passenger or damage to his luggage while they are carried by a coach belonging to the carrier from the marine station to the ship are covered by the word "carriage".

With regard to cabin luggage, the provisions of the Convention apply from the time during which the passenger is in a marine terminal or station or on a quay or in or on any other port installation if that luggage has been taken over by the carrier, his servant or agent, until re-delivery.

With regard to other luggage which is not cabin luggage, the provisions of the Convention apply from the time of its taking over by the carrier, or his servants or agent on shore or on board, until re-delivery.

International carriage: means any carriage in which, according to the contract of carriage, the place of departure and the place of destination are situated in two different States, or in a single State if, according to the contract of carriage or the scheduled itinerary, there is an intermediate port of call in another State. Thus, the carriage of a passenger from the Shetland Isles to a port in the United Kingdom when the ship is calling at a Norwegian port, is an international carriage.

Scope of application

Article 2 provides that the provisions of the Convention "apply to any international carriage if:

---

Republic of Germany held that the operations of embarkation commence in the airport waiting room (1962) Z.F.L.W.R. 78; the Court of Appeal of Paris decided that the Warsaw Convention applies to an accident caused by a luggage trolley on the way from the airport building to the aircraft (1971) R.F.D.A. 173.
From these decisions it seems that the courts rely upon three tests, namely:
(a) the authority of the carrier at the time of the accident;
(b) the degree of control exercised by the carrier over the movements of the passenger; and
(c) the location of the incident.

(a) the ship is flying the flag[1] of or is registered in a State Party to this Convention; or

(b) the contract of carriage has been made in a State Party to this Convention; or

(c) the place of departure or destination[2], according to the contract of carriage, is in a State Party to this Convention."

Article 2 is unfortunately misworded as it refers to international carriage rather than the contract of carriage[3]. (a) above is not an option but a condition for the application of the Convention. Furthermore, article 2 omitted the case of an agreement. Thus, a question may arise: can the parties by agreement inserted in the ticket stipulate for the application of the Convention?

The draftsmen of the Convention were anxious to avoid any conflict between the Convention and any of the compulsory existing transport conventions dealing with another mode of transport. In case such conflict exists, the provisions of the compulsory convention of the other mode of transport will prevail[4].

---

(1) The Convention applies to ships owned by the State or public authority and used for commercial purposes. See art.21.

(2) A subsequent change of the place of departure or destination would not affect the application of the Convention.

(3) Part I of Schedule 3 of the 1979 Act modified article 2. It states: "This Convention shall apply to any carriage if:

(a) it is international carriage and the contract of carriage is made in the United Kingdom; or

(b) it is international carriage and, under the contract of carriage, a place in the United Kingdom is the place of departure or destination; or

(c) under the contract of carriage, the places of departure and destination are in the area consisting of the United Kingdom, the Channel Islands and the Isle of Man and there is no intermediate port of call outside that area."

Although the substituted article is better than the one of the Convention, it is still in need of improvement.

(4) See paragraph 2 of article 2.

## Basis of liability

At common law, the carrier owes a duty to his passengers to exercise due care and diligence to ensure their safety(1) and his failure in carrying out this duty would give rise to his liability. The Convention adopted the same basis, i.e. fault or neglect. Article 3 states: "The carrier shall be liable ... if the incident ... was due to the fault or neglect of the carrier or his servants or agents acting within the scope of their employment."

## Liability of the carrier and performing carrier

As mentioned earlier, the "Contracting" carrier is the person primarily liable for any damage, loss, injury or death if the incident which caused the damage occurred in the course of the carriage(2) and was due to the fault or neglect of the carrier or of his servants or agents acting within the scope of their employment(3).

---

(1) *Readhead* v. *Midland Railway Company* (1869) LR 4 Q.B.379 where Montague Smith, J., said (at p.384): "An obligation to use all due and proper care is founded on reasons obvious to all, but to impose on the carrier the burden of a warranty that everything he necessarily uses is absolutely free from defects likely to cause peril, when from the nature of things defects must exist which no skill can detect, and the effects of which no care or foresight can avert, would be to compel a man, by implication of law and not by his own will, to promise the performance of an impossible thing ..." See also *Cockerton* v. *Naviera Aznar SA* (1960) 2 Lloyd's Rep. 451. See also the revised requirements for the submission of passenger returns by the masters of ships carrying passengers to or from United Kingdom ports. M.Notice 842.

(2) Carriage as defined in article 1(3).

(3) Where the act is done by an employee with no authority, it could not be said that such an act is done within the scope of his employment and that the employer becomes liable. An act of theft is not regarded within the scope of employment of the carrier's servants. Cf. Lord Denning in *Rose* v. *Plenty* (1976) 1 W.L.R. 141, where he said at p.144: "If it is done for his employers' business, it is usually done in the

The burden of proving the incident which caused the damage and also the extent of the damage lies with the claimant. This is usually not a heavy burden. The Convention goes even further and states that fault is presumed in two circumstances. First, if the death or personal injury of the passenger or the loss of or damage to his cabin luggage arose from or in connection with[1] the shipwreck, collision, stranding, explosion, fire or defect in the ship[2]; second, with regard to loss of or damage to any non-cabin luggage in any circumstances.

The passenger or after his death, his executors or administrators, may bring their action against the performing carrier if the incident which caused the damage occurred while the carriage was performed by him.

The measure of damages authorised by the Convention can be reduced by virtue of the claimant's contribution to the fault. However, article 6 of the Convention makes it clear that the effect of a claimant's contribution to fault depends on the effect of contributory negligence in the municipal law of the court seized of the Case.

Article 5 excludes the liability of the carrier for valuables such as monies, negotiable securities, gold, silverware, jewellery, ornaments and works of art unless they have been deposited with the carrier for safe-keeping.

Limitation of liability

At common law, the carrier[3] can limit his liability or even exclude it entirely[4]. The position

---

course of his employment, even though it is a prohibited act."

(1) The use of the term "in connection with" is to widen the application of the presumed fault to cases when shipwreck, collision, stranding, explosion, fire or defect were not the direct cause of the damage.

(2) Not any minor defect in the ship would be sufficient to bring about the presumed fault. It may be a direct, combined or a mixed fault.

(3) *Ludditt* v. *Ginger Coote Airways* (1947) A.C.233. P.C.

(4) There are a number of cases on the validity of exemption clauses to be found in passenger tickets. The two main issues in all these cases are: whether the document when the exemption

under the Athens Convention is quite different as articles 7 and 8 provide for a limitation of liability which is a kind of ceiling to the claims.

In 1976 a Protocol was signed to amend articles 7 and 8 in order to abandon the franc and replace it with a unit of account. The limits under the Protocol and their equivalent under the Merchant Shipping Sterling Equivalents (various Enactments) Order 1985 are as follows:

- Liability for the death or personal injury not exceeding 46,666 units = £38,636.90
- Liability for loss of or damage to cabin luggage not exceeding 833 units = £689.94
- Liability for loss of or damage to vehicles including all luggage carried in or on the vehicle not exceeding 3,333 units = £2,759.78
- Liability for loss of or damage to non-cabin not exceeding 1,200 units = £993.52

The carrier will lose the benefit of limitation if it is proved that the damage resulted from an act or omission of the carrier done with the intent to cause such damage, or recklessly and with knowledge that such damage would probably result (article 13). The second paragraph of this article deals in similar language to the loss of right of limitation for the servant or agent(1).

Accordingly, the carrier, his servant or agent will lose the right of limitation where there is:

(a) an intentional wrong act or omission; or

(b) a reckless(2) act without caring whether

---

clause is incorporated is a contactual document, and whether sufficient notice of such condition has been given to the passenger. See *The Eagle* (1977) 2 Lloyd's Rep. 70.

(1) It must be noted that the servant or agent, if he proves that he acted within the scope of his employment, is entitled to the same defences and limits of liability as the carrier (art.11).

(2) In *Reed* v. *London and Rochester Trading Co.* (1954) 2 Lloyd's Rep. 463, Devlin, J. held that: "recklessly ... means something more than mere negligence or inadvertence .. it means deliberately running an unjustifiable risk." See also *Frazer* v. *Furman* (1967) 2 Lloyd's Rep.1.

> it is right or wrong. In this case, the carrier, his servant or agent must know that the loss, damage or delay would probably result. Knowledge, in this respect, does not mean actual knowledge but covers cases of a presumed knowledge or where a person turns a blind eye on certain events(1).

Apart from cases of theft, it may be argued whether an unjustified deviation is covered by article 13.

It must be noted that the limitation of liability would not affect the right of the carrier to rely upon the limitation based on the tonnage, i.e. The Brussels Limitation Convention, 1957, or the Limitation of Maritime Claims Convention, 1976, in case it would be favourable to him (article 19).

The limits of liability apply to the aggregate of the amounts recoverable in all claims arising out of the death of or personal injury to any one passenger or the loss of or damage to his luggage.

Where the carriage is wholly or partly performed by a performing carrier, the aggregate of the amounts recoverable from the carrier and the performing carrier and from their servants and agents shall not exceed the amounts stipulated in the Convention as amended by the Protocol.

<u>Notice of loss or damage to luggage</u>

The passenger(2) must give written notice to the carrier(3) or his agent(4) indicating the general

---

(1) In *Compania Maritima San Basilio* v. *Oceanus* (1976) 2 Lloyd's Rep. 161, Lord Denning said: "and when I speak of knowledge, I mean not only positive knowledge, but also the sort of knowledge expressed in the phrase 'turning a blind eye'."

(2) The passenger is the only person entitled to give the notice.

(3) Presumably a notice given to the performing carrier is not valid. Where the damaged luggage is re-delivered by the performing carrier, it would be difficult for the passenger to give notice to the contractual carrier.

(4) Only an agent can receive the notice. The Convention is silent on whether the servant of the carrier can receive the notice.

nature of the loss or damage to the luggage. A written notice is required to indicate the passenger's intention to claim for the loss or damage to his luggage. The notice is not needed in case there has been a joint survey or inspection (article 15(3)).

Article 15(1) maintains a distinction as to the time of giving notice between apparent and non-apparent damage. In case of apparent damage to cabin luggage, the notice must be given before or at the time of disembarkation of the passenger. For all other luggage, the notice must be given before or at the time of the re-delivery of the luggage.

In the case of non-apparent damage, the notice must be given within fifteen days from the date of disembarkation or re-delivery or from the time when such re-delivery should have taken place.

Failure to give the notice within the prescribed period or the absence of any notice are considered as *prima facie* evidence that the carrier has delivered the luggage undamaged. If the passenger is still seeking to recover for damage to or loss of his luggage, the onus of proof lies upon him. In other words, the absence or delay in giving the notice results in *prima facie* proof of the good condition of the luggage; evidence, nevertheless, can refute this.

## Time limit for bringing the action

The time limit is two years. Article 16(1) states: "Any action for damages arising out of the death of or personal injury to a passenger or for the loss of or damage to luggage shall be time-barred after a period of two years." Thus, any action(1) which results from the carriage of the passenger or his luggage under the Convention is subject to the two-year time limit(2). An action from the carrier against the performing carrier can be brought after the expiration of the time limit.

Paragraph 2 of article 16 deals with the commencement of the time limit:

"(a) in the case of personal injury, from the date of disembarkation of the passenger;

---

(1) The term "any action" covers an action based on contract or tort.

(2) No reference is made as to whether the time limit applies to arbitration procedures.

(b) In the case of death occurring during carriage, from the date when the passenger should have disembarked, and in the case of personal injury occurring during carriage and resulting in the death of the passenger after disembarkation, from the date of death, provided that this period shall not exceed three years from the date of disembarkation;

(c) in the case of loss of or damage to luggage from the date of disembarking or from the date when disembarkation should have taken place, whichever is later."

The expiration, suspension and interruption of the time limit: Under certain civil legal systems, the time limit may be regarded as a "prescription"(1) or a "delai de déchéance". If the two-year period constitutes "prescription", this would mean that the period may be extended and the claim may survive more than two years. If it is considered as "delai de déchéance", the two-year period will not be extended(2).

Paragraph 3 of article 16 states that: "The law of the court seized of the case shall govern the grounds of suspension and interruption of limitation periods, but in no case shall an action under this Convention be brought after the expiration of a period of three years."

Can the two-year period be extended?: The answer to this question is provided for in paragraph 4 of article 16 which states that: "...the period of limitation be extended by a declaration of the carrier or by agreement of the parties after the course of action has arisen." An agreement in advance before the course of action has arisen is not valid.

---

(1) "Prescription" in common law is more nearly analogous to a statute "barring the remedy" than the one "extinguishing" or "being a condition upon" the right.

(2) Under English law, a suit must be brought on time and to the correct court, otherwise it will be barred. As to the extension of the time limit, the parties may agree that the two-year period can be extended.

Competent jurisdiction

Article 17 profides that the claimant, at his option, can bring his action before any of the following four courts:

(a) the place of the carrier's business or his permanent residence;

(b) the place of departure or destination;

(c) the place of the domicile or permanent residence of the claimant; and

(d) the place where the contract of carriage was made,

provided that the court is located in a State party to the Convention.

Option (d) is usually the same as (b). Further, the word "domicile" in (c) is ambiguous. More important is that article 17 failed to include the most popular option, i.e. an agreement between the parties on the court to have jurisdiction. Such an agreement, under article 17, can only be valid after the occurrence of the incident which has caused the damage.

Invalidity of contractual provisions

One of the objectives of the Convention is to invalidate any clause which relieves or lessens the carrier's liability below that provided in it. Article 18 states that: "Any contractual provision concluded before the occurrence of the incident which has caused the death of or personal injury to a passenger or the loss of or damage to his luggage, purporting to relieve the carrier of his liability towards the passenger or to prescribe a lower limit of liability ... or having the effect of restricting the option specified in .. article 17 shall be null and void."

References

The Carriage of Passengers and their Luggage by Sea (Interim Provisions) Order, 1980 (S.I.1092/1980).

The Carriage of Passengers and their Luggage by Sea (Interim Provisions)(Notice) Order, 1980 (S.I. 1125/1980).

Grime, R., The Carriage of Passengers and the Athens Convention in the United Kingdom, IMO first edition, pp. 252-276.

(v) SPECIAL TRADE PASSENGER SHIPS AGREEMENT, 1971

The carriage of large numbers of unberthed passengers in special trades, such as pilgrims, gives rise to problems of the allocation of space per passenger, of sanitary requirements, etc. In 1931, a set of rules known as the Simla Rules were adopted to govern special trades. However, over the years, these Rules became seriously out of date.

The IMO became aware of the problems associated with the carriage of pilgrims in a restricted sea area around the Indian Ocean. Therefore, it convened a conference to consider the safety requirements of special trades passenger ships in relation to the 1960 SOLAS Convention. To this end, an agreement was adopted in 1971(1) to safeguard ships and passengers(2). It provides for modification of Chapters II and III of the 1960 SOLAS Convention. A certificate called a Special

---

(1) The Agreement came into force on January 2, 1974.

(2) Rule 2(6) defines "special trade" as meaning "the conveyance of large numbers of special trade passengers by sea on international voyages within the area specified below (as illustrated in the chart in Appendix I to these Rules):

- on the south bounded by the parallel of latitude 20°S from the east coast of Africa to the west coast of Madagascar, thence the west and north coasts of Madagascar to longitude 50°C, thence the meridian of longitude 50°E to latitude 10°S, thence the rhumb line to the point latitude 3°S, longitude 75°E, thence the rhumb line to the point latitude 11°S, longitude 120°E, thence the parallel of latitude 11°S to longitude 141° 03'E;

  on the east bounded by the meridian of longitude 141°03'E from latitude 11°S to the south coast of New Guinea, thence the south, west and north coasts of New Guinea to the point longitude 141°03'E, thence the rhumb line from the north coast of New Guinea at the point 141°03 E to the point latitude 10°N, at the north-east coast of Mindanao, thence the west coasts of the islands of Leyte, Samar and Luzon to the Port of Sual (Luzon Island), thence the rhumb line from the Port of Sual to

Passenger Ship Safety Certificate[1] is required to be carried on board in addition to the Passenger Ship Safety Certificate (Rule 5). Rule 20 makes it clear that this type of ship shall comply with the International Health Regulations (1969).

Work on this issue was continued by the IMO in co-operation with the World Health Organization (WHO) to draw the technical rules on the safety aspects of the disposition of passengers on board such ships. As a result of this work, a Protocol on Space Requirements for Special Trade Passenger Ships was adopted in 1973[2]. Appendix I presents a table of space showing the minimum space allocation per passenger, as follows:

| Location | Duration of Voyage | Minimum Space Allocation per Passenger |
|---|---|---|
| Weather Deck (during the season of fair weather only) | Less than 24 hours | 0.74 $m^2$ (8 sq ft) |
| | 24 hours and over but less than 72 hours | 1.12 $m^2$ (12 sq ft) |
| Upper Deck | Less than 24 hours | 0.74 $m^2$ (8 sq ft) |
| | 24 hours and over but less than 72 hours | 1.12 $m^2$ (12 sq ft) |
| Upper Between Deck | Less than 24 hours | 0.88 $m^2$ (9½ sq ft) |
| | 24 hours and over but less than 72 hours | 1.12 $m^2$ (12 sq ft) |
| Lower Between Deck | Less than 24 hours | 0.88 $m^2$ (9½ sq ft) |
| | 24 hours and over but less than 72 hours | 1.40 $m^2$ (15 sq ft) |

Hong Kong;
- on the north bounded by the south coast of Asia from Hong Kong to Suez;
- on the west bounded by the east coast of Africa from Suez to the point latitude 20°C."

(1) See the Form of Certificate, Appendix II to the Convention.

(2) The Protocol came into force on June 2, 1977.

# CHAPTER VI

# NAVIGATIONAL RULES

The Law of Safe Navigation is of vital concern to the State, the shipping industry, seafarers and environmentalists. A great part of the law owes its existence to the IMO. Through this Organization, several measures were approved. The IMO has also lent its support to other organizations working on safety of navigation. It is important to note that the IMO rules form an integrated package. Therefore, the navigational rules should be considered in conjunction with other rules such as the one on the protection of the environment and ship construction. The rigorous regulations on construction, subdivision and stability ensure the structural strength of the hull and thus contribute to safe navigation. Similarly, the prevention, detection and extinction of fire is an additional guarantee for the safety of the ship as well as the crew and cargo. The efforts of the IMO in this respect cover almost every aspect of navigation.

"Black Box": A proposal to carry a "black box" to record the human and technical failures which lead to collisions and groundings was considered(1). The "black box" is to record:

(a) navigational and manoeuvring data for use in the analysis of collisions and groundings; and

(b) information for use in the investigation of total losses where there are no or few surviving witnesses.

During the discussion of the proposal, it was mentioned that a recorder is of particular importance to record commands given on the bridge and to monitor radiotelephone conversations. The recovery of the recorder in deep water may not always be possible. Some delegations believed that shipmasters should be protected against legal liability with respect to the use of information from recorders. The recorder would have to be installed in such a way that it would be released and would float to the surface automatically if the ship sank to a certain depth. The Sub-Committee on Safety of Navigation did not take any decision on this matter until the Japanese delegation presents technical details on experiments with data recorders.

---

(1) IMO News, No.2, 1980, p.5.

Relationship between the master and the shipowner: An *ad hoc* Group considered this issue and its relevance to maritime safety and pollution control. Among the matters raised for discussion were:

(a) the dependence of the master upon the shipowner;

(b) the degree of control of the shipping management over the shipowner; and

(c) the enforcement by the maritime administration for breaches by the shipowner and the master.

The Group agreed that there was a general need for a framework of protective provisions for the master against unjustifiable dismissal or other form of discrimination as a result of his action to ensure safety and protection of the marine environment. No restraints should be placed on the master's professional judgment. Resolution A.443 (XI) invited governments to ensure that:

"(a) The shipmaster is not constrained by the shipowner, charterer or any other person from taking in this respect any decision which, in the professional judgment of the shipmaster, is necessary;

(b) The shipmaster is protected by appropriate provisions, including the right of appeal, contained in, *inter alia*, national legislation, collective agreements or contracts of employment, from unjustifiable dismissal or other unjustifiable action by the shipowner, charterer or any other person as a consequence of the proper exercise of his professional judgment."

Deep sea pilotage: The term "deep sea pilotage" refers to the use of pilots outside coastal waters. Such pilotage is not compulsory and it is for the master or owner of the ship to decide whether to take a deep-sea pilot. In December 1978, a Council Directive 79/115/EEC was passed. It requires Member States which have coasts bordering on the North Sea or English Channel to take all necessary and appropriate measures to ensure that vessels availing themselves of the services of a deep sea pilot for pilotage in the North Sea or the English Channel be provided with adequately qualified deep sea pilots. As a result, Rules on Deep Sea Pilotage were drawn up by the North Sea Pilotage Commission and subsequently endorsed by the IMO.

Introducing a compulsory pilotage system outside the territorial waters needs an international agreement. Governments would not adhere to such an agreement unless a good case is made on the advantages of the system(1). Furthermore, the enforcement of an agreement on the high seas would certainly be a difficult task.

Resolution A.209 (VII) on manoeuvring: A Working Group looked at Resolution A.209 (VII) and agreed that:

"(a) the Resolution does not account for the results of more investigations concerning human factors and behaviour or the needs of shipmasters and pilots handling modern ships;

(b) the resolution is not precise in reflecting which manoeuvring characteristics are of direct importance to shipmaster and pilot. Further, it does not consider the most effective format for presentation of manoeuvring information."

The Group approved a revised version of Resolution A.209 (VII)(2) and draft Guidelines for Estimating Manoeuvring Performance in Ship Design(3).

Universal Time (UTC): Some consideration was given to a co-ordinated Universal Time (UTC) and the Sub-Committee on Safety of Navigation agreed(4) that for all practical navigation purposes, UTC can be considered as equivalent to GMT in matters related to navigation(5).

---

(1) A Code of good conduct for deep-sea pilotage, undertaken on a voluntary basis, has been developed through the North Sea Pilotage Commission (NSPC) which acts principally as an advisory body on pilotage matters of common interest to the eight countries bordering the North Sea: Belgium, Denmark, the Federal Republic of Germany, France, the Netherlands, Norway, Sweden and the United Kingdom.
(2) DE27/WP.4, of March 1, 1984.
(3) *Ibid*, Annex 3 to DE27/WP.4.
(4) NAV27/12, p.24.
(5) Among other matters related to navigation was

Ships' bridge and layout: The Sub-Committee decided that the guidelines on ships' bridge and layout should be restricted to the International Organization for Standardization (ISO) draft International standard for shipbuilding and marine structures - ships' bridge layout and associated equipment, requirements and guidelines(1).

Several delegations to the Sub-Committee stressed the importance of navigating bridge visibility for safety at sea. It was agreed to establish a working group on this subject to examine in detail the guidelines proposed by the United States(2) and the relevant extracts from the ISO draft Standard(3).

Ocean Data Acquisition Systems (ODAS): The Sub-Committee agreed that the rules on ODAS should be adapted in order to be in line with the provisions of the International Association of Lighthouse Authorities (IALA) Maritime Buoyage System as adopted by the IMO(4).

The International Code of Signals: The Sub-Committee prepared draft amendments to the Code. These amendments relate to the identification of hospital ships and their helicopters; the air to surface visual signals as provided for in MERSAR and IMCOSAR Manuals; and the introduction of reporting a ship's position by OMEGA and NAVSAT in replacement of the existing provisions for CONSOL(5).

Navigational charts: Charts based on out of date surveys could severely restrict the movement of the ship. Without full confidence in the charts, the master may reduce speed, follow round-about routes, reduce the draught by carrying less cargo and, in some cases, may be deterred from entering certain areas altogether. In brief, the use of charts with inadequate information could have severe economic

---

the French proposal that the IMO should prepare a standard list of information which any ship requiring towage assistance should be in a position to transmit without delay to a towing ship. *Ibid*, p.30.

(1) NAV27/INF.5.
(2) NAV27/10/1.
(3) NAV27/INF.5.
(4) NAV27/12, p.27.
(5) *Ibid*, p.29.

effects and place the ship at the risk of grounding(1).

For historic reasons, the United Kingdom(2) assumed responsibility for surveys and chart work in many parts of the World. The Admiralty chart series gives virtually worldwide coverage. However, as a result of financial constraints, the Hydrographer of the Navy(3) limited his activities to survey of areas deemed essential to the navy.

The United Kingdom, the United States and the Soviet Union maintain a worldwide series of charts, and France, Germany and Japan have series which cover most of the world. They compromise usually by including smaller scale charts which cover larger areas. This reduces the number of charts needed but also affects the adequacy of chart coverage.

Through bilateral agreements, a country could adopt the charts of another and correct them by its

---

(1) See *The Norman* (1960) 1 Lloyd's Rep. 1; *The Marion*, H.L. (1984) 2 Lloyd's Rep. 1.
Until 1960, the maximum draught of a ship was about 11 metres. Nowadays, the draught of a VLCC could be 20 m. or more and can even exceed 30 m.
In fact, there are serious difficulties in determining safe routes for deep-draught tankers off the West Coast of Scotland because of the inadequate hydrographic surveys of these waters. Furthermore, new routes had to be found in this area as a result of the various offshore activities and the safety zones around the rigs.

(2) Responsibility for surveys of U.K. waters, whether for defence or civil purposes, rests with the Ministry of Defence and the Hydrographer of the Navy.

(3) The Hydrographer of the Navy has published a Chart (Chart 5500) covering the English Channel and Dover Strait. It contains sections on planning the passage; the general and special provisions of ships' routeing in the area; recommendations applying to particular classes of vessels; radio reporting requirements; pilotage services; maritime radio services; tidal information and radiobeacon services. In fact, it brings together information which could only be found in a number of publications. Another advantage is the simplicity offered by presenting the information in the chart format which could be easily corrected.

own Notices to Mariners[1].

In 1967, the International Hydrographic Organization (IHO) took the first step to find a solution to the international charting problem. It formed a commission to study the feasibility of an international series of charts and to date almost 80 INT charts, covering the whole world, have been published.

The idea is that a number of countries undertake to compile a number of charts in the series in conformity with laid down specifications. Other countries, acting as printer-nations, can reproduce these charts. Corrections issued by the producer nation can be reproduced by the printer-nations within their own national Notice to Mariners.

The next step is to select from national series those charts needed by international shipping and to integrate national schemes. This has already been done for the North Sea and plans are far advanced for the Mediterranean and Black Sea.

The INT chart concept is that gradually a set of charts, uniform in style, based on the best surveys available, their limits conforming to an integrated scheme, will emerge as a worldwide series making available to international shipping the best available charts published.

The solution adopted by the IMO of adopting a worldwide series and augmenting it with odd charts from national series is considered to be piecemeal. The IMO should pay great attention to this matter[2] as the discussion within the IMO is

---

(1) The use of tracings to keep the charts up-to-date gives rise to the question of liability for inaccurate tracings. Many companies provide a service of tracings to save the officers the time of plotting. They usually provide the tracings with the appropriate Notices to Mariners. They also contain, in small print, a phrase to exclude their liability for any error. Thus, the officer in charge of the chart would have to check the correctness of the traces in the light of the Notices to Mariners.

(2) The Sub-Committee on Safety of Navigation in its 27th session (11-15 Oct., 1982) (NAV 27/12, p.27) considered only the issue of availability of navigational charts and Notices to Mariners. A questionnaire had revealed that difficulties were experienced in obtaining charts internationally. The IHO pointed out that more than

limited to whether an Assembly resolution should be made on this issue(1).

Issues for consideration: The Maritime Safety Committee has on several occasions amended and adopted new traffic separation schemes. Yet, the latest proposals for the amendment of the Collision Rules, if adopted, would fuel the controversy instead of resolving the difficulties.

Satellite communication including distress, urgency and safety messages through INMARSAT system is having top priority. INMARSAT and its important work in the field of satellite communication is the organization for the future. It is unique among international organizations since it is run on commercial terms. As a private enterprise it would have a more imaginative commercial way to make a profit. This could be in conflict with its role as an international body.

This chapter covers the important measures taken in the field of navigation, namely:

(i) traffic separation schemes and vessel traffic services;

(ii) the Collision Rules;

(iii) a Standard Marine Navigational Vocabulary and a new buoyage system;

(iv) Maritime Search and Rescue; and

(v) Satellite Communications.

---

20 chart-producing States published through Notices to Mariners or chart catalogues the names and addresses of agents from whom charts and publications may be obtained.

(1) NAV 27/WP.7.

## (i) TRAFFIC SEPARATION SCHEMES AND VESSEL TRAFFIC SERVICES

### 1. Traffic Separation Schemes

In order to ensure "the safety of navigation in converging areas and in areas where the density of traffic is great or where the freedom of movement of shipping is inhibited by restricted sea-room, the existence of obstructions to navigation, limited depths or unfavourable meteorological conditions", it was necessary to adopt traffic separation schemes.

Article 22 of the UN Convention on the Law of the Sea, 1983 states:

> "1. The coastal State may, where necessary having regard to safety of navigation, require foreign ships exercising the right of innocent passage through its territorial sea to use such sea lanes and traffic separation schemes as it may designate or prescribe for the regulation of the passage of ships"(1).

The objectives of the schemes include some or all of the following:

"(a) the separation of opposing streams of traffic so as to reduce the incidence of head-on encounters;

(b) the reduction of dangers of collision between crossing traffic and shipping in established traffic lanes;

(c) the simplification of the patterns of traffic flow in converging areas;

(d) the organization of traffic flow in areas of concentrated offshore exploration or exploitation;

(e) the organization of traffic flow in or around areas where navigation by all ships or by certain classes of ships is dangerous or undesirable;

(f) the reduction of risk of grounding by providing special guidance to vessels in areas where water depths are uncertain or critical;

---

(1) See also articles 41 and 53 of the UN Convention on the Law of the Sea, 1983.

(g) the guidance of traffic clear of fishing grounds or the organization of traffic through fishing grounds"[(1)].

Several traffic separation schemes throughout the world were adopted by the IMO. These schemes were recommended at the beginning on a voluntary basis and by Resolution A.228 (VII) the IMO asked its Member States to make the observance of the schemes mandatory[(2)].

Although the IMO revised the principles of navigation within these schemes, there was no guarantee that States when adopting the 1972 Collision Rules will also make the schemes compulsory. Therefore, the schemes were made part of the Rules by Rule 10.

At its fifty-first session the Maritime Safety Committee adopted amendments to the "General Provisions on Ships' Routeing"[(3)]. Article 2 provides for certain definitions such as "Inshore traffic zone" which means "a routeing measure comprising a designated area between the landward boundary of a traffic separation scheme and the adjacent coast, to be used in accordance with the provisions of rule 10(d) of the 1972 Collision Regulations".

Article 3 on Procedures and Responsibilities states in 3.1: "The IMO is recognized as the only international body responsible for establishing and recommending measures on an international level concerning ships' routeing." It is doubtful that this rule is valid under International Law. In fact, some of the IMO schemes are on the high seas where others are within the territorial waters of coastal states. Where the scheme is on the high seas, it will be an offence to proceed against the established direction of the traffic flow, only for ships flying the flag of a Contracting State. Where the scheme is within the territorial waters of a State which is party to the Collision Rules, foreign vessels, even if they fly flags of non-party States, must follow the rules of the scheme as they would be considered as part of the local rules of navigation.

---

(1) See the General Provisions on Ships' Routeing, NAV 30/11 of Jan. 18, 1985.
(2) The Dover Strait scheme became mandatory in 1977. On July 1, 1982, amendments were made to this scheme, see M.Notice 1029.
(3) See NAV 30/11 of January 18, 1985.

Article 4 describes the methods which may be used for separation. The following articles deal with: Planning (article 5); Design criteria (article 6); Temporary adjustments to traffic separation schemes (article 7); the use of routeing systems (article 8); and Symbols (article 9).

In addition to the new and amended traffic schemes[1], the IMO adopted routeing systems other than traffic schemes[2].

## 2. Vessel Traffic Services (VTS)

Traffic in certain areas created hazards to life, property and the marine environment. Since these matters are of national concern, some ports have introduced a traffic management service or a control system for ships within their jurisdiction.

A number of ports worldwide apply various systems to control the movements of the vessels. The functions of, say, a vessel traffic service are: (a) surveillance; (b) radio communications; (c) identification; (d) information; (e) monitoring; and (f) obtaining general information such as the position of navigation marks. The information may be couched in the form of an advice, directive or order. The lack of uniformity in the systems applied by the ports is inevitable because every port or waterway has its own system of operation. Furthermore, the legal powers given to the port authority or other competent authority are not the same[3].

---

(1) *Ibid*, Annex 3.

(2) For example, a routeing system was adopted for the navigation through the entrances to the Baltic Sea. As the maximum depth is 17 metres, ships of 20,000 gross tonnage and above should only enter the Baltic Sea with a draught at which it is safe to navigate through the area. *Ibid*, Annex 5.

(3) The utilisation of control systems poses the novel question whether there is a duty on the port organization to provide such a system. The answer to this question depends on various considerations such as the density of the traffic, the financial guarantees, the insurance covers effected by the port, etc. However, from the legal point of view, a court of law would only consider two factors. The first is whether

Where a control system is introduced in an area a legal duty[1] consisting of two components exist. The first is the duty to inform the controller[2] of the movement of the ship, and the second is the duty of the master to observe the information[3] received from the controller. The legal duty in this respect derives from the regulations of the port or from the concept of good seamanship. According to this concept, the master[4] is required to communicate

---

the control system is necessary for the safety of the port, and the second the regulations of the port.

(1) It can be argued that a vessel using a port which provides information, management or a control system assumes greater duty than when using a port without such a system.

(2) From the information received, the controller will have a complete view of the flow or the pattern of traffic.

(3) The information may be couched as an advice, directive or order, It is widely believed that the difference between an advice and directive from a controller is that the former is not binding as the master is free to accept or ignore it, while the latter would have to be followed. However, an advice, directive or an order from the controller may be actionable if his conduct was blameworthy. Liability in this respect is based on the failure to take reasonable precautions to avoid the accident. Although an advice is something to be accepted or rejected, it is far from being negligible. An advice may be given in a way that a set of predictable actions by the master have to be taken. On the other hand, a directive could leave the master with a choice. This is a question of fact which has to be decided by consideration of all circumstances. Thus, regardless of the form in which the information is provided, it is the duty of the master to use the information in a "reasonable" and "intelligent" way. What specifically constitutes such "reasonable" and "intelligent" use is a function of two factors. First, the techniques by which the information are to be made useful to the navigators. Second, the way in which the master utilises the information to the best advantage.

(4) The master enjoys a certain degree of discretion

with the port when approaching it and to take advantage of all safety devices at hand. The information received from the controller will be of great value to the master and will enable him to initiate positive action to avoid an accident.

Although the control systems are closely linked with Rule 10, the IMO decided[(1)] not to be involved in the adoption or approval of vessel traffic services. The only aspect which seems to escape this ban is the setting up of Guidelines on the operational procedures and planning for VTS. The Annex to the Guidelines made it clear that they do not deal with the questions of liability nor do they create rights or impose requirements on shipping.

The Guidelines[(2)] are divided into two chapters: Chapter 1 on Objectives and Procedures, and Chapter 2 on Planning. The Guidelines state in 1.1 that the reasons for establishing a VTS may include:

"- assistance to navigation in appropriate areas;
- regulation of movements to facilitate an efficient traffic flow in the VTS area;
- handling of data relating to ships involved;
- participation in actions in case of accident; and
- support of allied activities."

---

in observing the directions received from the controller. This view can be supported by the fact that the information service does not furnish an "excuse" for not observing the Collision Rules. The information service, by its nature, is to supplement and not to replace the rules of good seamanship.
Thus, where an accident occurs, the burden of proof is on the master. He must establish that:
(a) the reliance upon the information was the direct cause of the accident; and
(b) it was not reasonable under the "circumstances" to take an avoiding action.
The result is that an extensive reliance upon the information can under "certain' circumstances be considered as reasonable and give rise to the liability of the port. The concept of "creditworthiness" placed by the master in the new system may well be invoked. On the other hand, the "circumstances test" will ensure that the law accords with both the maritime requirements and the reality of modern techniques.

(1) MSC 48/25.
(2) NAV 29/WP.5 of June 21, 1984. See Appendix IV.

The functions of a VTS may include (article 4):

"- Data collection.
- Data evaluation.
- Information service.
- Navigational assistance service.
- Traffic regulation service.
- Support of allied activities."

The widespread utilization of VTS poses novel and complex problems and the IMO Guidelines offer little or no assistance in solving the liability of the controller and formulating a code of practice on the communication between ship and shore.

## (ii) THE COLLISION RULES

One of the effective measures to ensure safe navigation at sea is to observe the International Regulations for Preventing Collisions at Sea (herein called the Collision Rules or simply the Rules). The uniform Rules "apply irrespective of frontiers to matters which are of wider than national concern ... a law which is broader in scope than municipal law"(1).

The IMO revised the 1960 Rules(2) and in 1972 it adopted a new set of Rules which came into force at 1200 hours zone time on July 15, 1977.

The Rules are presented in a logical order. They are divided into five parts, A to E, followed by four annexes. Part A deals with the application of the Rules, responsibility to obey them and definitions which apply to all the Rules. Part B contains the steering and sailing rules. The technical details on lights and shapes are dealt with in Part C, while Part D is devoted to sound and light signals. Part E deals with exemptions.

Annex I on "Positioning and technical details of lights and shapes" contains details on the placing of lights. It also contains technical details on the navigation lights to ensure uniform colour intensities. Annex II on "Additional signals for fishing vessels fishing in close proximity" aims at the standardization of the signals. Annex III is entitled "Technical details of sound signal appliances" while Annex IV is on "Distress signals".

### The 1981 Amendments

On November 15, 1979, the Assembly adopted Resolution A.431 (XI) entitled "Recommendation concerning vessels restricted in their ability to manoeuvre when engaged in an operation for the maintenance of safety of navigation in a traffic separation scheme".

---

(1) C.N. Jenks, The Common Law of Mankind (1958), p.81. However, the Rules are not to be regarded as belonging to international customary law despite the fact that many States have ratified or adhered to them. Therefore, they will not be binding on non-party States.

(2) For the background of the Rules and the general principles on Collision, see the Author, Collision at Sea, A Guide to the Legal Consequences, published by North Holland, 1978.

As a result, the MSC adopted an amendment to Rule 10(k).

Subsequently the MSC (at its 44th session) included the above amendment with others[1] which came into force on June 1, 1983[2].

The 1981 Amendments brought slight changes to the opening of Rule 13(a), Rule 22(d), Rule 23(c), Rule 24(d)(e)(g)(i), Rule 25(b), Rule 27(b)(c)(d)(e)(f)(g), Rule 29(a)(iii), Rule 30(e)(f), Rule 33(a), Rule 34(b)(iii), Rule 35(d), Rule 36, Rule 37, Rule 38 and the Annexes.

1. Critical Review of Certain Rules

With attention focused on the second set of amendments, it may be appropriate to consider the deficiencies in some rules, to comment on the 1981 amendments and to evaluate the proposals for reform.

Rule 1 - Application

*(a) These Rules shall apply to all vessels upon the high seas, in all waters connected therewith navigable by seagoing vessels.*

*(b) Nothing in these Rules shall interfere with the operation of special rules made by an appropriate authority for roadsteads, harbours, rivers, lakes or inland waterways connected with the high seas and navigable by seagoing vessels. Such special rules shall conform as closely as possible to these Rules.*

Thus, the Rules apply to all vessels, i.e. merchant vessels, warships, state-owned ships used for non-trading or trading purposes and ships flying

---

(1) MSC XLIV/21, Annex 6 and T2/3.02 (NAV 3).

(2) Guidance for the Uniform Application of Certain Rules of the International Regulations for Preventing Collisions at Sea, 1972, were circulated to Member States. MSC/Circ.320. The aim was to "assist mariners and all others concerned with the correct application of the Collision Regulations". NAV 27/WP.9 of October 14, 1982. Some of the rules in the Guidance will be included in the second set of amendments. Once this task is accomplished the Guidance will disappear.

the flag of an international organization on the high seas. They also apply to all vessels when in waters connected with the high seas provided that these waters are navigable by seagoing vessels.

As for ships in the territorial or internal waters, the State may apply its own local rules which (using the language of paragraph (b)) shall conform as closely as possible to the Rules. The reason for inserting paragraph (b) is to avoid any interference with the State's jurisdiction over its territorial and internal waters.

However, accidents in ports and their approaches, rivers, canals, straits and confined waters are more frequent than on the high seas. One can argue that according to Rule 1, the general rule is to apply the Rules to vessels on the high seas where few accidents occur and the exception is to apply them to territorial and internal waters where many accidents happen. The situation should have been reversed. It is suggested that the language of Rule 1(b) should be changed in order to extend the application of the Rules to territorial and internal waters. Such an extension would not be considered as a kind of limitation on State jurisdiction because it has been freely accepted. A State should also be given the right, in certain circumstances, to apply its own local rules and this would be regarded as an exception to the application of the Rules.

The above issue has not been considered during the discussion on the amendments to the Rules. Only the word "shape" was added to para.(c) of Rule 1.

## Rule 3 - General Definitions

Rule 3 is entitled "General Definitions" and consists of twelve paragraphs (a) to (l). A careful examination of some of the definitions reveals that they are in fact illustrations. For instance, the word "includes" in paragraph (a) indicates that this is not a definition of the word "vessel"(1).

Apart from this observation, Rule 3 may give rise to a general debate on whether the definitions serve any purpose. It may be argued that they are of great value to mariners as they would assist them in the application of some of the Rules. In fact,

(1) See also paragraph (g) as amended in 1983.

they brought the link between the 1960 and 1972 Rules. The definitions spell out the accepted meanings of terms as developed under the 1960 Rules and in this way they were instrumental in the smooth application of the 1972 Rules. Against this view, one can say that the definitions may prove to be too rigid to apply to new situations.

Whatever the case may be on the merits of the definitions, the language of some of them needs to be improved. Also, the list of definitions is not complete and the meaning of some important terms[1] should have been included in the list.

Under the 1981 Amendments, paragraph (g) was amended to read as follows:

*(g) The term "vessel restricted in her ability to manoeuvre" means a vessel which from the nature of her work is restricted in her ability to manoeuvre as required by these Rules and is therefore unable to keep out of the way of another vessel.*

*The term "vessels restricted in their ability to manoeuvre" shall include but not limited to:*

*(i) a vessel engaged in laying, servicing or picking up a navigation mark, submarine cable or pipeline;*

*(ii) a vessel engaged in dredging, surveying or underwater operations;*

*(iii) a vessel engaged in replenishment or transferring persons, provisions or cargo while underway;*

*(iv) a vessel engaged in the launching or recovery of aircraft;*

*(v) a vessel engaged in minesweeping operations;*

*(vi) a vessel engaged in a towing operation such as severely restricts the towing vessel and her tow in their ability to deviate from their course.*

---

(1) The United Kingdom suggested in a note (on file with the Author) to include definitions on "Risk of collision"; "end on or nearly end on vessel"; "overtaking vessel" and "a giving way vessel".
Other important terms are "narrow channel" and "plotting".

The Guidance includes clarification of the definition "vessel constrained by her draught" and the definition of the word "underway"(1).

Rule 7 - Risk of Collision

The word "plotting" in Rule 7 is ambiguous. However, the representative of The Netherlands took the view that the words "not to impede" as appearing in Rules 9(b),(c) and (d), 10(i) and (j), and 18(d) are vague. Therefore, they proposed(2) a new paragraph (e) to clarify the meaning of "not to impede" to be added to Rule 7.

---

(1) In a note presented by The Netherlands to the Sub-Committee on Safety of Navigation (NAV 27/4/2), dated August 24, 1982, the following definition of Rule 3(h) on "Vessel constrained by her draught" was proposed:
"(h) The term "Vessel constrained by her draught" means a power-driven vessel which because of her draught in relation to the available depth of water and to the *available navigable width of water* is severely restricted in her ability to deviate from the course she is following."
Rule 3(i) - Underway
"(i) The word "Underway" means that a vessel is not at anchor, or made fast to the shore, or aground. *A vessel underway may be stopped and making no way through the water*."
It is most likely that these two proposed definitions will be accepted and introduced into the second set of amendments.

(2) The proposed paragraph is as follows:
"(e) A vessel which by one of these Rules is required not to impede, or to avoid to impede, the passage of another vessel, shall so far as the circumstances of the case admit, navigate in such a way as to avoid development of risk of collision. However, each of the two vessels approaching each other remain fully obliged to comply with the Rules of this part when, in spite of the requirement for one of the vessels not to impede the safe passage of the other vessel, a situation has developed involving risk of collision." NAV 27/4/2, August 24, 1982. See also Notice M.930 on Interaction between ships.

## Rule 8 - Action to Avoid Collision

It is very difficult to define a close-quarters situation mentioned in Rule 8. Its existence depends on many factors, such as the weather conditions, state of visibility, type of vessel, manoeuvrability and whether observations are carried out by visual means or by radar. However, the Working Group considered a submission from the Government of the German Democratic Republic concerning a definition of the term "close-quarters situation"(1).

## Rule 10 - Traffic Separation Schemes

Traffic in converging areas and in areas with dense traffic or where the movement of vessels is restricted could be hazardous. In order to ensure the safety of traffic in these areas, it was necessary to impose a degree of control. This control is expressed through measures on routeing, traffic separation schemes, deep water routes and areas to be avoided.

Rule 10 gives rise to many difficulties and perhaps it was a wrong policy to integrate the separation schemes with the Collision Rules despite the similarity of some of the objectives.

Suppose a traffic separation scheme is introduced in a narrow channel, which Rule will apply: Rule 9 or Rule 10? It is suggested that once a traffic scheme is adopted in a narrow channel, it will lose its status under Rule 9. With this interpretation, one can avoid a conflict between the two Rules.

Finally, there are too many schemes; some of them are unnecessary or of little use and therefore they do not add much to the safety of navigation.

There is no doubt that Rule 10 suffers from serious defects and therefore it was slightly amended in 1981, and further changes will be introduced to it in the second set of amendments.

### Summary of the Discussion on Rule 10

*(a) This Rule applies to traffic separation schemes adopted by the Organization.*

The Working Group considered a proposal to amend paragraph (a) to read as follows: "This Rule

---

(1) NAV 26/4/2 and NAV 27/4/3.

applies to traffic separation schemes adopted by the Organization *and does not relieve any vessel of her obligations under other Rules of these Regulations*." The purpose of this addition to para. (a) is to emphasize the link between Rule 10 and other Rules of Part B, in particular those in Sections II and III(1).

(b) *A vessel using a traffic separation scheme shall:*

> (i) *proceed in the appropriate traffic lane in the general direction of traffic flow for that lane;*
>
> (ii) *so far as practicable keep clear of a traffic separation line or separation zone;*
>
> (iii) *normally join or leave a traffic lane at the termination of the lane, but when joining or leaving from either(2) side shall do so at as small an angle to the general direction of traffic flow as practicable.*

According to this paragraph, vessels when using the separation schemes are required to proceed with the direction of traffic flow. But paragraph (b) does not make it compulsory for vessels to use the schemes. In other words, where there is an alternative route, vessels may ignore the scheme and go through the other route.

Again paragraph (b) is not clear on the issue of transference within the lane and therefore the representative of The Netherlands suggested the following amendments(3):

> "(i) Proceed in the appropriate traffic lane in the general direction of traffic flow for that lane, *except that a transfer within the lane from one side to the other may be made, provided such a transfer is accomplished at as small an angle to the general direction of traffic flow as is practicable.*"

---

(1) NAV 27/WP.9. The representative of Japan felt that the proposed amendment was not needed.
(2) The word "either" was added in the 1981 Amendments.
(3) NAV 27/4/2, August 24, 1982.

This proposal, however, was not accepted by the Working Group.

*(c) A vessel shall so far as practicable avoid crossing traffic lanes, but if obliged to do so shall cross as nearly as practicable at right angles to the general direction of traffic flow.*

Paragraph (c), on crossing traffic lanes, created an unnecessary risk of collision every time a vessel has to cross a traffic lane, by prescribing a course at right angles to the traffic. Such a manoeuvre involves a principle incompatible with that laid down in Rule 10(b)(iii) for vessels joining or leaving a traffic lane, that they should do so at as small an angle as possible with the general direction of the traffic[1].

Obviously in view of the importance of the issue, there was a lengthy discussion on it during the sessions of the Working Group. A majority of its members supported a certain text[2] which they believe to be flexible, while the minority[3] felt that the proposed text "would lead to an undesirable crossing situation which would not be in the best

---

(1) Cf. J. Paton, Ships' Routeing - Present Status and Future Trend, a paper presented to the Bremen Conference, 1981, on Vessel Traffic Services, where he said (at p.23): "...the two principles are in fact complementary rather than contradictory, provided again that the Rules are not interpreted in too literal a way."

(2) The majority of members were in favour of the following text:
"A vessel shall so far as practicable avoid crossing a traffic lane, but, if obliged to do so, shall, if the circumstances of the case admit, maintain a heading at as broad an angle as practicable to the general direction of traffic flow. Such vessel shall not maintain a heading of more than $30^{\circ}$ from the right angle to the general direction of traffic flow."

(3) The minority preferred the following text:
"A vessel shall so far as practicable avoid crossing traffic lanes, but if obliged to do so, shall (if the circumstances of the case admit), maintain a heading as nearly as practicable at right angles to the general direction of traffic flow."

interest of safety"[1].

(d) *Inshore traffic zones shall not normally be used by through traffic which can safely use the appropriate traffic lane within the adjacent traffic separation scheme. However, vessels of less than 20 metres in length and sailing vessels may under all circumstances use inshore traffic zones*[2].

Paragraph (d) prohibits through traffic from using the "inshore zone" which is normally used by coastal and local traffic. However, the words "normally", "through traffic" and "safely" are not easy to define. The Department of Trade issued Notice M.1029 which states:

> "It is the Department's view that any vessel which commences its voyage from a location beyond one limit of the zone and proceeds to a location beyond the further limit of the zone and is not calling at a port, pilot station or destination or sheltered anchorage within the zone is a 'through' vessel and for the purposes of Rule 10(d) should, if it can safely do so, use the appropriate traffic lane of the adjacent traffic separation scheme, unless some abnormal circumstances exist in that lane."

The Department also brought many prosecutions of masters of British ships who used the inshore traffic zones when not calling at a port or terminal within the zone[3].

During the discussion of the Working Group, three delegates and one observer supported a new text[4] for paragraph (d), but many delegates

---

(1) NAV 27/WP.9. The Japanese delegate was against any changes to para.(c).
(2) Adopted in the 1981 Amendments.
(3) See *The "Nordic Clansman"* Queen's Bench Division (1984) 1 Lloyd's Rep. 31 (Master used an inshore traffic zone contrary to the Collision Rules.
(4) "Inshore traffic zones shall not normally be used by through traffic which can safely use the appropriate traffic lane within the adjacent traffic separation scheme, but may be used by local traffic as specified in the description of the traffic separation scheme adopted by the

expressed concern because of the different interpretations given to this paragraph in many countries. Some delegates were of the opinion that "there should be no local rules governing the traffic of ships in inshore traffic zones, as such rules would not be in conformity with the need for uniform application of the Collision Rules". Other representatives were of the opinion that Coastal States have a sovereign right to establish local rules for inshore traffic zones totally or partly within their territorial waters and that the existence of local rules governing traffic in inshore zones is unavoidable[1].

The Working Group was unable to reach any agreement on this issue.

(e) *A vessel other than a crossing vessel or a vessel joining or leaving a lane shall not normally enter a separation zone or cross a separation line except:*

(i) *in cases of emergency to avoid immediate danger;*

(ii) *to engage in fishing within a separation zone.*

(f) *A vessel navigating in areas near the terminations of traffic separation schemes shall do so with particular caution.*

(g) *A vessel shall so far as practicable avoid anchoring in a traffic separation scheme or in areas near its terminations.*

(h) *A vessel not using a traffic separation scheme shall avoid it by as wide a margin as is practicable.*

(i) *A vessel engaged in fishing shall not impede the passage of any vessel following a traffic lane.*

(j) *A vessel of less than 20 metres in length or a sailing vessel shall not impede the safe passage of a power-driven vessel following a traffic lane.*

---

Organization. Vessels of less than 20 metres in length and sailing vessels may under all circumstances use inshore traffic zones."

(1) NAV 27/WP.9.

(k) *A vessel restricted in her ability to manoeuvre when engaged in an operation for the maintenance of safety of navigation in a traffic separation scheme is exempted from complying with this Rule to the extent necessary to carry out the operation.*

(l) *A vessel restricted in her ability to manoeuvre when engaged in an operation for the laying, servicing or picking up of a submarine cable, within a traffic separation scheme, is exempted from complying with this Rule to the extent necessary to carry out the operation*[1].

Rule 18 - Responsibilities between Vessels

In the Guidance it was stated that a clarification of the relationship between Rule 18(d) and the Rules of Part B, Sections II and III, was needed[2].

---

(1) The underlined parts were added in the Amendments of 1981.
(2) The Netherlands note (NAV/4/2, August 24, 1982) proposed the following:
Rule 18(d) - Relation between Rule 18(d) and the rules of Part B, Section II.
(d)(ii) "A vessel constrained by her draught shall navigate with particular caution having full regard to her special condition and shall have her *engines ready for immediate manoeuvre. It remains fully obliged to comply with the Rules of this Section when approached by another vessel as to involve risk of collision.*"
Rule 18 -"Responsibility of a vessel, such as a patrol vessel, approaching another vessel for a specific purpose."
Add a new paragraph (f):
(f) (i) "A vessel, such as a patrol vessel, approaching another vessel for a specific purpose, shall not endanger the safe passage of the vessel it is approaching and shall manoeuvre in such a way as to avoid collision;
(ii) A vessel being approached by a vessel exhibiting the signals prescribed by Rule 36(b) is relieved from any obligation to take action for avoiding collision with such vessel."

## 2. Proposed Second Set of Amendments

Work continued during 1985 on the preparation of proposed amendments to ensure that no further changes would be necessary in the foreseeable future. It is expected that these amendments would be submitted to the fifteenth regular session of the Assembly for adoption.

There was no agreement among the delegations on whether there was a need for a second set of amendments. The Japanese delegation, for example, opposed any attempt to amend the Rules in view of the absence of an assessment on their application. They added that "any amendments would not only cause undue confusion among seafarers but also lead to a hasty rule-making of steering and sailing rules[1]. Other delegations were in favour of changing certain rules or improving their language[2]. A summary of the proposed amendments is to follow.

### Rule 3 - Definitions related to terms used in Rule 10

The Federal Republic of Germany[3] proposed that definitions of certain terms used in Rule 10, which are defined in the General Provisions on Ships' Routeing, be included in a new Rule 3(m). This was considered necessary since the General Provisions may not be readily available to seafarers. The Sub-Committee on Safety of Navigation did not agree with this proposal because the current definitions in the General Provisions do not refer to the application of Rule 10[4].

### Rule 7 - New Rule 7(e) "not to impede"

There was a heated discussion on this issue. The Japanese delegation opposed any amendment because if draft Rule 7(e) is added, every fishing vessel will be obliged to "navigate in such a way as to avoid development of risk of collision". It may follow a different conduct of navigation from the one prescribed as "not to impede" under Rule 9(c)[5]. The

---

(1) NAV 29/4/5 of April 30, 1984.
(2) See Note by the Government of the United Kingdom, NAV 29/4/3 of April 11, 1984.
(3) NAV 30/4/4.
(4) NAV 30/11 of January 11, 1985, p.12.
(5) NAV 29/4/5 of April 30, 1984.

American delegation agreed with this view and recommended that no action be taken to define or limit the meaning of "not to impede"[1]. They added that the proposed amendments would limit the options currently available to mariners, when dealing with the situations covered by Rules 9(b) (c),(d), 10(i),(j) and 18(d). "Rule 28 provides the opportunity for a vessel to advertise her limitations in manoeuvring due to the safe water available, yet does not relieve her of the obligation to follow the other Rules which apply when there is risk of collision. A vessel directed by the rules "not to impede", after becoming aware of a vessel constrained by her draught, is directed to exercise the spirit of Rule 2 and manoeuvre, when possible to do so, in a manner to provide the sea room necessary for safe transit of the vessels involved. The proposed Rule 7(e) does not make this clear"[2].

The Dutch delegation proposed[3] an improvement to the draft text. They said that a ship which is obliged not to impede does not lose this obligation when approaching another ship so as to involve risk of collision. In such a case the ship which is obliged not to impede should contribute to avoid collision and to the safe passage of the other vessel. Consequently, they put forward the following text:

> "1. A vessel which by any one of these Rules is required not to impede the passage of another vessel shall, so far as the circumstances of the case admit, navigate in such a way that risk of collision is avoided. In circumstances, however, where risk of collision with another vessel exists or is deemed to exist, such vessel shall take appropriate action in compliance with the Rules of this Part.
>
> 2. This Rule does not relieve the other vessel of the obligation to comply with the Rules of this Part as required by the circumstances of the case"[4].

---

(1) NAV 30/4/5 of November 16, 1984.
(2) *Ibid*, p.2.
(3) NAV 29/4/6 of April 30, 1984.
(4) The delegation of the Federal Republic of Germany proposed that the new Rule 7(e) should: (a) be rearranged so that Rule 7(e)(i) provides

After consideration of these views, the Sub-Committee concluded that the Collision Rules should be amended to clarify the application of the requirement "not to impede" and decided to include the clarification in a new Rule 8(f)[1].

Rule 10(d) - Use of Inshore Traffic Zone

A Working Group proposed the following text[2]:

"(d)(i) A [power driven] vessel shall not use an inshore traffic zone when she can safely use the appropriate traffic lane within the adjacent traffic separation scheme. However, vessels of less than 20 metres in length, sailing vessels and vessels engaged in fishing may use inshore traffic zones;

(ii) Notwithstanding sub-paragraph (i) above, a vessel may use an inshore traffic zone when she is en route to or from a port, offshore installations, pilot station or any other place situated within that inshore traffic zone or is seeking shelter in such zone."

The ICS[3] believed that the above text will preclude a small, or relatively slow, vessel being allowed to seek a sheltered passage through an inshore traffic zone in anticipation of adverse weather conditions. It will amount to recognition of the potential hazards associated with vessels on coastal passages (starting and finishing) relatively near but outside an inshore traffic zone) crossing and recrossing the traffic streams associated with the adjacent traffic separation scheme. Finally the proposal is a recognition of the need for masters to exercise prudence and good seamanship - by executing a passage plan which, from the information available, the master's experience, the

---

for action to be taken by the vessel which is required "not to impede" and Rule 7(e)(ii) for the other vessel;

(b) include a requirement that the "not to impede" vessel shall avoid altering course towards the other; and

(c) ensure that avoiding action by the "not to impede" vessel is taken in good time.

NAV 29/WP.4.

(1) NAV 30/11, p.12.

(2) NAV 28/WP.9.

(3) NAV 29/4/10 of May 18, 1984.

condition of the ship, her equipment and other circumstances external to the ship, indicate that a safer route is via the inshore traffic zone.

The ICS proposed the following text:

"(d) Inshore traffic zones shall not be used by vessels which can use the appropriate traffic lane within the adjacent traffic separation scheme unless:

(i) a vessel is less than 20 metres in length or a sailing vessel;

(ii) a vessel is proceeding to or from a port, pilot stations or destination either within a zone or on the coast near to it, provided the vessel is heading opposite to the general direction of the traffic flow in the adjacent traffic lane;

(iii) a vessel is seeking a sheltered anchorage or passage within a zone;

(iv) the circumstances prevailing indicate that it is prudent and in the interests of good seamanship and safety to use a zone"(1).

The majority of the Sub-Committee did not support this proposal as it would allow varying interpretations of the term "through traffic"(2).

<u>Annex I (10)(b) - Vertical sectors of electric lights on sailing vessels</u>

Poland was of the opinion that Annex I (10)(b) should not apply to the anchor lights and not under command lights of sailing vessels, since their behaviour at anchor or aground is the same as that of power-driven vessels(3). Since Annex I (10)(b) only applies to lights required by Rule 25, the Sub-Committee concurred with this opinion and recommended that the following sentence is to be added following sub-paragraph 10(b)(ii):

---

(1) See also the Note by the International Association of Institutes of Navigation (IAIN), NAV 29/4/8 of May 14, 1984.

(2) The Government of the Federal Republic of Germany proposed that definitions of some of the terms used in Rule 10 which have been included in the General Provisions of Ships' routeing, should be revised. NAV 30/4/4 of Nov. 2, 1984.

(3) NAV 30/4 of July 23, 1984.

"The requirements of sub-paragraphs (i) and (ii) do not refer to the anchor and 'not under command' lights which should comply with the relevant requirements of paragraph 10(a)."

Annex IV - Distress signals

The International Council of Marine Industry Association (ITCOMIA) proposed[1] to add a white strobe light signal to the list of authorized distress signals in Annex IV and so a new sub-paragraph (c) to paragraph 1[2] will read as follows:
(c) "a high intensity white light flashing at regular intervals from 50 to 70 times per minute."

To Rule 36 on "Signals to Attract Attention" would be added the following sentence: "Such high intensity flashing white lights may be used only as signals to indicate distress and need of assistance as described in Annex IV to these Regulations"[3].

The American delegation supported this proposal because the strobe light is a technological advance which, if properly regulated, can greatly enhance maritime safety by serving as an effective, easy to use, and highly visible signal to indicate distress and need of assistance[4].

---

(1) NAV 28/4/3.
(2) NAV 29/4/1 of March 2, 1984.
(3) There was also a proposal for the following amendments to paragraph 1(n) of Annex IV: "(a) Signals transmitted for distress purposes by emergency position-indicating radio beacons and ship earth station", presented by the Sub-Committee on Radio-communications. See NAV 29/4/2.
The Federal Republic of Germany proposed in document NAV 28/4/4 of Sept. 5, 1983, to incorporate in Rule 34 a "keep-away" signal which must be given by vessels on which leakage of dangerous cargo or radioactive substances occurs or is likely to occur. However, the Working Group opposed this proposal on the ground that the Collision Regulations contain only signals for the prevention of collisions and the proposed signal would require measures to avoid the danger from other vessels, such as stopping, decrease in speed, with the possible beginning of a full-turn manoeuvre. NAV 29/4/9 of May 18, 1984.
(4) NAV 30/4/5.

Other delegations expressed concern that inclusion of the strobe light signal in Annex IV would lead to abuse of the signal and would not add to the safety of small craft[1]. For these reasons, the Sub-Committee refused to propose any amendments in this respect[2].

<u>Use of blue flashing and fixed lights by sea-going vessels and as signals to identify patrol boats</u>

The Sub-Committee considered the above proposal presented to it by the Federal Republic of Germany[3]. France[4], supported by many delegations, opposed this proposal as, in accordance with the International Code of Signals, the blue flashing light is used to identify medical transports in time of war and its use for other purposes might cause confusion. The Sub-Committee therefore considered it impracticable to standardize the use of blue lights and in the absence of proposals on other lights for identifying patrol vessels, did not discuss this matter further[5].

The foregoing are the issues considered for amendments. In 1979, the Governments of the United Kingdom and France proposed a draft resolution on the importance of imposing exemplary penalties on masters who contravene the Rules[6]. In fact, there should be a "tariff" for each kind of offence. In other words, offences should be measured and graded. Thus, by providing an elaborate scale of punishment, the offences could be classified according to their degree of dangerousness.

Closely connected with this matter is the case of "near misses" since there is no sanction against an offender who does not obey the Rules in case no accident occurs. Penalties of this kind and other contraventions should be agreed internationally in the Rules and not be left to the Contracting States.

---

(1) See the Note of the Government of the United Kingdom, NAV 29/4/3 of April 11, 1984.
(2) NAV 30/11, p.14.
(3) NAV 28/INF.10.
(4) NAV 30/4/2.
(5) NAV XXIII/5/2, July 6, 1979.
(6) Resolution A.432 (XI) adopted on Nov. 15, 1979, on Compliance with the Rules. The Annex to the Resolution gives the form of the report in case of contraventions.

## (iii) A STANDARD MARINE VOCABULARY AND A NEW BUOYAGE SYSTEM

### 1. THE STANDARD MARINE VOCABULARY

A great deal of human communication is based on the knowledge of a common language and this is especially important for radio conversations. Apart from the problem of the choice of the language for the sea, some of the words of any language may not mean the same thing to different listeners. The use of a local dialect may make it even more difficult for the listeners to understand it. Therefore, it is difficult to set up vocabulary which fits all situations without loss of meaning.

Despite these difficulties, the IMO recognized the needs of transmitting information among sailors of various nationalities and adopted the Standard Marine Navigational Vocabulary. It is designed to standardize the language used in communication for navigation at sea, in port approaches, waterways and harbours. The basic idea of the standard vocabulary is to make it second nature to those using it so that the terms will come without effort and mean the same thing to the listener as to the speaker. Thus the Vocabulary has been compiled:

(a) to assist in the safety of navigation and conduct of ships; and

(b) to standardize the language used in communications for navigation at sea, in port approaches, in waterways and harbours(1). English is considered to be the common language for international navigational communications.

The Standard Vocabulary(2) uses short words and is set out in a logical order. It is divided into various sections for easy reference.

---

(1) The Vocabulary is not intended to supplant or affect in any way the Collision Rules, the Code of Signals and Radio Regulations nor the Radiotelephone practice as set out in the ITU Regulations.

(2) See Resolution A.380 (X) adopted by the Assembly at its tenth session held on Nov. 14, 1977. Annex II of this Resolution states that amendments to the Vocabulary will normally come into

At its thirtieth session, the Sub-Committee on Safety of Navigation considered the possible relationship between the Standard Marine Vocabulary and the Seaspeak system[1]. The Seaspeak Manual is based on the Vocabulary and is designed to give detailed guidance on how to communicate clearly and unambiguously.

A number of amendments to the Vocabulary were adopted by the Maritime Safety Committee in accordance with the procedure laid down in Assembly Resolution A.380 (X)[2].

It must be noted that the use of the Standard Vocabulary is not compulsory. The IMO took the view that through constant repetition in ships and in training establishments ashore, the phrases and terms used will become normally accepted and commonplace among seamen. A legal question may arise here: suppose a seaman ignored the Standard Vocabulary and, by using his own language, he was unable to communicate with another ship. As a result a collision occurred. Can the seaman be blamed for not using the Standard Vocabulary? Since the use of the Vocabulary is not compulsory, a seaman is not required to use it. This, of course, is a great weakness in the Standard Vocabulary.

---

force at intervals of approximately five years. As for amendments which require urgent action, the period may be shortened to two years. Amendments will be notified to all concerned and will come into force twelve months after the date of notification.

(1) The following observations were made:
(a) Seaspeak complies with all existing IMO and ITU provisions on VHF radio-communications at sea.
(b) Seaspeak is in accordance with the vocabulary and, used in conjunction with it, allows the construction of all ship-ship and ship-shore maritime VHF messages.
(c) Seaspeak has been fully researched world-wide and is especially compatible with the requirements of vessel traffic services.
(d) Seaspeak achieves maximum clarity and minimum ambiguity, and thereby greatly enhances safety.
NAV 30/INF.2 of October 10, 1984.

(2) NAV 30/11 of January 18, 1985.

## 2. MARITIME BUOYAGE SYSTEMS

Since the end of the nineteenth century there has been disagreement on the use of buoy lights. Some countries installed red lights to mark the starboard side of a channel while others used the same light to mark the port side. Again, some countries adopted a lateral system in which buoys were fixed to mark the edges of channels. Others used a cardinal system in which buoys were laid out in the quadrants of a compass to show where the danger lies in relation to the mark. Wrecks around the British Isles were marked by a single green buoy, usually anchored over the wreck itself if submerged; a system of marking which was not followed by Continental countries.

Thus the "free for all" situation in the buoyage system was most unfortunate. In an attempt to remedy this deficiency, a Conference was held in Geneva in 1936 to set up a unified system, but met with no success. In 1955, at a conference held in Holland, it was decided to form the International Association of Lighthouse Authorities (IALA). The new organization was established on July 1, 1957, with the main objective: "to encourage the continued improvement of aids to navigation, through any appropriate technical means, for the safe and expeditious movement of vessels"(1).

In 1971, *The Brandenburg* struck in the Dover Strait a wrecked ship, *The Texaco Caribbean*, and sank. A few weeks later, in spite of the two wrecks being marked by two light vessels and 14 green buoys, another vessel, *The Niki*, ploughed into the wreckage and sank. Altogether 51 lives were lost and there was controversy over the effectiveness of the navigational marks.

This accident accelerated the efforts to bring radical reforms in this field. In 1976, the IALA adopted the Rules for System A(2) which gradually

---

(1) The IALA has its office in Paris. It has three different categories for membership: lighthouse authorities are members; port authorities are associated members; and manufacturers of aids to navigation are accepted as industrial members. The work of the Organization is carried out through an executive committee consisting of fifteen members.

(2) The System basically used red to port and green to starboard for lateral marks. This was

received acceptance in Europe(1), Africa, the Gulf, some Asian countries and Australia. The IALA continued its work with the assistance of the IMO and the International Hydrographic Organization (IHO) to formulate System B for those countries which were unable to accept System A. This task was completed and the Rules were concluded on April 15, 1982(2). The only difference between the regions is which colour is to port and which is to starboard. The MSC, at its forty-fourth session, adopted the IALA Rules. Fifty-six Lighthouse Authorities had become Parties to the Rules(3).

Thus there are two regions where either System A(4) or System B(5) is applicable. It must be noted(6) that both Systems have common features and it is unlikely in view of the costs involved, to have a unified system.

---

combined with a system of cardinal marks to be painted black and yellow, having distinctive top marks formed of two triangles variously arranged and light characters (with white lights) generally corresponding to the position of the buoys as set out on a clock face, e.g. three flashes at three o'clock for the eastern mark and six flashes at six o'clock for the southern mark.

(1) The Rules for System A were introduced in the Dover Strait in 1977.

(2) See IALA NP 735 ed.3, 1982.

(3) MSC 49/19 of April, 1984, p.14.

(4) Europe, Australia, New Zealand, Africa, the Middle East and most of Asia opted for the Region A scheme in which colour is to port. Implementation of the rules in this Region is already well advanced and is expected to be completed in 1985.

(5) The USA, with other countries of North, Central and South America, Japan, South Korea and the Philippines, chose to be in Region B, where red is to starboard.

(6) For marking of wrecks there used to be difference in the systems used in the United Kingdom and the Continent. Around the British Isles, wrecks were marked by a single green buoy, usually anchored over the wreck itself if submerged. The IALA, in an attempt to combine the best features of the lateral system which was used in British waters with the more widely used Continental cardinal system, adopted System A. Under it, the position of a wreck is shown by a

The difficulties in this field are:

(a) some countries have no buoys at all; and

(b) seamen tend to know the system applicable in their own region.

Suppose a seaman was unable to identify the System of buoyage applicable in a region other than his own region; can his conduct amount to an act of negligence? One may argue that System A and System B are applicable worldwide and the concept of good seamanship requires the knowledge of both Systems. However, in order that such an argument would succeed in a court of law, two conditions must be fulfilled:

(a) seamen should be required to know both Systems; and that

(b) the knowledge of the buoyage System should be made compulsory.

---

single "cardinal" buoy, a pillar buoy with a mark on top. A cardinal buoy marks safe water around the wreck by indicating the appropriate quarter of the compass in which it lies. In addition to the change in colour and the introduction of cardinal pillar or spar buoys, the colours of lights and their flashing sequences are altered as well. The light sequences for the cardinal buoys are quite ingenious, and should bring instant recognition to the navigator as the number of flashes is based on the clock face:

north - uninterrupted;
east - three flashes in a group;
south - six flashes (equivalent to six o'clock; and
west - nine flashes (nine o'clock).

The cardinal buoys also have distinctive "top marks" to aid their visual recognition - double cones apex up for north, double inverted cones for south, and so on.

## (iv) MARITIME SEARCH AND RESCUE

The duty to render assistance to persons in distress is one of the oldest traditions of the sea. It derives from the rules of chivalry and later received support from Christian teachings.

Several international conventions have provided for such a duty. Article 11 of the Convention for the Unification of Certain Rules of Law Relating to Assistance and Salvage at Sea 1910, states: "Every master is bound, so far as he can do so without serious danger to his vessel, her crew and her passengers, to render assistance to everybody, even an enemy, found at sea in danger of being lost."

Regulation 15 of Chapter V on Safety of Navigation of the Safety of Life at Sea (SOLAS) Convention 1974, provides:

"(a) Each Contracting Government undertakes to ensure that any necessary arrangements are made for coast watching and for the rescue of persons in distress at sea round its coasts. These arrangements should include the establishment, operation and maintenance of such maritime safety facilities as are deemed practicable and necessary having regard to the density of the seagoing traffic and the navigational dangers and should, so far as possible, afford adequate means of locating and rescuing such persons.

(b) Each Contracting Government undertakes to make available information concerning its existing rescue facilities and the plans for changes therein, if any."

However, the principle of save and assistance as stipulated for in these international instruments was left to be implemented by each State. Municipal law of many countries prescribes penal or disciplinary measures for failure to comply with such a duty.

Despite the national effort[1] made for coast watching and for search and rescue services, a

---

(1) The United States Coast Guard's AMVER (Automated Mutual-assistance Vessel Rescue) system is a computerised system which has improved the measures for search and rescue. Being able to forecast the locations of merchant vessels near an emergency, the computer is told where help is

number of weaknesses were apparent in the various systems. There was a lack of coordination and control between the individual countries in accordance with their own requirements and resources. As a result, national organizational plans have developed along different lines.

The dissimilarity of such plans and the lack of agreed and standardized procedures, on a worldwide basis, give rise to certain difficulties, although these are generally limited to the initial stages of an alert. In some cases, they can also result in an uneconomical use of SAR facilities, or in unnecessary duplication of effort. Furthermore, differences in procedures and lack of links of communication may result from the fact that the personnel and equipment used for SAR are part of the military services of the country concerned.

In certain regional areas, neighbouring countries have established regional arrangements which operate successfully, and have agreed on links of communication, standard procedures and areas of responsibility for co-ordination and control in cases of distress. The exchange of personnel and frequent contracts between those responsible for operating SAR services help in resolving operational difficulties and contributed to the effectiveness of the system[1]. Obviously, SAR operations would be greatly assisted if this type of co-operation could be extended and practices agreed to on a worldwide basis.

---

needed and the whereabouts of nearby ships. The rescue centre controller handling the incident can use the information to tell a suitable vessel that her help is needed. Accordingly, a ship when leaving the port had to send a sail plan to the AMVER Centre. While underway, she also had to send position reports to keep her plot accurate. At the AMVER Centre in New York, hundreds of ships' communications are fed daily into the computer.

(1) MERSAR: In 1971, the IMO Assembly adopted the Merchant Ship Search and Rescue Manual (MERSAR) which is designed as a guide to seafarers, in particular masters of ships who are called upon to conduct SAR operations during emergencies at sea. MERSAR is divided into eight chapters which deal with SAR co-ordination; action by a ship in distress; action by assisting ships; assistance by SAR aircraft; planning and

1. The SAR Convention, 1979

In order to improve the situation still further and to introduce an international agreed search and rescue policy, the IMO Maritime Safety Committee established a group of experts with the purpose of preparing a draft convention which aims to:

(a) standardize procedures to the maximum possible extent;

(b) facilitate direct contact between SAR services of various States;

(c) ensure efficient co-operation between surface and air units participating in search and rescue; and

(d) provide guidance for the development of SAR services where needed.

The Group prepared a draft convention which was adopted by a Diplomatic Conference held in Hamburg from 9 to 27 April, 1979. The aim of the Convention(1) as stated in its preamble is to establish a "plan responsive to the needs of maritime traffic for the rescue of persons in distress at sea". In fact it has two main features. Firstly, it combines sea and air in the services. Secondly, it relies

---

conducting the search; conclusion of search; communications; and aircraft casualties at sea. IMOSAR: The MSC adopted the IMO Search and Rescue Manual (IMOSAR) which contains guidelines for governments wishing to establish or develop their search and rescue organizations and for personnel who may be involved in the provision of search and rescue services. Appended to the Manual is a Maritime Search and Rescue Recognition Code which is intended to facilitate the communication of essential descriptive information regarding merchant vessels and small craft within and between maritime SAR organizations. The Assembly (Resolution A.439, X, 1, 15 Nov., 1979) adopted an Annex on Procedures for amending and updating the Manual. It provides that amendments by the MSC will become applicable after twelve months. For amendments of a very urgent nature, the period may be shortened at the discretion of the MSC.

(1) The Convention came into force on June 22, 1985.

for its effectiveness on the co-operation between the neighbouring States. The difficulty in this respect is that some of the organizations which are involved in the services are military and close co-operation may not be desirable for security reasons. However, it could be possible to reach a degree of co-operation by setting up regional bodies(1).

Thus, the Convention provides that each SAR region shall be established by agreement among the Parties concerned. It states that the delimitation of SAR regions is not related to and shall not prejudice the delimitation of any boundary between States.

With the Convention, an Annex and eight Resolutions were adopted. The Annex, which is considered as an integral part of the Convention, consists of six chapters. Chapter 1 defines certain terms which are used in the Annex. Chapter 2, entitled "Organization", deals with five issues:

(a) arrangements for provision and co-ordination of search and rescue services;

(b) co-ordination of search and rescue facilities;

(c) establishment of rescue co-ordination centres and rescue sub-centres;

(d) designation of rescue units; and

(e) facilities and equipment of rescue units.

It is the duty of the Parties to arrange that their SAR services can and do give prompt response to any distress call and must take urgent steps to provide the most appropriate assistance to any person in distress.

Information concerning SAR services must be submitted to the IMO and then circulated to all Parties. Parties are required to co-ordinate their SAR facilities and services nationally by establish-

---

(1) The basic requirements on SAR communications are embodied in Regulation 3 of the Convention on Safety of Life at Sea, 1974, Chapter IV. This specifies that all passenger and cargo ships of 1,600 tons gross and above must possess a radiotelegraph station, while Regulation 4 requires all cargo ships of 300 tons gross and above to be fitted with a radiotelephone.

ing rescue co-ordination centres (RCCs) and rescue sub-centres (RSCs). They must also ensure that each RCC and RSC has adequate means for receiving distress communication and communicating with its rescue units and with RCCs and RSCs in adjacent areas.

The chapter concludes with details of colour coding and other information to be used on containers and packages containing survival equipment for dropping to survivors.

Chapter 3 - Co-operation: This chapter requires the Contracting Parties to co-ordinate search and rescue operations with those of neighbouring States.

Authorization should be given for the immediate entry into or over its territorial sea or territory of rescue units of other Parties which are engaged in a search and rescue operation.

A Party which wishes its rescue units to enter into or over the territory of another Party solely for search and rescue purposes shall send a request to the RCC or other designated authority of that Party. This request must give full details of the intended mission and the need for it.

The Party receiving such a request must immediately acknowledge it and, as soon as possible, state any conditions under which the intended mission may be undertaken.

However, in order to prevent unnecessary delays and formalities, Parties are recommended to enter into agreements with neighbouring States on the conditions for entry of their rescue units into or over their respective territorial sea or territory.

The convention recommends that each Party should authorize its RCCs:

(a) to request and provide such assistance as may be needed from or by other RCCs;

(b) to grant any necessary permission for the entry of SAR units into or over its territorial sea or territory and to make the necessary arrangements with customs, immigration and other authorities.

Agreements with neighbouring States are also recommended for the pooling of facilities; the establishment of common procedures; the conduct of joint training and exercises; regular checks of inter-State communications; liaison visits by RCC personnel; and exchange of search and rescue information.

Chapter 4 - Preparatory measures: This chapter deals with the preparatory measures to be taken by RCCs and RSCs and the state of preparedness of rescue units. Each RCC and RSC must have available up-to-date information relating to its area, including details of available rescue units and coast watching units; resources such as transportation facilities and fuel supplies; means of communication including names, cable and telex addresses, telephone and telex numbers of shipping agents, consular authorities, international organizations and other agencies who may be able to assist in obtaining vital information on vessels; identities of maritime mobile service and other radio stations, and other information.

Each RCC and RSC should have ready access to all appropriate information concerning the vessels within its area which may be able to provide assistance to vessels or persons in distress at sea.

Each RCC and RSC must have detailed plans or instructions for the conduct of search and rescue operations in its area. These should contain details concerning action to be taken by those engaged in SAR operations in the area.

Chapter 5 - Operating procedures: It is the duty of the Parties to ensure that continuous radio watches are maintained on international distress frequencies when this is considered practicable and necessary.

Detailed requirements are given concerning the actions to be taken by coast radio stations which receive distress messages. Any element of the search and rescue organization which has reason to believe that a ship is in a state of emergency should as soon as possible give all available information to the appropriate RCC or RSC. These in turn must evaluate this information and determine the emergency phase and the extent of search and rescue operation required.

Procedures are laid down for the initiation of SAR operations for vessels whose position is unknown.

The chapter then deals with a number of other operational matters including:

(a) Co-ordination when two or more Parties are involved.

(b) Termination and suspension of SAR operations.

(c) On-scene co-ordination of SAR activities.

(d) Designation of the on-scene commander and his responsibilities.

(e) Designation of co-ordinator surface search and his responsibilities.

(f) Initial action and searches.

Chapter 6 - Ship reporting systems: Parties should establish a ship reporting system within any search and rescue region for which they are responsible, where this is considered necessary and practicable for search and rescue purposes.

A ship reporting system should provide up-to-date information on the movements of vessels. During a distress incident this could reduce the interval between loss of contact with a vessel and the initiation of search and rescue operations; permit rapid selection of vessels which are in a position to assist; limit the search area; and facilitate the provision of medical assistance or advice.

In order to achieve the above objectives, the ship reporting system should provide information which would make it possible to predict vessel movements, including sailing plans and position reports; maintain a shipping plot; receive periodic reports of participating vessels; be simple in design and operation; and use an internationally agreed standard ship reporting format and procedures.

A ship reporting system should incorporate the following reports, each containing the name and call sign or ship station identity:

(a) sailing plan giving the date, time and point of departure, next port of call, intended route, speed and expected date and time of arrival;

(b) position report with date, time, position, course and speed; and

(c) final report giving date and time of arrival at destination or of leaving the area covered by the system.

2. Resolutions

Resolution 1 - Arrangements for provision and co-ordination of SAR services: States are urged to co-ordinate all SAR services including those for aeronautical purposes. The IMO is invited to continue to work closely with ICAO to harmonize aeronautical and maritime SAR plans and procedures.

Resolution 2 - Cost to ships of participating in ship reporting systems: States are recommended to arrange for participation in such systems to be free to the ships concerned.

Resolution 3 - Need for an internationally agreed format and procedure for ship reporting systems: It invites the IMO to develop an internationally agreed format for ship reporting systems, using as a basis a format annexed to the resolution. Such a format was adopted by the 13th Assembly of the IMO in November, 1983 by Resolution A.531(13).

Resolution 4 - Search and rescue manuals: The resolution encourages the use of the MERSAR and IMOSAR manuals.

Resolution 5 - Frequencies for maritime search and rescue: It urges the allocation of one frequency for use exclusively for distress and safety purposes in the 4,6,8,12 and 16 MHz maritime mobile bands.

Resolution 6 - Development of a global maritime distress and safety system: The draft requirements have been agreed. The object of the system is to provide for adequate communications in order to promote safety of life at sea. It is designed to support the SAR.

Resolution 7 - Harmonization of SAR services with maritime meteorological services: The IMO is invited to work closely with the World Meteorological Organization to explore the practicability of harmonizing the areas of maritime meteorological forecasts and warnings with SAR regions.

Resolution 8 - Promotion of technical co-operation[(1)]: States are urged, in consultation with, and with the assistance of the IMO to support States requiring technical assistance for training personnel in SAR and for the acquisition of SAR equipment and the development of SAR facilities.

The foregoing exposé of the provisions of the Convention and the Resolutions does not mean that a

(1) See NAV 29/INF.8 of May 18, 1984, on SAR in the greater Caribbean area.

worldwide search and rescue system has immediately come into operation.

The Convention does not provide a time schedule nor stipulate any date on which the system should become operative. What it does is to describe the way in which an international SAR system and its component SAR areas should be established.

The world's oceans have been divided into 13 areas for search and rescue purposes. In each of these a maritime SAR plan has been developed by the countries concerned. The areas and the collector of information are as follows:

| Area and collector of information | Collection of information | Provision of SAR plans |
|---|---|---|
| 1 North Atlantic (USA) | Substantially complete | Substantially complete |
| 2 North Sea (UK) | Complete | Complete |
| 3 Baltic Sea (Sweden) | Complete | Substantially complete |
| 4 Eastern South Atlantic (-) | Incomplete | None |
| 5 Western South Atlantic (Argentina and Brazil) | Substantially complete | None |
| 6 Eastern North Pacific (USA) | Substantially complete | Substantially complete |
| 7 Western North Pacific (Japan) | Substantially complete | Progressed at Workshop in Jakarta, Indonesia, in October, 1984 |
| 8 Eastern South Pacific (Chile) | Substantially complete | None |
| 9 Western South Pacific (New Zealand) | Incomplete | Progressed at Workshop in Jakarta, Indonesia, in October, 1984 |
| 10 Indian Ocean(1) (Australia) | Incomplete | " |
| 11 Caribbean (-) | Substantially complete | Substantially complete |
| 12a Mediterranean (France) | Incomplete | None |
| 12b Black Sea | Substantially complete | None |
| 13 Arctic Ocean | Complete | None |

(1) It was agreed that area 10 should be divided into

## (v) SATELLITE COMMUNICATIONS

Nearly one hundred years ago, when a ship was in distress, she had to use flares in order to alert others to come to her rescue. If no vessel happened to be in the vicinity, no assistance could be rendered to a ship on fire or on the verge of sinking, and no links existed between the ship, her crew and the land.

The year 1895 saw the great invention of radio by MARCONI which brought revolution in telecommunications. Ships equipped with a radio were able to receive assistance and lives were saved in many recorded incidents(1) due to the use of radio on board the ship(2).

Regulations on radio communications were drafted in 1903 at the Berlin Conference. In 1906 the International Radiotelegraph Conference, held in Berlin, laid down the basis for the development of radio-communications at sea.

In 1912, at a conference in London, the letters SOS(3) were adopted as the international distress call. Subsequent several conferences were held to amend or update the regulations and the task in this respect was carried out by the International Telecommunications Union (ITU). Its activities are

---

three sub-areas (10a - North West Indian Ocean; 10b - South West Indian Ocean; 10c - East Indian Ocean).

(1) The first recorded incident of using the radio for saving life happened in March, 1899 when the lightship on the Goodwin Sands near Dover, used its radio to report that the ship *Elbe* had run aground. In January, 1900, an apparatus built by Alexander Popov was used to send a message to the icebreaker *Yermak*. As a result, the ship was able to rescue fishermen trapped in an ice-flow in the Gulf of Finland.

(2) In 1909, two ships, the *Republic* and *Volturno*, collided off the east coast of the United States. A radio distress message was picked up by a coast radio station and within 30 minutes the *Baltic* arrived at the scene. All 1700 people on board the two ships were saved.

(3) The letters are not an abbreviation and they were adopted because they are easy to remember and easy to transmit in Morse Code. The "Mayday" distress call used in radiotelephone derives from the French word "m'aidez" which means help me.

governed by the Montreux International Telecommunication Convention of 1965 with its Final Protocol and Additional Protocols(1). Article 48 of the Montreux Convention imposes upon member States of the ITU the duty to establish and operate radio stations "in such a manner as not to cause harmful interference to the radio services or communications of other Members...". Revisions of the ITU Regulations are done by Administrative Conferences.

In 1962 the first satellite(2) was put into orbit and thus it became possible to transmit messages to a satellite which in turn re-directs them to the desired locations on earth. This scientific ingenuity meant that high quality speech and television pictures can be transmitted instantly from one place on earth to another.

The scientific achievement brought with it a political struggle. European countries were anxious to improve their bargaining position towards the United States. Therefore, in 1963, they decided to set up the European Conference on Satellite Communication (CETS) to harmonize European views and to undertake discussion with the United States. On the other hand, the United States, Canada, the Western

---

(1) Although the ITU Convention still contains jointly structural and general technical provisions, the detailed technical rules have been shifted to separate regulatory texts. The ITU General and Administrative Regulations are divided into the Telegraph and Telephone Regulations, the Radio Regulations, and the additional Radio Regulations.

(2) An insurance policy can be effected for bringing the satellite into correct orbit. It was reported that the McDonald Douglas/Thiokol Payload Assit Module (PAM) motors failed to launch two satellites into correct orbit with the result that they were both circling the earth some 550/575 miles up, whereas they should have been in geosynchronous orbit at 22,320 miles. In case the satellite is back on earth, it will be the property of the underwriters and presumably it will be sold to offset part of the claim. See John Miller, Satellite bill spins into orbit, The Post Magazine, Feb.16, 1984, p.370; Graham Capel, Underwriters take a $10m satellite gamble, *ibid*, Oct.25, 1984, p.2542.

European countries, Australia and Japan reached agreements on August 20, 1964, to create an operational agency which would function side by side with the ITU. These agreements entered into force the same day and the International Telecommunications Satellite (INTELSAT) Consortium was established(1).

While the efforts of the international community continued in the field of satellite communication, the IMO devoted its work to the use of satellite communication for maritime purposes. In 1971, it decided to co-operate with the ITU and a panel of experts was set up to establish a system which would satisfy the following aims:

(a) improve distress, urgency and safety communications;

(b) relieve the present congestion in the medium frequency (MF) and high frequency (HF) bands;

(c) improve reliability, quality and speed of communications;

(d) improve geographical coverage and continuous availability of services;

(e) provide more reliable circuits and permit automation of radiotelephony and teleprinters;

(f) cater for services not possible at present in the MF and HF bands, such as high speed data transmission; and

(g) provide for radiodetermination.

Preparatory work continued and in 1976, the Convention on the International Maritime Satellite Organization (INMARSAT) was adopted. The Convention came into force in 1979 and thus a new independent organization, INMARSAT, was born.

Satellite communications offer many facilities such as: alerting and locating ships in cases of distress or emergency; assisting in search and rescue operations; issuing safety and urgent messages; reporting of ship's position; giving guidance to

---

(1) The United States had an initial quota of 61 per cent. This quota has now been decreased because of the accession of new members, but it is still more than 50 per cent.

traffic; giving warnings and weather information. In fact, satellite communication is expanding rapidly. It has brought fundamental changes to shipping(1) and development in this area will continue into the next century.

Thus, in this section the following points will be considered:

1. the general principles governing the orbit/spectrum;
2. INMARSAT; and
3. recent developments in satellite communication.

## 1. THE GENERAL LEGAL PRINCIPLES GOVERNING THE ORBIT/SPECTRUM

### A. Space and Outer Space Communication

For many years, the United Nations Committee on the Peaceful Uses of Outer Space has been concerned with the issues of delimitation of outer space and the rules governing the activities of the States in this area. No agreement has been reached, due mainly to the opposing views of the USSR and the United States. The former favours a limit of 110 km, with the right of innocent passage, while the United States argues that delimitation at the present time would be premature. Other countries have suggested a functional approach, i.e. asserting that the function of a particular object should determine whether the activity should be subject to international space law(2).

While the issue of delimitation has not been resolved, other important issues on outer space communication were established. The first one was that outer space belongs to all mankind to whom all the benefits of telecommunication services should be

(1) The impact of satellite communication on Shipping Law is profound. The master will soon lose his independent position as all decisions and the stowage plan could be made by the management and conveyed to him. On the other hand, it would create problems concerning the protection of the information or perhaps the development of "hunter-killer" satellites.
(2) UN.Doc. A/AC.105/C.2/L 141/Add.6 (April 7, 1983).

directed. Article 1 of the Outer Space Treaty, 1967[(1)] states that the outer space is deemed to be "the province of all mankind" and requires that it will be used "for the benefit and the interests of all countries, irrespective of their degree of economic or scientific development". The INTELSAT Agreement refers in article II to the use of the "most advanced technology available" for telecommunication services "for the benefit of all mankind", of "the most efficient and economic facilities possible consistent with the best and most equitable use of the radio frequency spectrum and of orbital space"[(2)].

State practice indicates an evolving rule of International Customary Law that earth orbit is to be regarded as part of outer space. In fact, International Law recognizes the principle of the full use of the channel dispersion of the new technology on geostationary satellite communication. It allows the development of the orbit/spectrum[(3)] resources so that satellite communication "pathways" (channels) would be available. The dimension of the channel is developing in its depth, distribution and directions. Channel depth refers to an increase in the number of messages which could be conveyed at

---

(1) The full title is The Treaty on Principles Governing the Activities of States in the Exploration and Use of Outer Space, Including the Moon and Other Celestial Bodies, 1967, 610 UNTS 205.

(2) See also the Agreement on the Rescue of Astronauts, the Return of Astronauts, and the Return of Objects Launched into Outer Space, 1968, 672 UNTS 119; The Convention on the International Liability for Damage Caused by Space Objects, 1972, 24 UST 2389, TIAS No.7762; the Convention on Registration of Objects Launched into Outer Space, 1972, 28 UST 695, TIAS No. 8480; and the Agreement Governing the Activities of States on the Moon and Other Celestial Bodies (the Moon Agreement) 1979, which came into force on July 11, 1984.

(3) The orbit/spectrum has three bands: the C band, the Ku band and the Ka band. Recently this area is subject to various exploration activities for both the geostationary orbit and the electromagnetic spectrum. The geostationary orbit is a ring of space above the equator where the satellite must be placed in order to serve

one time(1). International Law also supports the development of the channel to its full capacity in distributing the messages to different places. Through the INTELSAT and the ITU Agreements, many countries are committed to maximise channel distribution by promoting the establishment of geostationary satellite communication channels to different countries. Similarly, the Law encourages the efforts done to maximize channel directions to different places from which a message may be sent.

## B. Air Space and Radio Space

Scholars differ on the legal status of the air space. Arguing for the traditional view, Fauchille(2) and Oppenheim(3) maintain that the State has soverign rights in its airspace (atmosphere) and such rights include its radio space (frequencies) and the electromagnetic radio waves. The waves (frequencies) travel through the air space. No distinction exists in international law between the status of the air space and the radio space. The State has the right to transmit its radio waves and to stop (jam) waves (frequencies) coming from other States.

Lauterpacht, while agreeing in principle with the traditional view, introduced a refined element to it when he states that: "it is possible that the growing number of treaties in this field will contribute to the more general acceptance of the principle prohibiting the abuse of rights with regard to both the emission and the passage of waves."

It is clear that the traditional view is based on the distinction between air space and radio space. It is equally clear that accepting this view would create many difficulties. It could affect the efficiency of radio communication and perhaps bring utter chaos in this field. In fact, the International Telecommunication Union (ITU) developed an

---

as a relay platform for messages from various geographical areas.

(1) This is quite evident in the large number of agreements on "Table of Frequency Allocations" concluded through the ITU.

(2) Traite de Droit International Public, Vol.I, (1951), 848.

(3) International Law (8th ed. Lauterpacht), 1955, Vol.1, 529.

administrative machinery in this respect. Although the ITU Conventions are silent on the issue of the legal status of the air and radio space, they reject, by implication, the concept of a State legal title on them. Article 48 of the Montreux Convention imposes upon Member States of the ITU the duty to establish and operate radio stations "in such a manner as not to cause harmful interference[1] to the radio services or communications of other Members". In the Washington Radio Regulations of 1927, the ITU introduced a provision to the effect that member administrations should notify the Bureau of ITU of the establishment and operation of any radio station. Member administrations also undertook to assign frequencies to radio stations in such a way as not to interfere with frequencies which had been previously notified to the Bureau. A list of all frequencies which had been notified is published by the Bureau and the publication is aimed to bring to the attention of the international community the spectrum reality which no administration could afford to ignore. The procedure of notification and publication has been acted upon by the States and it tended to offer an alternative basis to that of the absolute right. The ITU procedure of assigning a frequency to be used, gave rise to another issue, namely that of priority.

Before World War II, the ITU Bureau compiled a comprehensive list on Frequency Allocations, known as the Bern List. When the Bureau, after the War, started to revise the List, the Soviet Union took the view that the allocation of frequencies as contained in the List gave Member States legal rights which could not be altered. The United States opposed this view, denying that the list created any priorities or titles to the frequencies. The Americans argued that the spectrum reality had changed to the extent that no right could be attached to the Bern List. The majority of the ITU Members subscribed to this view.

In practice, the present users of the frequencies are in a better position than newcomers. This

(1) Annex 2 of the Convention defines harmful interference as "any emission, radiation or induction which endangers the functioning of a radio-navigation service or of other safety services, or seriously degrades, obstructs or repeatedly interrupts a radio-communication service operating in accordance with the radio regulations".

privileged position is recognized in article 4 of the International Telecommunication Convention which requires the ITU:

"(1) to effect allocation of the radio frequency spectrum and registration of radio frequency assignments in order to avoid harmful interference between radio stations of different countries"; and

"(2) to coordinate efforts to eliminate harmful interference and to improve the use made of the radio frequency spectrum."

## 2. INMARSAT

In recent years, long delays(1), poor quality of transmission and areas of black-out are not infrequent(2). These deficiencies could be eliminated by the use of space technology. In fact, the main attractions of communication via satellite are to:

(a) relieve the pressure on the MF and HF bands;

(b) improve the quality of transmission;

(c) improve the geographical coverage; and

(d) improve distress communications.

---

(1) Long delays are mainly caused by:
(a) heavy congestion of frequencies which results in difficulty in having contact with coast stations; and
(b) most ships carry one radio officer keeping an eight-hour watch schedule which does not always coincide with the times of optimum propagation conditions.

(2) At the present rate of growth of maritime traffic, there may soon be acute congestion and saturation of the present maritime HF bands. At certain times of day, in some areas, this situation has already been reached and it is impossible to handle all the traffic because the number of bands is insufficient.
Shipowners have reported that the average delay on HF telegraph traffic is six hours and delays of 12 hours are not uncommon. In adverse conditions, as much as 36 hours delay has been known to occur.

For these reasons, the World Administrative Radio Conference for Space Telecommunications was held in June 1971 under the auspices of the ITU. Although the Conference had the opportunity to define the operational requirements for a maritime satellite system, it was unable to take these requirements into account when deciding on the frequencies to be allocated and on other technical matters. Nevertheless, the Conference considered Recommendations prepared by the IMO which state that space techniques could be used for the exchange of information by telephony and telegraphy - including data transmissions, direct printing and facsimile, teleprinter and wide band telegraphy - necessary for the administration and operational handling of ships and for passengers' and crews' requirements in the way of communications.

Following the allocation of frequencies to the maritime mobile service for the use of space techniques, it was necessary to study the practical problems connected with developing and setting up an operational maritime satellite system. Therefore, the IMO decided to prepare an organizational plan for an international maritime satellite system in full co-operation with the telecommunication authorities of its member governments.

## A. Establishment, Funding and Organs

Establishment: In March 1972, the MSC of the IMO[(1)] set up a panel of experts to study the above-mentioned problems in detail. The panel held six meetings and prepared a report which included the

---

(1) The IMO identified the following operational requirements which needed to be satisfied by the new system:
1. Handling of distress cases, including distress messages and search and rescue control communications, as well as determination by land-based stations of the position of any ship in distress and of search and rescue units involved.
2. Distribution of urgent safety messages, including requests for medical assistance.
3. Interrogation of the land-based station by the ship or other mobile craft to obtain position information. This could possibly be followed by environmental, meteorological and

following sections: reasons for establishing a maritime satellite system; operational requirements; basic technical parameters of a first-phase system; channel assignment and terrestrial interface; economic assessment; and organizational and institutional arrangements.

The report was submitted to a conference convened by the IMO. It held three sessions, the first in April,1975, the second in February,1976, and the third in September,1976. It adopted two instruments: the Convention on the International Maritime Satellite Organization (INMARSAT) and the Operating Agreement on the International Maritime Satellite Organization. Article 3 of the Convention states that the purpose of the organization is to make provision for the space segment for improving distress and safety of life at sea communications, efficiency and management of ships, maritime public correspondence services and radio determination capabilities. The Convention sets out the structure of the organization and the operating agreement spells out how the organization can raise its financial resources. The idea of having a separate operating agreement is to avoid the domination of the organization by the major investors. Governments are entitled to become parties to the Convention, whereas the operating agreement is open for

---

oceanographic information, or regular interrogation of the ship at appropriate time intervals by the land-based station, together with the transmission of position and other information.

4. Initial position determination, providing accuracies of the order of one to two nautical miles. As technology develops, and considering cost effectiveness, accuracy may be improved until the system is suitable for navigation near coasts, and in narrow passages and fairways.
5. Transmission of highly accurate standard frequencies and time signals.
6. Selective calling and multiple access technique to facilitate communications.
7. Selective calling of ships by coast stations for establishing public correspondence through terrestrial communications.
8. Public correspondence including ship's and company operational business carried out by telegraphy and telephony.

signature by governments or alternatively by competent entities designated by those governments which do not sign the operating agreement. These bodies could include, for example, private companies or corporations, public state-owned bodies or a mixed enterprise. It is interesting to note that INMARSAT is a combination of an inter-governmental organization enjoying privileges and immunities and a commercial enterprise formed by public and private "shareholders". This means that the Organization enjoys both the political authority and commercial flexibility. On July 16, 1979, the INMARSAT Convention came into force.

Capital contributions and investment shares: INMARSAT is funded by capital contributions from its Signatories. Each Signatory makes contributions in proportion to its investment share which is determined in the Operating Agreement. The largest shareholders are the USA with 23.4%, followed by the USSR with 14.1% and the UK with 9.9%. The initial investment share(1) of new Signatories joining

---

9. Data transmission, including facsimile, teleprinter and wide band systems.
10. Automatic warning of ships which are continuously tracked by the system, that they are approaching shallow waters, underwater constructions, drilling/production platforms, etc.
11. Advising ships which are continuously tracked by the system on anti-collision actions and on avoidance of continuously tracked navigational hazards, for example, icebergs.
12. Automation of the position-reporting system based on position information as mentioned in 3.
13. Traffic control, including collision warnings, especially in converging areas, subject to the radio determination system providing sufficient relative accuracy (see 4).
14. Distribution to ships of meteorological, hydrographic and oceanographic information.
15. Individual meteorological and oceanographic advice to ships by land-based stations (e.g. weather routeing, navigation through ice, etc.).
16. Collection from ships of meteorological, hydrographic and oceanographic observations.

(1) The initial investment share relates closely to

INMARSAT is 0.05%. Contributions go towards funding the costs of the space segment and the operating and administrative costs of the Organization. Signatories will receive capital repayment and compensation for use of that capital when revenues allow.

Organs: INMARSAT is composed of three bodies. The Assembly, the Council and the Directorate. The Assembly, where all member states are represented and have one vote each, meets once every two years to review the activities and objectives of INMARSAT and to make recommendations to the Council. The latter body is like a corporate board of directors; it consists of the 18 Signatories with the largest investment share in the Organization and four others elected by the Assembly on the basis of a just geographical representation and with due regard to the interests of developing countries. The Council meets at least three times a year and gives direction to the Directorate. The Signatories have a voting power equal to their investment shares. The Directorate, in turn, is headed by the Director General and carries out the Council decisions.

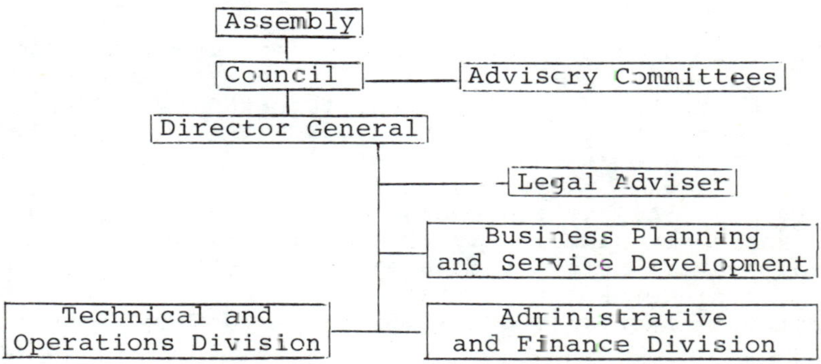


---

the prospective investment share on the basis of utilization, taking into account:
(a) the utilization of the new Signatory in relation to the total utilization of all other Signatories;
(b) the initial investment share requested by the new Signatory; and
(c) any other information that the new Signatory has provided regarding its projected utilization, e.g. terminal population, special projects, coast earth station provision.

## B. THE INMARSAT SYSTEM

The Elements: The services are provided through the satellite system, which comprises three elements: the satellite capacity leased by INMARSAT; the coast-earth stations, which are owned and operated by national telecommunications carriers; and the ship-earth stations.

The satellites are used to relay signals between the ship-earth stations and the coast-earth stations. INMARSAT uses capacity leased on three American Marisat satellites. More recently, INMARSAT has leased capacity on two Marecs satellites from the European Space Agency and the maritime packages on three INTELSAT satellites(1). Thus, INMARSAT has one operational and one spare satellite over each of the three oceans.

The coast-earth stations (CESs) provide the link between ships at sea and the terrestrial communications networks. These CESs comprise parabolic antennae constantly pointed at the operational satellite. They are owned and operated by national telecommunications administrations.

Finally, the third component is the ship-earth station which consists of two parts: the above and the below deck equipment. Above deck is a parabolic antenna mounted on a stabilized platform which enables it to constantly track the satellite despite ship manoeuvres. Below deck is the telephone, telex and other operational equipment.

Services: All telecommunications(2) services used on shore are also available to ships at sea. Examples of these services are: telephone, telex, distress alerts, information services, data communications, facsimile and slowscan television.

---

(1) See The inside story, drawings of Marecs and Intelsat published in Ocean Voice, the Journal of INMARSAT, Vol.2, No.2, October, 1982, pp.11-13.

(2) In the United Kingdom the telecommunications services were supplied by a government Department, that of Her Majesty's Postmaster General. The functions of that Department were transferred to the Post Office by the Post Office Act, 1969. Subsequently the telecommunications and data-processing business of the Post Office were transferred to a separate Corporation by the British Telecommunications Act, 1981. The Government still retains control of the tele-

Circuits can be leased for one or two hours per day for periods as short as one month. The leased circuit will be between a designated ship-earth station and a shore-based location via a designated coast-earth station.

Advantages: The INMARSAT system has been used by a wide range of users, including offshore operators, masters of oil tankers, chemical carriers, passenger vessels, tugs and cable-laying vessels. Oil rigs transmit data to shore for rapid processing and analysis. Oil tankers can be diverted to ports of loading or discharge at short notice. Seamen can get in touch with their families. Cargo manifest can be transmitted instantly. Distress alerts can be given to rescue co-ordination centres. Thus, the advantages of maritime satellite communications over conventional radiotelegraphy and radiotelephony are:

- almost global coverage;
- instantaneous, high-quality service at any time of the day or night, unaffected by weather or ionospheric disturbances;
- improved emergency reporting, with priority access to INMARSAT satellites for distress alerts;
- the interconnection of services with the worldwide public telecommunications networks;
- a direct dial capability for voice and telex communications;
- privacy of communications;
- short, medium and long range communications using the same equipment;
- mostly automatic connection; and
- telephone, telex and facsimile, data transmission and other specialized high-speed services can allow real-time, ship-to-shore computer communications.

Calls are placed to and from ships in virtually the same way as one would make a telephone call on

---

communications but it does so through a licensing system contained in the Telecommunications Act, 1984. See also the Cable and Broadcasting Act, 1984.

land and connections are made just as fast. Each ocean region has the equivalent of a country code. Calls are uplinked from the ship to the satellite at 1.6 GHz and downlinked from the satellite to a coast-earth station at 4 GHz. Going the other way, a call routed through the coast-earth station uplinks to the satellite at 6 GHz and travels from the satellite to the ship at 1.5 GHz.

## 3. RECENT DEVELOPMENTS IN SATELLITE COMMUNICATIONS

While satellites have a profound effect on distress-alerting and SAR capability worldwide, further efforts are made to improve its capability. One of the most important projects in this respect is the one currently considered by the IMO on "Future Global Maritime Distress and Safety System" (FGMDSS). The main objective of the system is to provide for adequate communications in order to promote safety of life at sea. It is designed to support SAR[1].

A. FGMDSS: The basic concept of the FGMDSS is that shore search and rescue authorities, as well as shipping in the vicinity of a distress incident, will be rapidly alerted to the distress and be capable of being involved in a co-ordinated rescue operation[2]. In order to operate effectively, the system would apply to all cargo and passenger ships on international voyages regardless of their geographical location. The system will provide for urgency and safety communications as well as the dissemination of navigational and meteorological information to ships.

Although many countries have some sort of search and rescue facilities for aiding ships at sea, these facilities vary and their efforts are not co-ordinated on a global basis. Again, the FGMDSS will provide for the establishment of rescue co-ordination centres (RCCs) and for a set of procedures for responding to distress alerts and carrying out rescue missions.

---

(1) An essential feature of the system will be the frequencies which need to be reserved for maritime distress and safety purposes.

(2) The legal status and the function of the operator in the FGMDSS is to be considered by the Sub-Committee on Safety of Navigation.

The FGMDSS system will use both coast radio station (Terrestrial) or Coast Earth Station (CES) (Satellite)[1]. It will lead to the amendment of a number of shipping conventions[2]. By 1990 it is anticipated that a co-ordinated communications network will be developed and implemented[3] together

---

(1) Terrestrial communications will no longer use Morse Code radiotelegraphy but will employ digital selective calling (DSC), radiotelephony and narrow band direct printing (NBDP). A report from the International Radio Consultative Committee (CCIR) on trials of the DSC system involving shore transmitting stations and ships from a number of Member States, considered that the results of the tests were impressive and that the DSC system could be considered viable providing the number and distribution of coastal stations was carefully selected.

(2) The introduction of the FGMDSS will involve amendments to Chapter IV of the International Convention for the Safety of Life at Sea, 1974 (SOLAS), the International Convention on Standards of Training, Certification and Watchkeeping for Seafarers, 1978 (STCW), and the Radio Regulations of the International Telecommunication Union.

(3) The Sub-Committee on Safety of Navigation prepared at its 30th session a work programme to study a proposed worldwide satellite navigation system. Members were invited to consider this programme. The terms of reference of the study include the following:
1. The operational requirements of a worldwide satellite navigation system which would be reliable, of low user cost and meet the needs of coastal and ocean navigation as well as the requirements of the future global maritime distress and safety system (FGMDSS), which is currently being developed by the IMO.
2. The organizational structure and arrangements which would be needed by an international organization or consortium for it to be recognized by the IMO as being suitable to provide, implement and operate such a system.
3. The arrangements, if any, by which a national or multi-national satellite navigation system might be recognized by the IMO or might be operated by a recognized international organiz-

with an international search and rescue plan(1).

The WARC and the FGMDSS: In 1983, the World Administrative Radio Conference (WARC) of the International Telecommunications Union (ITU) was held to revise the radio regulations applying to mobile services, including shipping. The primary task of the meeting was to take a series of decisions affecting the FGMDSS.

The WARC agreed to make all frequencies requested by the IMO available. A key decision involved acceptance of a "dispersed" approach to the allocation of frequencies for the FGMDSS. This means providing the necessary frequencies in those parts of the bands used for three principal methods of alerting - digital select calling (DSC), radiotelephony and narrow-band direct printing.

New radio regulations were adopted making it clear that the testing of radio-telephone alarms on the air at sea is prohibited. There is a clause allowing testing in port by government surveyors, provided certain conditions are satisfied.

The various attitudes towards the FGMDSS: European countries support the FGMDSS but the United States has strong reservations. The Americans believe that the idea of applying the system to vessels of 800 tons and over represents a heavy burden on small ships. Australia and New Zealand are willing to

---

ation or consortium.

4. The most economic method by which such a system might be provided, including the possible use of the system by other mobile services and the possible use of the facilities providing the system to meet other operational requirements.

(1) When the FGMDSS becomes operational, it is expected to require the carriage of NAVTEX which transmits navigational and meteorological information. This information is received on board ships in printed form on unattended receivers. The NAVTEX system is used in the North Sea, Baltic, Channel and part of the Atlantic. Many countries are at present testing the system. The Maritime Safety Committee (MSC) of the IMO agreed that the priority for the establishment of NAVTEX should be based on shipping density where its implementation would enhance navigational safety.

support the full development of the FGMDSS but they are anxious to avoid any interference with existing distress and safety systems until the FGMDSS has been fully proven.

Many developing countries have strong reservations on the acceptability of the FGMDSS. An interesting idea at the WARC, 1983, was a proposal for a recommendation that the FGMDSS facilities should be available in countries with large desert areas. This would provide emergency alert facilities for isolated populations. This proposal received the support of the Conference and it is hoped that a universal land/sea FGMDSS will win Third World support.

B. Emergency Position-indicating Radio Beacons (EPIRB): Distress signals could be provided in the FGMDSS through emergency position-indicating radio beacons(1) (EPIRBs). EPIRBs are designed to transmit an automatic distress message in the event of a sudden accident at sea. They are designed to float free if the ship sinks, thereby enabling an alarm to be given even if it is impossible to do so manually. They will have to use satellites as relays. Satellite EPIRBs could make use of the INMARSAT geostationary satellites(2) or the polar orbiting satellites in the COSPAS/SARSAT system which has been developed by Canada, France, the United States and the Soviet Union(3).

---

(1) The beacons are developed from aeronautical emergency systems. In essence an EPIRB is a device which will automatically transmit an alert signal and continue to do so until power runs out. The EPIRB will float and is similar in appearance to a marker buoy.

(2) The INMARSAT system is geostationary and uses three satellites placed over the Atlantic, Indian and Pacific Oceans.
Recently INMARSAT has made access to its system for trials carried out by several countries, including the United States, the Soviet Union, the United Kingdom, Norway, Japan and the Federal Republic of Germany. A series of demonstrations of EPIRBs are planned to take place later this year.

(3) Since 1980, four countries - Canada, France, the United States and the Soviet Union, recently joined by Norway and the United Kingdom, have

Thus, the EPIRB could be carried[1] on a buoy, in a lifeboat or held in hand. When it is carried on a buoy, it will float on the water and will then activate a transmitter to give a message on the ship's identification number and her position. Once the message is received a rescue mission could be alerted.

Financial funding of the new EPIRB services is giving rise to difficult problems. INMARSAT considered the possibility that its new satellites would carry a 406 MHz transponder, like those in the COSPAS/SARSAT system, but this idea was not accepted by its Member States[2]. Therefore, the new satellites will support only EPIRBs working at 1.6 GHz.

Changes will continue to take place in satellite communication and we will be constantly burdened with new regulations. Yet, in an evolutionary society, change is in itself an enduring feature.

---

been working on a system known as COSPAS/SARSAT which uses near polar orbiting satellites and operates on 121.5 MHz and 406 MHz.
In the 28th session the Sub-Committee on Radio Communications considered a proposal that a study be made on a system model of geostationary and polar-orbiting systems, each able to relay satellite EPIRB transmissions on the 406 MHz and 1.6 GHz bands.
At present, most EPIRBs can operate at either 121.5 or 243 megahertz. The 406 MHz frequency and the L-band, which is about 1.6 gigahertz, can also be used. In future, most EPIRBs would work on both these frequencies. See M.Notice 982.

(1) The equipment to be carried on ships will be designed for simple operation and will be largely automated. The equipment required to be carried will depend on a ship's area of operation. See MSC 49/4/3 of March 19, 1984.

(2) INMARSAT submitted to the IMO Sub-Committee on Radio Communications, estimates for providing 406 MHz and L-band transponders on its satellites. They showed that annual costs of L-band EPIRB services in 1988-95 would be in the range of $150,000 to $2 million a year. Annual costs of including a 406 MHz service were estimated to be in the range of $10-15 million. See MSC 49/4/2 of February 9, 1984. A note on Funding of INMARSAT Satellite EPIRB Services.

References

Alexandrowicz, C.H., The Law of Global Communications, Columbia University Press, 1971.

Cahill, R., Collisions and Their Causes, Fairplay Publications, 1983.

Conner, Timothy. Maritime Tort Liability, J. of Maritime Law and Commerce, Vol.11, No.3, pp. 226-292.

Couper, Frank. The Deep Draught Vessel, J. of Maritime Law and Commerce, Vol.8, No.3, pp. 295-335.

Holdert & Buzek, Collision Cases, Lloyd's of London Press, 1984.

Lundberg, Olof. INMARSAT: Improving Maritime Communications, Marine Policy, October,1984, pp. 337-345.

Mankabady, S., Collision at Sea, North-Holland.

Murphy, Thomas. The Legal Implications of Marine Radar, J. of Maritime Law and Commerce, Vol.7, No.4, pp. 573-614.

Ocean Voice, the Journal of INMARSAT.

Pineus & Roherke, Limited Liability in Collision Cases, Lloyd's of London Press, 1984.

Plant, G., International Traffic Separation Schemes in the new Law of the Sea, Marine Policy, April, 1985, pp. 134-147.

# CHAPTER VII

# RULES ON THE PROTECTION OF THE ENVIRONMENT

Oil enters the marine environment[1] by discharge during transport, drilling[2], shipping operations[3], accidents[4], dumping and from shore installations. Pollution is not, of course, confined to oil but it covers also chemicals and wastes. Some chemical substances are more dangerous to the environment than oil. Furthermore, radioactive substances may enter the marine environment by accident or through nuclear tests carried out on the high seas or in the space above them[5].

The protection of the marine environment is a complex subject for which a number of international conventions[6] were adopted. The complexity and

---

(1) The American National Academy of Sciences estimated that in 1980, 3.54 million tons of oil entered the sea every year; some 1.5 million tons from transport and the remainder from land-base activities.
(2) See the London Convention on Civil Liability for Oil Pollution Damage from Offshore Operations, 1976; and the interim voluntary agreement among oil companies known as OPOL.
(3) Operational discharges arise from two sources: the washing of oil cargo tanks and the pumping of machinery space bilges.
(4) The hazards of many of these substances are not limited to the environment but may extend to the crew on board the ship and persons handling the cargo.
(5) On January 17, 1966, an American military aircraft carrying nuclear weapons crashed off the coast of Spain. This incident illustrates the possibility that radioactive substances can be released accidentally into the marine environment.
Under article 1 of the Nuclear Test Ban Treaty signed in Moscow on August 5, 1963, each Party renounces the right to explode nuclear devices not only "at any place under its jurisdiction or control" and in the atmosphere; beyond its limits, including outer space; or under water including the high seas but also "in any other environment if such explosion causes radioactive debris to be present outside the territorial limits of the State under whose jurisdiction or control such explosion is conducted..."
(6) The SOLAS Convention, 1974, as amended by the 1978 Protocol, 1981 and 1983, are of great importance in preventing pollution. SOLAS has

comprehensiveness of the international rules are particularly appropriate in order to prevent or eliminate pollution and to compensate persons who suffer damage. Some of these conventions were amended on several occasions and implemented by municipal rules with the result of an expansion of the body of Environmental Law.

Before considering the rules on the protection of the marine environment, the following observations could be made:

(a) The protection of the marine environment can not just only be achieved through the introduction of legal rules, indispensable as this is. Other means such as the adoption of a manual(1) or a code(2) of

---

its own contribution in parallel with MARPOL. See Chapters II and VII.
See also article 194 of the UN Convention on the Law of the Sea, 1983, which states: "1. States shall take, individually or jointly as appropriate, all measures consistent with this Convention that are necessary to prevent, reduce and control pollution of the marine environment from any source, using for this purpose the best practical means at their disposal and in accordance with their capabilities, and they shall endeavour to harmonize their policies in this connection.
2. States shall take all measures necessary to ensure that activities under their jurisdiction or control are so conducted as not to cause damage by pollution to other States and their environment, and that pollution arising from incidents or activities under their jurisdiction or control does not spread beyond the areas where they exercise sovereign rights in accordance with this Convention."

(1) The Marine Environment Protection Committee (MEPC) of the IMO prepared an Anti-Pollution Manual. Sales No. 78.11.E. The Manual provides guidance to governments on ways of establishing response organizations and preparing contingency plans, both local and regional. The Manual consists of five sections: Prevention, Contingency Planning; Salvage; Methods for dealing with Spillages of Oil; and Legal Aspects.

(2) The Institution of Petroleum published a Code of Practice which is intended to assist local

conduct is equally important[1].

(b) The main responsibility for ensuring that agreed standards are observed rests with the flag State. But, it is increasingly apparent that port States should also have powers to carry out surveys on foreign ships.

(c) Regional co-operation[2] could be the most effective way to deal with environmental problems in view of the locality and the relationship between the parties concerned.

(d) The enforcement rules, in some countries, are not adequate. The adherence to the

---

government departments and seaside councils to use oil slick dispersants. The Code is written in simple and easy-to-grasp language, and is directed at those concerned with the actual clean-up operations.
The International Chamber of Shipping (ICS) and the Oil Companies International Marine Forum (OCIMF) published a Guide called "Perils at Sea and Salvage". Its purpose is to assist masters in making decisions when faced with a difficult situation. The Guide has been prepared principally with oil tankers in mind, but much of the advice is applicable to other types of ships. See also Oil Spills: Their Fate and Impact on the Marine Environment, 1980; Disabled Tankers, 1981; Drift Characteristics of 50,000 to 70,000 DWT Tankers, 1982; OCIMF recommendations on Equipment for the Towing of Disabled Tankers, 1981. All these publications are issued jointly by ICS and OCIMF.

(1) Far greater emphasis is needed for the co-operation of shipping, oil and chemical industries, shipbuilders, manufacturers of machinery and equipment, and classification societies.

(2) For the EEC countries, see Directive 464 of 1976 on Pollution caused by certain dangerous substances discharged into the aquatic environment of the community. Directive 319 of 1978 on Toxic and dangerous waste; Directive 501 of 1982 on the major accident hazards of certain industrial activities; Directive 631 of 1984 on the Supervision and Control within the Community of the transfrontier shipment of hazardous waste; and recently in 1985 a Directive on Environmental impact assessments for industrial installations.

> international rules is not strictly observed and the control is usually superficially exercised[1]. The difficulties of enforcement will reduce the effectiveness of control set up by MARPOL. A round-the-clock aerial surveillance would not be cost-effective. However, it may be practical to brief airline pilots flying regularly over busy shipping lanes so that they can report discharges of oil, chemicals or any other hazardous substances from ships.

The use of aerial surveillance coupled with sanctions is one of the means for securing more effective co-operation between States in the enforcement of international conventions. It would be inequitable if there were wide disparity between penalties imposed, say, on UK and foreign ships for similar offences.

In order to give a proper conception of the rules on the protection of the marine environment, it may be convenient to classify them into two categories: public and private international rules. It must be noted that this classification is adopted for illustration purposes as certain breaches of MARPOL provisions (public rules) may give rise to liability under the Civil Liability Convention (private rules).

Thus, this chapter is divided into two sections:

(i) the public international rules; and

(ii) the private international rules.

(1) There are serious difficulties in bringing proceedings against foreign owners.

## (i) THE PUBLIC INTERNATIONAL RULES

Historical background: Towards the end of World War I, pollution started to attract the attention of many governments. In 1921, a conference consisting of shipowners, oil companies and harbour officials was held in London to consider the problems arising from oil pollution. As a result of this conference, the Oil in Navigable Waters Act,1922, was passed in Great Britain. This Act prohibited the discharge of oil or oily water into the territorial waters of Great Britain and Northern Ireland and imposed a fine of £100 for any offence under it.

The prohibited zone established by this Act was considered by a committee of London and Liverpool shipowners which recommended the extension of the zone and the need for providing facilities for discharging oily waste ashore or into barges.

The measures on oil pollution taken in Britain attracted world attention and an international conference was held in Washington in 1926 to consider this issue. The conference did not succeed in formulating a convention. However, one of its results was the voluntary adoption by British shipowners of a 50 mile prohibited zone. This was followed by similar actions by shipowners in Holland, Belgium, Norway and Sweden. Shipowners in the United States even accepted a zone of 100 miles.

In 1934, the question of oil pollution was raised by Britain at the League of Nations and a special committee was set up to prepare a draft convention. The work of this committee was interrupted by World War II.

In 1952, the British Government established a committee known as the Faulkner Committee which published in 1953 a comprehensive report on the effects of oil pollution, the causes of pollution and the short and long term solutions. Following the publication of this report, the British Government held a conference in 1954 and the outcome of it was the International Convention[1] for the Prevention of Pollution of the Sea by Oil, 1954.

### The International Convention for the Prevention of Pollution of the Sea, 1954, and its Amendments

Ths 1954 Convention was primarily aimed at pollution

---

(1) The Convention came into force on July 26, 1958.

from routine tanker operations[1] and from discharge of oily wastes from machinery space. Oil is defined in article I(1) as "crude oil, fuel oil, heavy diesel oil and lubricating oil". Consequently, the provisions of the Convention applied only to certain persistent oils and non-persistent oils were not covered by them. The Convention[2] prohibited discharge from a tanker in certain zones, of oil or of mixtures containing more than 100 parts of oil per million. The zones were: (a) all sea areas within 50 miles from the nearest land; (b) certain special areas defined in Annex A; and (c) any area within 100 miles from the nearest land along the coasts of a State which has declared such a zone. Reception facilities were required to be provided in each main port to receive oil residues from machinery space bilges and oil fuel tanks that had been used for the carriage of water ballast. A new form of oil record book was required which was designed to show the movement of cargo oil and its residues from loading to discharging on a tank to tank basis. The rules of the Convention did not apply to naval auxiliaries vessels under 500 tons gross tonnage, whaling vessels and vessels on the Great Lakes (art.2)[3].

---

(1) Unloaded oil tankers must take on seawater for ballast to ensure proper submergence and vessel stability. Upon arrival in port, the tankers must then discharge this ballast, i.e. "deballast" before loading their cargo tanks with oil. Ballast held in empty oil tanks will contain oil residue.

(2) The Convention was deposited with the United Kingdom pending the establishment of the IMO.

(3) After the conclusion of this Convention, the Oil in Navigable Waters Act,1922 was repealed and the Oil in Navigable Waters Act,1955 was enacted. It followed closely the provisions of the Convention. The penalties for wilful infringement of the 1955 Act were more severe than those laid down by the 1922 Act. The master of a ship was liable to a fine of £1,000 on summary conviction, or to an unlimited fine on indictment if he permitted the discharge of persistent oils within the prohibited areas. The oil tanker record book, which was stipulated by the 1922 Act, was retained by the 1955 Act.

The 1962 Amendments: More control was still needed[1] and in 1962 the IMO called a conference to revise the 1954 Convention. The 1962 Convention[2] amended the 1954 Convention[3] by extending the area of the prohibited zones, widening the scope of the Convention by applying its provisions to all tankers over 150 tons gross and, so far as practicable, to all other vessels of whatever size; and finally by securing general acceptance of the principle that persistent oil should not be discharged into the sea.

Under both the 1954 Convention and the 1962 Amendments there were a number of loopholes. It was difficult to prove that the discharge had in fact taken place in a specified zone, or in the case of any oily mixture, exceeded the permitted level[4]. Moreover, the shipowner could have a good defence if he could show that the oil was discharged in order to secure the safety of the vessel, or to save life, or that the oil escaped because of damage to the ship or leakage which was not due to negligence of the master.

The 1969 Amendments - Load on Top (LOP): The oil industry developed a technique to remove as much water as possible from the residue in the slop tank[5]. The cargo tank washings are transferred

---

(1) In July,1959, the International Conference on Oil Pollution of the Sea held at Copenhagen, recommended that the IMO should prepare a further conference aiming at extending the prohibited zones to cover the Gulf of St.Lawrence, the Grand Banks of Newfoundland and the Eastern seaboard of North America.

(2) The 1962 Convention was enacted by the Oil in Navigable Waters Act, 1963.

(3) The Conference adopted fifteen Resolutions which were submitted to Governments and Other Bodies concerned for consideration and appropriate action.

(4) The so-called "clean" ballast is that which "if discharged from a vessel that is stationary into clean, calm water, would not produce visible traces of oil on the surface of the water or on adjoining shore lines". *Chevron U.S.A.* v. *Hammond* (1984) A.M.C., p.1028.

(5) On June 17, 1964, Shell, Exxon and British Petroleum announced that after three years of trial and research, their tankers would sail

through "stripping" pipes to the slop tank and, after settling, the water is discharged to sea(1) or to port reception facilities and the fresh cargo will be loaded on top of the slop tank oil residues. This technique, known as "load on top", has met with great success and about 80% of oil tankers are using it.

In spite of the success in using the LOT method, it has its own limitations. The settling needed to separate the oil required a certain period of time and consequently the LOT cannot be used in short voyages and for vessels engaged in coastal trade. Another problem is that the oil to be loaded on the next voyage may be incompatible with the persistent oil retained on board in the slop tank which usually contains a high level of salt. Finally, when the tanker enters a repair yard it should be cleaned to remove the oily residue and sludge. Some shipyards do not deny the entry of tankers with slops aboard while others insist on the removal of the heavy sludge material before entry into the yard.

The use of the LOT method by tankers of 20,000 tons gross or more was in need of certain clarification. To this end, the IMO passed a Resolution(2) to amend the 1954 Convention. According to the new Amendments of 1969, discharge from tankers is prohibited unless the following conditions are satisfied:

(i) the tanker is proceeding *en route*;

(ii) the instantaneous rate of discharge of oil content does not exceed 60 litres per mile(3);

(iii) the total quantity of oil discharged on a ballast voyage does not exceed 1/50,000th of the total cargo-carrying capacity;

(iv) the tanker is more than 50 miles from the nearest land.

---

clean across the seas as a result of using the LOT method. See S.Z. Pritchard, Load on Top, J. of Mar. L. & Comm., Vol.9, No.2, 1978, pp. 185-224.

(1) The effluents mixed with the water are considered to represent negligible pollution.

(2) IMO Resolution A.175 (VI); UK Misc. No.7 of 1970 (Cmnd.4347). The amendments came into force on January 20, 1978.

(3) This condition can be reached by adjusting the discharge rate with the speed of the vessel.

This amendment enables tankers to operate the "load on top" system without violating the Convention. For other ships to which the Convention applies, there are substituted for conditions (iii) and (iv) above the following conditions:

(iii) that the oil content of discharge is less than 100 parts per million of the mixture; and

(iv) that the discharge is made as far as practicable from land.

In fact, both the 1954 Convention and the 1962 Amendments are based on the philosophy that the discharge of oil is permissible unless it occurs inside the prohibited zones. The 1969 Amendment brought a fundamental change to this philosophy by allowing a discharge if the oil is sufficiently dispersed at sea(1).

---

(1) The provisions of the Convention were incorporated into the Prevention of Oil Pollution Act, 1971. The Act repealed the Oil in Navigable Waters Acts of 1955-1963 and 1971; section 5 of the Continental Shelf Act, 1964; section 21 (7) of the Sea Fisheries Regulation Act, 1966, and section 10(1)(c) of the Mineral Workings (Offshore Installations) Act, 1971, and it consolidated all these Acts.
The Act prohibits the discharge into UK territorial waters of any oil or any mixture containing oil by any vessel, irrespective of nationality. Section 2(2) provides that: "This section applies to the following waters ... (b) all other waters ... which are ... navigable by seagoing ships". In *Rankin* v. *De Coster* (1975) 2 Lloyd's Rep. 84, it was held that the waters in the dry dock fell within the general description, and could properly be called waters "navigable by seagoing ships". That fact that, when the oil was discharged into the dry dock, the waters were not navigable by seagoing ships did not affect their general character.
The Act prohibits the discharge by any UK registered ship of any crude fuel, lubricating or heavy diesel oils or a mixture containing these, into any part of the sea outside the territorial waters of the UK. Persons guilty of an offence under these provisions are liable to a fine of £50,000 on summary conviction or

The 1971 Amendments: These Amendments which concern operational pollution, redefined the phrase "nearest land" in article III so that the Great Barrier Reef is given the extra protection which it lost when Annex A was deleted in 1969. The Amendments also limited the size of tanks on oil tankers, thereby minimizing the amount of oil which could escape in the event of a collision or stranding.

---

unlimited fine on indictment.
In *Federal Steam Navigation Co. Ltd. v. Department of Trade and Industry (The 'Huntingdon')* (1974) 1 Lloyd's Rep. 520, the *Huntingdon*, a British ship, while on a voyage from Port Arthur to New York in August,1970, discharged a quantity of mixed oil and water into the sea off Nova Scotia contrary to s.1(1) of the Oil in Navigable Waters Act, 1955.
The shipowner and the master were fined £2,500 and £500 respectively. The shipowner appealed on the ground that according to s.1(1), only one (either the owner or the master) could be convicted of an offence. The House of Lords dismissed the owner's appeal. Lord Reid said that the word 'or' is used conjunctively and therefore the owner and the master were both liable to prosecution. Lord Wilberforce, dissenting, said: "I regret to express an opinion differing from that so strongly held by those who have preceded me in this House. The revelation of this difference of opinion may perhaps be salutary if the draftsmen are encouraged to use care in the use of 'or' and, or even if I dare say so, 'and/or'."
Where a master or owner is charged with one of the offences listed above, it will be a defence for him to show that the pollutant was discharged for:
(a) securing the safety of the vessel; or
(b) preventing damage to any vessel or cargo; or
(c) saving life.
Similarly, it is a defence to show that the pollutant escaped in consequence of damage to the vessel or through a leakage provided all reasonable steps were taken to stop or reduce the polluting process and, also, in the case of leakage, there was no want of reasonable care in either causation or discovery.
In order to assist in the enforcement of many of the provisions of the Act, an oil record book is to be kept on board the ship.

Despite the various amendments to the 1954 Convention, there was a need, in view of the increasing amount of chemicals carried by sea(1), to prevent pollution(2) by all noxious substances emanating from ships, not only oil. After four years of deliberation, the International Convention for the Prevention of Pollution from Ships (MARPOL) was adopted in 1973(3). MARPOL replaced the 1954 Convention and its amendments and its goal is eventually to eliminate all pollution except the disposal of land-generated waste into the sea by dumping.

Although MARPOL is the most important convention in this field, it is necessary to say a brief word on dumping at sea, the Intervention Convention, 1969, and co-operation between States to protect the environment. Thus, in this section, the following issues will be examined:

1. MARPOL 1973/78 and its Amendments;
2. dumping at sea;
3. the Intervention Convention, 1969; and
4. regional co-operation.

---

(1) Lloyd's Statistics Tables (1984) show that the number of ships carrying bulk chemical cargoes in the world was 1,206 ships with a total of 6,474,089 G/T.

(2) The strong policy statement of the US Ports and Tanker Safety Act (PTSA),1978 runs as follows: "(A) that the carriage by vessels of certain cargoes in bulk or in residue creates substantial hazards to life, property, the navigable waters of the United States (including the quality thereof) and the resources contained therein and to the adjoining land, including but not limited to fish, shellfish, and wildlife, marine and coastal ecosystems, and recreational and scenic values;
"(B) that existing standards for the design, construction, alteration, repair, maintenance, operation, equipping, personnel qualification, and manning of all such vessels which use any port or place subject to the jurisdiction of the United States must be more stringent and comprehensive for the mitigation of the hazards to life, property, and the marine environment."

(3) The Convention came into force on October 2, 1983. By November,1984, thirty-one States

## 1. THE INTERNATIONAL CONVENTION FOR THE PREVENTION OF POLLUTION FROM SHIPS (MARPOL) 73/78

The main goal of MARPOL is to reduce the total oil remaining on board to the minimum. If there is no cargo left on board the tanker, there can be no pollution from it. Residues and wastes should be retained on board for eventual discharge into shore reception facilities. MARPOL, in essence, is a combination of different sets of rules on oil, chemicals, noxious substances in packaged forms, sewage and garbage, with very little link between them[1]. It introduced several undertakings on the part of shipowners, masters, oil and chemical industries, to ensure the existence of certain equipment and the adherence to certain operational requirements. The Convention is addressed to States, ports and other authorities to ensure the establishment of reception facilities and an effective system of control. Several national regulations[2] had to be enacted to implement the Convention. The MARPOL Convention ran into difficulties due mainly to the fact that the original text was badly drafted as the control measures were expressed in a general way. Therefore, it was necessary to introduce several amendments to it.

---

representing 72% of the world's maritime fleet are parties to it. C53/7/Add.1 of September 20, 1984.

(1) Annex I on Oil entered into force and Annex II on Chemicals will enter into force on April 6, 1987.

(2) In the United States, the Coast Guard is the government agency in charge of drafting the national regulations for ship-shore interface, certifying the construction of the ship and enforcing pollution control regulations within the United States territorial waters. Another agency, the Environmental Protection Agency (EPA) is in charge of enacting regulations on legal liability for waste disposal, imposing fines and assessing a surcharge on waste activities.
While the Coast Guard has introduced a comprehensive inspection procedure, in European ports the Paris Memorandum will give the port authority the opportunity to exercise its control in respect of MARPOL.

MARPOL incorporates a "tacit acceptance" procedure, under which amendments automatically enter into force on a specific date unless rejected by one-third of the Contracting Parties or by Contracting Parties whose combined fleets of merchant shipping represent not less than 50 per cent of world gross tonnage(1).

The Protocols attached to the Convention

Two protocols are appended to the Convention; the first contains provisions concerning reports(2) on incidents involving harmful substances, and the second provides an arbitration machinery to solve the disputes.

Reporting of pollution incidents: After the entry into force of MARPOL, considerable attention was given to the format and procedures for the submission of mandatory reports on deficiencies of ships and certificates(3); discharges in contravention to the Convention(4); and incidents involving harmful substances(5).

At the 20th session of the MEPC, some delegations recommended that the Convention's reporting requirements should apply only to certain types and sizes of vessels and within limited geographic

---

evidence of the compliance (e.g. letter of compliance issued by the flag State or a recognized classification society), the ship would receive appropriate recognition by the port State inspector. MEPC 22/WP.16, Dec. 6, 1985, pp. 6,7.

(1) Protocol I is not applicable to incidents involving dangerous goods in packaged form. MEPC 21/11/2, Feb. 27, 1985. See also M.Notice 1152 which states that: "In the light of continuing incidents involving packaged dangerous goods that have affected our coastlines, there is a need to take action prior to the implementation of Annex III of the Convention. The Department would therefore urge Masters and Shipowners to report incidents involving packaged dangerous goods."

(2) See article 16 of MARPOL and article VI of the Protocol of 1978.

(3) Article 5 and Resolution A.542 (13).

(4) Article 6 and Resolution A.542 (13).

(5) Article 8 and Resolution A.447 (XI).

areas, while others opposed these limitations. Several delegations took the view that all vessel discharges or potential discharges of hazardous substances can pose a threat to a coastal State, and that all ships regardless of size, loaded conditions, or type, should be required to follow Protocol I and its associated Guidelines. The coastal State could then evaluate the environmental danger and take the necessary action.

The MEPC believed that it would be preferable to limit the number of different reporting requirements imposed upon vessels. This could be achieved if the reporting requirements adopted by MARPOL also satisfy the needs under other conventions such as the one on Salvage. One problem that may arise is that the guidelines, which contain much of the substantive standards for reporting, are not mandatory. The balance between the Protocol and Guidelines should be carefully considered(1).

Several delegations suggested(2) that the MEPC when considering any amendments to Protocol I to MARPOL, should insert the following provisions:

(a) requiring not only the master of the vessel in distress to submit reports on the incident, but also the master of the vessel providing assistance to make appropriate reports to the coastal State; and

(b) requiring(3) the assisting vessel and the vessel being assisted to provide detailed supplementary reports on all aspects of the progress being made in respect of the

(1) MEPC 21/11/2, February 27, 1985; MEPC 22/WP.16, December 6, 1985, p.20.
(2) MEPC 21/11/7, April 2, 1985.
(3) Under English law, reports should be made whenever:
(a) an accident occurs involving actual or probable spillage of oil or other harmful substances;
(b) any spillage of oil or other harmful substance is observed at sea;
(c) any ship is seen discharging oil.
In case of incidents or sightings in coastal regions, an immediate report should be sent to the authorities of neighbouring coastal States which may be affected by pollution, or to the nearest coast radio station. See M.Notice 876; and M.Notice 1141.

salvage operation(1).

## The 1978 Protocol

Many States were not prepared to ratify MARPOL 1973 because of the reception facilities and the discharge requirement for chemical tankers. For this reason a conference was held in 1978 to consider changes to MARPOL. The conference adopted a Protocol which approved changes to Annex I and deferred the implementation of Annex II. The Convention and the 1978 Protocol were amalgamated into one single instrument. By accepting the Protocol, the Contracting State will undertake to implement at the same time the requirements of the Convention.

## THE ANNEXES TO MARPOL

All the technical measures of MARPOL are included in five annexes dealing respectively with:

- Annex I - Oil
- Annex II - Noxious liquid substances carried in bulk (e.g. chemicals)
- Annex III - Harmful substances carried in packages (e.g. tanks and containers)
- Annex IV - Sewage
- Annex V - Garbage

Annexes III, IV and V are optional, but governments ratifying the convention must accept Annexes I and II.

---

(1) In fact, any reporting system would need to deal with the following issues:
  (a) the authority to which reports should be made;
  (b) when and where the duty to report would arise;
  (c) the consequences of non-reporting both from the civil and penal liability; and
  (d) the distance from the coastline where reporting would be required.

## ANNEX I (OIL)

The main objective of Annex I[1], as amended by the 1978 Protocol, is to eliminate the intentional pollution of the marine environment by oil and to minimize the accidental discharge of oil.

Oil is defined in Regulation 1(2) as follows:

> "Oil" means petroleum in any form including crude oil, fuel oil, sludge, oil refuse and refined products other than petrochemicals[2].

Discharge provisions: Annex I applies to all tankers of 150 gross tons and above and other ships of 400 tons and above. The oil discharge criteria contained in the 1969 Amendments to the 1954 Convention are maintained but the total amount of oil which can be discharged into the sea is halved to 1/30,000 of the cargo. For discharge from machinery space of all vessels, the ship must be underway - more than 12 miles from land - and the oil must be less than 100 ppm.

The exceptions are:

(a) any discharge into the sea of oil or oily mixture which is necessary for the purpose of securing the safety of a ship or saving life at sea; or

(b) any discharge into the sea of oil or oily mixture which results from damage to a ship or its equipment:

(i) provided that all reasonable precautions were taken after the occurrence of the damage or discovery of the discharge for the purpose of preventing or minimizing the discharge; and

---

(1) The Merchant Shipping (Prevention of Oil Pollution) Order, 1983, and The Merchant Shipping (Prevention of Oil Pollution) Regulations, 1983, which were made under that Order, gave effect to all of Annex I with the exception of Regulation 12 on Reception Facilities. Later, a separate Order, i.e. The Merchant Shipping Prevention of Pollution (Reception Facilties) Order, 1984, gave effect to both Regulation 12 of Annex I and Regulation 7 of Annex II. This Order came into force on July 25, 1984.

(2) For the list of those petrochemicals excluded from the definition, see M.Notice 1077.

(ii) unless the owner or the master acted either with intent to cause damage, or recklessly and with knowledge that damage would probably result; or

(c) any approved discharge into the sea of substances containing oil, when used for the purpose of combating specific pollution incidents in order to minimize the damage from pollution. Any such discharge shall be subject to the approval of any government in whose jurisdiction it is contemplated the discharge will occur.

Special Areas: The discharge of oil is completely forbidden in certain "Special Areas" where the threat to the marine environment is especially great. In some of these areas, the limited exchange of water with the oceans are considered to be particularly vulnerable to pollution.

The special areas specified in Regulation 16 of the Mediterranean Sea area(1), the Black Sea area, the Red Sea area and the Gulfs area.

The discharge provisions do not take effect for the Red Sea Area and the Gulfs area until a date which has yet to be established by the IMO. The establishment of this date will depend on the provision of adequate reception facilities at oil loading terminals and repair ports within those areas. However, vessels must comply when proceeding in these areas, with the discharge provisions mentioned above, and any local or national restrictions.

---

(1) Pollution of the Mediterranean is mainly caused by:
(a) tankers discharging dirty ballast and tank washings while on ballast voyages;
(b) all vessels discharging bilge and slop residue from machinery spaces; and
(c) the failure to provide deballasting facilities and bilge collection equipment at ports.
See Seminar on Reception Facilities for Wastes, organized by the IMO (30-31 August, 1984), p.228.
There are nineteen crude oil loading terminals in the Mediterranean handling approximately 360 million tonnes of crude oil. Only nine are provided with deballasting stations. *Ibid*, p.228. See also the Study of the EEC on this subject. *Ibid*, p.282.

Pollution prevention equipment: Oil tankers must carry the equipment necessary to operate the load on top system and to retain oily residues on board until they can be discharged into shore reception facilities. This equipment includes slop tanks, oily water separating equipment or filtering systems, oil content meters, oil discharge monitoring and control systems, sludge tanks and suitable pumping and piping arrangements.

All ships of 400 gross tons and above(1), including non-tankers, must be equipped with oily water separating equipment or a filtering system for the discharge of machinery space bilges. Since certain doubts were raised concerning the reliability of the equipment, Resolution A.393 (X)(2) states that the equipment has to satisfy the requirements of the

---

(1) Regulation 16 requires that any ship of 400 tons grt and above be fitted with oily water separating or filtering equipment such as will ensure that any oily mixture discharged to sea after passing through it has an oil content not exceeding 100 p.p.m. In addition, ships of 10,000 tons grt and above must be fitted *either* with an oil discharge monitoring and control system almost identical to that required for oil tankers *or* with an oil filtering system which accepts the discharge from the required separating system and reduces the oil content of the effluent from not more than 100 p.p.m. to not more than 15 p.p.m.
This is an additional requirement for all ships of 400 tons and above: by Regulation 17 they must be provided with sludge tanks of adequate capacity to accept the residues which cannot be dealt with in accordance with the requirements of Annex I, such as those resulting from the purification of fuel and lubricating oils and some oil leakages in machinery spaces.

(2) Since many delegations proposed a review of Resolution A.393 (X), a Working Group was set up to carry out this task. The Oil Companies International Marine Forum (OCIMF) undertook to provide the Group with information on the accuracy of monitors and the result of the research done by the Institute of Offshore Engineering (IOE) in Edinburgh.
The information received by the OCIMF from several manufacturers together with the IOE study, were included in a report dated March 25,

Recommendation[1] on International Performance and Test Specifications for Oily Water Separating Equipment and Oil Contents Meters. Similar doubts were raised on the accuracy of the oily water monitors and, as a result, Resolution A.543 (13) was adopted. It calls upon Administrations to recognize the shortcomings when dealing with any infringements of the discharge regulations[2].

New oil tankers[3] of 70,000 deadweight tons and above must be provided with segregated ballast

---

1985, presented to the MEPC (MEPC 21/9/8). It called for the following changes:
(a) granting a waiver on a ship-by-ship basis subject to certain conditions, and extending the entry into force for existing ships to October 2, 1988; and
(b) the Test and Performance Specifications for Type Approval of Oil Content Meters contained in part I of the Draft Guidelines and Specifications for Oil Discharge Monitoring and Control Systems for Oil Tankers, should be implemented on October 2, 1986, and should apply to all monitor installations made after that date.

(1) The ICS circulated a questionnaire (MEPC 19/5/2) and the replies showed that in many ports and terminals throughout the world, the reception facilities for oily waters were inadequate or not yet available.
In response to queries as to the course of action which should be followed by a tanker engaged on a ballast voyage within special areas in circumstances where operational discharge of oil is prohibited but the port lacked the necessary reception facility, the MEPC stated that it was not legally possible to grant any waiver from the requirements of the Convention. C52/8, March 20, 1984.

(2) A further concession was made whereby new ships would have an increased period of grace before the fitting requirements for monitor installations became mandatory.

(3) New oil tankers are those to which any of the following dates apply:
- contract placed after 1 June, 1979;
- keel laid after 1 January, 1980; or
- delivery after 1 June, 1982.

tanks (SBT)[1] of sufficient capacity to enable them to operate safely on ballast voyages without recourse to the use of cargo tanks for ballast purposes (except in very severe weather)[2]. In the SBT system, certain tanks are used for ballast only and these tanks are secured by their own dedicated pumps and pipeline. On new tankers, the SBT tanks are to be in "protective location" (PL)[3] which means that they are to be fitted around cargo tanks so as to protect the latter in case of collision[4]. Existing crude oil tankers of 40,000 tons dwt and above to be fitted with SBT, clean ballast tanks (CBT) or a crude oil washing system (COW)[5]. The CBT system is basically the same as a SBT system, but the pumps

---

(1) SBT means that sufficient tanks to contain adequate sea water ballast must be provided and used solely for that purpose; they cannot be used for the transport of oil. This measure is designed to eliminate the mixing of oil and water resulting from the carriage of ballast water. On the laden voyage, these tanks are simply kept empty.

(2) The fact that SBTs are not used for carrying oil means that no oil-water mixtures are produced, and consequently no pollution.

(3) PL means that the ballast tanks (which are empty on the cargo-carrying journey and only loaded with water ballast for the return journey) are positioned where the impact of a collision or grounding is likely to be greatest. In this way the amount of cargo spilled after such an accident will be greatly reduced.

(4) New subdivision and stability requirements have been introduced to ensure that tankers can survive assumed side or bottom damage to a degree which is specified on the basis of the ship's length.

(5) Instead of using sea water, tank cleaning is carried out by spraying the cargo tanks with crude oil itself. This is a more effective way of cleaning so as to avoid the mixture of oil and water. It may also benefit the cargo owner as almost all cargo can be delivered. It will cast doubts on the idea of a permissible or inevitable loss in the carriage of oil which is based on the assumption that slops and dirty ballast are covered by the customary trade allowance.

and lines used may also be employed for pumping cargo. There are stringent requirements for the fitting and emptying of CBT tanks and this is only approved as an interim solution before the adoption of the permanent systems of SBT or COW.

Certificate and record book: The tanker must carry an International Oil Pollution (IOPP) Certificate which states the selected system, e.g. SBT, CBT or COW. Owners of tankers using SBT/CBT may change[1] to COW so long as the requirements of the washing equipment and inert gas are met[2].

In order to obtain such a certificate[3], the ship is required to be surveyed and the 1978 Protocol introduced the following requirements[4]:

---

(1) Product carriers of 40,000 dwt and above, which carry both crude oil and dirty petroleum products, must operate both COW and SBT/CBT. When electing to carry products, they must be cleaned and gas freed for the issuance of an IOPP certificate as SBT or CBT tankers. Dual certifications, where COW is an option, can be obtained for tankers which have separate independent piping and pump arrangements for ballasting in accordance with the CBT option.

(2) Most oil charter-parties contain a clause known as "clean seas" or "Oil Pollution", to take account of the LOT system. These clauses seek to shift the burden of providing reception facilities from the owners to the charterers and require them to bear the cost of retaining oily wastes on board where no facilities are available. The undertaking extends to cover periods of drydocking and off-hire. Disputes may arise between the parties where the charterers leave the slops during drydocking.

(3) See the Form of Certificate International Oil Pollution Prevention Certificate, BIMCO Bulletin V-1982, p.6849, and the Form of Oil Record Book, *ibid*, p.6855.

(4) The IMO adopted guidelines for surveys under Annex I of MARPOL 73/78. They are intended to provide a general framework upon which Administrations can base their arrangements for carrying out surveys. The guidelines deal with the initial survey, mandatory annual survey, intermediate survey and periodical survey. They do not include standards for unscheduled surveys since both the Maritime Environment Protection

(a) an initial survey before the ship is put in service or before an International Oil Pollution (IOPP) Certificate is issued;

(b) periodical surveys at intervals not exceeding five years;

(c) a minimum of one intermediate survey during the period of validity of the Certificate; and

(d) unscheduled inspection or mandatory annual surveys must be carried out[1].

Tankers and other ships must carry and maintain an oil record book in which all operations involving oil are to be recorded. The book can be inspected by the authorities[2] of any State which is party to

---

Committee and the Maritime Safety Committee have expressed a preference for mandatory annual surveys.

(1) The United Kingdom has adopted mandatory annual surveys in substitution for unscheduled inspections of all ships requiring the IOPP certificate. Annual and intermediate surveys are not required. All United Kingdom oil tankers of 150 gross registered tons and above engaged in voyages to ports or offshore terminals under the jurisdiction of other parties to the Convention, are required to hold the IOPP Certificate. Oil tankers of less than 150 gross registered tons and other ships of less than 400 gross tons, must also comply with these rules but the survey will be less strict.

(2) Regulation 10 of the Merchant Shipping (Prevention of Oil Pollution) Regulations,1983 requires that every ship of 400 GRT and above and every oil tanker of 150 GRT and above shall be provided with an Oil Record Book Part I (Machinery Space Operations). It also requires that every tanker of 150 GRT and above shall additionally be provided with an Oil Record Book Part II (Cargo/Ballast Operations).
The master must record in it:
(a) loading, transfer during a voyage and discharge of oil cargo; ballasting and cleaning of cargo tanks; discharge of dirty ballast; of water from slop tanks, and discharge overboard of oily bilge water which has accumulated in machinery spaces, including

the Convention[1].

Oil Reception Facilities: Regulation 12 of Annex I requires that reception facilities should be provided in oil loading ports and terminals, repair ports and other ports in which ships have oily residues to discharge[2].

The detailed requirements for such facilities are left to be governed by national law. In the United Kingdom, the Merchant Shipping Prevention of Pollution (Reception Facilities) Order,1984 gave effect to both Regulation 12 of Annex I and Regulation 7 of Annex II. It repealed that section of the Prevention of Oil Pollution Act, 1971, that

---

pump rooms whilst in port, disposal of oil residues and the routine dicharge at sea of oily bilge water.

(b) Any occasion when oil or any oily mixture has to be discharged from a ship to maintain its safety or to prevent damage to any vessel or cargo or to save life.

(c) Any occasion when oil or any oily mixture has been discovered escaping, or to have escaped from a ship due to damage or to leakage from that ship.

(1) In November,1985, a Manual on Oil Pollution was published. It contains practical information on means of preventing pollution of the sea by oil. It summarises the main internationally agreed requirements for preventing oil pollution (Annex I) to which the Merchant Shipping (Prevention of Oil Pollution) Regulations, 1983 (S.I.1398/1983) gave effect.

(2) The MEPC circulated a questionnaire (Circ.117 of Dec. 23, 1983) to determine whether or not reception facilities were available and the information contained in the replies (MEPC/Circ. 135) was published in order to assist shipowners and masters to get in touch with the operators or proprietors of such facilities. See MEPC 21/8 of Jan. 22, 1985.
See also the Memorandum of Understanding signed in November,1976 between IMO and UNEP on "Special Area" reception facility. Recently the Regional Organization for the Protection of the Marine Environment (ROPME) consisting of Bahrain, Iran, Iraq, Kuwait, Oman, Qatar, Saudi Arabia and the United Arab Emirates carried out a feasibility study on reception facilities.

contained provisions for oil reception facilities, at the same time re-enacting certain of these provisions. The Order requires harbour authorities and terminal operators to provide reception facilities for ships which, in their opinion, are using the harbour or terminal for a primary purpose other than using the reception facilities. The facilities must be adequate to meet the needs of ships using them without causing undue delay to ships.

Furthermore, M.Notice 1156 was issued in December, 1984, giving instructions, advice and guidance to harbour authorities, terminal operators and others when assessing the type and capacity of facilities needed to satisfy the provisions of the Order. Although the M.Notice has no binding effect, it is invariably followed in practice. It is based on the IMO Guidelines and would serve as a basis for consultation between the Department of Transport and shipowners, harbour authorities and terminal operators when following up allegations of inadequate facilities.

The terms "adequate"(1) and "undue delay" need some explanation. For the first term, the M.Notice states: "In order for a harbour or terminal to be fully provided with reception facilities which satisfy the requirements of MARPOL 73/78, it is not sufficient simply to provide some facilities. The facilities provided must be of sufficient capacity and appropriate design to enable all ships which may be expected to use the harbour or terminal for

---

Oman is planning, with the assistance of Norpol (a Norwegian company) to use floating facilities.

Sweden sent a circular which contains the conditions that apply to the transfer of oil residues to reception facilities, thus enabling such matters as the intended time of transfer, the nature and form of the oily waste, the pumping rate, etc., to be notified to the appropriate authority 24 hours before the transfer was desired to take place. MEPC 33/WP. 16, December 6, 1985, p.15.

(1) Adequacy is defined in the Seminar on Reception Facilities for Wastes organized by the IMO in 1984 (on page 229) as covering:
- quality of the effluent; this limitation has a direct bearing on the type of treatment technology for the reception facilities; and
- deballasting time for average ships 6 hours, and for high percentage ships 8 hours.

a primary purpose other than utilizing the reception facilities to be able to do so without suffering any undue delay. It follows that in assessing the type and capacity of facilities needed, an authority must take into account not only the numbers, types and sizes of vessels and the trades they are engaged in but also any prospective changes. Changing ship designs and operating practices will also have an effect as will the speed with which the residues and substances discharged can be dealt with."

No undue delay should be caused when using the facilities. Examples of causes of delay are:

(a) a ship may have to move to a special berth to discharge oil residues and mixtures and this may involve the cost of using tugs;

(b) facilities may be provided at a nearby terminal but they may only be available to users of that terminal. Thus the overall facilities of a harbour may appear adequate but, in practice, a ship may have to move a considerable distance to gain access to a facility;

(c) the rate at which oil wastes and slops can be received by the reception facility is often criticised as being too low and to cause delay to the ship.

Under Article 4 of the Order, the Secretary of State may investigate allegations that a harbour or terminal does not have facilities sufficient to meet the requirements of MARPOL 73/78. If after consultation with any organization appearing to the Secretary of State to be representative of owners of ships registered in the UK, the harbour authority and, where appropriate, the terminal operator, the Secretary of State is of the opinion that the facilities provided are inadequate or, if there are no existing facilities, that there should be facilities, he has the power to direct(1) the harbour authority or terminal operator (as the case may be) to provide or to arrange for the provision of facilities. The

---

(1) Failure by a Harbour Authority or Terminal Operator to comply with a directive given by the Secretary of State within the time allowed is an offence. On summary conviction for this offence, a fine not exceeding £1,000 may be imposed.

direction may specify the facilities to be provided.

Harbour Authorities are given powers under Article 3 to provide reception facilities either on their own or in co-operation with others. Alternatively they may arrange for others to provide the facilities. The Harbour Authorities are also required under Article 3 to ensure that the reception facilities provided are adequate to meet the requirements of the Convention.

Harbour Authorities and Terminal Operators who provide reception facilities or others with whom an authority has an agreement to provide them may make a reasonable charge for their use. The owner of a ship is required to pay those charges(1) unless he has an agreement with the owner of the cargo that the latter will meet those costs. Conditions for the use of the facility may be laid down so long as those conditions are reasonable. Subject to compliance with these conditions, facilities provided by, or by agreement with, a Harbour Authority or by a Terminal Operator shall be open to all vessels which in the opinion of the Harbour Authority or Terminal Operator (as appropriate) are using the harbour or terminal for a primary purpose other than utilising the reception facilities (Article 5).

## The 1984 Amendments to Annex I

In September,1984 the first set of amendments to MARPOL 73/78 was adopted and they came into force on January 1, 1986. These amendments are only concerned with Annex I.

The main points of the amendments are as follows:

Regulation 10 - Method for prevention of oil pollution from ships while operating in special areas: The amendments introduce requirements for oily water separating equipment and a device to stop discharge

---

(1) It is suggested that the charges should be based not on the quantity of ballast actually discharged but on the deadweight tonnage of the ship and that the charge rate should decrease proportionally with the increase in size of the ship. *Ibid*, p.252.
Another point was raised before the MEPC that in some ports the costs of providing reception facilities are included in the harbour dues. MEPC 22/WP.16, December 6, 1985, p.16.

automatically once the oil content of the mixtures being discharged exceeds 15 ppm. Any residues which cannot be discharged in compliance with the regulation have to be retained on board the ship(1).

Regulation 13 - Segregated ballast tanks, dedicated clean ballast tanks and crude oil washing: This regulation was changed considerably in the 1978 Protocol and the 1984 amendments make some changes to the section which deals with the carriage of ballast water in cargo tanks. This is permitted in exceptional cases where the peculiar character of the operation of an oil tanker renders it necessary.

Regulation 14 - Segregation of oil and water ballast and carriage of oil in forepeak tanks: The amendment bans the carriage of oil in the forepeak tank or forward of the collision bulkhead in new tankers.

Regulation 15 - Retention of oil on board: The major changes here concern requirements regarding slop tanks. Their total capacity remains at not less than 3 per cent of the oil-carrying capacity of the tanker, unless it is equippped with a system to recirculate wash water. Where segregated ballast tanks, dedicated clean ballast tanks or crude oil washing is provided, for example, slop tanks capacity can be reduced to 2 per cent of capacity.

Regulation 16 - Oily discharge monitoring and control systems and oily-water separating and oil filtering equipment: As with Regulation 15, the existing requirements may be waived by Administrations for ships which are exclusively engaged on voyages within special areas, within 12 miles of the nearest land outside special areas provided that the ports from which the ship operates are in a State party to the convention or if the voyage itself is restricted, as determined by the Administration. Strict conditions have to be complied with before this can be done.

The amendments then go on to give detailed specifications of oil discharge monitoring and control systems, oily water separating equipment and oil filtering equipment.

Regulation 18 - Pumping, piping and discharge arrangements for oil tankers: A basic principle in

---

(1) See M.Notice 1081.

the original regulation is that all discharges of oily water should take place above the waterline so that an observer can see any floating oil and, if necessary, stop the discharge.

The amendments provide for some exceptions to the above criteria enabling certain discharges to take place below the waterline.

Regulation 20 - Oil Record Book: The format of the existing Oil Record Book is changed. Non-tankers will now have to carry an Oil Record Book Part I (Machinery Space Operations) while tankers will additionally have to carry Part II (Cargo/Ballast Operations). The amendments give details of the various operations which have to be recorded. Each completed operation has to be signed by the officer and officers concerned and each completed page by the master; originally officers only had to sign 'each section of the book'.

Regulation 21 - Special requirements for drilling rigs and other platforms: Outside special areas and more than 12 nautical miles from land the discharge into the sea of oily mixtures is banned when the oil content reaches 100 ppm or more (within these areas the limit is 15 ppm).

Regulation 22 - Damage assumptions: This regulation is intended to ensure that tankers can survive assumed side or bottom damage to an extent which is specific on the basis of the ship's length. The amendments strengthen the existing provisions[1].

## ANNEX II (LIQUID NOXIOUS SUBSTANCES)

Objective and categories: The main objective of Annex II is to limit the operational discharge[2] of noxious substances from chemical tankers. Products

(1) The MEPC (MEPC 20/19) approved a uniform interpretation of the requirements related to:
- Discharges from offshore platforms (Regulation 21).
- Survey requirements for ships solely engaged on domestic voyages (Regulation 4).
- Interpretation of "specific trade" (Regulation 15(5)).

(2) Operational discharges mean the discharge of noxious liquid substances or water contaminated

shipped in bulk were classified by the UN Group of Experts on Scientific Aspects of Marine Pollution (GESAMP) into four categories, A to D[(1)], according to the degree of damage caused to the environment. The considerations which were taken for evaluating the hazards of each product are: bioaccumulation, damage to living resources (aquatic toxicity), hazard to human health by oral intake, hazard to human health by skin contact and inhalation and reduction of amenities. Some 250 products were evaluated and appeared in a list attached to the

---

by these substances which are the result of cargo tank and line washing, deballasting of unwashed cargo tanks or other residues or contaminated water from cargo pump-room bilges. Accidental discharges mean the results of cargo containment damage or cargo spills.
The word "unloading" is used to refer to the unloading of cargo to receivers, terminals or ports.

(1) During the debate at the Sub-Committee on Bulk Chemicals, The Netherlands delegation suggested the division of noxious liquid substances into two groups for the purpose of controlling discharges. Group I would include Category A and B substances posing a "hazard or major hazard". Group II would include the Category C and D substances which present a "minor or less recognizable hazard". They argue that operational discharge of Group I substances could be reduced to the minimum by removing residues as far as possible before the ship leaves port.
If such a proposal is accepted, three conditions will be required: the ship is under way, the discharge is below the waterline, and the operation takes place over 12 miles from the nearest land.
The Dutch delegation also suggested that the rules on discharge applying to Group I could equally be made applicable to pollution-vulnerable "special areas" and non-special areas. Only one difference will remain: Group I rules would have to apply to certain Group II substances (the present Category C substances) when ships were operating in special areas. This regime could be progressively adjusted in the light of experience. For example, the list of Group I could be expanded to cover more Category C substances as the hardware require-

Convention[1].

Annex II is, to a quite considerable extent, a technical document and therefore it would not be possible to give a thorough analysis of its requirements. Nevertheless, the main requirements of the Annex could be described by considering:

- the restrictions on discharge;
- the amendments to the Annex; and
- the essential elements required.

Restrictions on discharge: Regulation 5 of Annex II specifies the conditions under which discharge of residues may take place. The severity of the restrictions depends on the category to which the product belongs. The discharge of products of Category A or tank washings, ballast water or other mixtures containing Category A substances is prohibited. The residue of substances of Category A and tank washing must be discharged in a reception facility until a predetermined concentration is attained[2] in the effluent and until the tank is empty. After diluting the remaining residue with a water volume of not less than 5 per cent of the tank volume, it may be discharged at sea provided:

(a) the discharge is made below the waterline;

(b) the vessel is more than 12 miles from the nearest land;

(c) the vessel is underway at a speed not less than 7 knots; and

(d) the vessel is in water deeper than 25 metres.

---

ments for efficient stripping were developed.

(1) Some 200 or more trade-named substances which would fall within Annex II are currently moved in bulk. They need to be given hazard profiles in order that they may be assigned ship type requirements and pollution categories.

(2) Some experts have called for the revision of the rules covering tank washing operations for Category A substances. The stipulation that residue concentration measurement of tank washing effluent continue until the required residual concentration is attained, seems to be impracticable.
The American delegation submitted a paper to

For certain sea areas identified as "special areas", more stringent discharge criteria are given. Under Annex II the special areas are the Baltic Sea Area(1) and the Black Sea Area(2).

Annex II also prohibits the carriage of Category B and C substances in tanks in which the residue quantities after unloading exceed the quantities given in the Annex.

For substances of Category B, the quantity of residue which may be discharged from a tank and its associated cargo piping is limited to 1 cubic metre. In case the vessel is unable to reach this limit, the discharge of the resultant residue should be made in a reception facility. It must be noted that the restrictions mentioned above under (a) and (d) for substances of Category A will also apply to substances of Category B. In addition, the residue concentration in the wake astern of the vessel may not exceed 1 ppm.

Substances of category C are subject to restrictions similar to those of Category B except that the quantity of residue discharged is limited to 3 cubic metres and the concentration in the wake may not exceed 10 ppm.

Thus, for each tank intended for the carriage of such substances, an assessment of the residue quantity has to be made. Only when the residue quantity as assessed is less than the quantity prescribed by the Annex may a tank be approved for the carriage of a Category B or a Category C substance.

As for the substances of Category D(3), restrictions (b) and (c) mentioned above will apply.

---

the Sub-Committee on Bulk Chemicals on the results of Annex II trials on Board US vessels and described the rules of the Annex as an unacceptable burden. There were no real means for the administration to ensure the compliance with the discharge rules although the use of the micro could be useful in this respect.

(1) The Baltic Sea area means the Baltic Sea proper with the Gulf of Bothnia, the Gulf of Finland and the entrance to the Baltic Sea bounded by the parallel of the Skaw in the Skagerrak at $57^{\circ}$ 44 8'N.

(2) The Black Sea area means the Black Sea proper with the boundary between the Mediterranean and the Black Sea constituted by the parallel $41^{\circ}$N.

(3) The MEPC agreed that a Noxious Liquid Substance (NLS) Certificate, rather than a Code Cert-

In addition, the residue content of any effluent discharged to the sea may not exceed 1 part in 10. Furthermore, restrictions apply to vessels discharging residues in certain special areas.

The Annex requires the use of a Cargo Record Book to provide a complete picture of the handling of noxious substances from the time they are loaded on the ship until they have been unloaded(1). Surveyors appointed by Contracting States would ensure the compliance with the rules of Annex II to substances falling under the four categories. Contracting Parties are required to issue detailed measures for the design, construction and operation of chemical tankers which contain at least all the provisions of the Code for the Construction and Equipment of Ships Carrying Dangerous Chemicals in Bulk(2).

---

ificate of Fitness, would be issued to:

(a) chemical tankers, including oil tankers and gas carriers carrying only Category D substances not included in Chapter 17 of the IBC Code and Chapter VI of the BCH Code;
(b) gas carriers carrying those Annex II substances presently listed in the Gas Carrier Codes;
(c) dry cargo ships carrying in deep tanks Category D substances; and
(d) supply vessels carrying substances included in Chapter 17 of the IBC Code.

MEPC 22/WP.16, Dec. 6, 1985, p.6.

(1) See Regulation 9 on Cargo Record Book. The book would be used as evidence showing the compliance or the breach to MARPOL. However, maintaining the record book could add significant additional tasks on the ship in view of the wide range of chemicals carried, the complex tank cleaning, and the control of discharge operations.

(2) Regulation 13 of the Annex requires compliance with the Bulk Chemical Code. This would lead to the assignment of the type of ship. Furthermore, there are a number of products included in the Code which can not be evaluated until certain data have been made available. For these products and in the absence of the evaluation, a ship of a type higher than the usual one would be required.

## The 1985 Amendments to Annex II

The Procedures and Arrangements for discharge (and cleaning by ventilation) for Category A, B and C must be based on "Standards" developed by the IMO in order to ensure uniformity. The task of developing these "Standards" was entrusted to the Sub-Committee on Bulk Chemicals (BCH) and the first attempt to draw up draft "standards" was made in 1977.

The 1977 "Standards" met with severe criticism from the industry and from many delegations to the IMO. Therefore, a drafting group met in January, 1982 and prepared a revised text which introduced two concepts: a manual(1) and a stripping system(2).

Trials were made to test the working of the 1982 "Standards" and the results showed that they suffered from a number of deficiencies(3) and that a major revision was needed. To this end, the BCH

---

(1) Since the controls were drafted in a general way, it would not have been easy for an Administration to apply them to individual ships which have their own characteristics, tanks and ancillary systems. Furthermore, the range of properties of the categories which the ship would be called upon to carry must be considered since not all cargo residues could be dealt with in the same way under the terms of the Annex. To overcome these difficulties, the procedures and arrangements for each ship or series of identical ships are to be prescribed in an approved Manual. Once it has been approved by the Administration, no alteration could be made to it without its prior approval.

(2) The concept of efficient stripping is based on one tenth of the permissible quantity. This is to be 0.1 $m^3$ for Category B and 0.3 $m^3$ for Category C substances when discharges are made to the sea outside Special Areas and 0.1 $m^3$ for Category C substances when discharges are made to the sea inside Special Areas.

(3) P. Bergmeijer said at the MariChem Conference, 1985:
"The trials demonstrated the following:
- a complete lack of adequate shore reception facilities;
- a clear indication that these facilities will also not be available in the future;
- an absence of any possibility for effective control whether or not the complex operational

Sub-Committee instructed a Working Group in 1984 to look again at the "Standards", propose the necessary amendments to the Annex and to the Chemical Codes. The Group completed its work which led to the adoption of the Amendments to Annex II on December 5, 1985(1). These Amendments will come into force on April 6, 1987.

The Essential elements of the Annex

The working of Annex II needs the following elements:

(a) the evaluation of the hazards of the noxious substances;

(b) the development of "Standards" for Procedures and Arrangements for discharge of noxious substances; and

(c) the formulation of Guidelines on the provision and maintenance of adequate reception facilities.

(a) The evaluation of the hazards: As mentioned earlier, GESAMP has evaluated and categorised many substances before the adoption of the Convention. GESAMP continues with this task for other substances. Where the substances that have not been categorised are shipped, the Annex requires the administration involved to assign the category provisionally. In case of disagreement, the more stringent category proposed must be assigned(2).

---

discharge requirements at sea are complied with; and
- an unacceptable increase in the workload for ships' crews."

(1) See MEPC 22/21.

(2) The MEPC agreed that if a change of hazard rating by GESAMP of a substance listed in appendix II of MARPOL, Annex II would result in an alteration of the category of such substance:
(a) any upgrading of category should be treated as an amendment to Annex II of MARPOL 73/78 in accordance with article 16; and
(b) a downgrading of category may be treated in a similar manner to the inclusion of new substances, i.e. circulation by an MEPC circular recommending that, pending the entry into force of the amendments covering introduction of these substances in the IBC

At its 20th session, the MEPC recognized that there were problems in evaluating the hazards of substances currently carried under trade names. They would have to be converted to proper chemical names to be included but this could present problems for GESAMP since some data had been submitted under conditions of confidentiality.

(b) The Procedures and Arrangements (P & A) for Discharge: As mentioned earlier, the "Standards" on (P & A) were formulated in 1977 and revised in 1982 and 1985. The main changes brought by the 1985 Amendments can be summarised as follows.

The requirements in Regulation 5A were phrased in such a way that the carriage of Category B and C substances is prohibited in tanks which cannot be emptied to residue quantity levels of 0.1 or 0.3 cubic metres for Category B and C substances respectively. The regulation further requires pumping efficiency[(1)] tests as prescribed in Appendix A to the Standards in order to demonstrate that the required residue quantity levels can be achieved. Some relaxation in respect of quantity levels are given for existing ships[(2)], i.e. efficient stripping levels are a factor 3 higher than for new ships and a period of grace is granted for retrofitting existing ships.

Regulation 8 provides that after unloading, a prewash shall be carried out in accordance with procedures laid down in the Standards and that the resulting tank washings shall be discharged to a reception facility at the unloading port, unless:

(a) the tank is to be reloaded with the same or a compatible substance and the tank will not be washed or ballasted; or

---

and BCH Codes, these new chemicals should be carried in compliance with the provisions of the amendments.

MEPC 22/WP.16, Dec. 6, 1985, p.5.

(1) The BCH Code and the IBC Code were amended to cover pollution aspects necessary for compliance with Annex II. They require the fitting of equipment and arrangements in a ship's Procedures and Arrangements Manual.

(2) The pump efficiency in cargo unloading in accordance with specified procedures will be the efficiency determined in the test of the tank.

(b) the residues in the tank, when suitable, will be removed by ventilation; or

(c) all tank washings and contaminated ballast water will be retained on board for discharge to a reception facility at another port where the government of that port has indicated that reception facilities are adequate for such purpose; or

(d) in respect of Category B and C substances, the cargo tanks have been efficiently stripped in accordance with the procedures and arrangements of the Standards.

Each ship must have a manual which serves to identify(1) to the ship's officers(2) all the operational procedures with respect to cargo handling, tank cleaning, slops handling, and cargo tank ballasting and deballasting(3).

---

(1) The Manual together with the ship's Cargo Record Book and the Certificate for the Carriage of Noxious Liquid Substances, or the Certificate of Fitness under the IBC Code, or the Certificate of Fitness under the BCH Code, will be used by the administrative body in the Contracting States as proof of full compliance with the requirements of Annex II.

(2) The master shall ensure that no discharges into the sea of cargo residues or residue/water mixtures containing Category A, B, C or D substances shall take place, unless such discharges are made in full compliance with the operational procedures contained in the Manual.

(3) Among the information and operational instructions in the Manual are:
  (a) a description of the main features of Annex II, including discharge requirements;
  (b) a table of noxious liquid substances which the ship is certified fit to carry and which specifies information on these substances as detailed in Appendix D;
  (c) a description of the tanks carrying noxious liquid substances; and a table identifying in which cargo tanks each noxious liquid substance may be carried; and
  (d) a description of all the equipment including cargo heating and temperature control systems which is on board the ship and for which requirements are contained in

(c) <u>Reception Facilities:</u> Under Regulation 7 of Annex II[1], The Contracting Parties undertook to ensure that cargo unloading terminals shall provide arrangements to facilitate stripping of cargo tanks of ships unloading noxious liquid substances at these terminals. Cargo hoses and piping systems of the terminal, containing noxious liquid substances received from ships unloading these substances at the terminal, shall not be drained back to the ship. The facilities are to be used for residues, slops, mixtures and ballast water containing Category A in all areas; Category B in special areas; Category C within special areas and Category C outside special areas. The last three cases apply only where the quantity of residue exceeds the required limits.

Under international law, Contracting States which ratified the Convention will be under an obligation to construct reception facilities. However, no remedies are available in case of the non-observance of such an obligation. Therefore, it would be more appropriate to regard the obligation in this respect as a promise to build the facilities rather than a legal undertaking.

## ANNEX III (HARMFUL SUBSTANCES IN PACKAGED FORMS)

The Annex[2] applies to all ships carrying harmful substances[3] in packaged forms[4], or in freight

---

Chapters 3 or 8 including a list of all tanks that will be used as slop tanks.
See MEPC 21/4, p.10.

(1) See *supra* on oil reception facilities. However it must be noted that the conditions and requirements are not the same as for oil.

(2) The Marine Directorate of the Department of Transport has estimated that packaged dangerous goods constitute some 5-10% of all cargo carried by commercial vessels.
MEPC 21/INF.12 of April 25, 1985.

(3) 'Harmful substances' are those substances which are identified as 'marine pollutants' in the International Maritime Dangerous Goods (IMDG) Code. See draft report to the MEPC at its 22nd session.
MEPC 22/WP.16/Add.1, December 6, 1984, p.4.

(4) 'Packaged form' is defined in regulation 1, i.e. "Unless expressly provided otherwise, the

containers, portable tanks or road and rail tank wagons. The Annex requires the issuing of detailed requirements on packaging, marking, labelling, documentation, stowage, quantity limitations, exceptions and notifications for preventing or minimizing pollution by harmful substances. The IMDG Code has been revised in order to take into account the requirements of Annex III. In accordance with the Code, packaged goods, including hazardous chemicals, are often carried as deck cargo. Hence they can be easily jettisoned in the event of an emergency such as a fire, to protect the ship and the crew. Improper stowage or adverse weather conditions have often resulted in the loss of deck cargoes overboard.

Thus, the objective of Annex III(1) is to prevent or minimize pollution of the marine environment by harmful substances carried at sea in packaged form(2).

The United Kingdom submitted a note(3) to the Sub-Committee on the Carriage of Dangerous Goods(4) indicating the following defects in the Annex.

(a) It should be made clear that the Annex is only concerned with cargo in packages and not the ships carrying them. Also the application of the provisions of the Annex should extend to cover shipborne barges.

---

regulations of this Annex apply to all ships carrying harmful substances in packaged form, including those in freight containers, portable tanks, road and rail vehicles and shipborne barges." MSC 51/21, p.11.

(1) The Annex is not yet in force.
(2) The floating packages lost from a ship are likely to come ashore where they present a considerable problem. Their labels are often obliterated and the IMO warning signs washed away.
(3) MEPC 21/10, Annex 5, January 25, 1985.
(4) See M.Notice 1152 where it is stated that: "In the light of continuing incidents involving packaged dangerous goods that have affected our coastlines, there is a need to take action prior to the implementation of Annex II to the Convention. The Department would therefore urge Masters and Shipowners to report incidents involving packaged dangerous goods."

(b) The substances listed in the appendix vary considerably in toxicity and potential threat to the environment.

(c) More precise requirements on stowage should be formulated for the more potentially pollutant substances.

(d) More clarification is required as to standard of packaging required.

(e) Further study is required on mixtures and diluted solutions. Entries for Class 9 for "Pollutant only" substances should be prepared for the IMDG Code.

In another note(1) to the same Sub-Committee, the United Kingdom asked for some additional requirements(2) to be inserted into the Annex to minimize the accidental loss to the sea of marine pollutants. Further studies(3) were needed to ensure that:

(a) The substances are not shipped in packagings which are likely to be disintegrated by short-term immersion in the sea.

(b) Except where stowage on deck is required for human safety reasons, underdeck stowage should be required in those types of ship lacking protected decks or protected positions on open decks.

(c) The security arrangments of such goods when stowed on exposed decks should be subject to the approval of the competent authority.

---

(1) MEPC 21/10, Annex 4, January 25, 1985.
(2) See the draft "Circular on the transport of marine pollutants in packaged form", annex to CDG 35/WP.7.
(3) A note from the Federal Republic of Germany to the Sub-Committee on the Carriage of Dangerous Goods expressed its satisfaction with the implementation of Annex III after ratifying it. The note pointed to the fact that similar regulations to those of Annex III are already in force for the Baltic Sea under the Convention on the Protection of the Marine Environment of the Baltic Sea Area.
MEPC 21/10, Annex 3, January 25, 1985.

ANNEX IV (SEWAGE)

Traditionally sewage was dumped into the sea as a matter of course. With the movement of the tide, most of the refuse was soon to reappear on the beaches. Under Annex IV, ships are not permitted to discharge sewage within four miles of the nearest land unless they have in operation an approved treatment plant. Between four and twelve miles from land, sewage must be comminuted and disinfected before discharge.

ANNEX V (GARBAGE)

Under this Annex(1), specific minimum distances have been set for the disposal of the principal types of garbage(2). Perhaps the most important feature of this Annex is the complete prohibition placed on the disposal of plastics into the sea.

---

(1) Annex III and Annex IV are optional. By November,1984, both Annexes were ratified by twenty countries whose combined merchant fleets represents 33.49 per cent of the world gross tonnage.

(2) A note from the Federal Republic of Germany to the Sub-Committee on the Carriage of Dangerous Goods expressed the need for a precise definition of the term "garbage". It also mentioned that compliance with Annex V was recognized to be contingent upon the availability of adequate reception facilities in ports for all garbage which ships are prohibited to dispose of into the sea.
A note from the United Kingdom stated that it would be impossible for cruise ships, which by the very nature of the cruise business, use the smaller remote ports which are least likely to have adequate facilities to comply with regulation 5 of the Annex. A ship calling at such a port would be unable to retain on board the garbage produced during the course of even a 3-day passage and would be prohibited from discharging into the sea. Even when some facilities exist they may not be adequate, and a cruise ship, operating a tight schedule, could not afford to be delayed through having to discharge high volumes of garbage through inadequate or badly sited reception facilities. MEPC

## Proposed Amendments to Annexes I, II and IV concerning the harmonized system of survey and certification

A joint MCC/MEPC Working Group (the GSI Group) studied the requirements for survey and certification under MARPOL(1) and the way to adjust it in order to follow those required under SOLAS. The Group found that although most of SOLAS provisions are applicable to MARPOL, there are certain areas of differences. Unlike SOLAS, MARPOL requirements for survey apply to ships engaged on international and domestic voyages(2). Despite these differences, the Group(3) proposed the following amendments to Annexes I, II and IV.

---

21/10, Annexes 3 and 6, January 25, 1985.

(1) The requirements for survey and certification under Annex II closely follow those under Annex I.

(2) Regulation 4A(2) prescribes that the examination of items related to the condition of the outside of the ship's bottom may be carried out at the time of the bottom survey under SOLAS. It is not clear whether, insofar as Annex I of MARPOL 73/78 is concerned, there is any survey item that is related to the condition of the outside of the ship's bottom, and how the IOPP Certificate should show that the examination of these items has been carried out at the time of the SOLAS survey.

(3) Work has been started to incorporate in the IBC and BCH Codes the requirements for the construction and equipment presently included in the standards for the Procedures and Arrangements. When this is completed, the survey and certification of all hardware items may be covered by the Code Certificate.
In such a case, there appears to be no survey item covered by the Noxious Liquid Substances (NLS) certificate which will not be covered by the Code Certificate, and a question would arise whether there is a need to include in Annex II the requirements for survey and certification. It may be argued that the NLS Certificate might be regarded as a "cover note" for the Code Certificate. If this view is right, a question would arise whether the NLS Certificate could be renewed independent of the renewal of the Code Certificate.

Annex I

.1 The date of each year corresponding to the date of expiry of the IOPP Certificate is defined as "anniversary date";

.2 the provisions for unscheduled inspections have been deleted and annual surveys are required to be carried out within three months before or after each anniversary date;

.3 intermediate surveys must be carried out within three months before or after the second or third anniversary date;

.4 new provisions have been included to allow the inspection of items relating to the outside of ship's bottom to be carried out at the time of the bottom survey under SOLAS;

.5 new provisions have been included for the extension of the renewal survey and the certificate.

Annex II

.6 The requirements for survey and certification are practically identical to those of Annex I.

Annex IX

.7 The requirements for annual surveys have been included;

.8 it is suggested that the survey requirements might be extended to domestic ships;

.9 provisions for the extension of the renewal survey and the certificate have been modified to bring them in line with the provisions of Annex I[1].

## 2. DUMPING AT SEA

Damage to the marine environment may be caused by discharge of oil or the disposal of wastes at sea. The extent of the harm by dumping depends on the source, composition of the waste[2] and the kind of

---

(1) MEPC 20/11, February 9, 1984.

(2) Wastes enter the sea from rivers used for waste disposal, effluent points located on the coast

treatment received.

Wastes dumped from ships: Two methods of dumping should be distinguished: wastes which are dispersed and wastes which are containerized. The latter is the usual method used for industrial wastes and in particular for dangerous materials(1) in the hope that they will remain containerized for a long period. However, it is not known how much containerized waste has been dumped in the oceans(2).

---

and dumping.
The term "waste" is a broad one covering materials of different chemical dispositions from many sources. This term is used in the sense that someone wants to get rid of the substances and not in the sense that they are the unwanted by-products of human activities.
Wastes are often divided into two categories: domestic and industrial. The former includes sewage, waste from food-processing, detergents and run-off from agricultural areas. The latter covers substances such as radioactive materials, toxic chemicals, mustard and nerve gas. Clearly, industrial wastes are more harmful to the environment than domestic wastes.

(1) The most important problem concerns the radioactive waste from nuclear power stations. If the use of radioactive materials in the world (by no means confined to the nuclear power industry) continues to grow, more easily monitored and controlled means of disposal will be needed.
In 1967, the North Atlantic Ocean 700 km to the North-East of Spain, was designated as the European dumping-site by the Nuclear Energy Agency under the auspices of the Organization for Economic Co-operation and Development (OECD). Eight countries carried out a total of 28 dumping operations at the site between 1967 and 1982, dropping more than 96,000 tonnes of radioactive waste into the sea.
This waste is sealed into steel drums, in an inner concrete matrix, and dropped into water 4000m deep. Tests carried out for the US Atomic Energy Commission on identical containers showed that one-third of the barrels were crushed by varying degrees during descent.

(2) Most governments refuse to reveal what they dump and where they dump. The fact is that dumping has been going on for some time and continues

Perhaps the greatest potential danger from containerized wastes arises from the uncertainty of when and how[1] the material in the container will be dispersed[2]. Containers are usually made of very strong material, often concrete or steel, or both. Concrete, however, does crumble and steel rusts. Earthquakes on the ocean floor can break

---

today. In August,1970, the United States sank a ship loaded with nerve gas, by rockets, in the Atlantic.
The incident of the Dutch tanker *Stella Maris* is a good illustration. The ship had planned to dump 600 tons of chemical wastes, from a factory in Rotterdam, in deep water some 110 km from the Norwegian coast. After vigorous representation by the Scandinavian governments, it was announced on 20 July, 1971, that the ship had been diverted to an alternative dumping ground in mid-Atlantic about 100 km south of Iceland and West of Ireland. This immediately evoked further protest, this time from the Icelandic, Irish and British governments. The ship was refused bunkering facilities at the Faeroes where a large public demonstration met it at the quay-side. On July 22, 1971, the ship was refused permission to refuel in the Hebrides on the order of the British government. In view of this vigorous protest, the Dutch government recalled the ship to Rotterdam.
Many other incidents have been reported; see for example *The Topaz* which is owned by the Gem Line of Glasgow and was chartered to the European Energy Agency to dump atomic waste off the Bay of Biscay. The Times, August 20, 1971.

(1) The monitoring systems can collect data through automated buoys and transmit the information throughout the world. This information will assist to determine the places where wastes were dumped and trace the dispersal patterns.
The Intergovernmental Oceanographic Commission collaborated with the IMO in studying the problem of the "Ocean Data Acquisition System" (ODAS). The study covers the establishment and maintenance of such devices

(2) In principle, it is a bad idea to put things that may be dangerous where you cannot keep an eye on them. Too little is known of the sea bed, underwater currents and the food-chains of marine life. Wastes dumped by the United States

open any container known. No-one expects the containers to last forever, even those who make them. The usual expectation appears to be that materials will escape from the containers slowly and be diluted in vast quantities of sea-water.

Registration of dumpings of dangerous materials would appear to be the most appropriate step. Registration need not be a mere report of the substances and the place of dumping but might include a detailed account of the safety measures taken in order to prevent any harm to the environment. Once registration is established, an appropriate scientific body might consider setting standards for dumping.

Different policies: Some States support the idea of "prohibition of dumping with licensed exceptions". For this purpose a scheme for registration would be set up and regulations concerning the exceptions would be clearly drafted. There would be no doubt about the list of materials that were prohibited nor would there be room for argument about the conditions under which other substances might be released into the environment. Other States advocate the need for flexibility and favour the idea of providing permits for dumping. They are against any scheme for registration on the ground that no-one can state the potential damage of many substances with any degree of certainty[1].

---

some thirty years ago, not under the existing precautions, have apparently leaked enough radioactivity for detectable levels to have been found in marine life.

(1) The division between the policies of "prohibition" and "permits" is a deep one. The extent of the divergence is reflected in another way. Those who support prohibition want to prevent dumping of substances that could degrade or endanger health, marine life and damage the economic uses of the ocean. Those in favour of "permits" see dumping as an economic use of the ocean. They argue that the costs and risks of putting such materials elsewhere are greater. Also, they justify dumping on the assumption that the sea's absorptive and neutralizing properties were inexhaustible.
In the United Kingdom, see the Deposit of Poisonous Waste Act, 1972. This is an Act to penalise the depositing on land of poisonous,

This background information indicates that there was a need to have both regional and international rules to prohibit and control dumping. Article 210(5) of the UN Convention on the Law of the Sea, 1983, states: "dumping within the territorial sea and the exclusive economic zone or onto the continental shelf shall not be carried out without the express prior approval of the Coastal State, which has the right to permit, regulate and control such dumping after due consideration of the matter with other States which by reason of their geographical situation may be adversely affected thereby."

The Oslo Convention (February 15, 1972)

The Convention is a regional agreement for the North-East part of the Atlantic Ocean. It deals with marine pollution by dumping(1) from ships and aircraft. The Parties to the Convention considered that States bordering the North-East Atlantic have a particular responsibility to protect the waters of that region.

Under article 1, the Parties bind themselves to take all possible steps to prevent pollution of the sea by harmful substances. This general duty is not limited to dumping. The Parties in article 3 agree to supply the measures in a way as to prevent diversion of dumping into seas outside the Convention area. Article 4 provides a duty to harmonize the policies of the Contracting States in any measures taken to prevent pollution of the sea by dumping.

The most important part of the Convention is spelled out in articles 5, 6 and 7. Article 5 prohibits dumping of certain substances listed in Annex I (the so-called black list). Article 6

---

noxious or polluting waste so as to give rise to an environmental hazard, to make offenders liable for any resultant damage and to require the giving of notices in connection with the removal and deposit of waste.

The United Kingdom is responsible for ninety per cent of the sea dumping of wastes (partly as an agent for others). Japan would like to begin dumping in the Pacific on a scale similar to that of the United Kingdom in the Atlantic.

(1) Under article 19, dumping does not include "immersion" which is regarded as incidental to the normal shipping operations.

provides that dumping of the substances contained in Annex II (the grey list) is subject to special control. Article 7 contains a general rule that no dumping shall take place without the approval of the appropriate national authority. Annex III states the considerations which could be taken into account by the national authorities in deciding matters relating to dumping.

Under article 16, a Commission was established with the duty to supervise the implementation of the Convention, to consider any changes in the control measures and to review the lists of substances in the Annexes. In 1977 the Commission adopted a Code of Practice on incineration at sea which was converted in 1981 to legally binding rules. The Protocol to amend the Convention and a new Annex IV containing the incineration rules were opened for signature in Oslo in 1983.

The London Dumping Convention (December 29, 1972)

Despite the Oslo regional agreement, there was wide concern over the disposal of radioactive waste at sea and a need to reduce the quantity of waste to which other means of disposal could be found(1). This goal could be achieved by a multilateral treaty(2). To this end the London Dumping Convention (LDC)(3) was adopted(4). It is based on similar principles to those of the Oslo Convention

---

(1) Three methods could be used:
 (a) improvement of industrial processes;
 (b) reducing waste outputs; and
 (c) recycling and reusing wastes.

(2) See article 210 on Pollution by Dumping in the UN Convention on the Law of the Sea, 1983.

(3) It would have been more appropriate to call it the Anti-Dumping Convention.

(4) See the text of the Convention, IMO Sales No. 76.14.E. The provisions of the Convention were introduced into English law by the Dumping at Sea Act, 1974.
Dumping is prohibited unless a licence is obtained from the Ministry of Agriculture, Fisheries and Food. Licences granted by the appropriate authority in other Contracting States may be recognized. The definition of dumping under the Act is much wider than the one under the Convention. S.1(2) states that: "substances and articles are dumped in the sea

but is regarded as providing "a global basis for the control of waste disposal at sea"(1).

To the Convention which covers the legal framework, the following annexes are attached:

Annex I on Prohibited materials;

Annex II on Materials requiring special care; and

Annex III on Provisions for developing regulatory criteria and the technical framework.

Article I of the Convention states that the: "Contracting Parties shall individually and collectively promote the effective control of all sources of pollution of the marine environment, and pledge themselves especially to take all practicable steps to prevent the pollution of the sea by the dumping of waste and other matter that is liable to create hazards to human health, to harm living resources and marine life, to damage amenities or to interfere with other legitimate uses of the sea"(2).

---

for the purposes of this Act if they are permanently deposited in the sea from a vehicle, ship, aircraft, hovercraft or marine structure, or from a structure on land constructed or adapted wholly or mainly for the purpose of depositing solids in the sea."
Unauthorised dumping may result in a fine or a term of imprisonment or both, s.1(6). Defences similar to those of the Convention are allowed under the Act.
The task of enforcing the provisions of the Act lies with a British enforcement officer, who may inspect vehicles, aircraft and hovercraft in the UK, ships in UK ports and UK vessels wherever they may be. During such an inspection, he may take samples, examine equipment and require the production of licences and records of which he may take copies. Any person who, without a reasonable excuse, impedes the enforcement officer shall be liable to a fine not exceeding £200, s.7.

(1) LDC 8/10, March 8, 1984, p.5. See also the Resolution of the Third Consultative Meeting (of the Contracting Parties to the Convention) on Incineration at Sea, Oct. 12, 1978.

(2) Non-Contracting States are not bound by the provisions of the Convention. Consequently,

Definitions

Article III contains definitions[1] of certain terms such as "dumping"; "vessels"; "sea"; "wastes"; "special and general permit". The most important term is "dumping" which is defined as meaning:

" (i) any deliberate disposal at sea of wastes or other matter from vessels, aircraft, platforms or other man-made structures at sea;

(ii) any deliberate disposal at sea of vessels, aircraft, platforms or other man-made structures at sea.

Dumping does not include:

(i) the disposal at sea of wastes or other matter incidental to, or derived from, the normal operations of vessels, aircraft, platforms, or other man-made structures at sea and their equipment, other than wastes or other matter transported by or to vessels, aircraft, platforms or other man-made structures at sea, operating for the purpose of disposal of such matter or derived from the treatment of such wastes or other matter on such vessels, aircraft, platforms or structures.

The disposal of wastes or other matter directly

---

dumping from those States of harmful materials on the high seas will not be carried out under the supervision of any national or international authority. However, non-Contracting States must observe the rules of international customary law which are not clear on dumping.
By March,1985, fifty-three States were Contracting Parties to the Convention. C52/10, March 20, 1984.

(1) Many legal and technical terms were ill-defined or even undefined, leaving to the Contracting Parties the difficult task of implementing the provisions of the Convention. However, the LDC meets annually and conducts its work on a consensus basis. Technical and legal issues can be referred to intersessional groups for further study or resolution. The LDC is an active and dynamic treaty that tries to incorporate the state of the art in its deliberations, while remaining responsive to many opposing views regarding ocean disposal.

arising from, or related to the exploration, exploitation and associated off-shore processing of sea-bed mineral resources will not be covered by the provisions of this Convention."

Dredging, which is a process by which sediments are removed from the bottom of streams, rivers, lakes and coastal waters; transported via ship, barge, or pipeline; and discharged to land or water, is covered by the Convention. However, guidance adopted by the Consultative Meetings (7th, 1983) to the LDC has recognized that all the factors used to evaluate the ocean disposal of some material may not be applicable to dredged material and may in fact be excluded from the rigorous evaluation. The "Interim Guidelines of the Implementation of Paragraphs 8 and 9 of Annex I (prohibited materials) to the LDC" provide that, with respect to dredged material, the test procedures to be used for determining the potential for toxic effects, persistence, inhibition of life processes and bio-accumulation.

This information is used to determine whether Annex I materials are "trace contaminants" or "rapidly rendered harmless" and thus exempt from the prohibitions of Annex I. This information may not be needed if chemical characteristics of the material and knowledge of the receiving area allow an assessment of the environmental impact. In addition, Appendix 1 to the Interim Guidelines, "Test Procedures for the Interpretation of 'Trace Contaminants' and Harmlessness" exempts dredged material, in the absence of appreciable pollution sources, from the chemical and biological testing requirements of the Annex I prohibitions.

The LDC meeting in February, 1983, was asked to consider whether or not dredged material contaminated with prohibited substances could be capped with clean material under the provisions of the LDC by its Scientific Group. They make technical and scientific recommendations to the LDC concerning the ecological aspects of regulating dumping at sea. It was generally agreed that capping techniques are considered to be technically and scientifically feasible in low-energy environments and should continue as field research and the projects monitored until sufficient information is obtained as to the acceptability of capping for a broader selection of ocean environments.

There is controversy between States on whether "disposal into the sea-bed of high-level radioactive wastes" is covered by the LDC. Some States(1) hold the view that disposal into the sea-bed or sub-soil did not feature in the discussion during the preparations of the Convention nor can be supported by the definition of "dumping" as provided for in article III. Others believe that disposal into the sea-bed would be incompatible with the obligations under the Convention(2).

---

(1) The Russian delegation said: "it would be unreasonable and arbitrary to expand the scope of the London Dumping Convention by interpretation. This delegation could find no legal basis for extending the commitments of sovereign States beyond those which they had assumed." LDC 8/10, March 8, 1984, p.28.
The delegation of the United Kingdom agreed and said: "they could not accept a resolution implying that the sub-seabed disposal of high-level wastes was covered by the London Dumping Convention." They added that: "the only major commitment required at this stage, which the United Kingdom would be ready to give, was to ensure that no State proceeded to disposal into the sea-bed of dangerous wastes until it was proved feasible and environmentally acceptable." *Ibid*, p.29.
At the Eighth Consultative Meeting of Contracting Parties held from 20 to 24 February, 1984, it was concluded (without prejudice to the applicability of the London Dumping Convention to this form of disposal) that:
(a) the consultative Meeting was the appropriate international forum to address the question of the disposal of high-level radioactive wastes and matter into the sea-bed, including the question of the compatibility of this type of disposal with the provisions of the LDC; and
(b) no such disposal should take place unless and until it is proved to be technically feasible and environmentally acceptable, including a determination that such wastes can be effectively isolated from the marine environment, and a regulatory mechanism is elaborated under the LDC to govern the disposal into the sea-bed of such radioactive wastes. See C52/10, March 20, 1984, p.4.

(2) The Spanish delegation believed that sea-bed disposal is covered and prohibited by the London Dumping Convention because it falls within the

Apart from the question of the legal status of the sea-bed and sub-soil and whether dumping *at sea* would extend to areas under the water of the sea, an accident occurred where containers of harmful wastes were lost at sea. Such an incident is not covered by the LDC as the disposal was not "deliberate"(1).

At the Eighth Consultative Meeting held on 20-24 February, 1984, the American delegation presented a document in which particular attention was drawn to the need for a definition of the term "comprehensive total waste management strategy"(2).

---

definition of "dumping at sea". *Ibid*, p.27. The American delegation, while prepared to set aside those differences of interpretation as part of a consensus resolution, still maintained the view that the obligation under the Convention to protect the marine environment included an obligation not to engage in disposal into the sea-bed of high-level radioactive waste unless and until it has been determined that the activity was technically feasible and could be undertaken in compliance with vigorous criteria, ensuring protection of the marine environment. *Ibid*, p.31.
The definition of dumping is under review and it is possible to extend the scope of the Convention to cover disposal of waste caused by accidents or even to cover marine pollution from river and atmospheric sources. There is also a trend to define the role of the Contracting Parties in developing plans for total waste management.

(1) In August, 1984, the *Mont Louis* (4,210 tons gross), carrying highly toxic uranium hexafluoride in containers, sank after colliding with the ferry *Olau Britannia* (14,981 tons gross) in the English Channel. As a result of this accident, some containers were lost at sea. MEPC 21/INF.2 of Nov. 30, 1984, which is a document of an incident whereby 80 drums containing the chemical DINOSEB were lost from a Danish vessel in the North Sea. The incident happened at the beginning of January, 1984 and by the end of May, 72 drums were salvaged. The prohibition of the use of DINOSEB is a consequence of re-evaluation of pesticides.

(2) Document No. LDC 8/4/1.

The three Annexes: Article IV followed the same principles as the Oslo Convention by stating that dumping of waste or other matter listed in Annex I is prohibited. The dumping of waste or other matter listed in Annex II requires a prior special permit while dumping of all other waste or matter requires a prior general permit[(1)].

The LDC set up a Scientific Group which meets intersessionally to make technical and scientific recommendations to the Consultative Body concerning the ecological aspects of regulating dumping at sea. The Group met in September 1977 and has since met annually approximately six months prior to each LDC meeting.

A Task Team 2000 has been organized to identify the long-term goals of the LDC. The team's specific objective is to project the role of the Convention in the Year 2000. An *ad hoc* Legal Experts Group on Dumping also meets intersessionally on an as-needed basis to discuss and/or resolve legal interpretation of the LDC. Critical issues under discussion by this Group are incineration[(2)] at sea and sed-bed emplacement of high-level radioactive wastes.

Before the Scientific Group on Dumping, the Canadian delegation proposed to include lead and lead compounds in Annex I[(3)]. However, no decision

---

(1) Guidelines were approved on the Implementation and Uniform Interpretation of Annex III.

(2) With regard to the surveillance of cleaning operations of incineration vessels, the Ninth Consultative Meeting adopted Resolution LDC 20(9) containing interim provisions for the surveillance of such operations carried out at sea. These provisions could be later on adopted as mandatory requirements. MEPC 22/WP.16, p.35. The controversy over the incineration at sea of hazardous materials was considered by the US House of Representatives. It was alleged that insufficient is known about incineration of hazardous or toxic materials at sea and the default of a US-flag company to finance the two incineration ships under construction. Lloyd's List, December 5, 1985.

(3) The Consultative Meeting adopted the proposed revision of the term "significant amounts" for "lead and lead compounds" and for "pesticides and their by-products" listed in Annex II of the Convention to the effect that special care has to be taken and a special permit issued when

on this issue was taken nor any recommendation on the removal of organosilicon compounds from the list of substances contained in Annex II(1).

The Russian delegation stated that "The Annexes to the Convention should be kept under continuing review and the list of substances contained in the Annexes should be extended in the light of new scientific and technological data on disposal methods and effects on the marine environment"(2).

In fact, the allocation of substances to Annex I or II is not easy and the Scientific Group on Dumping felt that before setting up criteria on this subject, there is a need to clarify the purpose and concepts of the Annexes(3).

Non-application of the provisions of article IV: Article V allows dumping and the non-observance of article IV in the following circumstances:

(a) when it is necessary to secure the safey of human life or of vessel; or

(b) when there is a danger to human life or a real threat to the vessel provided that dumping appears to be the only way of averting the threat.

Article III(1) of the LDC excludes the disposal at sea of materials incidental to, or derived from, the normal operation of vessels. Accordingly, the force majeure requirements of Article V(1) would apply only to vessels loaded for the purpose of dumping (or incineration) of waste or other matter at sea.

---

wastes containing these compounds in concentrations of 0.05% or more by weight were dumped at sea. It also adopted a working plan for the development of criteria for the allocation of substances in Annexes I and II. *Ibid*, p.9.

(1) *Ibid*, p.7.

(2) *Ibid*, p.14.

(3) *Ibid*, p.7. The Scientific Group then considered as a matter of high priority:

(a) practical and technical criteria for determining the appropriate assignment of substances to the Annexes; and

(b) the nature of "special care" techniques to the disposal of Annex II substances. *Ibid*, p.7.

Dumping

A Contracting Party may issue a special permit[1] in emergencies, posing unacceptable risk relating to human health and admitting no other feasible solution existed[2].

Article VII states that each Contracting Party shall apply the measures required to implement the Convention to:

(a) vessels and aircraft registered in its territory or flying its flag;

(b) vessels and aircraft loading in its territory or territorial seas, matter which is to be dumped; and

(c) vessels and aircraft and fixed or floating platforms under its jurisdiction believed to be engaged in dumping.

## The Helsinki Convention, 1974

The Convention on the Protection of the Marine Environment of the Baltic Sea Area was adopted on March 22, 1974. Seven States bordering the Baltic

---

(1) The Secretariat in a note (LDC 8/3/4) drew attention to the existing procedures and formats and reminded Contracting Parties that any special permit for dumping and incineration at sea should be notified immediately after they have been issued and that annual records of all permits issued in a calendar year should be submitted to the Secretariat by 1 August of the following year. Attention was also drawn to the requirement that the Secretariat should be notified of actual amounts dumped or incinerated per calendar year and of the monitoring of dump sites (LDC 8/3/4, Annexes 3 and 4).

(2) The London Dumping Convention, 1972, was amended in 1978 and 1980. The 1978 Amendments concern Procedures for the Settlement of Disputes. Future work will include:
(a) the relationship between the London Dumping Convention and the Law of the Sea Convention;
(b) problems related to the import/export of wastes for disposal at sea;
(c) waste disposal for deep sea mining; and
(d) monitoring of international waters for the purpose of the London Dumping Convention. C52/10 of March 20, 1984.

Sea signed the Convention in order to regulate the protection of the Baltic from any kind of pollution.

Article 6 obliges the Contracting Parties to co-operate in the development and adoption of specific programmes, guidelines, standards of regulations. It also states that the substances and materials listed in Annex II should not be introduced into the Baltic Sea environment in significant quantities without a prior special permit, issued by the appropriate national authority.

Dumping is given a similar definition to the one adopted under the London Convention except that burning at sea is included. Under article 9, the Contracting Parties are obliged to introduce a general prohibition of dumping into their municipal law. Only dredged spoils may be dumped subject to a prior permit by the competent authority. The Helsinki Convention contains detailed provisions on the prevention of pollution from ships. Under article 12, a Commission was established with functions similar to those of the Osló Convention(1).

## 3. THE INTERVENTION CONVENTION, 1969

The history of the above Convention goes back to the grounding of the *Torrey Canyon* (100,000 dwt) in April, 1967, off the North-West Coast of England. Oil was discharged from it and polluted some parts of the English and French beaches. As a result of this incident, the International Convention Relating to Intervention on the High Seas in Cases of Oil Pollution Casualties was adopted on 18 November, 1969(2).

The right of intervention is not new for coastal States as it is well established by international customary law and is based on both the concept of

---

(1) The IMO receives regular reports from the Oslo Commission Secretariat on the measures taken under its regional convention on the prevention and control of marine pollution by dumping. However, no reports have been received from the commissions set up under the Helsinki Convention and the Barcelona Dumping Protocol. See LDC 8/10, p.13.

(2) The Convention came into force on May 6, 1975. The provisions of this Convention were incorporated into the Prevention of Oil Pollution Act, 1971.

necessity and self-preservation. Nonetheless, the Intervention Convention states precisely the circumstances and the conditions required for exercising such right.

Scope of application

The scope of application of the provisions of the Convention is limited in four ways: firstly it relates to intervention on the high seas; secondly it concerns oil; thirdly it is limited to cases where a maritime casualty has occurred; and fourthly it deals with ships. Article I(1) states: "Parties to the present Convention may take such measures on the high seas as may be necessary to prevent, mitigate or eliminate grave and imminent danger to their coastline or related interests from pollution or threat of pollution of the sea by oil, following upon a maritime casualty or acts related to such a casualty, which may reasonably be expected to result in major harmful consequences."

The first limitation is that the provisions of the Convention apply to the high seas. As for territorial waters, coastal states enjoy sovereign rights and exercise their jurisdiction over foreign vessels. Consequently, the conditions for intervention required by the Convention or its compulsory arbitration machinery are applicable for cases of intervention in territorial waters(1).

Oil is the only cargo which gives the right of intervention under the Convention. It is defined by Article II(3) as "crude oil, fuel oil, diesel oil

---

(1) This may lead to the adoption of two standards for intervention, depending on whether the casualty occurred in the territorial waters or the high seas. According to art.12 of the Prevention of Oil Pollution Act, 1971, three conditions are required: an accident, pollution on a large scale, and the measures are urgently needed. However, for intervention on the high seas, the Oil in Navigable Waters (Shipping Casualties) Order,1971, art.2 states that the intervention will be "in any case in which the Secretary of State is satisfied that there is a need to protect the coast of the United Kingdom or the waters in or adjacent to the United Kingdom up to the seaward limits of territorial waters against grave and imminent danger of oil pollution."

and lubricating oil"[1]. The Convention does not give the coastal state the right to intervene with gas carriers, chemical carriers or vessels carrying nuclear materials, which may be more dangerous than ships carrying oil.

The Convention is limited to cases where a maritime casualty has occurred. A "maritime casualty" is defined in Article II(1) to mean "a collision of ships, stranding or other incident of navigation, or other occurrence on board a ship or external to it resulting in material damage or imminent threat of material damage to a ship or cargo".

The fourth limitation is that the Convention applies to ships. The term "ship" is defined in Article II(2) as meaning:

> "(a) any sea-going vessel of any type whatsoever; and
> (b) any floating craft, with the exception of an installation or device engaged in the exploration and exploitation of the resources of the sea-bed and the ocean floor and the sub-soil thereof."

Article I(2) excludes warships and ships owned or operated by a State and used for non-commercial services.

## Circumstances in which the coastal state may intervene

Article I(1) states: "Parties to the present Convention may take such measures on the high seas as may be necessary to prevent, mitigate or eliminate grave and imminent danger to their coastline or related interests from pollution or threat of pollution of the sea by oil, following upon a maritime casualty or acts related to such a casualty, which may reasonably be expected to result in major harmful consequences."

Intervention is, thus, justified when there is a "grave and imminent danger"[2] to the coastline or "related interests". In the original draft of the

---

(1) This definition is wider than the one adopted by the Civil Liability Convention (CLC) and was intended to cover non-persistent oils.

(2) The IMO Legal Committee at its thirty-seventh session held on Dec. 5, 1978, LEC XXX VII/7, felt (at p.11) that the requirement that "a grave and imminent danger" must precede any

Convention, the words "disastrous consequences" were used, but in the final draft the word "extreme" was deleted and the word "grave" was used instead of "disastrous".

The words "related interests"(1) are defined in Article II(4) as meaning: "the interests of a coastal State directly affected or threatened by the maritime casualty, such as:

(a) maritime coastal, port or estuarine activities, including fisheries activities, constituting an essential means of livelihood of the persons concerned;

(b) tourist attractions of the area concerned;

(c) the health of the coastal population and well-being of the area concerned, including conservation of living marine resources and of wild-life"(2).

<u>Conditions required for intervention</u>

The coastal State must(3) enter into consultations with other States affected by the maritime casualty, particularly with the flag State. It may also consult independent experts from the list maintained by the IMO. Furthermore, the coastal State is required to notify the proposed measures without delay to any person who has interests which can be reasonably affected by those measures. In cases of extreme urgency, the prior notification and

---

intervention measures may be a source of frustration or delay and therefore a new criterion should be established.

(1) In the Legal Committee, a delegate proposed that the term "related measures" should be made clearer so as to cover continental shelf interests. *Ibid*, p.10.

(2) The Legal Committee regarded the concept of "intervention measures" as encompassing acts of salvage and assistance, if the intervening State so decided. *Ibid*, p.7. It also agreed to study when the right of intervention terminates.

(3) The Legal Committee agreed to study whether the intervening State should be required to prove that it was compelled to intervene, or on the contrary for the flag State to show that the intervention was not warranted. *Ibid*, p.12.

consultations are not required[1].

In intervening, the coastal State must avoid any risk to human life and must give assistance to persons in distress (Article III, e).

Article V(1) provides that the measures should be "proportionate" to the damage. The type of measures, their effectiveness and the extent of damage are to be taken into account[2]. Article VI states that: "Any Party which has taken measures in contravention of the provisions of the present Convention, causing damage to others, shall be obliged to pay compensation to the extent of the damage caused by measures which exceed those reasonably necessary to achieve the end mentioned in Article I."

Claims under the Convention will be settled by arbitration. Article VIII(1) states: "Any controversy between the Parties as to whether measures taken under Article I were in contravention of the provisions of the present Convention, to whether compensation is obliged to be paid under Article VI, and to the amount of such compensation shall, if settlement by negotiation between the Parties involved or between the Party which took measures and the physical or corporate claimants has not been possible, and if the Parties do not otherwise agree, be submitted upon request of any of the Parties concerned to conciliation or, if conciliation does not succeed, to arbitration as set out in the Annex to the present Convention."

## 4. REGIONAL CO-OPERATION

Many environmental problems which extend beyond national jurisdiction require regional co-operation between the States concerned[3]. Article 197 of the

---

(1) The Legal Committee agreed that the rules on notification and consultation with other interested States concerning the action intended to be taken should be examined. *Ibid*, p.11.

(2) At the fortieth session (June 19, 1979) of the Legal Committee, some delegations considered that the "proportionality" requirement was not necessary and could be substituted with the test of "reasonableness". See LEG XL/5, at p.6.

(3) Examples are the joint US/Canadian Plan for response to oil spills and the US/Mexico Plan. The US Coast Guard has established an oil spill

UN Convention on the Law of the Sea, 1983, spells out the broad principle in this respect by stating that:

"States shall co-operate on a global basis and, as appropriate, on a regional basis, directly or through competent international organizations, in formulating and elaborating international rules, standards and recommended practices and procedures consistent with this Convention, for the protection and preservation of the marine environment, taking into account characteristics regional features."

It must be recalled that protection of the environment was not one of the main objectives of the UN Convention on the Law of the Sea. However, since the policy of the draftsmen was to codify the various aspects of the law of the sea, it was necessary to deal in general terms with the environment. Another principle laid down by the 1983 Convention was that the obligation to protect and preserve the marine environment rests with the Contracting Parties (Article 192).

The IMO recognized that the protection of the marine environment is too large a problem to be tackled by governments in isolation. Therefore, a number of resolutions(1) were passed to encourage co-operation and to report incidents to the Organization.

---

altering mechanism for the Caribbean and participated heavily in negotiation of the environmentally-oriented Cartagena Convention.

(1) See for example Resolution A.448 (XI) adopted on Nov. 15, 1979. At the 10th session, the MEPC agreed:
- (a) to elaborate guidelines for the development and implementation of regional anti-pollution arrangements;
- (b) to ask governments in areas where regional arrangements neither exist nor are being developed to give consideration to establishing them;
- (c) to ask governments and industry to consider international arrangements for dealing with pollution emergencies whereby specialised equipment and expertise could be made readily available; and
- (d) to explore ways of promoting regional arrangements through the IMO. See IMO News, No.1, 1979, p.17.

It would be beyond the scope of this book to cover fully the work done by the various regional organizations(1). However, a brief word is necessary to describe the important ones.

1. The Bonn Agreement, 1969: The area which is subject to this Agreement is limited to the North Sea and the English Channel. Articles 5 and 6 provide for a detailed system of regional co-operation to ensure that timely information is received of casualties or oil slicks. Article 5 states: "(1) Whenever a Contracting Party is aware of a casualty or the presence of oil slicks in the North Sea area likely to constitute a serious threat to the coast or related interests of any Contracting Party, it shall inform that Party without delay through its competent authority..." Thus, masters of vessels flying the flags of the Parties should report all pollution incidents. In case of a grave oil pollution incident, the area is divided into zones in order to avoid any duplication in cleaning-up operations. The Agreement came into force on August 9, 1969.

Since 1977 the Contracting Parties have met annually and have established a technical working group to consider the appropriate method to deal with an oil spill and to develop the procedures for mutual assistance in joint combating operations. A Manual has been developed which describes the operational command structure for dealing with oil pollution incidents and lists all the equipment which might be available to other Contracting Parties in the event of an emergency.

In September, 1983, the Contracting Parties with the addition of the EEC, signed a new Bonn Agreement extending their field of co-operation to harmful substances other than oil. The new Agreement

---

(1) A special centre for combating pollution was recently established in the Philippines in which three States - Indonesia, Malaysia and the Philippines - are involved. Pollution is a continual threat in South-East Asia, which is a major route for tankers. See IMO News, No.3, 1985, p.18.
Regional plans have been developed in the Red Sea and the Gulf of Aden; the Caribbean; West and Central Africa; East Asian Waters; the South East Pacific; the South-West Pacific and South Asia.

contains provisions governing the financial arrangements for combating pollution on a bilateral or multilateral basis[1].

2. <u>The Copenhagen Agreement, 1971</u>: The Parties to this Agreement are: Norway, Denmark, Finland and Sweden. Under it, the Parties undertake to inform each other of the sighting of any significant oil slick which may drift towards the territory of another Party. In addition to reporting the incident, the Agreement contains duties on co-operation and maintaining stocks of fighting equipment.

3. <u>The Paris Convention, 1974</u>: The Convention was signed by all the States which ratified the Oslo Convention with the exception of Finland (which has no land-based discharges to the area concerned) but with the addition of the EEC. The Convention applies to the same areas as the Oslo Convention and defines pollution from land-based sources as the pollution of the maritime area:

- through watercourses;
- from the coast, including introduction through underwater or other pipelines; and
- from man-made structures placed within the limits of the area to which the Convention applies.

Under the Paris Convention, the substances are divided into groups according to their characteristics for persistence in the marine environment, toxicity or other noxious properties and tendency to bioaccumulation. List I, the "black list" includes those substances which are not readily degradable or rendered harmless by natural process. The "grey list" covers substances which require strict control. A third group is radioactive substances including radioactive wastes, which is subject to measures laid down by the IAEA.

The Paris Commission is active in drawing up programmes and measures for the elimination or reduction of pollution from land-based sources.

---

(1) See the Manche Plan which is concerned with the English Channel. See also the Baltic Convention, 1974, which follows the lines of the Bonn Agreement and concerns the Baltic Sea.

4. <u>The Mediterranean Action Plan, 1976</u>: About 600 million tonnes of oil crosses or is landed in the Mediterranean ports. As the journeys are often too short to use the load on top system, pollution in the Mediterranean is proportionately far greater than in the rest of the world. However, the most serious kind of pollution is from land-based sources, i.e. industrial waste, municipal sewage and agricultural chemicals[1].

Under the auspices of the UNEP[2] a meeting was held at Barcelona where an Action Plan for the Protection of the Mediterranean was adopted on February 4, 1975[3]. The Plan consists of three parts: legal, scientific and integrated planning matters. The legal part covers a framework convention supported by a number of protocols while the scientific consists of seven pilot projects to be carried out by a network of Mediterranean laboratories. The third part on integrating planning programme deals with studies in selected critical areas to provide governments with data on which to base national planning on combined socio-economic development and environmental preservation.

In February, 1976, a Conference of Plenipotentiaries of the Coastal States of the Mediterranean was held in Barcelona when the Convention, a Protocol for the Prevention of Pollution of the

---

(1) Pollution is caused by:
  (a) tankers discharging dirty ballast and tank washings while on ballast voyages;
  (b) all vessels discharging bilge and slop residue from machinery spaces; and
  (c) failure to provide deballasting facilities and bilge collection equipment at ports as required by MARPOL.

(2) The UNEP is the United Nations organization concerned with the protection of the environment. In the marine field, it encourages and supports the development and implementation of plans to prevent oil pollution. This involves promoting international and regional conventions and guidelines for assessing and monitoring the state of pollution, supporting training schemes and providing a focal point for the exchange of information. Its headquarters is in Nairobi, Kenya.

(3) UNEP/IG.II/4. See Louis J. Saliba, Protecting the Mediterranean - Co-ordinating regional action. Marine Policy, Vol.2, 1978, p.171.

Mediterranean Sea by Dumping from Ships and Aircraft and the Protocol concerning Co-operation in Combating Pollution of the Mediterranean Sea by Oil and Other Harmful Substances in Cases of Emergency were adopted[(1)].

The Convention is merely a framework and the specific duties of the Contracting Parties are provided for in the protocols[(2)]. Thus, the Convention provides for its Members to take appropriate measures to prevent, abate, and where necessary combat pollution caused by, or resulting from: dumping, discharge, exploration and exploitation of the natural resources, rivers and other land-based sources. It stipulates for complementary or joint monitoring programmes in the fields of science and technology. The Dumping Protocol follows the London and Oslo Convention, 1972, on Dumping. The prohibited list includes all levels of radioactive waste. Annex III specifies the sites, the amount and the kind of materials allowed to be dumped. The second Protocol on Co-operation is concerned with monitoring and reporting pollution or the threat of it in the area and provides in Articles 7, 8 and 9, measures for coping with emergencies.

In 1985, a meeting was held in Genoa to review progress in respect of: the Mediterranean Action Plan (Barcelona, 1975)[(3)]; the Convention for the

---

(1) The Convention with its two Protocols came into force on February 12, 1978.

(2) No country may become a party to the Convention unless it becomes party to at least one of its Protocols. The Contracting Parties to the Conventions are: Algeria, EEC, Cyprus, Egypt, France, Greece, Israel, Italy, Lebanon, Libya, Malta, Monaco, Morocco, Spain, Syria, Tunisia, Turkey and Yugoslavia.

(3) A meeting was held in Monaco in January,1978 (UNEP/IG.II/4) where a sub-committee was established to prepare a study on:
   (a) the appropriate procedures for determination of liability and compensation for damage resulting from pollution of the marine environment deriving from violations of the provisions of the Barcelona Convention and its Protocols; and
   (b) the Interstate Guarantee Fund for the Mediterranean Sea Area.

   During this meeting the delegations received the preliminary draft protocol for the protection

Protection of the Mediterranean Sea against Pollution (Barcelona, 1976) and its related Protocols; and Recommendations of the Meeting on the contribution of Mediterranean bilateral and multilateral Programmes to the objectives of the Mediterranean Action Plan (Brussels, 1984). Several recommendations(1) were taken at this meeting to strengthen the Mediterranean Action Plan.

---

of the Mediterranean Sea against pollution from land-based sources. They recommended that the United Nations Environment Programme (UNEP) would set up a working group to seek agreement on the questions raised during the discussion and to prepare a revised protocol.
As part of the environmental assessment of the Action Plan, it was agreed to carry out studies on:
(a) the role of sedimentation in pollution of the Mediterranean;
(b) the monitoring of pollution in Mediterranean open waters; and
(c) the assessments of pollutants from land-based sources.
The delegations to this meeting also considered activities aimed at achieving environmentally sound socio-economic development throughout the region.
At the Intergovernmental Meeting in Yugoslavia in 1977, two major programmes within the socio-economic field - the Blue Plan and the Priority Actions Programme - were approved. The main objectives of the Blue Plan are:
(a) to assist States to identify points of reinforcement or conflict between development activities and the environment;
(b) in the light of these interactions, to suggest alternative, environmentally sound development strategies to be followed in the long run; and
(c) to identify specific actions to be taken immediately.
See UNEP/IG.II/INF.6.

(1) It recommends, *inter alia*:
- to implement at national level strategies involving appropriate measures aimed at the protection of the Mediterranean Sea;
- to increase mutual aid;
- to examine the possibility of financing projects contained in document UNEP/WG.104/4;

5. Kuwait Regional Convention, 1978: In 1978, a conference was held in Kuwait where the Convention(1) concerning Regional Co-operation in Combating Pollution by Oil and Other Harmful Substances was adopted(2). The Kuwait Action Plan (KAP) considered many important issues on the protection of the marine environment such as monitoring, training and the setting up of a data bank. Recently, the Regional Organization for the Protection of the Marine Environment (ROPME), set up under the Action Plan, carried out a feasibility study for the allocation and installation of reception facilities in the region. The feasibility report was approved at a meeting held in Bahrain in October, 1984 and it is regarded as a guideline in the planning and establishment of reception facilities(3).

6. The Eastern African Action Plan, 1985: In June, 1985, the UNEP convened a conference(4) in Nairobi, as part of its Regional Seas programme, which is designed to protect the marine environment and promote sound and sustainable use of marine resources. These objectives could be achieved by the adoption of protection and conservation measures on a regional basis.

The Conference adopted an Action Plan and a Convention for the Protection, Management and Development of the Marine and Coastal Environment of

---

and
- to provide a secretariat.

See MEPC 21/8 of January 22, 1985.

(1) The Convention came into force on June 30, 1979.

(2) Following the terms of the Convention, the Marine Emergency Mutual Aid Centre (MEMAC) was established to pursue the following functions:
   (a) to collect information on the laws and regulations on pollution, emergency plans, equipment and materials available for cleaning-up;
   (b) to assist in the preparation of laws and regulations on pollution and drafting emergency plans;
   (c) to assist in training programmes; and
   (d) to exchange information.

(3) MEPC 21/8, January 22, 1985.

(4) It was attended by delegates from France, Kenya, Madagascar, Mozambique, Seychelles, Somalia, the United Republic of Tanzania and the European Economic Community.

the East African Region[1]. It decided, subject to the availability of resources, upon the priorities to be followed in the implementation of programme activities for the period 1985-87. Contingency planning in cases of maritime pollution emergencies was listed third in the order of priority.

---

(1) With the Convention, two Protocols and three resolutions were adopted.
The first Protocol concerns Co-operation in Combating Marine Pollution in Cases of Emergency and the second deals with protected areas and wild fauna and flora.
The resolutions relate to the implementation of the programme, institutional arrangements and financial arrangements.

## (ii) THE PRIVATE INTERNATIONAL RULES

The *Torrey Canyon* incident of 1967 raised a number of legal difficulties. The first was to determine the country where legal proceedings could be taken. Pollution may cause damage in more than one State. The ship could be registered in a different State and the charterer, who is usually the oil company with the financial assets, may be resident in another State. Legal procedures could be taken in any of these States. The second problem was the different principles on civil liability applicable in various countries. Strict liability, i.e. pollution damage regardless of negligence, may be sufficient under certain legal systems, while in others, proof of negligence would be required. Further, the various legal systems differ on whether the owner or the charterer would be the party to be liable for pollution damage. Finally, even if the jurisdictional problem was solved and liability was established, there was still the possibility that the compensation would not be sufficient to indemnify the persons who suffer the damage as a result of the application of the limitation of liability based on the tonnage of the ship.

After considering all these deficiencies in the existing regime, the Legal Committee of the IMO prepared a draft convention on civil liability. This draft was submitted to a Diplomatic conference held in November,1969, which adopted the International Convention on Civil Liability for Oil Pollution Damage (CLC). The CLC came into force on June 19, 1975.

The Conference also passed a resolution requesting the IMO to consider and adopt a scheme to compensate victims of oil pollution unable to obtain full compensation under the CLC. To this end a conference was held in Brussels from November 29 to December 18, 1971, and resulted in the adoption of an International Convention on the Establishment of an International Fund for Compensation for Oil Pollution Damage.

On 25th May, 1984, two Protocols were adopted, the first to amend the CLC and the second to amend the Fund Convention in order to provide for improved scope and enhanced compensation(1).

---

See the preamble to the Protocol.

Thus, this section[1] will consider:

1. the CLC, 1969, as amended by the 1984 Protocol[2]; and
2. the Fund Convention, 1971, as amended by the 1984 Protocol.

## 1. THE INTERNATIONAL CONVENTION ON CIVIL LIABILITY FOR OIL POLLUTION DAMAGE (CLC), 1969

The principal rule of the Convention[3] is contained in art. III(1) which provides:

"Except as provided in paragraphs 2 and 3 of this Article, the owner of a ship at the time of an incident, or where the incident consists of a series of occurrences at the time of the first such occurrence, shall be liable for any pollution damage caused by oil which has escaped or been discharged from the ship as a result of the incident."

---

(1) A Conference was held in 1984 (30 April to 25 May) to consider a draft convention on the liability and compensation for damage in connection with the carriage of Noxious and Hazardous substances by Sea (HNS). After a lengthy discussion and disagreement on many provisions, the Conference decided to request the IMO to prepare a new draft.

(2) The Protocol will enter into force twelve months after being accepted by ten States, including six with tanker fleets at least 1 million gt.

(3) The United Kingdom enabling legislation is the Merchant Shipping (Oil Pollution) Act, 1971 (as amended by section 9 of the Merchant Shipping Act, 1974). It created a statutory tort on the shipowner for any damage in the United Kingdom caused by an escape or discharge of oil from his ship. The shipowner's liability covers the cost of preventive measures and of any damage such measures may have caused. The only defences are that the discharge of oil resulted from an act of war or from an "exceptional, inevitable and irresistible natural phenomenon", or was due wholly to the act of another individual (who was not the owner's servant or agent) done with intent to cause damage, or the negligent or wrongful act of an authority charged with the function of maintaining navigational aids. The

Accordingly, the shipowner (or shipowners) is strictly liable regardless of fault[1] for oil pollution[2] damage. Such a liability covers matters such as the costs of cleaning-up, loss to hoteliers and fishermen, and for measures taken to prevent or minimize the damage[3]. However, the scope of application of the provisions of the CLC is limited in three ways:

---

Act excludes any Common Law action the plaintiff might otherwise have brought. Common law remedies are, however, still available against persons other than the shipowner and his agent. Shipowners are permitted to limit their liability per incident to amounts which are specified in terms of Special Drawing Rights (SDRs) of the International Monetary Fund. The sterling values of these units vary depending on movements in the SDR/sterling exchange rate but, roughly speaking, they are approximately £84 per ship's ton, subject to an absolute ceiling of £8.8 million.

Under the Convention, a Convention country is obliged to require such ships, wherever registered, carrying more than 2000 tons of persistent oil in bulk as cargo,to maintain insurance (or other financial security) against oil pollution liability when entering or leaving a port in its territory, or arriving at or leaving an offshore terminal in its territorial sea, and to carry a certificate that the ship is so insured (or covered by a financial security).

(1) The liability is not absolute since the owner can exclude it in certain cases. However, it is strict in the sense that no proof of fault is necessary to establish it.

(2) GESAMP proposed the following definition of maritime pollution: "Introduction by man of substances into the marine environment resulting in such deleterious effects as harm to living resources, hazards to human health, hindrance to maritime activities including fishing, and reduction of amenities". See M. Tomczak, Jr., Defining Marine Pollution, Marine Policy, Oct. 1984, p.311.

(3) Tanker owners set up a scheme called the "Tanker Owners' Voluntary Agreement Concerning Liability for Oil Pollution" (Tovalop). Its aim is to deal with the claims by governments or local authorities. By signing Tovalop, a tanker owner

(a) it applies only to ships;

(b) it concerns oil; and

(c) it covers pollution damage caused in the territorial sea and to preventive measures.

The 1984 Protocol brought changes[(1)] to these limitations by extending the scope of application of CLC.

Scope of application

(a) Ship: Article I(1) defines ship as any "sea-going vessel and any seaborne craft of any type whatsoever, actually carrying oil in bulk as cargo". Thus, vessels exclusively used for carrying oil in lakes or rivers and oil rigs fixed or mobile are excluded. Furthermore, tankers on ballast voyages, even if they are carrying bunkers and slops are excluded[(2)].

The Convention does not apply to warships or

---

makes an admission to pay any government compensation for pollution damage up to a certain limit per tanker. For this reason he must have insurance cover for this sum. Such insurance can be provided by a P & I Club, the International Tanker Indemnity Association, or any insurer acceptable to it.
Tovalop came into operation in October,1969, and it was designed to fill a gap in national and international legislation.
As mentioned, the CLC came into force on June 19, 1975. Before that time, many countries had no legislation on liability for oil pollution damage and therefore the acceptance of Tovalop agreement by a coastal State in case of a pollution incident was an attractive offer. This situation has changed since many countries have ratified the CLC. However, many charter-party forms still contain a term by which the owner undertakes to be party to Tovalop in case his flag State is not party to CLC. This is a necessary term since many tankers are fixed in the spot market and some of them belong to non-party States.

(1) It also raised the amount of limitation.

(2) Tankers carrying oil in bulk as cargo are subject to the Convention even though the oil which escaped and caused damage is bunker oil.

vessels owned or operated by a State for non-commercial purposes.

The discharge must have been "from the ship". Thus, where a ship is connected with the refinery or a single mooring buoy (SMB) through flexible pipes and the oil escaped through a burst in the pipes, the Convention applies if the pipes are considered part of the ship. If the pipes are part of the shore installations or the flexible pipes are part of the (SMB), the Convention will not apply to the pollution damage.

The 1984 Protocol brought changes to the definition of "Ship" which means "any sea-going vessel and sea-borne craft of any type whatsoever constructed or adapted for the carriage of oil in bulk as cargo, provided that a ship capable of carrying oil and other cargoes shall be regarded as a ship only when it is actually carrying oil in bulk as cargo and during any voyage following such carriage unless it is proved(1) that it has no residues of such carriage of oil in bulk aboard".

Thus, the Protocol extends the definition of "ship" to include unladen tankers in ballast after carrying crude oil provided that it has no residues. The definition also applies to combination carriers engaged in the carriage of crude oil in bulk. Consequently, the application of CLC and its Protocol is limited to spills by tankers and oil combined tankers. It must be noted that the whole philosophy of the Convention is not to create a regime of compensation of damages caused by oil from all kinds of sources but only to establish a scheme for damages in the course of the carriage of oil in bulk by sea.

(b) Oil: Article I(5) defines oil as "... any persistent oil such as crude oil, fuel oil, lubricating oil and whale oil, whether carried on board a ship as cargo or in bunkers of such a ship."

In redefining "oil"(2), the 1984 Protocol is clear that it covers only persistent hydrocarbon mineral oil. Whale oil and non-persistent hydro-

---

(1) The burden of proof is on the claimant.
(2) Oil is defined as meaning: "any persistent hydrocarbon oil such as crude oil, fuel oil, heavy diesel oil and lubricating oil, whether carried on board a ship as cargo or in the bunkers of such a ship."

carbon are excluded[1].

The oil must have "escaped or been discharged" from the ship and thus both accidental and intentional discharge are covered. In case there was a grave and imminent or serious threat of pollution damage prevented at considerable costs, the provisions of the Convention will not be applicable because of the absence of actual escape or discharge[2]. Furthermore, the Convention applies where the oil has escaped "as a result of the incident". The word "incident" is defined in article I(8) as "... any occurrence, or series of occurrences having the same origin, which causes pollution damage".

Clearly the exclusion of the pre-spill preventive measures from the scope of the Convention is not in line with its objective and therefore the Protocol attempts to remedy this deficiency by covering the "threat" situation so long as it is

---

(1) Some delegations pointed out the difficulties which could arise from the change of the definition of oil. They stated that national laws in certain countries include non-persistent oils in the list of polluting or toxic substances. It was also argued that the exclusion of non-persistent oils from the scope of the Convention would run against its aims. However, the majority of delegations maintained that non-persistent oils were unlikely to cause real damage to the marine environment and could, at any rate, be covered by the Limitation for Maritime Claims Convention, 1976. There still remains the difficulty of a clear distinction between persistent and non-persistent oils.

(2) See the case of the *Tarpenbek* on June 21, 1979, (Appendix V). After the collision, the *Tarpenbek* was towed to a port of refuge and the cargo was pumped out. The owner claimed the expenses incurred in preventing the spill of cargo from the Fund, but the latter refused such a claim. As a result, a number of writs were issued in June,1982 against the Fund by the Treasury Solicitor of the UK, the Isle of Wight County Council and South Wight Borough Council, the owners of the *Tarpenbek* and the P & I Club. The claims are based on the ground that the Fund was liable under the UK Merchant Shipping Acts, 1971 and 1974 irrespective of whether there was any spill of persistent oil.

"serious" or is regarded as "grave and imminent". Thus, incident is defined as meaning: "any occurrence, or series of occurrences, having the same origin which causes pollution damage or creates a grave and imminent threat of causing such damage."

(c) <u>Areas where the damage occurs or the preventive measures are taken</u>: It states that: "This Convention shall apply exclusively to pollution damage caused on the territory including the territorial sea of a Contracting State and to preventive measures taken to prevent or minimize such damage." Measures taken outside the territorial sea in order to prevent damage threatening the territory or the territorial sea of the coastal State are also covered. However, the precise meaning of the term "pollution damage" is not clear despite the fact that it is defined in the Convention as meaning "loss or damage caused outside the ship carrying oil by contamination resulting from the escape or discharge of oil from the ship, wherever such escape or discharge may occur, and includes the costs of preventive measures and further loss or damage caused by preventive measures (art. 1(6))"(1). Preventive measures are defined as "any reasonable measures taken by any person after an incident has occurred to prevent or minimise pollution damage (art. 1(7))"(2). Thus, "loss or damage" covers cleaning-up costs, loss of income to hoteliers and fishermen, as well as consequential economic loss. The extent of loss or damage is to be determined according to civil liability in each country.

Thus, only damage caused by contamination is covered and not damage caused by fire or explosion(3). This is quite clear, but the definition fails to indicate the extent of the damage. This important issue was left to be decided by the courts in the country where the damage occurred. The courts will apply their own civil law rules with the inevitable different results.

---

(1) See also art. 1(2) of the Fund Convention.
(2) See art. 1(2) of the Fund Convention.
(3) The CLC does not cover physical damage caused by an explosion, for example a tanker blow-up at an installation resulting in its destruction. However, it applies to pollution damage caused by the escape of oil as a result of the explosion.

The Protocol brought two major changes in this respect. The first on the geographical scope by extending the application of the Convention to pollution damage in the territory, the territorial sea and in the exclusive economic zone (EEZ) of a Contracting State(1). In case an EEZ has not been established, the application of the Convention will extend to no more than 200 nautical miles. Furthermore, the Convention applies to preventive measures whenever taken, to prevent or minimize such damage (art.3 of the Protocol).

As for the definition of "pollution damage" which was a controversial issue, some delegations asked only for clarification as the ultimate interpretation of these words lies with the national courts of Member States. Others argued that the definition should make it clear that economic loss in the exclusive economic zone is also covered.

In fact, no attempt was made to clarify the issue whether the measures were "reasonable" or "directly related to the incident" as these were left to national law. However, the Protocol contains a provision on the environmental damage. A claim for such damage is allowed where the claimant has suffered quantifiable economic loss. The fact that the remaining oil may affect the environment can not be a basis of a valid claim, unless it has an effect on the economic interests. Thus, the Protocol defined "pollution damage" as meaning:

"(a) loss or damage caused outside the ship by contamination resulting from the escape or discharge of oil from the ship, wherever such escape or discharge may occur, provided that compensation for impairment

---

(1) Many delegations opposed this extension on the ground that the preventive measures as defined by the Convention cover actions taken anywhere. Furthermore, the extension would lead to unnecessary preventive measures on the high seas and consequently to doubtful claims for the costs of such measures. It would be very difficult to ascertain whether the measures taken within the EEZ were reasonable.
Other delegations supported the extension as it will be in line with the rules of the Law of the Sea Treaty 1983, which widened the State's jurisdiction in environmental protection and therefore compensation should be available for damage in areas beyond the territorial limits.

of the environment other than loss of profit for such impairment shall be limited to costs of reasonable measures of reinstatement actually undertaken or to be undertaken;

(b) the costs of preventive measures and further loss or damage caused by preventive measures."[1]

As mentioned above, the new definition allows for recovery of damages to the marine environment. It limits such recovery to the costs of reasonable measures of reinstatement actually undertaken or to be undertaken. It excludes claims for the intrinsic value of the environment. The words costs "to be undertaken" were added to a proposal by the Director of the Fund so as to allow for costs in respect of measures not actually undertaken at the time of the claim.

With these limits on the application of the Convention, the liability under CLC as amended by the Protocol does not apply to:

(a) vessels exclusively used for carrying oil on lakes and rivers;

(b) oil escaping from dry cargo ships and tankers on ballast if it has no residues;

(c) offshore installations;

(d) damage caused by non-persistent oil[2]; and

(e) pollution damage suffered outside the territorial sea and the EEZ of a Contracting State and pollution damage suffered by a non-Contracting State.

<u>Persons liable and the basis of liability</u>: Under the Convention, one person is liable and that is the owner[3] of the vessel. Article III(1) defines "owners" as "... the persons registered as the owner of the ship or, in the absence of registration, the

(1) Measures taken before the incident has occurred are not covered by the Convention but will be covered under the Protocol.
(2) i.e. spills of gasoline, light diesel oil, kerosene, etc.
(3) No claim can be made against the servants or agents of the owner. However, the owner may have a recourse action against third parties.

person or persons owning the ship". However, in the case of a ship owned by a State and operated by a company which in that State is registered as the ship's operator, owner shall mean such company.

The 1984 Protocol(1) states that: "... the owner of a ship at the time of an incident, or where the incident consists of a series of occurrences at the time of the first such occurrence, shall be liable for any pollution damage caused by the ship as a result of the incident."

Accordingly, the owner cannot escape liability by selling his ship after the incident. Contracting out of liability is not permitted.

The Convention does not exclude claims against other persons involved in the incident. However, the Protocol extends the protection of the Convention to the servants of the owner, pilot, salvor, or charterer including a bareboat charterer. The reason for this change is to avoid those persons from taking an insurance policy. This article states:

"(a) the servants or agents of the owner or the members of the crew;

(b) the pilot or any other person who, without being a member of the crew, performs services for the ship;

(c) any charterer (howsoever described, including a bareboat charterer), manager or operator of the ship;

(d) any person performing salvage operations with the consent of the owner or on the instructions of a competent public authority;

(e) any person taking preventive measures;

(f) all servants or agents of persons mentioned in sub-paragraphs (c), (d) and (e); unless the damage resulted from their personal act or omission, committed with the intent to cause such damage, or recklessly and with knowledge that such damage would probably result."

---

(1) During the debate on the 1985 Protocol, some delegations suggested that claimants should be allowed to sue bareboat charterers operating vessels as well as registered owners. Others were in favour of a "joint and several" liability

Under the original Convention, article IV states: "when oil has escaped or has been discharged from two or more ships, and pollution damage results therefrom, the owners of all the ships concerned, unless exonerated under article III, shall be jointly and severally liable for all such damage which is not reasonably separable."

In the Protocol, the above article is replaced by the following text: "When an incident involving two or more ships occurs and pollution damage results therefrom, the owners of all the ships concerned, unless exonerated under Article III, shall be jointly and severally liable for all such damage which is not reasonably separable."

Exceptions from liability

According to paragraph 2 of Article III, the owner is not liable if he proves that the damage "(a) resulted from act of war, hostilities, civil war, insurrection, or a natural phenomenon of an exceptional, inevitable and irresistible character". An example of a natural phenomenon of an exceptional character is an earthquake.

The second exception is stated in (b) which states the case where the discharge "was wholly caused by an act or omission done with intent to cause damage by a third party". This case covers acts by terrorist groups.

The third exception is where the owner can prove that the discharge "(c) was wholly caused by the negligence or other wrongful act of any government or other authority responsible for the maintenance of lights or other navigational aids in the exercise of that function"(1). Examples of this exception are negligence in marking a wreck or marking a channel.

The draftsmen of the Convention regarded all the three exceptions stated in paragraph 2 of article III as uninsurable risks.

---

of the owner and the bareboat charters. However, these proposals were not accepted because no person other than the shipowner need be insured for pollution damage.

(1) An attempt to abolish this exception during discussion of the 1984 Protocol was not successful. Some delegations asked to what extent a ship's master had to rely on navigational aids and whether out-of-date navigational charts are to be considered as part of navigational aids.

## Limitation and amounts of liability under the Convention

The owner is given by article V(1) the right to limit his liability under the Convention in respect of any one incident to an aggregate amount[1] of 2,000 francs[2] for each ton of the ship's tonnage. However, this aggregate amount shall not in any event exceed 210 million francs (about $14.6 million).

The owner is not entitled to limit his liability if the incident occurred as a result of his actual fault or privity (art. V(2)). The 1984 Protocol allows the breaking of shipowner's limitation only "if it is proved that the loss resulted from his personal act or omission, committed with the intent to cause such loss, or recklessly and with knowledge that such loss would probably result"[3].

It is only the owner who can limit his liability and it is the liability under the Convention which is subject to the limitation if the incident occurred as a result of his actual fault or privity (art. V(2)). The owner must establish a fund for the total sum representing his limit of liability with the court or other competent authority of any one of the Contracting States in which action is brought.

The Protocol establishes in article 6 a liability limit of 3 million SDRs for ships not exceeding 5,000 gt (about $3.1 million)[4]. Above this figure, liability will increase by 420 SDRs[5] per ton above 5,000 gt, reaching a maximum of 59.7

---

(1) There is no minimum liability but the industry has introduced a minimum of $1m.

(2) A Protocol was adopted in 1976 which alters the unit of account from the Poincaré francs to the Special Drawing Rights. See IMO Sales No. 77.05.E and Cmnd. 7028.

(3) See *infra*, the comment on the identical provision in the Protocol of the Fund.

(4) The minimum limit of liability for small tankers would avoid the involvement of IOPC in small claims.

(5) The unit of account in the Protocol is the SDR of the International Monetary Fund (IMF). States which are not members of the IMF may use the Poincaré or gold franc. The Protocol states that the SDR equals 15 gold francs (art.6).

million SDRs at 140,000 gt (about $62 million)(1).

Transitional period (Article 9)

The conference considered a number of ways of dealing with the transition from the 1969/1971 regime to the new system. It decided to adopt the "phased-in" approach which embodies a transitional period during which States may be bound by both the new and the old systems.

For States which are parties to the 1969/71 and 1984 regimes, the following will apply during the transitional period:

(1) where damage falls within the scope of the Protocol "liability shall be deemed to be discharged if and to the extent that it also arises under the 1969 CLC";

(2) where there is liability remaining under the Protocol, it shall arise "only to the extent that pollution damage remains uncompensated after application of the 1971 Fund Convention".

---

(1) One of the changes brought by the Protocol is the introduction of the "tacit acceptance" procedure for future amendments. This would enable the limitation amounts to be changed more simply and quickly.
Proposals containing changes to the limitation amounts would be submitted to the IMO Legal Committee. The proposals will be adopted if they are accepted by a two-thirds majority, providing that at least one half of the Contracting Parties are present at the time of voting (art.15).
Amendments will be deemed to have been accepted eighteen months after being notified to all Contracting States, unless they are rejected during that period by at least one-quarter of Contracting Parties and they will enter into force after a further eighteen-month period.
No amendments can however be considered for at least five years after the Protocol is opened for signature, nor less than five years after the entry into force of a previous amendment to Article V. The Protocol further stipulates that no amendment may be considered before the Protocol has entered into force.

Time limit for bringing an action: Article VIII provides that "Rights of compensation under this Convention shall be extinguished unless an action is brought thereunder within three years from the date when the damage occurred. However, in no case shall an action be brought after six years from the date of the incident which caused the damage. Where this incident consists of a series of occurrences, the six years' period shall run from the date of the first such occurrence".

Compulsory insurance: Article VII(1) provides that: "The owner of a ship registered in a Contracting State and carrying more than 2,000 tons of oil in bulk as cargo shall be required to maintain insurance or other financial security, such as the guarantee of a bank or certificate delivered by an international compensation fund, in the sums fixed by applying the limits of liability prescribed in Article V, paragraph 1, to cover his liability for pollution damage under this Convention". Thus, the duty to provide an insurance policy or a financial security arises only when the ship is carrying more than 2,000 tons of oil in bulk as cargo. Consequently, where a tanker is on a ballast voyage carrying 2,000 tons of bunkers or more, the owner is not required to have such an insurance.

The State of registry provides that proceedings may be made directly against the insurer or other persons providing financial security for the owner's liability for pollution damage, and that the insurer may limit his liability even though the owner is guilty of fault or privity. The insurer will have all the defences which the owner could have invoked against the assured. Furthermore, the insurer may raise the defence that the pollution damage resulted from the wilful misconduct of the owner.

Limitation of liability based on the tonnage of the ship

As mentioned earlier, the owner can limit his liability arising under the CLC according to its own

---

No limit may be increased "so as to exceed an amount which corresponds to the limit laid down in the Protocol increased by six per cent a year, nor so as to exceed the limit contained in the Protocol" (i.e. 59.7 million SDRs) multiplied by three.

limits and subject to its requirements. For other types of liabilities which are not covered by CLC such as: pollution damage from dry cargo ships, from non-persistent oil for other persons not liable under CLC such as charterers, the limitation of CLC cannot be invoked. These types of liabilities and persons other than owners can invoke the 1957 Convention(1) and benefit from its limitation.

It must be noted that claims for oil pollution damage are covered by the provisions of the Convention on Limitation of Liability for Maritime Claims, 1976(2). However, there are three main exceptions relating to: the CLC, drill ships and offshore installations.

(a) Article 3(b) provides that: "The rules of this Convention shall not apply to ... (b) claims for oil pollution damage within the meaning of the International Convention on Civil Liability for Oil Pollution Damage, dated 29 November,1969, or of any amendment or Protocol thereto which is in force..."

Thus, all claims for oil pollution damage as defined by the 1969 Convention are excluded from the limitation system of the 1976 Convention. As mentioned earlier, oil pollution damage outside the territory or territorial sea of a Contracting State and all damage suffered in the territory or territorial sea of a non-Contracting State are not governed by the 1969 Convention. Even if an action for compensation for such damage is brought in a State party to both the 1976 and the 1969 Conventions, the liability will not be subject to limitation under either Convention. Also, in the case of a claim for compensation which is brought in a non-Contracting State to the 1976 Convention, such as the action of the French Government in the *Amoco Cadiz* incident, the limitation system of the 1976 Convention will not be applicable. In brief, in cases where oil pollution damage as defined in the 1969 Convention would not result in a liability governed by this Convention, such liability will not be subject to limitation neither under the 1976 nor the 1969 Conventions.

---

(1) See *supra*, Chapter V, section (iii).
(2) See *supra*, Chapter V, section (iii).

(b) Article 17(4) states: "The Courts of a State Party shall not apply this Convention to ships constructed for, or adapted to, and engaged in drilling: (a) when that State has established under its national legislation a higher limit of liability than that otherwise provided for in Article 6; or (b) when that State has become Party to an international Convention regulating the system of liability in respect of such ships".

(c) Article 17(5)(b) excludes floating platforms constructed for the purpose of exploring or exploiting the national resources of the sea-bed or the sub-soil thereof.

## Claims for oil pollution damage in the United States

The *Amoco Cadiz* case before the American courts raised comments that the US is a "forum shopping" and its legal rules lead to opening a "floodgate" of litigation. In principle, a claim for compensation as a result of oil pollution damage may be based on tort, trespass or nuisance. In *Burgess* v. *M/V Tamano*(1), it was said that an individual could recover in tort for invasion of public rights only if he had suffered damage different in kind from that sustained by the public generally. The injury of which the fishermen complained had resulted from the defendants' interference with their direct exercise of the public right to fish. It would be an incongruous result to hold that a man engaged in commercial fishing and dependent thereon for his livelihood, would be denied any rights to recover for his loss on the ground that his injury was no different in kind from that sustained by the general public. A different situation pertains for businessmen who complained only of loss of customers, indirectly resulting from pollution of the coastal waters and beaches, in which they did not have a proprietary interest. Although, in some instances, their damage might be greater in degree, the injury they suffered, which was different from the public at large, was common to all business and residents of the area.

---

(1) 370 F. Supp. (D.Me.1973). See also *Union Oil Co.* v. *Oppen* (1975) A.M.C. 416, where it was held that commercial fishermen might recover damages for loss of profit due to the reduction of fishing caused by oil spillage.

The 1851 Limitation Act gives the owner the right to limit his liability(1) to the value of the ship at the termination of the voyage. Where the ship is lost or damaged, the Act limits the owner's liability to its diminished or salvage value(2).

<u>The Water Pollution Control Act (WPCA), 1972</u>: The Act modified and incorporated some of the provisions of the Water Quality Improvement Act (WQIA), 1970, and added certain protective rules(3). It states that the owner or operator of any vessel which discharges oil or a hazardous substance in violation of its provisions, is liable(4) to the Federal Government for the cost of clean-up to an amount not exceeding $100 per gross ton or $14 million, whichever is lesser. The exceptions allowed under the Act are: (a) act of God; (b) act of war; (c) negligence on the part of the US Government; and (d) act or omission of a third party(5). The limit was increased to $150 per gross ton and the ceiling of

---

(1) The United States is not yet party to the CLC.
(2) In *Matter of Thebes Shipping Co.*, the US District Court for Southern district of New York held on February 7, 1980, that the shipowner was not entitled to limitation of liability for damages resulting from the foundering of the *Argo Merchant* on the ground that the ship was unsafe. The Judge added that: "although there were frequent superficial repairs in various ports, there was no thorough-going systematic effort to prevent the use of worn-out and obsolete equipment. The causes of the grounding were general mismanagement and neglect by the owner, combined with navigation errors of the officers..." Lloyd's Maritime Newsletter, Issue No.9, 1980, p.3.
(3) The Act extended the clean-up liability to discharges of other hazardous substances. The Act was further amended by the Clean Water Act of 1977, 33 U.S.C. 1251-1376.
(4) The liability is for the actual costs of removal and not for the "reasonable" costs. See *U.S.* v. *Beatty Inc.*, 401 F.Suppl. 1040 (W.D.Ky. 1975).
(5) 33 U.S.C., s.1321 (f)(1). The provisions of this Act are the basis for most of the Coast Guard's marine environmental activities. Under it the Coast Guard has placed into effect pollution prevention regulations which provide for equipment requirements, operating procedures and

$14 million was removed by the Clean Water Act of 1977[1].

The Act provides that the limits apply only when the spill was caused without wilful negligence or misconduct within the privity and knowledge of the owner[2]. It also gives the Federal Government the right to remove spillage of oil or hazardous substances and establishes a $35 million fund to carry out the duties of cleaning-up. The Government may proceed directly against any insurer or other person holding a financial security on behalf of an owner[3].

The State and Federal Acts: When the State of Florida passed the 1970 Oil Spill Prevention and Pollution Control Act (a State Act), it was challenged by the shipping interests in *Askew v. American Waterways Operators*[4]. The District Court held that the State Act was unconstitutional as it conflicted with federal maritime law-making powers. However, the Supreme Court reversed this decision and said that it would not be proper "to allow

---

training of personnel.

(1) 33 U.S.C., § 1321 (g) (Supp.1978).

(2) In the *Ocean Eagle* (1974) A.C. 1629, the owner failed to limit his liability because he knew prior to the commencement of the voyage that the ship was overloaded and did not have manuals to assist in determining the stress created by the distribution of the cargo. See also *Complaint of Tug Ocean Price Inc.* (1978) A.M.C. 1786 (2 d Cir.).

(3) See also The Trans-Alaska Pipeline Authorization Act, 1973, Pub. L. No.93-153. The provisions of the Act apply to "oil that has been transported through the trans-Alaska pipeline" and to vessels operating "between the terminal facilities of the pipeline and ports under the jurisdiction of the United States". The Act holds the owner liable for all damages, clean-up costs sustained by any person or entity, public or private, including residents of Canada, as a result of discharges of oil. A fund of $100m was set up to compensate US citizens or West Coast Canadians suffering damages by a spill from a ship carrying oil that has passed through the Port Valdez, Alaska, terminal.

(4) 411 U.S. 325 (1973).

federal admiralty jurisdiction to swallow most of the police power of the States over oil spillage". The Court declined to decide on whether damage under the State Act would be subject to the 1851 Limitation of Liability Act.

This decision paved the way for any State to have her own Act beside the Federal Act and in fact many States such as Alaska, California, Florida, Maryland and New York passed acts to redress oil pollution damages incurred by the State or individuals.

Thus the WPCA(1) is a Federal Act under which the Federal Government can recoup the clean-up costs. It does not protect private claims nor claims by the State for clean-up costs and these are left to the State Act(2). Consequently, the scope and the protection afforded by the Federal and the State Acts are different(3). It is clear that if

---

(1) The Act makes it clear that it is not to affect or modify in any way the obligations of owners or operators of the vessel to any other person or agency for damages to any public or privately owned property resulting from discharge of oil or for removal of oil, nor is the Act to be construed as affecting the right of any State with respect to the discharge of oil in her waters. See U.S.C., s.1321 (o).

(2) An owner can limit his liability against the State and private claims. See *Complaint of Habor Towing Corp.* (1972) A.M.C. 597; *Portland Pipe Line Corp.* v. *Environmental Improvement Commission* (1973) A.M.C. 1341. See also re *Oswego Barge Corp.* and re *Stewart Transport Co.*, J. of Maritime Law & Commerce, Vol.9, No.3, p.397.

(3) However, the interaction of these Acts with the Limitation Act of 1851 gives rise to difficult problems. The following example illustrates how these Acts work together. Suppose a ship of 10,000 tons caused pollution damage and the cost of the Federal clean-up reached $1½ million. Under the WQIA, the vessel is liable to the extent of $1 million ($100 per ton). If the value of the vessel after the incident is $400,000 and the anticipated freight is $100,000, this half million dollars will make up the fund for the other injured parties not the Federal Government. Thus, Federal clean-up claims are the only claims protected against the limitation (but within its ceiling) as the WQIA and limitation are fully independent.

the owners of an oil polluting vessel are able to limit their liability under the 1851 Act, the recovery of State and private claimants would be affected. However, "privity and knowledge" could be established more easily under American law by, for instance, invoking the concept of unseaworthiness, i.e. to some defect in the vessel or equipment, and consequently avoid the limitation.

## 2. THE INTERNATIONAL CONVENTION ON THE ESTABLISHMENT OF AN INTERNATIONAL FUND FOR COMPENSATION FOR OIL POLLUTION DAMAGE, 1971

At the end of the International Legal Conference on Marine Pollution Damage held in Brussels from November 10-29, 1969, a Resolution was adopted requesting the IMO to convene an international legal conference for the consideration and adoption of a scheme to compensate victims of oil pollution unable to obtain full compensation under the CLC. Such a conference was held in Brussels from November 29-December 18, 1971, and resulted in the adoption of an international Convention on the Establishment of an International Fund for Compensation for Oil Pollution Damage, simply called the "Fund Convention" or the "IOPC Fund".

Close links exist between the CLC and the Fund Convention[(1)], the former establishes the shipowner's liability while the latter provides for supplementary compensation from the cargo-owner.

The Fund Convention came into force[(2)] in October, 1978[(3)]. In May, 1984, a Protocol to amend

---

(1) LEG XLIV/4.

(2) At the time of writing, the Convention has been ratified by the following States: Algeria, Bahamas, Denmark, Fiji, Finland, France, Gabon, Federal Republic of Germany, Ghana, Iceland, Indonesia, Italy, Japan, Kuwait, Liberia, Maldives, Monaco, The Netherlands, Norway, Papua New Guinea, Spain, Sri Lanka, Sweden, Syrian Arab Republic, Tunisia, Tuvalu, United Kingdom and Yugoslavia.

(3) The Contract regarding an Interim Supplement to Tanker Liability for Oil Pollution damage (Cristal) fulfils the same function as that of the Fund Convention. It supplements the compensation for pollution damage made available by a tanker owner under Tovalop, CLC and other

the Convention was adopted(1) in order "to provide for improved scope and enhanced compensation"(2). The Protocol(3) will enter into force twelve months after being accepted by at least eight States whose combined total of contributing oil amounted to at least 600 million tons during the previous calendar year (art.30 of the Protocol).

---

regimes.
At the first Extraordinary Session of the Assembly of the Fund held in October,1980, it was mentioned that non-Contracting States have certain doubts whether the ratification of the Fund Convention was advisable since Cristal provided a comparable cover. Contributions to Cristal were to be paid by their companies even if the State becomes a Member of the Fund. One delegation observed that the existence of Cristal after the entry into force of the Fund Convention was no longer required and asked States to encourage their oil companies to withdraw membership of Cristal.
Other delegations explained that it was necessary that Cristal went on providing cover for incidents which were not covered by the Fund Convention such as damages occurring in non-Member States and expenses for threat removal measures, and that it was for the companies to decide on their own whether or not continued membership in Cristal was in their interest.
In view of the increase in the limitation amount, a new scheme called Pollution Liability Agreement between Tanker Owners (PLATO) is under consideration by the oil companies. It will come into effect in March,1986 if fifty million tonnes deadweight of tankers sign up. INTERTANKO opposed the PLATO proposal and preferred updating Tovalop and the revision of Cristal.

(1) LEG/CONF. 6/67, 25 May, 1984.

(2) See the preamble to the Protocol.

(3) The "tacit acceptance" procedure has been introduced into the Protocol. It also makes provisions for denunciation by Contracting Parties. If another Contracting Party considers that such a denunciation may significantly increase the level of contributions to the Fund of other Contracting Parties, it may request the Director of the fund to convene an extraordinary session of the Assembly. The Director is also entitled to convene such a session on his own

The transitional period, during which both the 1971 Fund and the new Fund are in existence, will end twelve months after this figure has reached 750 million tons (art.31 of the Protocol).

<u>The Fund objectives</u>: The Fund has two objectives(1): firstly, to allow any person suffering pollution damage to have full and adequate compensation in case he has been unable to obtain it under the CLC, and secondly, to indemnify shipowners of part of their liabilities or, in the words of the 1984 Protocol, "to give effect to the related purposes set out" in it (art.3 of the Protocol).

<u>Providing full and adequate compensation</u>: The case of full and adequate compensation applies only to "pollution damage" and preventive measures taken to minimize or to prevent such damage caused on the territory or on the territorial sea of a State party to both CLC and the Fund Convention (art.3.1). The Protocol widens the scope of the application of the Fund Convention so as to cover pollution damage in the territory, the territorial sea or the Exclusive Economic Zone (EEZ) of a Contracting State. In the absence of an EEZ, the application of the provisions of the Convention to an area of 200 nautical miles. Furthermore, the Protocol extends the application of the provisions of the Convention to preventive measures, wherever taken, to prevent or minimize such damage (art.3 of the Protocol).

Article 4(1) states:

"For the purpose of fulfilling its function under Article 2, paragraph 1(a), the Fund shall pay compensation to any person suffering pollution damage if such person has been unable to obtain full and adequate compensation for the damage under the terms of the Liability Convention.

(a) because no liability for the damage arises under the Liability Convention."

Accordingly, the compensation paid out of the Fund would be available where (a) the damage resulted from a natural phenomenon of an exceptional,

---

initiative.

(1) A third objective which has not been exercised, is to assist a Member State to take preventive measures against pollution damage by giving advice or providing financial or technical aid.

inevitable or irresistible character; (b) the damage was wholly caused by an act or omission done with intent to cause damage by a third party; and (c) was wholly caused by the negligence or other wrongful act of the government or other authority responsible for the maintenance of lights or other navigational aids.

Article 4(1)(b) provides for the second situation where a person is unable to obtain full and adequate compensation. That is "because the owner liable for the damage under the Liability Convention is financially incapable of meeting his obligations in full..." An example of such a situation is the case where the owner becomes insolvent.

The third situation is stated under (c) where the "damage exceeds the owner's liability under the Liability Convention as limited pursuant to Article V, paragraph 1, of that Convention or under the terms of any other international convention". Thus, where a ship flying a flag of a State which is not party to the CLC but to the 1957 Convention and the oil escaped or discharged caused pollution damage to a State which is party to both the CLC and the Fund Convention, the Fund will supplement the compensation over the limits of the 1957 Convention.

Article 4 states that: "expenses reasonably incurred or sacrifices reasonably made by the owner voluntarily to prevent or minimize pollution damage shall be treated as pollution damage for the purposes of this Article."

The Fund, however, is not liable in two cases:

(a) where the pollution damage resulted from an act of war, hostilities, civil war or insurrection; and

(b) where the pollution damage was caused by warships or vessels owned by a State and used for non-commercial purposes (art. 4,2,a).

Furthermore, Article 4(3) provides for partial or complete exoneration in cases of the contributory negligence or intentional causative act of the claimant[1].

---

(1) Para.3 of article 4 was replaced in the 1984 Protocol by the following text:
"If the Fund proves that the pollution damage resulted wholly or partially either from an act

<u>Providing relief or "roll back" the limit of shipowner's liabilities:</u> Shipowners whose ships are registered in a State party to both the CLC and the Fund Convention can only obtain the relief provided for in Article 5. However, the damage need not have happened in a State party to both these conventions. It is sufficient that it happened in the territory or territorial waters of a State party to the CLC.

Article 5(1) states that the Fund shall indemnify the owner and his guarantor for a portion of his liability under the CLC. The limit of indemnification payable by the IOPC Fund is 500 (gold) francs (US $35), or 85 million (gold) francs (US $6 million), whichever is the less[(1)].

The Fund may not be liable where:

(a) the pollution damage resulted from the wilful misconduct of the owner himself; or

(b) as a result of the actual fault or privity of the owner, the ship did not comply with the Convention for the Prevention of Pollution of the Sea by Oil, 1954, as amended in 1962, the SOLAS Convention, the Load Line Convention and the Collision Regulations 1972, and that the incident or the damage was caused wholly or partially by such non-compliance.

<u>The compensation limits:</u> The aggregate amount of compensation payable[(2)] by the Fund was originally 450 million francs. It was raised to 675 million francs (about $47.7 million) and the higher amount has been applied to incidents occurring after

---

or omission done with the intent to cause damage by the person who suffered the damage or from the negligence of that person. The Fund may be exonerated wholly or partially from its obligation to pay compensation to such person, the Fund shall in any event be exonerated to the extent that the shipowner may have been exonerated under Article III, paragraph 3 of the 1984 Liability Convention. However, there shall be no such exoneration of the Fund with regard to preventive measures."

(1) The 1984 Protocol abolished this function because it restored the balance of liability between the shipping and oil industries.

(2) The time limit for actions against the Fund is three years from the date of damage.

April 20, 1979[(1)].

The Protocol adopts a two-tier system. The basic coverage available from the Fund provides a maximum of 135 million SDRs (about $140 million). This includes the amount of compensation actually paid under the CLC.

The maximum compensation available will rise to 200 million SDRs (about $208 million) when there are three Parties to the Convention whose contributing oil amounts to at least 600 million tons[(2)].

It must be noted that the amounts mentioned above will be converted into national currency on the basis of the value of that currency by reference to the SDR on the date of the decision of the Assembly of the Fund as to the first date of payment of compensation.

Where the amount of established claims against the Fund exceeds the aggregate amount of compensation, the amount available will be distributed in such a manner that the proportion between any established claim and the amount of compensation actually recovered by the claimant will be the same for all claimants (art.6, para.4 of the Protocol).

In exceptional cases, the Assembly of the Fund may decide that compensation will be paid to the victims despite the fact that the owner has failed to constitute a fund in accordance with the CLC (art.6, para.5 of the 1984 Protocol).

On payment of the compensation, the Fund acquires by the right of subrogation all the rights against the owner or his guarantor (art.11 of the Protocol).

---

(1) According to a resolution adopted by the Assembly of IOPC at its first session, the term "franc" is to be converted into national currencies in a way which follows the method adopted by the Protocol of November 19, 1976, to the Fund Convention. Accordingly, 15 francs equal one Special Drawing Right and the conversion of the Special Drawing Right is made in accordance with the method of evaluation applied by the International Monetary Fund in effect on the date in question for its operations and transactions.

(2) Since the USA contributing oil approximates 450m tons per year, the USA ratification would virtually assure bringing the higher limit.

<u>Contributions to the Fund</u>: Importers of oil who <u>have received[1] in total</u> quantities exceeding

---

(1) In the first extraordinary session of the Assembly of the Fund held on Oct. 8-10, 1980, it approved the interpretation of art. 10.1:
(a) Discharge of oil into a floating tank within the territorial waters of a Contracting State (including its ports) constitutes a receipt of oil irrespective of whether the tank is connected with on-shore installations via pipeline or not. Ships are considered to be floating tanks in this connection only if they are "dead" ships, i.e., if they are not ready to sail.
(b) Traffic within a port area shall not be considered as carriage by sea.
(c) Ship-to-ship transfer shall not be considered as receipt, irrespective of where this transfer takes place (i.e. within a port area or outside the port but within territorial waters) and whether it is done solely by using the ship's equipment or by means of a pipeline passing over land. This applies for a transfer between two sea-going vessels as well as for a transfer between a sea-going vessel and an internal waterway vessel and irrespective of whether the transfer takes place within or outside a port area. When the oil, after having been transferred in this way from a sea-going vessel to another vessel has been carried by the latter to an on-shore installation situated in the same Contracting State or in another Contracting State, the receipt in that installation shall be considered as a receipt of oil carried by sea. However, in the case where the oil passes through a storage tank before being loaded to the other ship it has to be reported as oil received at that tank in that Contracting State.

With regard to the question of which person has to be included in the report as the "receiver" of oil, the Assembly agreed that, within the scope of Article 10 of the Fund Convention, Contracting States should have a certain flexibility to adopt a practical reporting system allowing an effective and easy checking of the figures and taking into account the peculiarit-

150,000 tons during a calendar year[1], contribute to the Fund[2]. Contracting States transmit to the Fund the names and addresses of the persons who are liable to make contribution and the quantity of oil in respect of which they are so liable.

Thus, the Assembly of the Fund decides the total amount of contribution to be levied[3]. On the basis of that decision, the Director of the Fund calculates for each oil trader the amount of his annual contribution. The IOPC Fund does not collect a fixed premium but assesses the amount required in

---

ies of the oil movement and the local circumstances of a particular country and that, failing payment by persons reported other than the physical receivers, the physical receivers should ultimately be liable for contributions irrespective of whether the persons reported have their place of business or residence in a Contracting State or not. It was agreed that this interpretation of the Fund Convention should not lead to amendments of previous reports on contributing oil receipts and is only to be taken into consideration for future reports. The Director was asked to include the decisions in the explanatory notes attached to the forms for contributing oil receipts.

(1) The place of loading is irrelevant.

(2) During the preparation of the 1984 Protocol, some delegations voiced their dissatisfaction with the system of the contributions to the Fund which is based on oil import total. The Indonesian delegation called for a more balanced and fair system. In their view, the assessment of contributions should take into account factors such as the country's risk of massive pollution damage, density of shipping traffic, tanker tonnage owned, etc. They noted that some Fund Members pay nothing at all, yet they enjoy full rights of access to the benefits. Therefore, they proposed that those Fund Members not liable for contribution under article 10, should make a minimum annual payment. The Indonesian proposal ran into opposition as it was considered to be vague and impracticable. Most delegations believed that while the existing system was not perfect, it was fair and workable.

(3) There are initial and annual contributions. Initial contributions are due when a State becomes a Member of the Fund Convention. They

the light of the incidents which have occurred, the expected claims and for the administration of the Fund(1).

Article 16 of the 1984 Protocol states that: "Where a Contracting State does not fulfil its obligation to submit to the Director the communication ... and this results in a financial loss for the Fund, that Contracting State shall be liable to compensate the Fund for such loss ..."

Structure of the IOPC Fund: The IOPC Fund has three organs: an Assembly, an Executive Committee and a Secretariat.

The Assembly is the supreme organ and consists of all Members. It appoints the Director, approves the budget and decides the total amount of contributions to be levied. The Assembly meets at least once a year.

The Executive Committee was set up to carry out the functions of the Assembly in its absence and in particular to settle the disputes. However, the frequent change in its membership prevented it from carrying out its tasks effectively. Therefore, the 1984 Protocol abolished it.

It must be noted that under article 18 of the Fund Convention, the Assembly may "establish any temporary or permanent subsidiary body it may consider to be necessary" and this reference has been expanded in the Protocol by giving the Assembly powers "to define its terms of reference and to give it the authority needed to perform functions entrusted to it". The Protocol also emphasizes the importance of securing an adequate geographic representation on the body and ensuring that the largest contributors are appropriately represented.

The head of the Secretariat is the Director,

---

are calculated on the basis of 0.04718 (gold) francs (US $0.003) per tonne of contributing oil received by each contributor. If there is no-one who has received contributing oil exceeding 150,000 tonnes in the year preceding that in which the State becomes a Member of the Fund Convention, no initial contributions from the State will be due.

(1) After the annual contribution is fixed, the Director issues an invoice to each person liable to it. Annual contributions are due on 15 January of the year following that in which the Assembly decides to levy contributions.

who is the chief administrative officer of the Fund. He is assisted by a small number of staff. In principle their work is governed by the provision of the Fund Convention, the Interval Regulations adopted by the Assembly and the instructions of the Assembly, although the Director enjoys wide powers in the settlement of claims.

Handling the claims: Since February 13, 1979, the IOPC started to handle claims(1) for oil pollution damage. Decisions have been taken in each incident and a careful study of these cases gives some indication of the policy adopted by the Fund on certain claims. Procedures were set up for provisional payment (internal regulations 8.6-6.8); for payment before the commencement of the limitation of liability under article V(1) of the CLC; and for payment in respect of the agreed items without waiting for the investigation on the rest of the claim.

In the early years, the Fund relied heavily upon the P & I Clubs in the settlement of claims. Surveyors and lawyers were appointed on behalf of both the Fund and the Club. Negotiations for the settlement of disputes were usually carried out jointly by the two bodies. In 1980, the Memorandum of Understanding between the Fund and the International Group of P & I Clubs laid down the terms of co-operation. It provided for exchange of views and consultation when considering pollution damage of each incident.

More recently, the Fund started to develop its own rules on fishing claims, loss of profit to hoteliers(2), restaurant owners, loss of tax revenues from diminution of income of persons and businesses in a town dependent on tourism(3), and ecological damage.

Fishermen's claims: A good illustration of the formulation of new methods for calculation of compensation for damage is to be found in the case of fishermen(4). Firstly, the quantity of fish has to

---

(1) See Appendix V which covers the claims settled by the Fund.
(2) The Tanio claim, Appendix V.
(3) This claim was not accepted; the Tanio claim, Appendix V.
(4) The IOPC Fund has issued a "Claims Manual" in which basic information on how to present a claim is explained.

be ascertained and this could be reached by deducting the quantity of fish sold in the year which pollution happened from the average catch sold in the preceding years (the average is taken from two and up to five years). Secondly, the damage to the polluted area has to be measured in terms of percentage, i.e. 1/2, 1/3, 2/3, etc. Thirdly, the price of the sea products before the pollution damage must be ascertained. Fourthly, the average costs incurred by fishermen after selling their fish has to be found. So by multiplying the average of these four times, namely: the quantity of fish; extent of the damage to the area; average market price; and average costs after selling, then compensation for damage to fishermen could be ascertained.

Costs: The thorny problem which causes much discomfort to the Fund is "costs" and for its own convenience, it is divided into two categories: additional and fixed costs.

Additional costs cover the following:

(a) the price paid to the contractors for cleaning-up, the salaries and allowances for personnel employed to deal with the spill;

(b) costs of materials bought to deal with the spill, and depreciation of these materials;

(c) insurance premiums to carry out the above operations and tasks;

(d) costs of removal of the oil collected; and

(e) taxes, duties and fees which may be imposed.

The fixed costs cover:

(a) salaries and allowances for personnel permanently employed by the authorities(1) and capital costs for the equipment;

---

(1) See *Maritime Services Board of N.S.W.* v. *Posiden Navigation (The World Encouragement and Stolt Sheaf)* Supreme Ct. N.S.W. Australia, LMLN 71, 22 July, 1982, where the Maritime Services Board undertook the cleaning-up operations and submitted itemised bills for the costs to the owners of the ship. The latter admitted liability but contested the right of the Board to

(b) insurance costs; and

(c) taxes, duties and fees likely to be imposed.

The *Antonio Gransci*[1] settlement indicates that the Fund accepts the additional costs but is not willing to take the same position with respect to fixed costs.

Ecological damage: Claims for items such as "global ecological damage" and "loss of enjoyment of coastal area" could be admissible only if the claimant had suffered a direct quantifiable economic loss. The Fund Assembly passed a Resolution[2] on October 10, 1980, that the assessment of compensation paid by the Fund would not be made "on the basis of an abstract quantification or damage calculated in accordance with theoretical models". Furthermore, the Assembly's Fifth International Working Group reached the conclusion that compensation for environmental damage could be claimed: "only if a claimant having a legal right to claim under national law had suffered quantifiable economic loss. States suffering pollution damage were, of course, entitled to restore the environment by cleaning the water and beaches but the possible remaining effect of the oil on the marine environment could not lead to a claim for compensation if it did not have any effect on economic interests. It would be impossible to identify the person having a legal right for such a claim if no such interests were affected."

Wildlife: Another related issue is the damge to wildlife, as it is difficult to assess and there are

---

charge for its equipment and permanent employees. These arguments were that the words "expenses" and "costs" in the Australian Act refer to those paid to other. The Court said the Board was entitled to calculate the actual costs of it using its own employees, including overheads and administration charges, as well as the actual cost of using its own plant. Accordingly a port authority or a council is entitled to charge for using its men and machines in cleaning-up operations.

(1) The *Antonio Gransci* grounded on February 27, 1979, off the Soviet Union, spilling 5,500 tons of crude oil.

(2) Fund/A.4/10. July 15, 1981, Annex, p.7.

no proprietary interests involved. In fact, two problems have to be solved:

(a) who owns the wildlife? or who can assert a claim to ownership of wildlife?[1] and

(b) how can compensation be assessed?

On the second point the difficulty is to assess damage to wildlife in terms of money. An American court could not see such difficulty and in *Commonwealth of Puerto Rico et al* v. *S.S. Zoe Colocotroni*[2] it was held that the shipowner would be liable for the cost reasonably to be incurred by the sovereign or its designated agency to restore or rehabilitate the environment in the affected area to its pre-existing condition, or as close thereto as is feasible without grossly disproportionate expenditures.

---

(1) Some scholars invoke concepts of international law and in particular the trusteeship or the quasi-sovereign rights of the State while others rely on rules of national law to establish ownership of wildlife.
Under the trustee concept, the State is the trustee and the public is the beneficiary. The State as a trustee can claim compensation on the ground of her duty to protect and preserve wildlife. The weakness of this concept lies in the fact that the State holds sovereign interest only and not a proprietary interest. Furthermore, the trusteeship concept is not universally accepted by States. Since the rules of international law offer very little help, scholars turn to the rules of municipal law on the ownership of wildlife. Obviously these rules differ from one country to another. Under English law, wildlife birds are ownerless unless they are too young to move away or have been tamed. The landowner, or the person to whom he has granted sporting rights, has the exclusive right to catch them or to take eggs, whereupon they become his property. The Wild Creatures and Forest Laws Act, 1971, abolished any prerogative right of the Crown to wild creatures. However, white swans, unmarked and in open rivers, belong to the Crown. See also the Wildlife and Countryside Act, 1981.

(2) (1980) 628 Fed: R. 2d. 652, US Ct. of App. 1st Circuit.

Fund

This case, which was governed by the local Puerto Rican legislation, carries very little weight. In fact, several ideas based on economic principles were advocated to assist the court in determining the compensation for wild and marine life. According to the replacement value test, the compensation would be based on the estimated cost of replacing the birds. Factors to be taken into account are the time needed to replace the birds and the type of birds which could be difficult to replace.

The ecological and environmental test is based on repairing the harm done to the environment and compensating for the loss of enjoyment of birdlife and marshland. Therefore compensation could be assessed on various propositions such as the contribution made by the public for previous appeals to preserve wildlife. The difficulty with all these tests is the absence of quantification(1). One may conclude that it is too early to say that the Fund has established certain principles in the settlement of disputes. The decided incidents by the IOPC Fund give some indication of what seems to be acceptable for compensation. They may also be considered as a starting point for the development of rules on the settlement of oil pollution damage disputes.

---

(1) At the session held in October, 1980, the Oil Pollution Fund Assembly took the following resolution:
"Confirms its intention that the assessment of compensation to be paid by the International Oil Pollution Compensation Fund is not to be made on the basis of an abstract quantification of damage calculated in accordance with theoretical models."

## References

Bates, John. United Kingdom Marine Pollution Law. Lloyd's of London Press, 1985.

Boehmer, Christiansen. Dumping Nuclear Waste into the Sea, International Control and the Role of Science and Law. Marine Policy, No.1, Jan.,1983, pp. 25-36.

Brown, E.D., The International Oil Pollution Compensation Fund: an analytical report on fund practice. Oil & Petrochemical Pollution, Vol.1, No.4, p.269.

Code of Good Management Practice in Safe Ship Operation, 1981, published by the ICS and the International Shipping Federation.

Ganten, R., Oil Pollution Liability. Oil and Petrochemical Pollution, Vol.2, No.1, 1984, p.13.

Guidelines on the Provision of Adequate Reception Facilities in Ports: Part I (Oily Wastes). IMO Publication No.280, 77.02.E. Part II (Residues and Mixtures Containing Noxious Liquid Substances). IMO Publication No. 582, 80.03.E. Part III (Sewage) and Part IV (Garbage). IMO Publication No.584, 78.12.E.

Hayward, P., Environmental Protection: Regional Approaches. Marine Policy, April,1984, pp. 106-119.

International Environmental Law, edited by Ludwick A. Teclaff and Albert E. Utton. Praeger Publishers, New York.

Marine Safety Council (US) MARPOL 73/78, Proceedings 160 (June,1984).

Mensah, Thomas. Environmental Protection: International approaches. Marine Policy, April,1984, pp. 95-105.

Resolution A.544(13) "Standards for Procedures and Arrangements called for by Annex II of the International Convention for the Prevention of Pollution from Ships, 1973, as modified by the Protocol of 1978 relating thereto" (document MEPC 18/18/Add.1, Annex 3). These Standards will be available from the IMO in publication form in late 1984.

Recommendation on International Effluent Standards and Guidelines for Performance Tests on Sewage Treatment Plants. IMO Publication No. 592,

Fund

77.03.E (English); 593 77.03.F (French).

Schachtu, O. & Sermer, D., Marine Pollution Problems and Remedies. American Journal of International Law, Vol.65, 1971, p.111.

Silverstone, Deana, Ship Source Oil Pollution Damage. Marine Policy, April,1985, pp. 108-119.

Tanker Safety Guide (Chemicals), four volumes published by ICS.

United States Environmental Protection Agency, Office of Planning and Management, D.C., several reports.

# APPENDICES

## Appendix I

### MEMBERSHIP OF THE ORGANIZATION AS AT 31 MARCH,1985

| Members | Date of receipt of the instrument of acceptance |
|---|---|
| ALGERIA | 31 October,1963 |
| ANGOLA | 6 June,1977 |
| ARGENTINA | 18 June,1953 |
| AUSTRALIA | 13 February,1952 |
| AUSTRIA | 2 April,1975 |
| BAHAMAS | 22 July,1976 |
| BAHRAIN | 22 September,1976 |
| BANGLADESH | 27 May,1976 |
| BARBADOS | 7 January,1970 |
| BELGIUM | 9 August,1951 |
| BENIN | 19 March,1980 |
| BRAZIL | 4 March,1963 |
| BRUNEI DARUSSALAM | 31 December,1984 |
| BULGARIA | 5 April,1960 |
| BURMA | 6 July,1951 |
| CAMEROON | 1 May,1961 |
| CANADA | 15 October,1948 |
| CAPE VERDE | 24 August,1976 |
| CHILE | 17 February,1972 |
| CHINA | 1 March,1973 |
| COLOMBIA | 19 November,1974 |
| CONGO | 5 September,1975 |
| COSTA RICA | 4 March,1981 |
| CUBA | 6 May,1966 |
| CYPRUS | 21 November,1973 |
| CZECHOSLOVAKIA | 1 October,1963 |
| DEMOCRATIC KAMPUCHEA | 3 January,1961 |
| DEMOCRATIC YEMEN | 2 June,1980 |
| DENMARK | 3 June,1959 |
| DJIBOUTI | 20 February,1979 |
| DOMINICA | 18 December,1979 |
| DOMINICAN REPUBLIC | 25 August,1953 |
| ECUADOR | 12 July,1956 |
| EGYPT | 17 March,1958 |
| EL SALVADOR | 12 February,1981 |
| EQUATORIAL GUINEA | 6 September,1972 |
| ETHIOPIA | 3 July,1975 |
| FIJI | 14 March,1983 |
| FINLAND | 21 April,1959 |
| FRANCE | 9 April,1952 |
| GABON | 1 April,1976 |
| GAMBIA | 11 January,1979 |
| GERMAN DEMOCRATIC REPUBLIC | 25 September,1973 |

| Members | Date of receipt of the instrument of acceptance |
|---|---|
| GERMANY, FEDERAL REPUBLIC OF | 7 January, 1959 |
| GHANA | 6 July, 1959 |
| GREECE | 31 December, 1958 |
| GUATEMALA | 16 March, 1983 |
| GUINEA | 3 December, 1975 |
| GUINEA-BISSAU | 6 December, 1977 |
| GUYANA | 13 May, 1980 |
| HAITI | 23 June, 1953 |
| HONDURAS | 23 August, 1954 |
| HUNGARY | 10 June, 1970 |
| ICELAND | 3 November, 1960 |
| INDIA | 6 January, 1959 |
| INDONESIA | 18 January, 1961 |
| IRAN (ISLAMIC REPUBLIC OF) | 2 January, 1958 |
| IRAQ | 28 August, 1973 |
| IRELAND | 26 February, 1951 |
| ISRAEL | 24 April, 1952 |
| ITALY | 28 January, 1957 |
| IVORY COAST | 4 November, 1960 |
| JAMAICA | 11 May, 1976 |
| JAPAN | 17 March, 1958 |
| JORDAN | 9 November, 1973 |
| KENYA | 22 August, 1973 |
| KUWAIT | 5 July, 1960 |
| LEBANON | 3 May, 1966 |
| LIBERIA | 6 January, 1959 |
| LIBYAN ARAB JAMAHIRIYA | 16 February, 1970 |
| MADAGASCAR | 8 March, 1961 |
| MALAYSIA | 17 June, 1971 |
| MALDIVES | 31 May, 1967 |
| MALTA | 22 June, 1966 |
| MAURITANIA | 8 May, 1961 |
| MAURITIUS | 18 May, 1978 |
| MEXICO | 21 September, 1954 |
| MOROCCO | 30 July, 1962 |
| MOZAMBIQUE | 17 January, 1979 |
| NEPAL | 31 January, 1979 |
| NETHERLANDS | 31 March, 1949 |
| NEW ZEALAND | 9 November, 1960 |
| NICARAGUA | 17 March, 1982 |
| NIGERIA | 15 March, 1962 |
| NORWAY | 29 December, 1958 |
| OMAN | 30 January, 1974 |
| PAKISTAN | 21 November, 1958 |
| PANAMA | 31 December, 1958 |
| PAPUA NEW GUINEA | 6 May, 1976 |
| PERU | 15 April, 1968 |

Appendix I

| Members | Date of receipt of the instrument of acceptance |
|---|---|
| PHILIPPINES | 9 November, 1964 |
| POLAND | 16 March, 1960 |
| PORTUGAL | 17 March, 1976 |
| QATAR | 19 May, 1977 |
| REPUBLIC OF KOREA | 10 April, 1962 |
| ROMANIA | 28 April, 1965 |
| SAINT LUCIA | 10 April, 1980 |
| SAINT VINCENT AND THE GRENADINES | 29 April, 1981 |
| SAUDI ARABIA | 25 February, 1969 |
| SENEGAL | 7 November, 1960 |
| SEYCHELLES | 13 June, 1978 |
| SIERRA LEONE | 14 March, 1973 |
| SINGAPORE | 17 January, 1966 |
| SOMALIA | 4 April, 1978 |
| SPAIN | 23 January, 1962 |
| SRI LANKA | 6 April, 1972 |
| SUDAN | 5 July, 1974 |
| SURINAME | 14 October, 1976 |
| SWEDEN | 27 April, 1959 |
| SWITZERLAND | 20 July, 1955 |
| SYRIAN ARAB REPUBLIC | 28 January, 1963 |
| THAILAND | 20 September, 1973 |
| TOGO | 20 June, 1983 |
| TRINIDAD AND TOBAGO | 27 April, 1965 |
| TUNISIA | 23 May, 1963 |
| TURKEY | 25 March, 1958 |
| UNION OF SOVIET SOCIALIST REPUBLICS | 24 December, 1958 |
| UNITED ARAB EMIRATES | 4 March, 1980 |
| UNITED KINGDOM OF GREAT BRITAIN AND NORTHERN IRELAND | 14 February, 1949 |
| UNITED REPUBLIC OF TANZANIA | 8 January, 1974 |
| UNITED STATES OF AMERICA | 17 August, 1950 |
| URUGUAY | 10 May, 1968 |
| VENEZUELA | 27 October, 1975 |
| VIET NAM | 12 June, 1984 |
| YEMEN | 14 March, 1979 |
| YUGOSLAVIA | 12 February, 1960 |
| ZAIRE | 16 August, 1973 |

| Associate Member | |
|---|---|
| HONG KONG | 7 June, 1967 |

## Appendix II

## NON-GOVERNMENTAL ORGANIZATIONS IN CONSULTATIVE STATUS

INTERNATIONAL CHAMBER OF SHIPPING (ICS)
INTERNATIONAL ORGANIZATION FOR STANDARDIZATION (ISO)
INTERNATIONAL SHIPPING FEDERATION LTD (ISF)
INTERNATIONAL ELECTROTECHNICAL COMMISSION (IEC)
INTERNATIONAL UNION OF MARINE INSURANCE (IUMI)
INTERNATIONAL CHAMBER OF COMMERCE (ICC)
INTERNATIONAL CONFEDERATION OF FREE TRADE UNIONS (ICFTU)
INTERNATIONAL ASSOCIATION OF LIGHTHOUSE AUTHORITIES (IALA)
INTERNATIONAL RADIO-MARITIME COMMITTEE (CIRM)
PERMANENT INTERNATIONAL ASSOCIATION OF NAVIGATION CONGRESSES (PIANC)
INTERNATIONAL FERTILIZER INDUSTRY ASSOCIATION (IFA)

jointly with

EUROPEAN NITROGEN PRODUCERS' ASSOCIATION (APEA)
INTERNATIONAL MARITIME COMMITTEE (CMI)
INTERNATIONAL ASSOCIATION OF PORTS AND HARBORS (IAPH)
THE BALTIC AND INTERNATIONAL MARITIME CONFERENCE (BIMCO)
INTERNATIONAL ASSOCIATION OF CLASSIFICATION SOCIETIES (IACS)
INTERNATIONAL LAW ASSOCIATION (ILA)
INTERNATIONAL CARGO HANDLING CO-ORDINATION ASSOCIATION (ICHCA)
EUROPEAN COUNCIL OF CHEMICAL MANUFACTURERS' FEDERATIONS (CEFIC)
LATIN AMERICAN SHIPOWNERS' ASSOCIATION (LASA)
OIL COMPANIES INTERNATIONAL MARINE FORUM (OCIMF)
EUROPEAN TUGOWNERS' ASSOCIATION (ETA)
INTERNATIONAL MARITIME PILOTS' ASSOCIATION (IMPA)
INTERNATIONAL SHIPOWNERS' ASSOCIATION (INSA)
ENGINEERING COMMITTEE ON OCEANIC RESOURCES (ECOR)
FRIENDS OF THE EARTH INTERNATIONAL (FOEI)
INSTITUTE OF INTERNATIONAL CONTAINER LESSORS (IICL)
INTERNATIONAL ASSOCIATION OF DRILLING CONTRACTORS (IADC)
INTERNATIONAL ASSOCIATION OF INSTITUTES OF NAVIGATION (IAIN)
INTERNATIONAL ASSOCIATION OF PRODUCERS OF INSURANCE AND REINSURANCE (BIPAR)
INTERNATIONAL COUNCIL OF MARINE INDUSTRY ASSOCIATIONS (ICOMIA)

Appendix II

INTERNATIONAL FEDERATION OF SHIPMASTERS' ASSOCIATIONS (IFSMA)
INTERNATIONAL LIFE-SAVING APPLIANCES MANUFACTURERS' ASSOCIATION (ILAMA)
INTERNATIONAL SALVAGE UNION (ISU)
OIL INDUSTRY INTERNATIONAL EXPLORATION AND PRODUCTION FORUM (E AND P FORUM)
ASSOCIATION OF WEST EUROPEAN SHIPBUILDERS (AWES) (on a provisional basis)
INTERNATIONAL ASSOCIATION OF INDEPENDENT TANKER OWNERS (INTERTANKO)
INTERNATIONAL GROUP OF P AND I ASSOCIATIONS (P AND I)
THE INTERNATIONAL TANKER OWNERS POLLUTION FEDERATION LTD (ITOPF)
INTERNATIONAL UNION FOR CONSERVATION OF NATURE AND NATURAL RESOURCES (IUCN)
ADVISORY COMMITTEE ON POLLUTION OF THE SEA (ACOPS)
SOCIETY OF INTERNATIONAL GAS TANKER AND TERMINAL OPERATORS LIMITED (SIGTTO)
INTERNATIONAL LIFEBOAT CONFERENCE (ILC) (on provisional basis)*

* Subject to final approval by the Assembly.

## Appendix III

## LIST OF CODES, GUIDELINES AND MANUALS

Anti Pollution Manual
Code for Dynamically Supported Craft (A.373 (X))
Code for the Construction and Equipment of Ships
Code for the Construction and Equipment of Ships Carrying Dangerous Chemicals in Bulk, known as the Bulk Chemical (BCH) Code
Code for Existing Ships Carrying Liquefied Gases in Bulk
Code of Mobile Offshore Drilling Units (MODU) (A.414 (XI))
Code for Portable Tanks and Road Tank Vehicles for the Carriage of Liquid Dangerous Goods in Ships
Code of Good Conduct for Deep-Sea Pilotage
Code of Safe Practice for Ships Carrying Timber Deck Cargoes, 1973 as amended in 1978
Code of Safe Practice for Solid Bulk Cargoes (BC) 1984
Code of Safety for Nuclear Merchant Ships (A.491 (XII))
Code of Safety for Diving Systems
Code of Safety on Special Purpose Ships (A.534 (13))
Code on Noise Levels on Board Ships (A.648 (XII))
FAO/ILO/IMO Document for Guidance for Fishermen's Training
Guidelines for Reporting Incidents Involving Dangerous Goods in Packaged Form
Guidelines for the Application of Principles of Safe Manning
Guidelines for Estimating Manoeuvring Performance in Ship Design
Guidelines for Surveys under Annex I of MARPOL 73/78
Guidelines on Emergency Towing Requirements for Tankers (A.535 (13))
Guidelines for Acceptance of Non-duplicated Rudder Actuators for Tankers, Chemical Tankers and Gas Carriers (A.467 (XII))
Guidelines on the Operational Procedures and Planning for VTS
Guide to Helicopter/Ship Operations
IMO/ILO Guidelines for Packing of Cargo in Freight Containers
IMO Search and Rescue Manual (A.439 (XI))
International Bulk Chemical (IBC) Code
International Code of Signals
International Gas Carrier (IGC) Code
International Maritime Dangerous Goods (IMDG) Code

Appendix III

International Safety Guide for Oil Tankers and Terminals (ISGOTT)
Manual on Oil Pollution
Medical First Aid Guide (MFAG) for Use in Accidents involving Dangerous Goods, 1982
Merchant Ship Search and Rescue Manual (Mersar) (A.229 (VII))

# Appendix IV

## GUIDELINES FOR VESSEL TRAFFIC SERVICES

### PREAMBLE

1. These guidelines describe only operational procedures and planning for vessel traffic services (VTS). They should be followed only where they are in accordance with national or international law, as some of the functions are not appropriate for all the VTS areas. The guidelines do not deal with the questions of liability or responsibility, nor do they create new rights to enact legislation which impose requirements on shipping.

2. VTS authorities or those planning VTS are recommended to follow these guidelines, as appropriate to their needs, in the interests of achieving harmonization internationally and improving maritime safety.

3. This document describes the possible functions of VTS and defines guidelines for designing and operating VTS once it has been decided that such a system, whether very simple or highly sophisticated, is necessary. It further aims at harmonizing them internationally. It addresses the procedures used by VTS and takes into account current practices. It is based on IMO recommendations and resolutions on this subject, in particular, it supplements the draft Assembly resolution A.531(13) on "General Principles on Ship Reporting Systems'.

### CONTENTS

These guidelines contain the following chapters and sections:

Appendix IV

## CHAPTER 1 - OBJECTIVES AND PROCEDURES

### 1. Vessel traffic services

A VTS is any service, implemented by a competent authority, designed to improve safety and efficiency of traffic and the protection of the environment. It may range from the provision of simple information messages to extensive management of traffic within a port or waterway.

1.1 The reasons for establishing a VTS may include:

- assistance to navigation in appropriate areas;
- regulation of movements to facilitate an efficient traffic flow in the VTS area;
- handling of data relating to ships involved;
- participation in actions in case of accident; and
- support of allied activities.

1.2 VTS is particularly appropriate in the approaches and access channels of a port and in areas having one or more of the following characteristics:

- high traffic density;
- traffic with noxious or dangerous cargoes;
- navigational difficulties;
- narrow channels; and
- environmental sensitivity.

### 2. VTS authority

2.1 "VTS authority" is the authority operating a VTS. It may include a single port authority, a governmental maritime administration, a pilotage organization or any combination of them.

2.1.1 The authority establishing a VTS should delineate its area of coverage, declare it as a VTS area and disseminate to mariners full details concerning the service provided and the procedures to be followed (see section 7). It should state the classes of ships which are required or recommended to participate in a VTS and indicate the VTS centres responsible for the VTS tasks.

2.1.2 The authority should establish appropriate qualifications and training requirements for VTS operators in accordance with section 6.

2.1.3 The VTS authority should ensure that the effects of vessel traffic services, routeing, aids to navigation, pilotage, etc. are fully inter-related.

2.1.4 Care should be taken to ensure that traffic regulations do not encroach upon the master's responsibility for the safe navigation of his vessel or disturb the traditional relationship between master and pilot.

2.1.5 When planning or designing a VTS, the authority should take into account the factors and criteria of chapter 2.

3. Elements of a VTS

3.1 General

A VTS consists of the following elements:

- VTZ organization.
- Vessels using VTS.
- Communications.
- Common language.

3.2 VTS organization

3.2.1 The VTS organization should be equipped with communication facilities and may have radar surveillance equipment and other equipment in accordance with the tasks to be performed by the VTS. The VTS organization should be equipped with the appropriate frequencies, as prescribed in Appendix 18 of the Radio Regulations, including the international distress, safety and calling frequencies.

3.2.2 "VTS centres" are centres from which VTS are operated.

3.2.3 "VTS operators" are the persons who perform the functions of the VTS (see section 4).

3.3 Vessels using a VTS

3.3.1 Vessels participating in a VTS are assumed to be fitted with the navigational and communications equipment in accordance with the 1973 SOLAS Convention, as amended, Chapters IV and V.

3.3.2 The decisions concerning the effective navigation and manoeuvring of the vessel remain with the master. Neither the sailing plan (see paragraph 5.3.1) nor requested or instructed changes to the sailing plan can supersede these decisions.

3.3.3 If voluntary or compulsory pilotage exists in the VTS area, the pilot will, in a manner agreed with the master, take part in the navigation and manoeuvring of the ship. Pilotage plays an important role in a VTS. The functions of a pilot is to provide:

- the master with assistance in manoeuvring his vessel;
- the master with local knowledge both concerning navigation and national/local regulations; and
- assistance with communicating between ship and shore particularly where there are language difficulties.

### 3.4 Communications

Communications between the VTS centre and the ship must exist and should follow the prescribed communication rules. These communications generally involve VHF/UHF radio links which however can be duplicated or complemented, for example, with traffic signals. The number of VHF/UHF channels required will depend upon the amount of radio traffic.

### 3.5 Common language

3.5.1 The language used must enable the VTS authority and the ship to understand each other clearly.

3.5.2 In international waters communication in a VTS should take place primarily in the English language. When in addition to the English language a local language is used to communicate with a specific vessel, navigational information relevant to other vessels should be repeated in English.

3.5.3 In national waters the primary language should be the appropriate working language of the country where the system is established and English should be used where language difficulties exist. Systems established in areas where there are many international ships may designate English as the primary language.

3.5.4 The IMO Standard Marine Navigation Vocabulary should be used where possible.

## 4. Functions of a VTS

### 4.1 General

The functions of a VTS may include:

- Data collection.
- Data evaluation.
- Information service.
- Navigational assistance service.
- Traffic regulation service.
- Support of allied activities.

4.2 Data collection

Data collection may include:

- Gathering data on the fairway and traffic situation by appropriate equipment, e.g. hydrological and meteorological sensors, radar, VHF-Direction Finder, etc.
- Maintaining a listening watch on the designated marine safety and distress frequencies.
- Receiving ships' reports.
- Obtaining reports on the ship's conditions with regard to hull, machinery, equipment or manning.

4.3 Data evaluation

Data evaluation may include:

- Monitoring the manoeuvres of ships for compliance with international, national and local requirements and regulations.
- Interpreting the total traffic situation and its developments.
- Monitoring the fairway situation (hydrological and meteorological data, aids to navigation).
- Coordinating the information flow and distributing the relevant messages to the participants of organizations concerned.
- Collecting information for statistical purposes.

4.4 Information service

An information service is a service provided by broadcasting information at fixed times, or at any other additional time if deemed necessary by the VTS centre, or on request of a vessel and may include:

- Broadcasting information about the movements of traffic, visibility or the intentions of other vessels, to assist all vessels including small craft that are only participating in the VTS by listening.
- Exchanging information with vessels on all relevant safety matters (notices to mariners, status of aids to navigation, meteorological and hydrol-

ogical information, etc.).
- Exchanging information with vessels on relevant traffic conditions and situation (movements and intentions of approaching traffic or traffic being overtaken).
- Warning vessels about hindrances to navigation such as hampered vessels, concentrations of fishing vessels, small craft, other vessels on special operations, and giving information on alternative routeing.

### 4.5 Navigational assistance service

A navigational assistance service is a service given on request of a vessel, or if deemed necessary by the VTS centre, or when required by regulation and may include assistance to vessels in difficult navigational or meteorological circumstances or in case of defects or deficiencies.

### 4.6 Traffic regulation service

A traffic regulation service is concerned with the forward planning of movements in order to avoid development of dangerous situations and to provide safe and efficient movement of traffic within the VTS area, which may be accomplished on the basis of sailing plans and may include:

- Establishing and operating a system of traffic clearance and reports for specific manoeuvres and conditions.
- Scheduling vessel movements through special areas such as where one-way traffic is established.
- Regulating the traffic by means of advice or instructions requiring a vessel to remain in or proceed to a safe position, whenever the safety of life or protection of environment or property warrants it.

### 4.7 Support of allied activities

Support of allied activities may include:

- Coordinating the information flow and distributing the relevant messages to the participants or organizations concerned.
- Supporting activities allied to those of the VTS authority such as pilotage services, port services, marine safety, pollution control and search and rescue.
- Calling upon and requesting action by rescue and emergency services and, if appropriate, participating in the actions of these services.

## 5. Procedures

### 5.1 General

5.1.1 Every VTS should follow procedures based on these guidelines to the extent required by its functions and needs.

5.1.2 Reporting procedures should be clear, simple and contain only the information consistent with maintaining to a minimum the additional bridge duties of masters, officers of the watch and pilots.

5.1.3 When detailed and extensive information has to be exchanged with one ship which is not relevant to other ships, the VTS operator may decide to communicate with that ship on an alternative VHF channel.

5.1.4 To avoid an unnecessary repetition of information by the ship, basic information should be reported once, be retained in the system and be complemented or updated according to the requirements and should be made available to shore services as appropriate.

5.1.5 All ships participating in a VTS should, unless otherwise permitted by the authorities, maintain a continuous listening watch on the appropriate frequency of the VTS. This listening watch shall be carried out from the position from which the ship is navigated.

5.1.6 Status of the message

Any message to a vessel should make it clear whether it is information, advice or instruction.

5.1.7 Information by VTS

The times for regular bulletins should be clearly published in relevant nautical documents and should take account of transmission times of neighbouring VTS centres. They should be drawn up in a standard format and only contain essential information (see section 7). Bulletins in special circumstances should be preannounced in an appropriate way. Information can also be requested by a vessel.

### 5.2 Initial contact - Identification

5.2.1 Generally, the ship contacts the VTS centre by VHF and this is the first direct link between the ship and the VTS. This initial exchange of data enables the ship to confirm certain preliminary advice, if any (see paragraph 5.2.2). It also enables the ship to request certain specific data from the VTS operator. In most cases a ship through its dialogue with the VTS operator provides its identification. This identification may be assisted by technical means such as shore based radar or VHF direction finder.

5.2.2 A vessel's arrival in a port area is normally anticipated as the agent will have given an Estimated Time of Arrival (ETA) and request a berth or anchorage. In the case of vessels carrying dangerous substances, IMO Circular MSC 299 dated December, 1980 "Safe transport, handling and storage of dangerous substances in port areas" which recommends notification of specific information should be followed, as well as any local rules which may be applicable.

5.3 Reporting within a VTS

Ships participating in a VTS should report, if required, at the designated positions and times and in accordance with the agreed reporting format. The master should, as far as practicable, ensure correct and timely reporting. Other vessels not required to report but wishing to avail themselves of the services offered by the CTS should follow the relevant procedures. The types of reports described in the IMO "General Principles for Ship Reporting Systems" should be used as follows within the VTS procedures:

5.3.1 Sailing Plan

5.3.1.1 It should be sent before departure from a berth or entering the area covered by the VTS. The VTS authority should specify the information required in the sailing plan for all or for special ships according to local circumstances. In exceptional circumstances the sailing plan may on request of the VTS operator be amplified.

5.3.1.2 On account of the traffic situation or of special circumstances the VTS operator may advise changes to the sailing plan.

5.3.1.3 After the sailing plan is agreed between the vessel and the VTS operator, the vessel is permitted to participate in the VTS and should, as far as practicable, try to maintain the plan.

5.3.1.4 If special circumstances so require and for the purpose of the safety of the traffic the VTS operator, after indicating the reason, may request the vessel to follow a changed sailing plan. Such changes should be limited, as far as practicable, and may include:

- time of passing the next reporting point or another specific point;
- extra position reports;
- a new destination;
- remaining at a specified location;
- request not to enter the VTS area;
- request to stay alongside the berth; and
- request to follow a certain route.

5.3.1.5 When special circumstances or the safety of the traffic so requires and when the VTS operator has the authority, a vessel can be instructed to maintain a specific sailing plan or implement changes to the sailing plan in accordance with paragraphs 5.3.1.4 and 3.2.2.

5.3.1.6 If a vessel does not comply with the requested action the reasons should be reported to the VTS operator.

5.3.2 <u>Position report</u>

When there is no automatic tracking after reception of sailing plan and identification of the ship, position reports are necessary to update the movement data of a ship. Ships may be required to send position reports at the prescribed positions.

5.3.3 <u>Deviation report</u>

If the sailing plan cannot be maintained the vessel should send a deviation report to the VTS operator and an amended sailing plan be agreed between the vessel and the VTS operator.

5.3.4 <u>Final report</u>

When leaving the VTS area or arriving at the final destination of the sailing plan, the vessel should send a final report.

5.3.5 <u>Any other reports</u>

Any other report prescribed by the VTS authority should be made in accordance with IMO principles. For example, a "deficiency report" is one which should be made to inform the VTS centre of defects, damage, deficiencies or other limitations.

5.4 <u>Assistance to navigation</u>

When a vessel requests navigational assistance or when such assistance is prescribed by regulation, the

VTS operator should ensure positive identification and location of the vessel by reliable means and obtain other relevant information. After the identification and location is established, the messages on navigational assistance should be sent at short intervals. When the vessel needs no further navigational assistance, clear notice should be given to the VTS operator. In open waters, navigational assistance will mainly contain a description of surrounding traffic and warnings with respect to the closest point of approach (CPA) and time of closest approach (TCA) of other ships and, if necessary, advice on course. In confined waters, navigational assistance will usually contain also position data (e.g. distance to "reference line" and to "way point").

5.5 Traffic rules

In certain places, traffic rules exist. Such rules may cover the movement of special ships, limitations in a channel or passing or overtaking situations. Where such rules exist, and where the VTS operator has the authority, the VTS operator may need to issue instructions to ensure that these traffic rules are complied with by the traffic as appropriate.

6. Personnel

The authority should ensure that VTS operators have specialized training appropriate to their tasks within the VTS and meet the language requirements as mentioned in paragraph 3.4, in particular, with regard to VTS operators authorized to issue traffic instructions or to give navigational assistance.

7. VTS publications for users

7.1 A VTS authority should ensure that the rules and regulations in force, the services offered and the area concerned are appropriately promulgated.

7.2 The publication should be convenient for use by mariners and should, where possible, include chartlets showing the area and sector boundaries, general navigational information about the area together with procedures, radio frequencies or channels, reporting lines and reporting points.

## CHAPTER 2 - PLANNING A VTS

1 The safety of maritime traffic in a VTS is necessarily a co-operative activity between those ashore and those at sea. It is therefore important, wherever a VTS is being planned and designed, that amongst others the mariner's views on the need for and operation of the service are taken into account. The level of need should also be considered. This will assist in the effective implementation of VTS and facilitate the co-operation and the confidence of all the future participants in procedures to be followed.

2 When considering the introduction of a VTS, the authority should verify that its operation will be in accordance with international and national law and ensure that, should ships be required to participate, appropriate legislation exists or is enacted.

3 When planning a VTS, the VTS authority should be guided by criteria such as:

.1 the general risk of marine accidents and their possible consequences and the density of traffic in the area;

.2 the need to protect the public and safety of the environment, particularly where dangerous cargoes are handled;

.3 the operation and economic impact on users of the system and the marine community as a whole;

.4 the availability of the requisite technology and expertise;

.5 existing or planned vessel traffic services in adjacent waters and the need for co-operation between neighbouring States;

.6 existing or proposed traffic patterns or routeing systems in the area, including the presence of fishing grounds and of small craft;

.7 existing or foreseeable changes in the traffic pattern resulting from port or offshore terminal developments or offshore exploration in the area;

.8 the adequacy of existing communication systems and aids to navigation in the area;

.9 meteorological factors such as weather and ice

conditions;

.10 hydrological factors such as tides, tidal ranges and currents; and

.11 narrow channels, port configuration, bridges and similar areas where the progress of vessels may be restricted.

4 A VTS area can be divided into sectors but these should be as few as possible. The boundaries should be indicated in appropriate nautical documents.

5 Area and sector boundaries should not be in places where vessels normally alter course or manoeuvre or where they are approaching convergence areas, route junctions or where there is crossing traffic.

6 VTS centres in an area or sector should use a name identifier.

7 Reporting points should be clearly identified, for example by number, sector, name and a geographical position or description. They should be kept to a minimum and as widely separated as possible.

## Appendix V

## CLAIMS SETTLED BY THE FUND

The following claims[1] have been settled by the Fund.

1. *Antonio Gramaci*: The *Antonio Gramaci* (27,694 grt) flying the Russian flag, grounded on February 27, 1979, off the Swedish coast. About 5,500 tonnes of oil were spilled and the Swedish authorities had to carry out the clean-up operations. The owners limited their liability to 2 431 584 Rbls and the amounts paid by the Fund to the Swedish authorities were as follows:

| | |
|---|---|
| clean-up costs | S Kr. 89 057 717 |
| interest | 6 649 440 |
| total | S Kr. 95 707 157 (US $ 11 671 604) |

2. *Miya Maru No.8*: The *Miya Maru No.8* (997 grt), flying the Japanese flag, was involved in a collision on March 22, 1979, and about 540 tonnes of oil were spilled. The Fund paid the following sums:

| | |
|---|---|
| clean-up costs | Yen 108 589 104 |
| fishery damage | 31 521 478 |
| indemnification | 9 427 585 |
| total | Yen 149 538 167 (US $ 626 731) |

3. *Tarpenbek*: The German tanker *Tarpenbek* (999 grt) loaded with about 1600 tonnes of lubricating oil, collided with the Royal Fleet auxiliary *Sir Geraint* off Selsey Bill (England) on June 21, 1979. The *Tarpenbek* was towed to a port of refuge and the cargo was pumped out. The owner of *Tarpenbek* claimed the expenses incurred in the pumping, parbuckling and towage operations. The United Kingdom Government and local Councils carried out various measures to prevent a possible spill of oil. The Fund refused to pay the claims because of the lack of evidence of an

(1) The survey of these claims is based on the Annual Report of the Fund published in 1983.

actual spill of persistent oil after the collision. The claimants subsequently issued writs against the IOPC Fund in which the owners claimed £594 358 and the UK Government and local authorities claimed £1 177 215 plus interest. The outcome of the settlement of this important incident depends on the decision of the High Court(1).

4. *Mebaruzaki Maru No.5*: The tanker of 19 grt, flying the Japanese flag, sank on December 8, 1979, off the Japanese coast and a quantity of about ten tonnes of oil was spilled. The Fund paid:

| | |
|---|---|
| clean-up costs | Yen 7 477 481 |
| fishery damage | 2 710 854 |
| indemnification | 211 370 |
| total | Yen 10 399 705 (US $ 43 586) |

5. *Showa Maru*: The tanker of 199 grt, flying the Japanese flag, was involved in a collision on January 9, 1980, off Mebaru Port, Japan, and about a hundred tonnes of oil were spilled. In this incident, the Fund settled the claims as follows:

| | |
|---|---|
| clean-up costs | Yen 10 408 369 |
| fishery damage | 92 696 505 |
| indemnification | 2 030 785 |
| total | Yen 105 135 659 (US $ 440 635) |

6. *Unsei Maru*: The tanker of 99 grt, flying the Japanese flag, was involved in a collision on January 9, 1980, off the Japanese coast. About a hundred and forty tonnes of oil were spilled. The estimated claim is Yen 6 903 461. However, as a recourse action against the insurer is available, no compensation by the Fund is likely to be paid.

---

(1) The Director of the Fund entered into discussion with the UK Government to settle the claim while maintaining the IOPC Fund's position. No agreement has yet been reached and legal proceedings are pending. See International Oil Pollution Compensation Fund, Annual Report, 1984, p.6.

7. *Tanio*: The Malagasy tanker *Tanio* (18,048 grt), carrying 26,000 tonnes of fuel oil, broke amidship in heavy weather conditions off Brittany, France. About 13,500 tonnes of oil spilled from the wreck. More than 200 kilometres of the Brittany coast were polluted and the Channel Islands were also affected. The stern section, with about 7,500 tonnes of oil aboard, remained afloat and was towed to the port of Le Havre. The bow section, with about 5,000 tonnes of oil, sank to a depth of 90 metres. The oil contained in the sunken bow section had to be pumped out in order to prevent further pollution from the wreck.

Claims for compensation were submitted by nearly one hundred claimants, and the total sum of these claims amounted to FFr. 517 248 887 plus £39,483 plus US $878 608 (totalling £43,498,885). The claim from the French Government amounted to more than 90% of the total sum. This claim consisted of expenses for pumping the oil from the sunken bow section, clean-up operations, and for compensation paid by the French Government to victims for their loss of earnings. Claims from local authorities related to the costs of clean-up work, road repairs, beach restoration and to the loss of earnings of municipal camping sites. Private persons submitted claims for loss of earnings in their business. The shipowner's insurer claimed for expenses incurred for the survey of the sunken fore-section and provisional sealing of holes in the wreck.

The total claims (in round figures) were as follows:

| | |
|---|---|
| French Government | 490m FFr. |
| French local authorities | 14m FFr. |
| Private claimants (hoteliers, camping sites) etc. | 13m FFr. |
| UK P & I Club | 8m FFr. |
| | 525m FFr. |

The Fund accepted liability for FFr. 350m. Since the Fund's liability is limited to FFr. 245 millions, the claimants received only about 70 per cent of their claims.

During the settlement of this claim, the Fund laid down important principles on the admissibility of claims. It approved as admissible claims for "pollution damage" costs and for the repair of damages caused to roads, dunes, etc., during the clean-up operations. It also accepted as compensatable the economic loss suffered by the tourist industry which was directly hit by the contamination of the beaches.

The Fund after paying FFr. 216 443 221 (US $ 25 270 662) to the claimants, together took legal action before the Court of Brest against the owner to recover the amount paid by the Fund and the sums which exceeded its limits. The ground for the action is that the owner was guilty of fault or privity and thereby he was deprived of the right to limit his liability.

8. *Furenäs*: The tanker (999 grt), flying the Swedish flag, collided with another vessel on June 3, 1980, off Oresund (Sweden). As a result, about two hundred tonnes of oil were spilled causing damage to both the Swedish and Danish coasts. The Fund paid the following:

| | | |
|---|---|---|
| clean-up costs by the Swedish authorities | S Kr. | 2 911 637 |
| clean-up costs by Swedish private claimants | | 276 050 |
| total: | | 3 187 687 |
| clean-up costs by the Danish authorities | D Kr. | 408 633 |
| clean-up costs by Danish private claimants | | 9 956 |
| total: | | 418 589 |
| indemnification | S Kr. | 153 111 |

(Total US $ 448 291)

9. *Hosei Maru*: The tanker (983 grt) was involved in a collision on August 21, 1980, off Miyagi (Japan) and about 270 tonnes of oil were spilled. The Fund paid:

| | |
|---|---|
| clean-up costs | Yen 163 051 598 |
| fishery damage | 50 271 267 |
| indemnification | 8 941 480 |
| total | 222 264 345 |
| | (US $ 931 535) |

10. *Jose Marti*: On January 7, 1981, the Russian tanker *Jose Marti* (27,706 grt), while carrying 40,000

tonnes of heavy fuel oil, grounded in a narrow channel near Dalarö, Sweden. About 1,000 tonnes of oil were lost and polluted the Stockholm Archipelago. The clean-up costs by the Swedish authorities reached S Kr. 19 296 000, and by private persons amounted to S Kr. 850 000. The Swedish Government started an action against the owner of the tanker and the latter denied liability for the oil pollution damage on the ground that the accident was caused by the negligence of the Swedish Government in maintaining navigational aids. No payment has been paid by the IOPC Fund until a decision has been made in the dispute between the Swedish Government and the owner.

11. *Suma Maru No.11*: The Japanese tanker *Suma Maru No.11* (199 grt) grounded on November 21, 1981, off the Japanese coast and about ten tonnes of oil were spilled. The Fund paid:

| | | |
|---|---|---|
| clean-up costs by the shipowner | Yen | 6 426 857 |
| indemnification | | 1 849 085 |
| total | Yen | 8 275 942 |
| | (US $ | 34 685) |

12. *Globe Asimi*: The Gibraltar tanker *Globe Asimi* (12,404 grt) was carrying 16,000 tonnes of heavy fuel oil when she ran aground on November 22, 1981, and broke up near the port of Klaipeda, USSR. Several thousand tonnes of oil were spilled into the port and later drifted out to sea. The pollution damage caused by this incident was reported to be approximately Rbls 813 million (£721 million), but no damage was suffered in the territory of any Fund Member State and no claim for compensation of pollution damage was therefore made to the Fund. However, the shipowner after limiting his liability under CLC to Rbls 1 350 324 (£1,198,158) claimed indemnification from the Fund in accordance with Articles 3.2 and 5 of the Fund Convention. Accordingly the Fund paid to the shipowner the sum of US $ 467 952.

13. *Ondina* On March 3, 1982, the Dutch tanker *Ondina* (31,030 grt) lost a quantity of oil while discharging her cargo of crude oil at the Shell storage tank in the port of Hamburg. It was estimated that between 200 and 300 tonnes of oil

escaped from the tanker because of defects in the valves.

The costs of clean-up, plus interest paid by the Fund, was DM 10 165 879 (US $ 3 643 684). It must be noted that the owner had no right of indemnification under article 5 of the Fund Convention since the ship was flying the flag of The Netherlands which was not a Member of the Fund Convention at the time of the incident.

14. *Shiota Maru No.2*: On March 31, 1982, the Japanese tanker *Shiota Maru No.2* (161 grt) was carrying 300 tonnes of heavy fuel oil when she went aground on Takashima Island, Japan. About twenty tonnes of oil spilled from the fractured tank causing pollution damage to the coast and fish farms. The Fund paid Yen 72 573 189 (US $ 304 162) for the clean-up costs and fishery damage. The shipowner's limitation fund amounted to Yen 6 304 300 (£21,600).

The investigation into the grounding of the tanker revealed that the incident happened without any fault or privity on the part of the owner. Consequently, the Fund paid Yen 71 095 714 (£200,237) as compensation in March, 1983, and Yen 1 576 075 (£4,953) as indemnification in June, 1984.

15. *Fukutoku Maru No.8*: On April 3, 1982, the Japanese tanker *Fukutoku Maru No.8* (499 grt), while carrying 850 tonnes of heavy bunker oil, collided with the gravel carrier *Koshu Maru* (486 grt) in Tachibana Bay, Japan. Over 85 tonnes of oil escaped from the tanker causing damage to the coasts and fishing areas. The Fund paid:

| | | |
|---|---|---|
| clean-up costs | Yen | 130 419 443 |
| fishery damage | | 233 312 312 |
| total | Yen | 363 731 755 |
| | | (US $ 1 524 441)(1) |

(1) The investigation into the incident established that it was caused by an error in navigation and the absence of any fault or privity on the part of the owner. Therefore, compensation amounting to Yen 363 731 755 (£947,256), as shown above, was paid in early 1983. Following the end of the limitation proceedings, the Fund paid indemnification to the owner amounting to Yen 5 211 110 (£16,720) in September, 1984.

16. *Kifuku Maru No.35*: On December 1, 1982, the Japanese tanker *Kifuku Maru No.35* (107 grt) had 250 tonnes of heavy duty oil. While moored at the quay in the port, the ship's stern became lodged under the quay and water got into the engine room. As a result, about 33 tonnes of oil were spilled.

The clean-up costs undertaken by the owner amounted to Yen 3 801 851 (£10,084). No third party claims were made against the Fund. Since the total amount of claims arising out of this incident was less than the owner's liability under the CLC (Yen 4 271 560), no compensation was payable by the IOPC Fund. However, indemnification to the owner, under articles 3.2 and 5 of the Fund Convention, was fixed at Yen 598 181 (US $ 2 507) and was paid by the Fund.

17. *Shinkai Maru No.3*: On June 21, 1983, the Japanese tanker *Shinkai Maru No.3* (48 grt), loaded with 105 tonnes of heavy fuel oil, spilled an estimated 3.5 tonnes of oil while refuelling the cargo ship *Ageshio Maru* in the port. The claims for the clean-up operations amounted to Yen 886 100 (£8,577). The owner's liability under the CLC was Yen 1 880 940 (£6,500).

The Executive Committee agreed that in view of the fact that the claim is relatively small, compensation could be paid without the limitation fund being established. Furthermore, the enquiry into the cause of the incident showed that it was due solely to the negligence of the master. Since the master was at the same time the owner, two questions were raised. The first was whether the owner/master was entitled to limit his liability under the CLC and the second was whether the owner/master could recover his expenses for voluntary preventive measures. The Committee took the view that the owner/master was entitled to limit his liability in so far as the negligent act was committed in his capacity as master. With this view, the answer to the second question was easy and so claims for expenses voluntarily incurred by the owner/master for taking preventive measures were accepted by the Fund. Accordingly, compensation of Yen 1 005 160 (£3,295) and indemnification of Yen 470 235 (£1,541) were paid in November, 1984.

18. *Eiko Maru No.1*: On August 13, 1983, the Japanese tanker *Eiko Maru No.1* (999 grt), loaded with 2,459 tonnes of heavy fuel oil, collided with a Panamanian cargo ship *Cavalry* (4,827 grt) in dense fog off the Japanese coast. About 357 tonnes of oil were spilled causing pollution damage to the coast and fishing areas. Expenses for the clean-up work have been agreed at Yen 52 726 595 (£156,691). The fishery damage has been settled at Yen 4 million (£11,887). The limitation amount of the *Eiko Maru No.1* under the CLC was Yen 39 445 920 (£13,500) and the indemnification of the owner will amount to Yen 9 861 480 (£34,000). The inquiry into the cause of the incident has not yet been completed but the compensation amounting to Yen 24 735 109 (£76,722) was paid in March, 1984.

19. *Koei Maru No.3*: On December 22, 1983, the tanker *Koei Maru No.3* (81 grt), laden with about 100 tonnes of heavy oil, collided with the ferry boat *Albireo* in the port of Nagaya, Japan. As a result of the collision, the tanker capsized and spilled about 50 tonnes of oil into the sea. The clean-up expenses were estimated at Yen 10 million (£30,000), and the shipowner's liability under CLC was Yen 3 091 660 (£9,200).

The Fund accepted to settle claims for compensation of fishery damage at Yen 10 million (£34,000) and clean-up expenses and other preventive measures at Yen 20 013 208 (£69,000). The claim for compensation was also settled in 1984 at Yen 26 921 548 (£89,233).

20. *Tsunehisa Maru No.8*: The master of the Japanese tanker *Tsunehisa Maru No.8* found on August 26, 1984, that the stern section of the vessel had sunk. The tanker was laden with 46 tonnes of heavy oil and as a result of this incident, about 30 tonnes of oil was spilled.

Claims for clean-up expenses amounted to Yen 15.3 million (£52,000) whilst the claims for the repairs amounted to Yen 2.3 million (£8,000). These claims have not yet been settled.

21. *Koho Maru No.8*: Another Japanese tanker, laden with 500 tonnes of heavy oil, ran aground and

about 20 tonnes of oil were spilled and drifted away with the tide. The area is well known for its fishing grounds and extensive clean-up operations were undertaken.

Claims were submitted to the Fund. They amounted to Yen 197 million (£70,000) but they have not yet been settled.

INDEX